The Capitalist Dilemma
in China's
Communist Revolution

This page is intentionally left blank.

The Capitalist Dilemma in China's Communist Revolution

edited by
Sherman Cochran

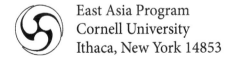

East Asia Program
Cornell University
Ithaca, New York 14853

The Cornell East Asia Series is published by the Cornell University East Asia Program (distinct from Cornell University Press). We publish books on a variety of scholarly topics relating to East Asia as a service to the academic community and the general public. Address submission inquiries to CEAS Editorial Board, East Asia Program, Cornell University, 140 Uris Hall, Ithaca, New York 14853-7601.

Cover images: The photograph of capitalists lining up to register during the Five Anti campaign in Shanghai in 1952 is from *Tupian Zhongguo bainian shi* (A history of one hundred years of photographs in China) (Jinan, Shandong: Shandong huabao chubanshe), v. 2, 425. The cartoon showing capitalists as targets of workers' accusations during the Five Anti campaign in Canton appeared in the newspaper, *Nanfang ribao,* February 3, 1952.

Number 172 in the Cornell East Asia Series
Copyright ©2014 Cornell East Asia Program. All rights reserved.
ISSN: 1050-2955
ISBN: 978-1-939161-52-9 hardcover
ISBN: 978-1-939161-72-7 paperback
Library of Congress Control Number: 2014945478

To the new generation of scholars and students in Chinese business history

This page is intentionally left blank.

CONTENTS

Part Three

CAPITALISTS WHO RETURNED TO CHINA

Part Four

CAPITALISTS WHO REMAINED ABROAD

Acknowledgments

The chapters in this volume were originally presented as essays at a conference that was sponsored by the American Council of Learned Societies and the Chiang Ching-kuo Foundation, with additional funding from a loyal Cornell alumnus, Mr. Lincoln Yung. I am grateful to ACLS, CCK, and Mr. Yung for their generous support. The conference was held at Cornell University and was hosted by the faculty and staff in Cornell's East Asia Program. The Cornell faculty members who made the most critical contributions were those who served as discussants of papers at the conference: Allen Carlson, Chen Jian, Andrew Mertha, Victor Nee, Mark Selden, and Xu Xin. Other members of Cornell's East Asia Program who played vital roles in the conference included Ellen Avril, Curator of the Asian Collection at the Johnson Museum of Art; Liren Zheng, Curator of the Wason Collection on East Asia in Olin Library; and Hongnan Ma, manager of the East Asia Program. My thanks to them all.

Thanks, too, to two conference participants, Morris Linan Bian and William Kirby, who presented papers that are not included in this volume. Each of their papers was well received at the conference, but when the authors discovered that they had not addressed the conference theme as closely as the other presenters had done, they graciously withdrew their papers from consideration for this conference volume.

I have been fortunate to work on this volume with Mai Shaikhanuar-Cota, managing editor of the Cornell East Asia Series, and I wish to thank her for her serious professionalism and her warm good humor. She recruited two anonymous reviewers of the manuscript, whom I also wish to thank for their thoughtful and detailed comments on all the essays in this book. I am also grateful to two Cornell graduate students: Xiaojia Hou for her work in the early stages of the book's preparation and Yuanchong Wang for his contributions in the later stages, particularly in the preparation of the book's glossary.

It is not customary for the editor of a collection of essays to thank its contributors, but in this case, I think it is appropriate to do so. In general, conference volumes are notorious for their lack of thematic coherence because they contain disparate essays, leaving the editor with pieces of a puzzle that do not fit together. But at our conference and ever since, the contributors to this volume have closely adhered to our theme, and I am grateful to them for making my job easier.

This page is intentionally left blank.

A Note on Romanization

The Chinese names and terms used in this book are generally given in the pinyin system of romanization, but there are some exceptions. Most of these exceptions are historical figures' names that have become widely used or are difficult to recognize in pinyin: Sun Yat-sen, Chiang Kai-shek, Madame Chiang Kai-shek, Chiang Ching-kuo, T.V. Soong, H.H. Kung, K.P. Chen, Robert Ho Tung and members of his family (in chapter 10), Koo Chen-fu and members of his family (in chapter 11), and Hsia Pin-fang and members of his family (in chapter 12). In addition, romanization other than pinyin has been used in place names for cities along China's borders: Hong Kong, Canton, Macao, Taipei, Keelung, Kaohsiung. To avoid confusion, a table at the back of the book lists each personal name and place name first in pinyin, then in other romanizations, and finally in Chinese characters.

This page is intentionally left blank.

1 INTRODUCTION

Sherman Cochran

After the People's Republic of China (PRC) was founded on October 1, 1949, did capitalism and communism become compatible in China? Later Mao Zedong as leader of the Chinese Communist Party (CCP) launched a series of campaigns—notably the Anti-Rightist campaign of 1957, the Great Leap Forward of 1958–1961, and the Cultural Revolution of 1966–1976—that carried China down the road to Stalinist state socialism and left no room for capitalism under communism until after Mao's death in 1976. But immediately after the new government took power in 1949, was China inevitably destined to take this path? Was it the only way that capitalism could go under any Communist revolution?[1]

In this book, the contributors have reached a variety of conclusions about the relations between the Chinese Communist Party and Chinese capitalists in the early 1950s, but they all have taken positions that are relevant to one of two themes: the speed and decisiveness of the CCP's transition from capitalism to socialism; and the importance of nationalism as the motivating force behind capitalists' decisions whether to stay in the People's Republic, leave it, or return to it from abroad.

The contributors have humanized these themes by focusing on individual capitalists in relation to the CCP, and they have provided fresh insights by consulting previously unused archival materials and making new discoveries. In particular, they have differed with each other on the question of how fast the CCP carried out the transition to socialism, and they have proposed a wide variety of alternatives to nationalism as the explanation for capitalists' decisions whether or not to live and work in China after 1949.

---

1. These questions parallel one raised by Arif Dirlik about an earlier historical moment. Based on Chinese Marxist thinkers' ideas before 1920, he has asked whether they were necessarily attracted to the doctrines of state socialism at that time, and he has suggested that they might well have been more open to republicanism, anarchism, or some other option. See Dirlik, *The Origins of Chinese Communism* (New York: Oxford University Press, 1989), 3–42.

1

THE SPEED OF THE CHINESE COMMUNIST PARTY'S
TRANSITION TO SOCIALISM

How fast did the CCP make the transition from capitalism to socialism? The answer is critical because it is a potential indicator of the CCP's attitude toward capitalism: if the process was slow, it suggests that the CCP allowed for the possibility that capitalism would develop under communism; if fast, it suggests that the CCP did not allow for this possibility.

On the question of how fast the transition to socialism occurred, the contributors to this volume all agree that in this process there were certain key events:

• the victories of the People's Liberation Army over Chiang Kai-shek's Nationalist forces in Chinese cities in 1949 (particularly in Tianjin on January 15, 1949, Shanghai on May 27, 1949, and Canton on October 14, 1949);

• the founding of the People's Republic with its capital in Beijing on October 1, 1949;

• the outbreak of the Korean War on June 25, 1950;

• the completion of the Five Anti campaign (against "bribery, tax evasion, theft of state property, cheating on government contracts, and stealing of state economic information"), January 26 to October 25, 1952;

• the PRC government's retention of direct control over all Chinese banks in December 1952;

• the PRC government's retention of direct control over all Chinese industrial enterprises in 1956.[2]

And yet, even though the contributors generally accept this basic chronology for the transition to socialism in China on a national scale, they reach strikingly different—even conflicting—conclusions about how fast it occurred based on their investigations into the experiences of particular Chinese capitalists.

In his chapter, Karl Gerth characterizes the CCP's treatment of capitalists in the transition to socialism as one of "slow strangulation." He acknowledges that the CCP established a legal basis for nationalizing industry as early as 1949, but he emphasizes that it did not implement this policy rapidly or abruptly. Instead, it went through three stages: utilization (1949–1952), restriction (1952–1953), and transformation (1953–1956) as outlined in the People's Republic's constitution in 1954. The CCP

---

2. For a close and precise study of this sequence of events from the standpoint of Mao and the CCP, see Hua-yu Li, *Mao and the Economic Stalinization of China, 1948–1953* (Lanham: Rowman and Littlefield, 2006).

would have taken faster action if it could have, but Chinese capitalists prevented its leaders from doing so. The party's "need to move to the left quickly was slowed by accumulated legacies such as the creation of 'patriotic' and 'national' capitalists like Wu Yunchu [China's MSG King who is the central figure in Gerth's chapter]."

Kai Yiu Chan similarly stresses that the CCP and Chinese capitalists took time to work out their relations with each other. His example of prolonged negotiations between the CCP and a capitalist focuses on Zhang Jianhui, an industrialist who thought seriously about leaving and returning to China at least three times—in 1949, 1951, and 1957–1958. In each instance, members of the CCP approached him differently. First, in 1949–1950, they emphasized their positive appeal to capitalists as expressed in Mao's policies under New Democracy and United Front, which persuaded Zhang to stay in China. Later, in 1951, they campaigned against counterrevolutionaries, which frightened Zhang into fleeing to Hong Kong. Finally, in 1957–1958, they played the CCP's "trump card" of permitting a family reunion, which induced Zhang to pay an extended visit to China but not to move his residence back from Hong Kong. Chan argues that on all three occasions, the CCP and Zhang seriously negotiated about whether he would settle permanently in China, and he warns that it would be a mistake to assume that the CCP and Chinese capitalists suddenly or definitively determined their relationship with each other when the revolution was launched in 1949. "The Communist Revolution of 1949 itself did not have an immediate or decisive impact on the Chinese capitalists," he contends. "It was those events that followed the revolution, including the terror, the purge, the violence, and so on that gradually pushed some capitalists into the position where they made clear-cut decisions."

Pui-Tak Lee also argues that Chinese capitalists took time to reach their decisions about how to deal with the Revolution of 1949. He suggests that historians have underestimated how long the process took because they have assumed that for each Chinese capitalist it ended as soon as he left China and arrived in the British colony of Hong Kong. In his study of the banker K.P. Chen, Lee has discovered that after Chen made his departure from Shanghai and resettled in Hong Kong in 1949, he maintained his connections with his bank's branches not only in Shanghai but also in other cities under Communist rule—Tianjin, Nanjing, Beijing, and Hankou. Even while Chen arranged to remit funds from his former headquarters in Shanghai to his new one in Hong Kong, he tried to retain his bank's license for exchange business in China and avoid confiscation of its foreign reserves there. In the process, he corresponded with Premier Zhou Enlai and other top CCP leaders. For that matter, after relocating in Hong Kong, he also continued to hear from officials in Chiang Kai-shek's Nationalist government, which by then had retreated from the mainland to Taiwan. In April 1950, he received invitations to attend meetings of both of the two rival boards of directors of the Bank of China—one in Beijing and the other in Taipei—and decided to accept the one from Taipei. In the early 1950s, even after making this decision, he continued to have ambivalent feelings and confided at the time that his heart was still in Shanghai.

Even though Gerth, Chan, and Lee have suggested that these examples show that the transition from capitalism to socialism in China was gradual, other contributors to the volume have come to contrary conclusions. Brett Sheehan has contended that the CCP's actions in the first phase of its dealings with Chinese capitalists between 1949 and 1951 were indicative of its decisiveness—not its gradualism—and that its subsequent actions were mere continuations, if not redundancies, in the wake of these definitive first steps. As early as April 1949, he notes, Liu Shaoqi, who was second only to Mao among leaders of the CCP at the time, paid a month-long visit to Tianjin and announced that the party would cooperate with the city's capitalists, including the industrialist Song Feiqing, who is the central figure in Sheehan's essay. This early phase of the relationship between the CCP and Chinese capitalists has often been characterized as a "honeymoon period," but Sheehan suggests that it was more like a "shotgun wedding." As he puts it, "even during this honeymoon period, the party was able to impose its will on private industry leaving little freedom for capitalist maneuver." In April 1949, before Liu had ended his brief visit to Tianjin, the CCP had already begun to weave its "web of controls" over Song's Dongya Corporation, and in May 1950 Song fled to Hong Kong, never to return to China. Such actions indicate, Sheehan concludes, that the party had already shown its determination to take fundamental managerial control away from capitalists at the time of Song's emigration, which was only eight months after the founding of the People's Republic and well in advance of the CCP's Five Anti campaign of 1952 and other efforts to deal with capitalists.

Like Sheehan, Man Bun Kwan emphasizes how fast the transition to socialism took place. Whereas Gerth concludes that the CCP's transition was slowed down by a capitalist like the MSG King Wu Yunchu, Kwan finds that it was speeded up by the capitalist Li Zhuchen, the head of Jiuda Salt Refinery, China's largest enterprise in the salt industry. In fact, Kwan shows that Li nationalized Jiuda faster than top CCP leaders would have preferred. At the time, Li was in touch with Chairman of the CCP Mao Zedong, Premier Zhou Enlai, and the CCP's chief economic planner Chen Yun (three members of the five-man "standing committee" of the Polituro that stood at the pinnacle of the new government's structure), and while presiding over Jiuda as its manager, Li concurrently held a high-level official position. In 1952, when Li announced to China's political leaders that he would voluntarily share authority over Jiuda with the government, he was cautioned by them not to move too quickly, but he forged ahead anyway, completing the process on July 1, 1952, and making Jiuda the first business in Tianjin to become officially designated as "jointly public and private" (*gongsi heying*).

While Sheehan and Kwan maintain that the transfer of managerial authority from capitalists to the state occurred swiftly, and Gerth, Chan, and Lee say that it happened gradually, Tomoko Shiroyama describes a case in which it was not completed at all—at least not in the 1950s. The subject of her chapter, Ma Xuchao, was a Cantonese who specialized in finance, not industry, and he managed to avoid government regulation of his remittance agency both before and after 1949. In this agency, he funneled funds from overseas Chinese in Canada, the United States, and Central America through the British colony of Hong Kong to members of their families and fellow villagers in south China's Guangdong province. After 1949, he had to adjust his operation to cope with efforts at intervention by two governments: the People's Republic, which tried to divert remittances from informal agencies like Ma's to official institutions like the Bank of China; and the United States, which tried to prevent Chinese-Americans from sending remittances to China as part of a Cold War strategy against communism.[3] And yet, despite the imposition of these political barriers, Ma's remittance agency continued to conduct its transnational business with clients in China throughout the 1950s.

Is it possible to reconcile these seemingly contradictory conclusions that the CCP carried out the transition to socialism slowly (as Gerth, Chan, and Lee say), quickly (as Sheehan and Kwan maintain), or not at all (as Shiroyama concludes)? One possible basis for reconciliation may be found in the geographical locations of the capitalists' enterprises. CCP leaders who were based in Beijing moved quickly and decisively in nearby Tianjin (the setting for essays by Sheehan and Kwan); they took longer and groped more tentatively as they reached out to the more distant and highly sophisticated urban economy of Shanghai (the setting for essays

---

3. Richard T. Devane, "The United States and China: Claims and Assets," *Asian Survey* 18.12 (December 1978): 1267–1279.

by Gerth, Chan, and Lee); and they took the most time and established control least fully in very distant Guangdong province in south China, especially along its porous border with Hong Kong (the setting for the chapter by Shiroyama).[4]

Whether the contradictions in these chapters can be reconciled or not, the contributors have taken sides on an issue that is well worth debating because it may help to explain why the CCP ardently appealed to Chinese capitalists to stay in China after the revolution or return there from abroad. Several of the contributors have described these appeals in detail, leaving no doubt that the CCP made them.

Those who interpret the transition to socialism as gradual maintain that the CCP was interested in capitalists' talent, technical know-how, and capital, which were needed to carry out an economic recovery in the aftermath of two devastating wars, the Sino-Japanese War of 1937–1945 and the Chinese Civil War of 1946–1949. Only with help from capitalists, in Gerth's words, could the CCP imagine building "a wealthy, powerful, and independent China" in the early 1950s.

By contrast, those who consider the transition to have been rapid express doubts that the CCP appealed to capitalists for these reasons. The high speed of the transition to socialism, according to Sheehan, "belies any thought that the party really wanted to take advantage of the managerial and entrepreneurial skills of capitalists such as Song Feiqing." If so, then why did the CCP make such a concerted effort to court Song and other capitalists? As Parks Coble has remarked in chapter 7 in this volume, if the CCP truly had no interest in making use of capitalists' skills, its aggressive appeal to them "seems almost perverse."[5] Perverse or not, the CCP is clearly shown here to have recruited capitalists, but did it do so as part of a gradual or fast transition to socialism? If the contributors' disagreements are any indication, this question is open to debate.

---

4. For detailed coverage of the CCP's approaches to Tianjin in north China, Shanghai in the lower Yangzi region, and Canton in south China during the early years of the People's Republic, see Kenneth Lieberthal, *Revolution and Tradition in Tientsin, 1949–1952* (Stanford: Stanford University Press, 1980); Frederic Wakeman, Jr., "'Clean-up': The New Order in Shanghai," in Jeremy Brown and Paul G. Pickowicz, eds., *Dilemmas of Victory: The Early Years of the People's Republic of China* (Cambridge: Harvard University Press, 2007), 21–58; and Ezra Vogel, *Canton under Communism: Programs and Politics in a Provincial Capital, 1949–1968* (New York: Harper and Row, 1969).

5. In his essay, Sheehan does not pretend to have a definitive answer to the question of why the CCP recruited capitalists, but he makes the tentative suggestion that "something about the existence of overseas Chinese capitalists' rejection of party orthodoxy, either Communist or Nationalist, was simply untenable to either party's sense of itself, threatening to its own sense of legitimacy."

CAPITALISTS' DECISIONS WHETHER TO
STAY, LEAVE, OR RETURN

While contributors to this volume differ with each other over how fast the transition to socialism was carried out in China, they also differ over why capitalists made their decisions to stay in China, leave it, or return from abroad after 1949. Up to now it has generally been assumed that those Chinese capitalists who chose to live in China under communism did so because they were nationalistic and those who fled and stayed abroad did so because they were not nationalistic. In 1947 on the eve of the revolution, Mao Zedong drew a sharp distinction between "national capitalists" (*minzu zibenjia*) who would be welcome in China under socialism and "compradore bureaucratic capitalists" (*maiban guanliao zibenjia*) who would be targets of the revolution. Since then, whether embracing Mao's distinction wholeheartedly or evaluating it critically, contemporary observers and historians have commonly accepted his point that Chinese capitalists who chose to live in China were motivated primarily or even exclusively by nationalism, and those who chose to leave and stay abroad were motivated by the lack of it.[6]

The contributors' essays challenge this assumption that nationalism was the sole determinant of whether capitalists chose to live in China under socialism. To be sure, their findings show that nationalism was one of the determinants. Li Zhuchen, the manager of Jiuda Salt Refinery in 1949, as described by Man Bun Kwan, became a passionate nationalist as early as the 1930s. In 1937, when the Japanese invaded his hometown of Tianjin in north China, he escaped from the occupied area, moving his company to Chongqing, Chiang Kai-shek's wartime capital in western China. During the Sino-Japanese War of 1937–1945, Li became, in Kwan's words, "a capitalist who considered profitmaking secondary to national salvation." After the war, on his return to Tianjin, Li had difficulty keeping Jiuda afloat, and in June 1949, after the People's

---

6. For recent examples of Chinese scholars' emphasis on nationalism as the motivation for decision making by Chinese "national capitalists," see the sketches in Li Zhancai, ed., *Shizi lukou: Zou haishi liu? Minzu zibenjia zai 1949* (At the crossroads: Leave or stay? National capitalists in 1949) (Taiyuan: Shanxi renmin chubanshe, 2009). For other examples of historical writing in China around this theme and a helpful historiographical analysis of it, see Tim Wright, ed., *The Chinese Economy in the Early Twentieth Century: Recent Studies* (New York: St. Martin's Press, 1992); and Tim Wright, "The Spiritual Heritage of Chinese Capitalism," in Jonathan Unger, ed., *Using the Past to Serve the Present* (Armonk: M.E. Sharpe, 1993), 205–238.

Liberation Army had taken the city but before the People's Republic had been founded, he began appealing to the Communists in Beijing for aid. He dealt directly with top leaders of the CCP, who recognized him as a model national capitalist and appointed him to high official posts at the national level, including Minister of Food Industry (later known as Minister of Light Industry), his post during the last years of his life, 1956–1968.

If Li was a fervent nationalist, Gu Zhun, an accountant responsible for reforming taxation in Shanghai under the People's Republic, as described by Christopher Leighton, was a committed localist. Born, raised, and educated in Shanghai, Gu became tightly enmeshed in professional networks consisting of his mentor, teachers, and clients whom he came to know through his training and career as an accountant. In the 1930s, he became attracted to communism and left Shanghai to go to a Communist base area where he became a member of the CCP, and as soon as the People's Liberation Army took over his hometown in 1949, he returned there to serve as a tax administrator. Rising swiftly to an influential position in Shanghai under communism, he succeeded in increasing the collection of tax revenue in Shanghai in 1950 and 1951, and he devised a scheme for retaining a substantial share of it in the city through investments in decentralized enterprises rather than channeling all of it to Beijing as the capital of the nation. His scheme failed, and he was denounced, losing his position as early as March 1, 1952, and among the reasons for his downfall was his advocacy of Shanghai-based localism as opposed to Beijing-centered nationalism.

Another capitalist, Ma Xuchao, as characterized by Tomoko Shiroyama, also continued to operate in China after 1949, but unlike Li and Gu, Ma made his primary commitment there not to China as his nation or a big Chinese city like Shanghai as his hometown. Instead his allegiance was above all to a rural locality, Taishan in Guangdong province, his native place. The head of a remittance agency, he delivered funds and letters that were sent home by Taishan natives living abroad. In the process, he built up a large network of émigrés who had left Taishan and taken up residences in widely scattered locations mainly in North and South America, and he funneled their funds and letters through Hong Kong, recruiting fellow Taishanese as couriers to make the final deliveries to recipients in Taishan. To this extent, Ma was extremely native place-oriented, but according to Shiroyama's analysis, he could not rely entirely on personal and native-place ties to keep his network functioning. To prevent couriers from absconding with funds, he kept track of the flow of money by requiring signatures on contracts, receipts, and other documents. So his success at continuing to deliver overseas remittances through Hong Kong and across the border into China throughout the 1950s suggests that he based his operation not only on a native place-based personal network but also an effective use of written documents.

While Li, Gu, and Ma demonstrated their commitments in China to their nation, hometown, or native place, other capitalists chose to live and work there for reasons that were not identified so fully with geographical locations. Zhou Zuomin, as described by Parks Coble, was a banker who made his decision to return and live in the People's Republic because of his attachment not to a place but rather to an institution, the Jincheng Bank. Zhou founded this bank at Tianjin in 1917, moved it to Shanghai in 1936, and kept it operating by deftly adapting to efforts at intervention by the Nationalist government before and after the Sino-Japanese War and by the Japanese occupying forces during the war. In 1948, a year before the People's Liberation Army's takeover of Shanghai, Zhou fled to Hong Kong. Once there, his business associates who had also fled advised him not to return to China, but in 1950 he decided to go back because his Jincheng Bank was in Shanghai, and he believed that he might continue to be the head of it as he had been under previous governments. Even if it became converted into a joint public-private institution, he thought that it might remain under his guidance, especially in promoting investment in industry. Between 1950 and 1952, he achieved his goal to the extent that he participated in the reorganization of Jincheng Bank and its consolidation with other banks in China. Until mid-1952 he apparently held out hope that Jincheng would retain its identity and that he would exercise a measure of control over it. Then in December 1952 any such hope was dashed when it was nationalized and placed directly under the control of the People's Bank in Beijing like other private banks at the time. At the end of 1952, after guiding Jincheng for thirty-five years, including two years following his return from Hong Kong to Shanghai, Zhou finally lost even a semblance of control over his beloved bank.

Like these capitalists who stayed in China or returned there, the ones who chose to stay abroad also made decisions based on a variety of considerations. Many who fled to Hong Kong and Taiwan (including some described in this book) moved there merely because these were the two most accessible and convenient temporary way stations available to them as they departed from China at the time. But others who chose to live in Hong Kong and Taiwan became politically attached to these places and took actions to prevent China from encroaching on them.

Robert Ho Tung, as characterized by Siu-lun Wong and Victor Zheng, was at the time of the Communist Revolution the richest of all Chinese, and his experience was illustrative of Chinese capitalists who became committed to Hong Kong. Before 1949, he and his family had long been based in the British colony and had received honors bestowed in the British empire. But they also had large stakes in presocialist China: a vast and dense network of compradores and a valuable portfolio of real estate holdings. After 1949, when the PRC's new government dismantled Robert Ho Tung's network and confiscated his family's property in China, he found no way to salvage his assets there, but he unflinchingly defended his base in Hong Kong. He took a firm political stand in support of his son, Ho Shai-lai, a military officer in Chiang Kai-shek's Nationalist army, and on April 2, 1950, he even went so far as to lend a car for his son's use in a daring commando raid to blow up airplanes that the People's Republic had claimed in Hong Kong. Following this successful raid, his son rose to prominence in the Taiwan-based Nationalist government and held high diplomatic posts as well as military ones. In the meantime, Robert Ho Tung prospered in Hong Kong, and when he died at the age of ninety-four in 1956, he bequeathed his fortune to heirs in Hong Kong and elsewhere outside China. In his will, he pledged funds for philanthropic purposes in China, implying that he was not devoid of nationalism, but his donations did not go to China because he set conditions for their acceptance that the government of the People's Republic refused to meet.

Just as Robert Ho Tung was politically committed to Hong Kong, so too was Koo Chen-fu politically committed to Taiwan. As portrayed by Tsai-man Ho, Koo had grown up in Taiwan like his ancestors before him and had considered it his home under Japanese colonial rule, which ended in 1945. In 1947, after Chiang Kai-shek's Nationalist government began its retreat from China to Taiwan, the newly arrived mainland officials arrested the Taiwanese Koo as a traitor and war criminal for collaborating with the Japanese during the Sino-Japanese War of 1937–1945, and they imprisoned him for nineteen months. Once released, he fled to Hong Kong, where he remained from 1949 to 1952—the same years that many Chinese capitalists fled from China to Hong Kong. Then, after receiving Chiang Kai-shek's personal guarantee for his safe return, Koo went back to Taiwan, and as the leader of Taiwan's third largest land-owning family, he participated in the Nationalist government's land reform and became the head of the Taiwan Cement Corporation. Unlike the other Chinese capitalists described in this book, he conceived of his homeland as the post-colonial island of Taiwan rather than the British colony of Hong

Kong, the nation of China, a Chinese city like Tianjin or Shanghai, a native place like Taishan, or anywhere else on the mainland.

If Robert Ho Tung and Koo Chen-fu chose to live outside China because they aligned themselves against its government and supported the governments of Hong Kong and Taiwan, not all Chinese capitalists refused to return to China for such politically charged reasons. A case in point is the banker Hsia Pin-fang, who, as described by Elisabeth Köll, was self-consciously apolitical. In 1951, after serving as a manager for the Bank of China in New York (1939–1945) and London (1946–1951), he decided not to take up a residence any place in Asia, and instead he spent the rest of his life in the West. According to Köll's analysis, he made this decision not to return to China or Taiwan based on the ethics of his profession as a banker. His belief in this code is perhaps traceable all the way back to 1925–1927 when as a young man he earned an M.B.A. with a concentration in investment banking at Harvard Business School. Subsequently throughout his career, when his superiors urged him to bend the rules, he adamantly refused, establishing a reputation for financial probity and even moralistic rigidity. Between 1949 and 1951, he was aggressively courted by banking officials in Beijing and Taipei, and he chose to reject positions offered to him by both the Communist and the Nationalist governments on the grounds that their approaches to banking were politically motivated and morally repugnant. In Köll's words, his decision not to serve as a banker in China or Taiwan and to remain in the West for the remainder of his life was "foremost guided by professional and personal values, not by dogmatic political convictions."

Taken together, these interpretations for explaining why Chinese capitalists chose to live and work in or outside the People's Republic encompass a wide array of possible motivations. They do not exclude nationalism, but they offer a variety of other alternatives: urban localism, rural native-place affiliation, political alignment with a government outside the mainland, and apolitical loyalty to an institution or a profession. Moreover they do not discount the possibility that a single capitalist adopted more than one of these rationales at various stages of his thinking about the difficult decision whether to live in China. For that matter, they include the possibility that such an individual entertained more than one of these rationales simultaneously.[7]

---

7. For example, it is easy to imagine that Zhang Jianhui, the subject of Chan's essay, shifted his loyalties as he traveled from place to place and job to job in tumultuous times; and it seems likely that Gu Zhun, as portrayed by Leighton, remained committed to the nation even while he defended the interests of his hometown. On the compatibility of na-

CHINA IN COMPARATIVE PERSPECTIVE

On these two issues—the speed of China's transition to socialism and the motivations of capitalists for staying or returning to China or leaving it—the contributors to this book have given contrasting and in some cases conflicting interpretations that are well worth debating in the context of Chinese history. In raising these issues, have they posed challenges that go beyond Chinese history and have implications for the history of communism and capitalism in other settings? If similar issues arise in the history of other Communist revolutions, do these other cases yield comparisons that might help resolve the issues in the case of China? In search of answers, it is worth considering how these two issues have been addressed by historians writing about three other Communist revolutions: the ones in Russia, Vietnam, and Cuba.

During the Russian Revolution, the transition from capitalism to socialism seems to have been abrupt and violent. The Bolsheviks launched their revolution in 1917, and they completed the transition to socialism by 1920. Historians generally agree that prerevolutionary private capitalists were virtually all killed or driven out of Russia by "wartime communism," 1918–1920, although they differ about whether the Bolsheviks or two wars—first World War I and then the Russian Civil War—were primarily responsible for this outcome. In 1921, after private capitalists had been eliminated from Russia, V.I. Lenin introduced his New Economic Policy, which included some forms of state capitalism. But it produced "Nepmen" (small-scale entrepreneurs and traders), not large-scale capitalists, and it ended abruptly when Joseph Stalin shut it down in 1928.[8]

By contrast, during the Vietnamese revolution, the transition from capitalism to socialism was slower and less violent. In 1945, Ho Chi Minh founded the Democratic Republic of Vietnam, based in Hanoi and confined to the northern part of the country, and in the 1950s Vietnamese leaders were well aware of precedents set by Russian and Chinese Communist revolutionaries in their treatment of capitalists. But not until 1958 did Vietnamese Communist leaders launch a campaign to "transform capitalism," and although it lasted for two years, 1958–1960, this campaign did not eliminate capitalism in North Vietnam,

---

tionalism, localism, and native place identity in the thinking of Chinese in presocialist Shanghai, see Bryna Goodman, *Native Place, City, and Nation: Regional Networks and Identities in Shanghai, 1853–1937* (Berkeley: University of California Press, 1995).

8. Alan Ball, *Russia's Last Capitalists: The Nepmen, 1921–1929* (Berkeley: University of California Press, 1990).

much less the entire country. It bore some resemblance to the CCP's Five Anti campaign of 1952 in China, but as Tuong Vu has observed, it included fewer public mass denunciations or trials than China's Five Anti campaign and was "timid by Chinese standards."[9] Not until nearly twenty years later, 1978–1980, after winning the war against South Vietnam and the United States, did the Vietnamese Communist Party carry out a more radical policy toward capitalists throughout the country.[10]

Compared to the transitions from capitalism to socialism in Russia and Vietnam, the one in Cuba was fastest and most decisive. Before taking power in January 1959, Fidel Castro was receptive to capitalists to the extent that he accepted financial aid from them, but within the next twenty-two months—by October 1960—he fully nationalized all private enterprises, causing Cuban capitalists to flee from Havana to Miami (only ninety miles away) and other cities abroad.[11] Unlike Lenin in Russia or Ho Chi Minh in Vietnam, Castro was not in the midst of fighting a long or bloody war during the transition to socialism, and perhaps he felt free to adopt an uncompromising policy toward capitalists because he was not experiencing wartime devastation and did not feel the need for capitalists' help in carrying out a postwar economic recovery. Subsequently he did not compensate for this elimination of private capitalism by introducing state capitalism (as Lenin had done with his New Economic Policy), and he still has not welcomed capitalists back into Cuba (as the governments of Russia, China, and Vietnam have all done under market reforms since the late twentieth century).

Within this comparative framework, where can we place China? If the speed of its transition to socialism is measured strictly by the time taken between the founding of a Communist government and the nationalization of private enterprises, then the length of time taken in China (seven years) was longer than the time taken in Cuba (less than two years) or Russia (three years not counting seven years of state capitalism under the New Economic Policy); and it was shorter than

---

9. Tuong Vu, *Paths to Development in Asia: South Korea, Vietnam, China, and Indonesia* (Cambridge: Cambridge University Press, 2010), 102; Nguyen Thi Ngoc Thanh, "The Reform of Capitalists and Capitalism in North Vietnam (1958–1960)" (Hanoi: unpublished paper, 1999). I am grateful to Tuong Vu for providing me with a copy of this unpublished paper.

10. Nguyen Van Canh, *Vietnam under Communism, 1975–1982* (Stanford: Hoover Institution, 1983), chap. 2. According to this interpretation, Vietnam's transition to socialism in the late 1970s "did not imply a philosophy of gradualism" (26).

11. Alfred L. Padula, Jr., "The Fall of the Bourgeoisie: Cuba, 1959–1961" (unpublished Ph.D. dissertation, University of New Mexico, 1974), chaps. 6 and 7.

the length of time in Vietnam (thirteen years before the first campaign against capitalism in the north and another fifteen years before the nationalization of enterprises nationwide).

But in measuring speed, shouldn't a Communist party's goals for itself in approaching capitalists during the transition to socialism also be taken into account? If so, then the CCP's aggressive courting of capitalists during the revolution in China (as documented in this book) seems to set it apart from Communist parties during the revolutions in Russia, Vietnam, and Cuba. Only in China did the party dispatch emissaries throughout the country and abroad to convince capitalists that they should serve their country under communism during the revolution. Or did the Communist parties in these other countries also make appeals to capitalists that have not yet come to light because they were made in secret? The findings by historians of China in the following essays pose this question for researchers in Russian, Vietnamese, and Cuban history.

On the issue of whether Chinese capitalists reacted nationalistically to a Communist revolution, it is also helpful to make comparisons with the Russian, Vietnamese, and Cuban revolutions. In these three cases, capitalists seem to have been even less inclined to take nationalistic stances than Chinese capitalists were.

In Russia, a group of Moscow-based entrepreneurs became proponents of economic nationalism for "Great Russia" in the nineteenth and early twentieth centuries, but they failed to broaden their ideology to include political nationalism and found no justification in it for staying in their homeland during the Communist revolution. At that time Russian capitalists were, in Steve Smith's characterization, "politically unassertive, deeply segmented by region and branch of industry and tied to the traditional merchant estate."[12] Moreover, even if Russian capitalists had been more politically nationalistic, they had no incentive to espouse nationalism during the revolution because as capitalists they were categorically condemned by the Bolsheviks whether they were identified as nationalists or not. As Sheila Fitzpatrick has observed, "The Bolsheviks considered themselves to be part of an international proletarian revolutionary movement [against capitalism], and hoped that their success

---

12. S.A. Smith, *Revolution and the People in Russia and China: A Comparative History* (Cambridge: Cambridge University Press, 2008), 195. On the emergence of the Great Russian nationalists and other entrepreneurs in nineteenth-century Russia, see Alfred J. Rieber, *Merchants and Entrepreneurs in Imperial Russia* (Chapel Hill: University of North Carolina Press, 1982).

in Russia would spark similar revolutions throughout Europe; they did not originally think of the new Soviet Republic as a nation state."[13]

During the revolution in Vietnam, unlike the one in Russia, capitalists had incentives to portray themselves as nationalistic because Vietnamese Communist leaders, following Mao Zedong's example, drew a sharp distinction between "national capitalists" (who were encouraged to remain in the country and live and work under socialism) and "compradore bureaucratic capitalists" (who were not). After defeating the French and ending colonial rule in 1954, Vietnamese Communists gave credit to Vietnamese capitalists who had demonstrated independence from French imperialists. In late 1955, these party members credited Vietnamese national capitalists as being "one of the four masters of the new regime" and considered them to be "a friend of the working class with many shortcomings but also many positive traits."[14] During and after the Vietnamese Communists' campaign of 1958–1960 to "transform capitalists" (as described above), many Vietnamese sought identification as national rather than compradore capitalists, and those who failed to acquire this designation disguised or doctored their records to give the impression that no one in their families had ever been a capitalist so that they could qualify for jobs as workers in state enterprises.[15]

In Cuba, the Communist leaders were more like those of Vietnam than those of Russia insofar as they bristled with nationalism, and in the initial phase of the revolution, some of the Cuban capitalists responded favorably to Castro's calls for economic nationalism. In 1958, as he claimed the victories that brought him to power, they made financial contributions to his movement, and after he established his new government in January 1959, they supported his drive for "the economic liberation of Cuba," which they found appealing because it included the idea of persuading consumers to "buy Cuban." By all these means Cuban capitalists tried, in the words of Alfred Padula, "to wrap themselves in the Cuban flag whatever defense it might afford."[16] But their nationalism, if not totally rootless, was shallow and weak as a result of their historically

---

13. Sheila Fitzpatrick, *The Russian Revolution, 1917–1932* (Oxford: Oxford University Press, 1982), 62.

14. Quoted by Tuong Vu, "Workers and the Socialist State: North Vietnam's State-Labor Relations, 1945–1970," *Communist and Post-Communist Studies* 38 (2005): 338. In the late 1970s, when the Vietnamese leadership extended its nationalization of capitalist enterprises nationwide, it also made use of the distinction between national and compradore capitalists. See Nguyen Van Canh, *Vietnam under Communism*, 25–26 and 35–37.

15. Vu, "Workers and the Socialist State," 345.

16. Padula, "The Fall," 282.

strong ties with the United States.[17] In the past, they had seen the United States intervene when Cuba had become politically unstable, and with these precedents in mind, even while they courted Castro, they assumed that if he turned against them and posed a threat to their businesses, they could count on the United States to oust him and protect them. Accordingly, their nationalism did not prevent them from fleeing to Miami and other cities abroad when the new government nationalized first the country's banks in August 1960 and then its private enterprises a few months later in October. As they departed, they remained confident that the United States would soon clear the way for their return, and they did not lose this confidence until April 17–19, 1961, when Cuban exiles under the sponsorship of the United States failed in their attempt to invade Cuba at the Bay of Pigs.

By comparison with capitalists in the Russian, Vietnamese, and Cuban Communist revolutions, the ones in China, as portrayed in this book, are similar in some respects and different in others. The most striking similarity is that Chinese capitalists, like Russian, Vietnamese, and Cuban ones, did not base their decisions to stay, leave, or return to their home countries solely on nationalism. In China, as in Vietnam (and not Russia or Cuba), the leaders of the new Communist government encouraged capitalists to espouse nationalism by placing a value on national capitalists as distinct from compradore bureaucratic capitalists. But even those that the government designated as national capitalists did not all choose to live in China under socialism for nationalistic reasons.[18]

How can capitalists' motivations during a Communist revolution be reliably documented and fully understood? Up to now, the answer to this question has generally eluded scholars who, for lack of nonofficial sources, have fallen back on Communist governments' official explanations. But the essays in this volume confirm that, at least in the case of the Communist revolution in China, it is finally possible to make new and fresh interpretations. By focusing closely on individuals and

---

17. Padula has concluded that Cuban capitalists "never ... thought in terms of the nation." See his "The Fall," 573. Jorge Dominguez agrees that Cubans in general were not nationalistic at the time of the revolution in 1959, but he has added historical nuance to this conclusion: "Nationalism was a useful theme in the Cuba of the 1930s and of the 1960s, but not in that of the two decades in between." see Dominguez, *Cuba: Order and Revolution* (Cambridge: Harvard University Press, 1978), 119.

18. For the case of a Chinese capitalist who chose to live in China for non-nationalistic reasons and questioned whether he should be designated as a national capitalist, see Sherman Cochran, "Capitalists Choosing Communist China: The Liu Family of Shanghai, 1948–1956," in Brown and Pickowicz, eds., *Dilemmas of Victory*, 359–385.

probing deeply into their thinking and experience, the authors of these essays have discovered a wide range of reasons for why Chinese capitalists did or did not choose to live and work under communism. The contributors to this volume have all concentrated on the dilemma for capitalists in China's Communist revolution. But their approach to their subject through archival research and rigorous analysis may also serve as a guide for future thinking about a variety of other historical figures. This approach is well worth adopting to explain how any members of society (not only capitalists) have resolved comparable dilemmas in all revolutions—the ones in China, Russia, Vietnam, Cuba, or anywhere else.

This page is intentionally left blank.

PART ONE
CAPITALISTS WHO LEFT CHINA

This page is intentionally left blank.

2 SHOTGUN WEDDING |
Song Feiqing, the Dongya Corporation, and the Early Communist Regime

Brett Sheehan

The Communist Revolution came early to Tianjin. The city fell to Communist forces on January 15, 1949, four months before the fall of Shanghai and a full eight and a half months before declaration of the founding of the People's Republic of China. It was not the first large city Communist forces took, but it was the largest city to date, and the largest business center. As such, it became the vital test case for the Chinese Communist Party's (CCP's) moderate policies toward urban elites of the so-called New Democracy period spoken of by Mao beginning in 1939 and especially in his "On New Democracy" of January 1940.[1] In Tianjin, as elsewhere, the period between Communist takeover and the Five Anti campaign of 1952 is often portrayed as a honeymoon of patriotic United Front cooperation between the CCP and China's capitalists. During this honeymoon period the Communist Party aggressively courted particular "patriotic" capitalist representatives and simultaneously implemented policies supposedly favorable to the inclusion of private business within the structures of the new China. Sherman Cochran, however, has recently shown that capitalists had complex reasons for cooperating with the new regime. Standard explanations of patriotic motivations did not necessarily hold true.[2]

The research for this essay was made possible by generous support and assistance from the University of Wisconsin graduate school, the Fulbright Foundation, the Teaching Asian Cultures Foundation, the Sung family, and the University of Southern California.

1. Mao himself dated the New Democracy period to the 1910s and 1920s, but party policies accepting capitalists did not begin until about 1940. See Stuart Schram, *The Thought of Mao Tse-tung* (Cambridge: Cambridge University Press, 1989), 75–79.
2. Sherman Cochran, "Capitalists Choosing Communist China: The Liu Family of Shanghai, 1948–56," in Jeremy Brown and Paul G. Pickowicz, eds., *Dilemmas of Victory: The*

Similarly, the picture in Tianjin was more complicated than normally thought. The initial months of Communist control produced unsuccessful results as labor activists and wary capitalists battled. In response, the party dispatched Liu Shaoqi, organizer extraordinaire and second only to Mao in the party hierarchy, for a month-long stay in Tianjin in the spring of 1949 to see if he could make the party's new urban policies work. In a series of talks with local officials, labor representatives, and business leaders, Liu managed to perform a shotgun wedding between socialism and capitalism. He chastised local party officials, reined in labor, and buttered up capitalists.

After this shotgun wedding, the party promoted Tianjin as the model of how to apply moderate policies to business. For example, the party passed out propaganda to local businesspeople in Chengdu in southwest China pointing to Tianjin as a successful case of cooperation between patriotic capitalists and the Chinese Communist Party.[3] In spite of the use of Tianjin in party propaganda as an instance of a successful marriage between socialism and capitalism, I will use the experience of Song Feiqing (1899–1955) and the company he managed, the Dongya Corporation, to show that even during this honeymoon period, the party was able to impose its will on private industry, leaving little freedom for capitalist maneuver.[4] Although Song and the Dongya Corporation had a highly visible presence in Tianjin and in Communist attempts to court capitalists, the company's experience shows that long before the Five Anti campaign of 1952 and even before the "Resist America, Aid Korea" campaign of late 1950, the party constructed a web of controls on work methods, production goals, finance, markets, and disposition of company resources that eliminated any possibility for autonomous capitalist activity. This one-sided marriage looked happy in public and allowed private enterprises to make money, but simultaneously quickly subordinated capitalist enterprises and their workers to party goals in a process of partification of economic life.[5]

Early Years of the People's Republic of China (Cambridge and London: Harvard University Press, 2007), 359–385.

3. Personal communication from Regina Abrami.

4. In a similar manner, Kenneth G. Lieberthal saw the period in Tianjin prior to 1952 as one of providing a foundation that made later campaigns possible. *Revolution and Tradition in Tientsin, 1949–1952* (Stanford: Stanford University Press, 1980), 8. Some sources say Song Feiqing died in 1956, but the notes of his widow, Li Jingfang, and other family sources state 1955.

5. By partification, I mean the subordination of private capital and private resources to direction by the Communist Party.

A STORMY COURTSHIP:
EARLY COMMUNIST RULE OF TIANJIN

In a pattern that repeated itself all over China, the fall of Tianjin looked as much like a collapse of the Nationalists as a victory for the Communists. In a later retrospective look at the period, an executive of the Dongya Corporation remembered the chaotic currency situation, difficulty purchasing materials after a state-decreed price freeze, and "coercive buying" when "wounded soldiers came in groups and disrupted things to the extent that ... the staff did not dare go to work."[6] With the collapse of the Nationalists, Tianjin faced the third regime change in the city in twelve years. The Dongya Corporation had survived the two previous regime changes, the Japanese invasion in 1937 and then Nationalist reassertion of power at the end of the war in 1945, by shifting production from its core business of knitting yarn to gunny sacks. The latter was an essential item in the transport of foodstuffs and other commodities, and the demand for gunny sacks actually increased at times of turmoil and war for transport of military supplies.

Amid the chaos, the Chinese Communist Party made its opening move in the long-term campaign to recruit Song Feiqing as an ally. One evening at home, Song Feiqing, who had been feeling "restless and anxious," received a telephone call from Shi Xiaodong, a Dongya employee long known to have leftist sympathies who had disappeared from the factory at the end of October.[7] In spite of blackout and curfew, Shi Xiaodong negotiated the streets and came to see Song at his home. He brought a message from the CCP Northern Bureau asking for Song Feiqing's help first in protecting the city during fighting and then his cooperation under future Communist rule. Song expressed concerns about foreign intervention in the event of Communist victory and about the possibility of a divided China with Communists in the north and Nationalists in the south. The former could lead to World War III and the latter to an isolated north China unable to survive economically. The meeting concluded with Song's pledge to remain at Dongya's helm. Song even showed Shi the new sofa he had purchased that could be made into a bed. He had bought it with the intention of moving into Dongya to supervise management during the coming fight.[8] Other than this, Song Feiqing made no further commitments to the party.

---

6. Report to Dongya Shareholders, March 26, 1950, History Museum (03).
7. On Song Feiqing's mood at this time, see Li Jingshan (7).
8. This account is based on the recollections of Song family and friends, including Shi

Good to Song Feiqing's word, on December 18, Dongya's management announced measures taken to address the tense political situation by issuing part of the wages for the first half of December early, as well as issuing flour and corn for employee consumption.[9] Two days later the company established a committee to oversee emergency measures during the coming political transition.[10] As Dongya employees hunkered down, so did at least some Nationalist troops in Tianjin. Authorities built a dyke around the city to serve as a bulwark; they expelled villagers and burned down their villages to create a clear line of fire.[11] Tianjin's local elites feared complete destruction of the city and petitioned Nationalist authorities to spare the city the ravages of war.[12] Song Feiqing joined eighty-one local-elite petitioners drawn from the ranks of scholars, professors, lawyers, National Assembly delegates, city councilors, merchants, industrialists and gentry. Their petition asked Fu Zuoyi, the Nationalist commander, to "remove troops from the cities of Peiping and Tientsin [Beiping and Tianjin] and fight the Communists outside their [city] limits. Should this be found impossible under the circumstances, we [the petitioners] sincerely request that the fight be discontinued forthwith in order to save millions of lives from unnecessary sacrifices."[13] Along with many other local elites, Song Feiqing apparently had become reconciled to Communist victory and saw surrender as preferable to continuation of the destructive war.

In the end the Nationalist will to fight disintegrated and the final battle for Tianjin lasted only five hours at mid-day on January 15. By three o'clock, the Communists were in control of the city. The Dongya factory did not have any losses, except for one shell that landed and put a hole in the corner of the wall of the worker personnel department. No one was hurt.[14]

In possession of their largest urban prize to date, the Communists launched their administration of Tianjin with a combination of admir-

---

Xiaodong in Song Yunzhang and Wang Weigang, *Tade meng: Song Feiqing* (His dream: Song Feiqing) (Hong Kong: Wenming, 2006), 323–326. See also Li Jingshan (7).

9. "Announcement (27) No. 93," December 18, 1948, Dongya Corp., 1-77-2-09.

10. "Committee for Facing the Political Change, Notice 18-83-quan-37," December 20, 1948, and various documents related to the work of the Committee for Facing the Political Change, December 23, 1948, Dongya Corp., 1-84-9-01.

11. This description is included in a petition of local dignitaries to Chiang Kai-shek to spare the cities and is preserved in a Reuters dispatch, December 30, 1938, in Siguret to Meyriet, December 31, 1948 (Nantes), box 100.

12. Siguret to Foreign Ministry, December 24, 1948 (Paris).

13. Reuters dispatch, December 30, 1938, in Siguret to Meyriet, December 31, 1948 (Nantes), box 100.

14. Li Jingshan (7).

able self-discipline and understandable lack of direction. The People's Liberation Army had become a well-oiled machine and the military occupation went smoothly. Frederic Wakeman memorably called the conquering Communist soldiers an "army of adolescents."[15] In Tianjin these adolescents demonstrated remarkable discipline and restraint.[16] Day-to-day urban administration, however, posed different challenges to the Communists. An American observer in Tianjin wrote that even though "The military occupation was well planned, well organized and well executed ... the civil administration seems not nearly so well prepared. A great lack of competent administrators, executives and officials is evident."[17]

At Dongya company management had proved adept over the years at coming to accommodation with regimes of varied political outlooks. In spite of the early message of cooperation sent by emissary Shi Xiaodong, however, accommodation with the Communists appeared much harder than with previous regimes. Underground party workers among Dongya employees organized anti-capitalist demonstrations and activities. Employee activists even went so far as to resume production on the third day after the fall of the city without consulting with factory management. The employees turned on the machines in response to party calls to resume production and restore Tianjin's economy, but company president Song Feiqing was appalled at the thought that the factory was running without concern for either supplies of raw materials or sales outlets.[18] In addition to facing the challenge posed by previously underground party members among Dongya's employees, the company also had to deal with a team from the party government's general municipal union, which arrived at Dongya only a few days after the fall of Tianjin.[19]

Even the union work team that came to Dongya did not seem to know what to do, and it soon issued a self-criticism saying it had not had proper time to truly listen to employee concerns.[20] A few days after this self-criticism, conflicts with workers across Tianjin reached a crest at the time of the Chinese New Year just under a month after the party took control of Tianjin. At that time, many workers made demands for back

---

15. Frederic Wakeman, "'Cleanup': The New Order in Shanghai," in Brown and Pickowicz, eds., *Dilemmas of Victory*, 22.

16. See Jobez (Hong Kong) to Meyrier (Nanjing)—Situation in Tianjin, April 12. 1949, (Paris); and ECA, "General Situation Report, January 10–31, 1949," Griffen, box 4, 5.

17. ECA, "General Situation Report, January 10–31, 1949," Griffen, box 4, 6.

18. Song and Wang, *Tade meng*, 330.

19. Dongya Corp., 2-86-2-01.

20. Dongya Corp., 2-86-2-01.

pay, bonuses and rehiring, and city officials were reluctant to ask workers to be moderate.[21] At Dongya a hundred plus workers surrounded the factory managers' office and shouted slogans such as "we will not continue to accept capitalist exploitation," "overthrow Song Feiqing," and "workers should be the masters of Dongya."[22] In the initial days of Communist rule, it appeared as if Song Feiqing had completely lost control of the company, as if capitalism and communism were implacable opponents. In a speech at a work conference on private enterprises, municipal Second Assistant Party Secretary Huang Huoqing admitted that many workers had taken advantage of capitalists' initial fear to make excessive demands during the first days of Communist rule prior to the New Year.[23]

On February 20 the Dongya board of directors held their first meeting since the fall of Tianjin. The minutes nostalgically looked back at the period of unity of only a month before when "more than 1,000 of our workers and employees enthusiastically formed a factory protection brigade." Now, under Communist rule and at the crest of labor activism, the board regretted the dissolution of this spirit of unity. After the fall of Tianjin, previously underground party members "organized a dispute brigade (*jiufen dui*) which caused the disbandment of the factory protection brigade." Clearly management faced new and difficult challenges. In addition, "inventories of supplies and produced goods were very short, perhaps only [enough] to maintain production for two or three months." Nonetheless, in spite of labor conflict and lack of raw materials, company management, experienced with years of wartime chaos, prepared to preserve its cash hoard and barter for supplies.[24] To raise additional cash, the company undertook an advertising campaign to promote sales and began running ads in the newly renamed *Progressive Daily* (*Jinbu ribao*, formerly *Dagong bao*, or *The Impartial*) to sell both gunny sacks and knitting yarn.[25]

As Dongya management tried to restore some sense of normalcy, and party officials continued to juggle the many balls involved with

---

21. Huang Xiaotong and Li Wenfang, *Liu Shaoqi yu Tianjin jianghua* (Liu Shaoqi and the Tianjin talks) (Kaifeng: Henan daxue chubanshe, 1998), 56.

22. Song and Wang, *Tade meng*, 332.

23. "Huang Huoqing tongzhi zai siying qiye weiyuanhui huiyi shang de tan hua" (Comrade Huang Huoqing's speech at the meeting of the Private Enterprise Commission), Zhonggong Tianjin shiwei dangshi ziliao zhengji weiyuan hui, Zhonggong Tianjin shiwei tongzhan bu, Tianjinshi dang'anguan, eds., *Zhongguo zibenzhuyi gongshangye de shehuizhuyi gaizao, Tianjin juan* (The socialist transformation of Chinese capitalist business and industry, Tianjin volume) (Tianjin: Zhonggong dangshi chubanshe, 1991), 26.

24. Board of directors meeting of February 20, 1949, Dongya Corp., 2-91-7-02.

25. *Jinbu ribao* (Progressive daily, formerly *Dagong bao*), February 27, 28, and March 2, 1949.

municipal administration. A pall of uncertainty and confusion hung over the city. Looking back, a Dongya manager later described this period as a time of "no clear understanding of the government policies."[26] Party officials seemed perplexed at the difficulty of balancing Communist ideology and capitalist production. Mayor Huang Jing eventually did intervene in Dongya's labor conflict, and Dongya's union representatives came to realize that satisfying worker demands would bankrupt the company.[27] Nonetheless city officials were still very tentative. Huang Jing later admitted that he refused to shake Song Feiqing's hand the first time they met.[28] At about the same time, less than a month after beginning its administration, the Tianjin Party Committee submitted a self criticism admitting to lack of experience in administering cities.[29] Bo Yibo, head of the CCP's Northern Bureau, submitted a report on February 27 outlining the serious problems in Tianjin, most of them economic. He pointed to the lack of capital, shortage of raw materials, poor transport, and decline of foreign trade, and thus shortage of foreign exchange.[30] In addition to the problems pointed out by Bo Yibo, inflation continued to rage and a black market developed in U.S. dollars.[31]

Communist Party leaders were certainly aware of the potential problems with administering cities.[32] Nonetheless, cities fell to the Communists with such speed that earlier lessons had yet to sink in. In one more attempt to get serious about developing new urban policies, the CCP's Seventh Central Committee took up the matter at its famous second plenum in March of 1949 held at Xibaipo in Hebei province.[33] At that meeting, Liu Shaoqi gave a speech emphasizing the need to change party policies to include strategies for cities as well as the countryside. Although much of his speech focused on taking over those industries formerly run by the Nationalist government, Liu also pointed to the problem of getting private industries back to work as soon as possible.[34]

---

26. Report to Dongya Shareholders, March 26, 1950, Tianjin History Museum (03). On confusion in Communist policy, see also French Chamber of Commerce (Tianjin) to Meffreys, March 3, 1949 (Nantes), box 100; and ECA, "General Situation Report of Tientsin [Tianjin] for February 1–March 19, 1949," Griffen, box 4, 1.

27. Song and Wang, *Tade meng*, 332.

28. Huang and Li, *Liu Shaoqi*, 54.

29. Ibid., 26.

30. Ibid., 27–28.

31. ECA, "General Situation Report, January 10–31, 1949," Griffen, box 4, 2.

32. Wakeman, "'Cleanup,'" 22.

33. On Mao's attitude at this meeting see ibid., 25.

34. Huang and Li, *Liu Shaoqi*, 34.

Even after this plenum, the confusion and ambivalence of party cadres toward capitalists was still evident in Tianjin as seen in a long, two-part article on Dongya that appeared in *Progressive Daily* at the end of March 1949. It included quotes from interviews with Song Feiqing, Chen Xisan, a vice president at Dongya, staff members and workers. It also liberally quoted from Chairman Mao's speeches and writings about the New People's Democracy. The content of the article ended up as a hodgepodge of justification by Dongya of its need for foreign exchange to purchase raw materials, criticism by the reporter of Dongya's sins, and a plea that everyone should be able to unite to build a strong and new China under the enlightened policies of unity and New People's Democracy.[35] In opening and closing sections, the reporter got to the crux of the political questions surrounding Dongya, Song Feiqing and, by extension, other capitalists in Tianjin. The reporter noted, "On March 6 the employees of the Dongya Corporation held a meeting and Song Feiqing denied he was an exploiter." Apparently unrepentant and unused to Communist-style self-criticism, Song Feiqing held to his belief that he had treated workers well. The reporter then asked Song Feiqing's opinion about the party's New Democracy slogan of "Increased Production, Flourishing Economy, A Matter for Both Public and Private, Benefit to Both Labor and Capital" (*zengjia shengchan, fanrong jingji, gongsi jiangu, laozi liangli*). Song Feiqing responded ambivalently that

> This principle is very good and there is no problem benefiting labor and capital. But, in the future there will be difficulties as an individual. For a lifetime I expended money and effort, took great pains in management and accomplished certain achievements. Now I have received a label as a "capitalist" it is truly ...

Choking on the words, Song stopped in mid sentence, the reporter explained. The article then instructed readers,

> In truth ["capitalist"] is only a social scientific name. Under the New People's Democratic Society, the capitalist class is a necessary element ... Chairman Mao has already made this clear ... President Song Feiqing who has been trained in the natural sciences, can certainly understand this point.[36]

---

35. *Jinbu ribao*, March 27, 1949, and March 28, 1949, both 1–3.

36. *Jinbu ribao*, March 28, 1949, 1–3. The idea that the party could decide whether or

With Song Feiqing properly chastised about his unscientific mis-understanding of party policies, the article ended on a note of anti-capitalist rhetoric by mentioning the story of a woman worker at Dongya surnamed Du whose unexplained tragedy should never be repeated.[37] If nothing else, it was clear that the Dongya Corporation had come to the forefront of local discussions and propaganda on the meaning and place of capitalism in Tianjin and the new China.

Otherwise, implementation of the party's policies seemed a confused mess. As local officials struggled to understand and implement the party's policies toward business, the party dispatched Vice-chairman Liu Shaoqi to Tianjin to see if he could find out what was wrong in the city and fix it.

THE SHOTGUN WEDDING:
LIU SHAOQI'S VISIT TO TIANJIN

At the time Liu Shaoqi prepared to visit Tianjin, party leaders had just moved to Beijing where Liu paid a call on the family of his new wife, Wang Guangmei. The visit gave Liu a chance to ask the Wangs about conditions in Tianjin, the family's former home. Wang Guangmei's brother, Wang Guangying, still had business affairs in Tianjin and his conversation with Liu Shaoqi has been reported based on Wang Guangmei's later recollec-tions in conversations with a party historian.[38] After a long discussion of Tianjin's economic and business conditions, Wang asked Liu about joining the party. Liu Shaoqi responded by saying, "The party has lots of members and cadres, but there are very few people who understand commerce and industry. If you can wear the clothes of a businessperson and still be on the side of the party and the workers, then that would be great!" Liu clearly wanted to give the impression that the party sought an alliance with business, not partification of the business world.

On April 9, the day before Liu Shaoqi left for Tianjin, Northern Party Bureau chief Bo Yibo submitted another report to party leaders summarizing the problems in Tianjin. Among a host of economic problems, he noted difficulties handling capitalists because party cadres

---

not individual capitalists were good or bad echoes Zhou Enlai's conversation with Liu Hongsheng. See Cochran, "Capitalists," 370.

37. *Jinbu ribao*, March 28, 1949, 1–3.

38. These recollections are recorded in Huang and Li, *Liu Shaoqi*, 36–37; and, almost word-for-word in Chen Yingci (apparently the party historian who actually visited Wang Guangmei), "Guanyu jiefang chu Liu Shaoqi de Tianjin zhi xing" (Liu Shaoqi's trip to Tian-jin in the early period of Liberation) *Yahuang chunqiu* 4 (1996): 2–8.

were afraid they would be judged too "rightist" if they spoke moderately to capitalists, and at the same time they were reluctant to discipline workers and tell them to discontinue activism. Thus, they simply "did not express opinions about worker struggles [with capitalists]."[39] A report from the Tianjin party pointed out that industry was particularly slow to get back to work because of mistrust on the behalf of capitalists. Even those factories reporting resumption of production, the report complained, often did so just to satisfy the authorities, but the reports did not represent reality.[40] Clearly the party needed to do something to get production on track.

Liu Shaoqi's train arrived in Tianjin on the evening of April 10. During his twenty-eight day visit to the city he heard reports from city officials, held meetings with various groups, visited companies (most state-run), participated in five conferences, and took two tours of the city.[41] During this time, he gave a series of speeches later collectively referred to as the "Tianjin Talks" (*Tianjin jianghua*). The texts of these talks became fodder for later political struggle during the Cultural Revolution when Liu Shaoqi was attacked for his activities in Tianjin in 1949 as one of his biggest "crimes" and proof of his secret identity as a "capitalist roader."[42] The subsequent controversies surrounding the "Tianjin Talks" have long obscured the events of 1949 themselves. Fortunately, study of the Dongya Corporation and Song Feiqing provides an excellent means to understand Liu Shaoqi's directives at the time. The company and Song Feiqing himself both had prominent roles in Liu's activities. In fact, Dongya was one of only two private companies Liu visited while in Tianjin.[43]

The night Liu Shaoqi arrived in Tianjin he heard reports from the Tianjin mayor and other high municipal officials. Huang Kecheng, secretary of the Tianjin Party Committee and head of the military administration, admitted that since taking control of Tianjin city officials had been "cold"

---

39. Huang and Li, *Liu Shaoqi*, 37–38.

40. "Tianjinshi gongshangju guanyu fugong fuye wenti de zongjie" (General conclusion by the Tianjin Municipal Industry and Commerce Bureau on the problem of restarting industry and employment), in Zhonggong Tianjin shiwei et al., *Zhongguo zibenzhuyi*, 25–26.

41. Huang and Li, *Liu Shaoqi*, 47.

42. On the history of the "Tianjin Talks," see Kenneth G. Lieberthal, 42, starred footnote; and a variety of Chinese publications which appeared at the time of Liu Shaoqi's posthumous rehabilitation in 1980 such as Huang and Li, *Liu Shaoqi*; and Ye Wuxi and Shao Yunrui, "Chongping 'Tianjin Jianghua'" (A New Evaluation of the Tianjin Talks), *Lishi yanjiu* 2 (1980): 47–58.

43. Huang and Li, *Liu Shaoqi*, 47. The other private company was the wool carpet company Renli.

to capitalists. Liu Shaoqi responded that the party needed to "learn from its enemies."[44] As a first step to learning from these enemies, the city asked several important capitalists, including Song Feiqing, to a meeting on April 11. Liu Shaoqi did not attend this meeting, but Song Feiqing took the opportunity to courageously present the city officials with nineteen opinions about conditions in Tianjin and China, and these became the basis for discussion. Among his opinions, Song noted that state policies were unclear on the amount of profit considered acceptable, that spiritual attacks on capitalists undermined morale, that workers and peasants did not have the education to run enterprises, that business needed consistent trade policies, that only the board of directors empowered by the shareholders could represent capital, and that investigations into business activities should not be too intrusive. Song also wondered, if capital and labor were to share profits, would they also share losses?[45]

With the opinions of the business community on the table, Liu Shaoqi began the job of delivering the party's message. In the following weeks in Tianjin, he spoke to all the parties involved in the shotgun marriage between socialism and capitalism that he had come to perform. This included party members, businesspeople, government cadres, and workers. First, in a talk to the Tianjin Party Committee he outlined the basic thrust of party policy and the ideas he would repeat later in public talks. Liu gave clear instructions that the party's work in the city must turn from establishing control to expanding production. He emphasized that Tianjin cadres were still not clear on the fact that national capitalists, as opposed to bureaucratic capitalists, were objects of work toward unity, not struggle. Likewise he noted that Tianjin's newspapers had not yet adopted an attitude of cooperation, but instead unsuitably "emphasized attack." He went on to speak of the need to discipline, or in his words "educate" the working masses who wanted to struggle against capitalists and who should realize that "now the emphasis is on cooperation." Working hours should not change. Wages should not increase unless they are truly too low, and then only by a limited amount. Capitalists should have the freedom to hire and fire.[46]

With party members suitably informed, the next day on April 19 Liu invited a small number of capitalists, including Song Feiqing, to a

44. Ibid., *Liu Shaoqi*, 54–56.

45. The text of Song's opinion paper is reprinted in ibid., 134–139.

46. "Liu Shaoqi tongzhi zai Zhonggong Tianjinshi weiyuanhui shang de jianghua" (Comrade Liu Shaoqi's talk to the Tianjin Party Committee), April 18, 1949, Zhonggong Tianjin shiwei et al., *Zhongguo zibenzhuyi*, 47, 48, 54.

meeting.[47] At that meeting Liu told the capitalists that he felt they still did not understand the party at its base. In addition, he promised the capitalists a bright future. He told Song Feiqing

> Now you manage one factory. In the future you can manage two, three, or eight factories. When socialism comes … you can hand the factories over to the state or the state will purchase them … Then the state will give the factories back to you to manage … Because you are capable, the state might give you eight more factories to manage, a total of sixteen factories to manage. Your salary will not be reduced, and will even be increased, but you have to manage well![48]

It is impossible to know exactly what Liu Shaoqi was thinking at the time, but in hindsight, this vision of high-paid former capitalists running state enterprises under socialism was Liu Shaoqi's pipe dream, his intentional deception of the capitalists, or, perhaps, just an ad hoc attempt to find a formula to bring socialism and capitalism together.

After his talk to businesspeople, Liu Shaoqi began speaking to larger and larger groups to broadcast his message, and these speeches were widely covered in Tianjin's newspapers. On April 24, he spoke to a meeting of Tianjin cadres where he reiterated the party line on capitalism. He stated, "We have three enemies and four friends. Imperialism, the feudal class and the bureaucratic capitalist class, these are our enemies and the objects of struggle and revolution, whereas workers, peasants, petty capitalists, and national capitalists are on our side."[49] At that meeting, he also repeated the idea that "The exploitative capitalist system still cannot be eliminated now."[50] Following this meeting with cadres, on April 28 he spoke to a large group of workers and white collar employee representatives where he included an appeal for discipline from labor.

---

47. Ibid., 50.

48. Huang and Li, *Liu Shaoqi*, 141. Liu repeated this conversation at a May 2 meeting with capitalists. See "Liu Shaoqi tongzhi zai Tianjinshi gongshangyejia zuotanhui shang de jianghua" (Talk to the Tianjin industrialists and businesspersons discussion meeting), May 2, 1949, Zhonggong Tianjin shiwei et al., *Zhongguo zibenzhuyi*, 89–93.

49. "Liu Shaoqi tongzhi zai Tianjinshi ganbu hui shang de jianghua" (Comrade Liu Shaoqi's Talk to the Tianjin cadre meeting), April 24, 1949, Zhonggong Tianjin shiwei et al., *Zhongguo zibenzhuyi*, 57.

50. Ibid., 68.

Some workers are demanding wages be doubled, tripled, quintupled, that laid-off workers be reinstated, that temporary workers be made permanent, or that factory regulations do not need to be obeyed ... Today I take responsibility for affirming to you: workers must correct these overly "leftist," unreasonable errors. If you do not do this, it will bring about terrible consequences. Factories will close, go bankrupt, production will drop ...[51]

He dismissed worker claims that they could run factories without capitalists by arguing that not a single cooperative was actually run well.[52] Four days later when speaking again with capitalists on May 2, he sounded positively ebullient in extolling the future of capitalism under party leadership. "How much profit is legal? I say any amount of profit is legal!"[53] Also, "Today capitalist exploitation is legal, the more the better."[54]

Besides giving these talks where he had slapped down worker activism and encouraged capitalist exploitation, Liu visited a number of factories in Tianjin. While most were state-owned, two, Dongya and Renli, were private. These two latter firms had special status as the examples chosen to provide a model of how the marriage between socialism and capitalism would work. In particular, Liu's visit to Dongya and his repeated references in talks to Song Feiqing and the Dongya Corporation show the importance of this company and its founder to the Communists' plans.

Liu Shaoqi and Wang Guangmei visited the Dongya Corporation on April 21, fairly early in their Tianjin sojourn. Liu and Wang arrived at Dongya in an aged limousine and spent several hours talking with Song Feiqing, company management, and worker representatives, including representatives of laid-off workers. One worker, charged with cleaning up the meeting room, recalled that his talk with workers lasted long enough for Liu to smoke two packs of cigarettes.[55] Recollections differ on the exact sequence of events of Liu's visit and to whom he said what. All accounts

---

51. "Liu Shaoqi tongzhi zai Tianjinshi zhigong daibiao dahui shang de jianghua" (Comrade Liu Shaoqi's Talk to the Tianjin professional staff and worker representatives meeting), April 28, 1949, Zhonggong Tianjin shiwei et al., *Zhongguo zibenzhuyi*, 80–81.

52. Ibid., 80–81.

53. "Liu Shaoqi tongzhi zai Tianjinshi gongshangyejia zuotanhui shang de jianghua," Zhonggong Tianjin shiwei et al., *Zhongguo zibenzhuyi*, 89–91.

54. Ibid., 89–95.

55. Zhang Boyang, "Yi Liu Shaoqi huijian 'Dongya' zhigong daibiao" (Liu Shaoqi's meeting with Dongya employee representatives), *Tianjin wenshi ziliao*, 79 (1998): 107.

agree, however, that both Liu and Song Feiqing made efforts to cooperate. For his part, Song Feiqing agreed to hire back about two hundred laid off workers. In turn Liu Shaoqi allayed Song's fears by telling him that "'Exploitation is not a scary word under the New People's Democratic Society.' [Then he asked] 'How many workers do you have now?' Song replied, 'A few more than one thousand.' Liu said, 'You are exploiting too few. You can expand ten times [that number]. The more [workers] you exploit the better because that shows that the economy is developing and that has benefit for the New People's Democratic Society.'"[56]

Contact between Liu Shaoqi and Song Feiqing did not end with this factory visit. Song Feiqing dusted off a plan he called "My Dream" about expanding Dongya into a conglomerate of more than ten companies. He had previously presented this to the Nationalist government at the end of World War II and now he presented it as a plan for development to the Communists.[57] Song Feiqing also wrote a letter to Liu Shaoqi who responded a few days later. The Tianjin press avidly covered Liu Shaoqi's visit to Dongya and the subsequent exchange of letters. *Progressive Daily* reprinted the texts of two letters in their entirety.[58] First Song Feiqing wrote, "After listening to your Excellency's wise instructions to our humble factory, all of the employees have a new understanding of the government's industrial policy and new hope for a mission of rebirth and destiny, [we] are very happy."[59] Liu Shaoqi's letter then responded, "Because your honored company is following the policy of benefiting both labor and capital, with continued hard work, the future will be

---

56. Zhao Runnian, "Yi Liu Shaoqi jianghua" (Remembering Liu Shaoqi's talk), *Tianjin wenshi ziliao* 79 (1998): 108. For alternative but largely similar tellings of Liu Shaoqi's visit to Dongya see also Ding Xiuzhu, "Yi Liu Shaoqi, Wang Guangmei shicha 'Dongya'" (Remembering Liu Shaoqi and Wang Guangmei's tour of Dongya); Song Yuzan, "Liu Shaoqi zai 'Dongya'" (Liu Shaoqi at Dongya); Zhang Guojun, "Huiyi Liu Shaoqi shicha 'dongya'" (Remembering Liu Shaoqi's tour of Dongya); and Zhang Guoxun, "Yi Liu Shaoqi 'Dongya' zhi xing" (Remembering Liu Shaoqi's trip to Dongya). These recollections by former Dongya employees are published in *Tianjin wenshi ziliao* 79 (1998): 102–103, 104–105, 109–110, and 111, respectively. In addition the papers of Li Jingshan (2) contains an account later expanded by Li Jingshan's daughter and two other authors and published as Liu Shaochun, Sun Jian and Li Yulian, "Huiyi Liu Shaoqi tongzhi shicha Dongya Gongsi" (Remembering Comrade Liu Shaoqi's visit to the Dongya Company), *Tianjin dangshi* 4 (1999): 50–52.

57. Li Jingshan (2). "My Dream" has been reprinted a number of times including in Song and Wang, *Tade meng*, 341–347. The original version presented to the Communists, complete with a drawing of hands clasping as a symbol of management and labor working together, was at the Tianjin History Museum in 2000.

58. The letters are also reproduced in Huang and Li, *Liu Shaoqi*, 143–144.

59. *Jinbu ribao*, May 6, 1949, 1–3.

bright. The restoration of the country and people can be realized soon."[60] Apparently Song Feiqing and Liu Shaoqi had agreed on a set of common goals, and publication of this exchange of letters gave the reading public a clear picture of cooperation between the party and capitalists while at the same time it amplified Dongya's symbolic importance in the coming marriage between socialism and capitalism. In fact, Liu Shaoqi himself frequently referred to Dongya and Song Feiqing as examples of how his policies would work. He did so in his talks to Tianjin cadres, to representatives of workers and professional staff from Tianjin, and in his talk to businesspeople where he recounted telling Song Feiqing he might end up managing sixteen factories on behalf of the socialist state.[61]

The marriage between socialism and capitalism required reconciliation between the party and capitalists on one hand and between capitalists and labor on the other. The highly publicized understanding between Song Feiqing and the party as well as that between Dongya and its employees culminated with a meeting at Dongya in early May between company management and employees. *Progressive Daily* covered the meeting, reporting that "Song Feiqing will go to Hong Kong soon to negotiate purchase of raw materials and machinery for the new factory. Before leaving, he and the employees' association called a meeting." At that meeting, the head of the employees' association, who only three months before had called for the overthrow of Song Feiqing, now addressed company employees in praise of Song Feiqing's sincerity "about development of the factory." He went on to chastise worker activists by saying that "A few comrades without enough class awakening perhaps don't fully understand the government's policy. I would like to take this opportunity to pass on what I heard from Liu Shaoqi and Mayor Huang." He declared, "It is a mistake to think the patriotic capitalists are enemies. Because we want the revolution to succeed, it is necessary to develop patriotic commerce and industry ... we must unite with private management and work together. Only then can we quickly advance toward socialism." For his part, Song Feiqing first "made a self-criticism about former mistakes saying, 'After Liberation because I did not understand the government's direction I was concerned and could

---

60. *Jinbu ribao*, May 6, 1949, 1–3.
61. "Liu Shaoqi tongzhi zai Tianjinshi ganbu hui shang de jianghua," Zhonggong Tianjin shiwei et al., *Zhongguo zibenzhuyi*, 69; "Liu Shaoqi tongzhi zai Tianjinshi zhigong daibiao dahui shang de jianghua," Zhonggong Tianjin shiwei et al., *Zhongguo zibenzhuyi*, 79–80; and "Liu Shaoqi tongzhi zai Tianjinshi gongshangyejia zuotanhui shang de jianghua," Zhonggong Tianjin shiwei et al., *Zhongguo zibenzhuyi*, 89–93.

not come up with an idea … It became anarchic.'" With his self-criticism out of the way, Song looked toward the future. "Our employees should unite together and establish a great goal and recognize clearly that our duty is the movement now of China from an agricultural country to an industrial country." *Progressive Daily* then reported that "[a]fter the speeches, there was entertainment and the whole group ate together before adjourning."[62] Unity seemingly had returned to the Dongya Corporation. Liu Shaoqi had succeeded in making Dongya a model of a marriage between socialism and communism.

A ONE-SIDED MARRIAGE

In spite of Liu Shaoqi's encouragement to capitalists in the spring of 1949, his vision did not allow for unrestrained capitalism. In his talk to cadres he pointed to efforts already underway to unify the purchase and sale of goods.[63] Later, during his May 2 talk to businessmen he spoke of a need for government allocation of resources.[64] As for finance, Liu promoted a system that unified and planned lending with a share for both public and private.[65] Close analysis of subsequent events shows four areas in which economic activity began to change: the adoption of party work methods and rhetoric by managers and workers alike, agreement, tacit or otherwise, with state-set production goals, party control of both finance and distribution channels, and party demands for financial support. The process of partification began even while Liu Shaoqi was still in Tianjin, picked up speed during 1950 and then accelerated again with China's intervention in the Korean War at the end of 1950.

Dongya began imitating party work methods as soon as employees and management came to their public reconciliation after Liu Shaoqi's visit. Song Feiqing outlined ways to market Dongya medicine in two-pill packets rather glass jars, and he decided to "only produce one kind of medicine."[66] Repackaging the product in single- or dual-dose bags, and focusing on a one-medicine-treats-all kind of production, Dongya could hope to make the price cheap enough to allow even peasants to

62. *Jinbu ribao*, May 12, 1949, 1–3.
63. "Liu Shaoqi tongzhi zai Tianjinshi ganbu hui shang de jianghua," Zhonggong Tianjin shiwei et al., *Zhongguo zibenzhuyi*, 58.
64. "Liu Shaoqi tongzhi zai Tianjinshi gongshangyejia zuotanhui shang de jianghua," Zhonggong Tianjin shiwei et al., *Zhongguo zibenzhuyi*, 86.
65. Ibid., 88.
66. *Jinbu ribao*, May 12, 1949, 1–3.

purchase it. In addition, the company redrafted its advertising to appeal to revolutionary themes. On May 1 the company placed an ad "In Celebration of Labor Day."[67] Three days later, Dongya placed a similar ad under the heading "Remembering May Fourth."[68] By July, Dongya began marketing its "special edition wool yarn," an inferior product that came from Chinese domestic, not Australian, wool as "Suitable for use by workers and peasants, public officials and students!"[69] Besides incorporating Communist rhetoric about peasants and workers in marketing plans, Song Feiqing made even more explicit references to party work methods when he announced at the public reconciliation meeting between Dongya management and workers that "Our method will be: study (absorbing new knowledge), self-criticism (work, moral character, and thought all need self-criticism in order to advance), and self-government (that is, if you have an opinion, raise it, don't wait)."[70] The use of the term "self-criticism," in particular, had Communist overtones. One former manager even remembered Song Feiqing's request that each staff member read a progressive book while Song went to Hong Kong to line up sources of suppliers of wool. Song himself prepared to read *Das Kapital* on board the ship to Hong Kong and he told his staff that he would give them exams on their progressive education when he got back.[71]

Over time, use of Communist work methods would become more pronounced as production became the number one goal for capitalists and workers alike. Dongya's workers and managers quickly began subordinating issues of personal gain to priorities of national production. When Dongya became the first company in Tianjin to form a collective labor-management bargaining committee, both the union and internal company accounts point out that the resolution of labor-capital disputes had resulted in increased production.[72] Tellingly, many of new worker demands made at the end of August 1949 revolved around increasing production. One workroom needed more wooden forks (used to push material through machines) and another proposed a method to repair torn threads quickly in order to avoid shutting down production.[73]

---

67. *Jinbu ribao*, May 1, 1949, 2–8.
68. Ibid., May 4, 1949, 2–5.
69. Ibid., July 19, 1949, 1–1.
70. Ibid., May 12, 1949, 1–3.
71. Li Jingshan (2).
72. *Jinbu ribao*, January 27, 1950, 2–1, and Report to Dongya Shareholders, March 26, 1950, History Museum (03).
73. Memo dated August 5, 1949, Dongya Corp., 2-86-2-02.

The focus on production reinforced the use of Communist Party work methods. By May of 1951 Dongya was operating under target production levels set by the government and it had adopted some of what would come to be hallmark Communist work methods, such as a production competition run by the union. In a sign of paranoia to come, the board of directors concentrated some of its attention on reporting shareholders who were war traitors or bureaucratic capitalists.[74] The board increasingly adopted the language and attitude of Communist control. In July of 1951 management reported to a meeting of shareholders, "With great help from the people's government and with the development of international socialism and warm advancement of patriotism to resist America and aid Korea and protect the nation with a production competition, this company's gunny sack production has increased greatly and has broken all existing records."[75] They attributed the production increase to the awakening of the political consciousness of all employees "under the leadership of Chairman Mao and the Communist Party. The union has led a competition to expand production and recently held a patriotic production competition."[76] Likewise, in October, managers proudly reported to the board that they had exceeded their production goal for gunny sacks by 5.21 percent.[77]

Besides work methods and production goals, party control of the economy most importantly came from intrusion in sources of finance and channels of distribution. Markets for both purchase of jute and sale of gunny sacks came into government hands with considerable speed. By the end of 1950 all purchase of jute in north China had to be made through government "unified purchase and allocation."[78] Likewise, as early as March of 1950, Dongya had stopped selling gunny sacks through representative agents, but sold either to the government-owned Xintuo Company or the government-controlled Bank of Communications to repay loans based on orders.[79] After May of 1951, even the latter quasi "private" sales declined as purchase of gunny sacks rapidly shifted from private to public hands. In the months preceding May 15, 1951, private purchase made up almost 53 percent of all gunny sack sales. For the

---

74. Board of directors meeting of May 19, 1951, Dongya Corp., 2-91-7-20.

75. Shareholders' Meeting July 29, 1951, Dongya Corp., 2-99-5-01.

76. Ibid.

77. Board of directors Meeting of October 20, 1951, Dongya Corp., 2-91-7-16.

78. In this report, the unification of purchase is dated to the previous autumn, Shareholders' Meeting July 29, 1951, Dongya Corp., 2-99-5-01; see also Shareholders' Meeting October 30, 1950, Dongya Corp., 2-91-7-09.

79. Report to Dongya Shareholders, March 26, 1950, History Museum (03).

remainder of the year the percentage fell to 12.3 percent. Even knitting-yarn sales, which were minimal, went primarily to state-run customers. Prior to May of 1951, all yarn sales had gone to private customers. For the remainder of the year, private customers only accounted for 7.8 percent of sales.[80]

The state dominated finance as well, placing Dongya at the mercy of the government-controlled banking system and centrally directed economic policies. For example, in October of 1950, the People's Bank notified Dongya that it would temporarily withdraw the company's loan because "it had the mission of shrinking loans throughout China." In order to make jute purchases, Dongya presold as yet unproduced gunny sacks. By the end of October the company had presold 160,000 gunny sacks. It had also used up its entire stock of Australian wool and most of its wool yarn stocks had been sold.[81] Although the cash flow problem eventually eased, reliance on the banking system had made Dongya very vulnerable to state pressures.

Finally, demands on private enterprise to finance party projects added another aspect to the partification of economic life. In his Tianjin talk to businesspeople, Liu Shaoqi had said, "If you have problems, we will help solve them. If we have problems, you help solve them."[82] In an extension of the "we will help you, you will help us" policy announced by Liu Shaoqi in his Tianjin speeches, financial demands on private enterprises progressively increased. By March of 1950, in addition to tax levies, the government pressured Dongya and other companies to purchase public bonds. The vehicle for this pressure came from Communist-organized trade associations and local street committees. Unfortunately, as the company tried to purchase raw materials and ramp up production, cash was tight. Finally, Dongya only managed to pay for the bonds with high-interest loans from state-controlled banks.[83] With the Korean War at the end of 1950, the Resist America Aid Korea campaign took off and Tianjin's industries heeded the call to mobilization. Dongya established its own "Resist America Aid Korea" branch committee, which put on performances, solicited donations from board members, and coordinated Dongya's contributions to the cause. "Dongya donated two airplanes in

---

80. Reports discussed at board of directors meetings, Dongya Corp., 2-91-7-20 and 2-91-7-17.

81. Board of directors meeting of October 30, 1950, Dongya Corp., 2-91-7-09.

82. "Liu Shaoqi tongzhi zai Tianjinshi gongshangyejia zuotanhui shang de jianghua," Zhonggong Tianjin shiwei et al., *Zhongguo zibenzhuyi*, 87.

83. Board of directors meeting of March 21, 1950, Dongya Corp., 2-91-7-06, and board of directors meeting of March 29, 1950, Dongya Corp., 2-91-7-07.

June of a value of three billion," then in November, when management saw that other large corporations donated enough money to purchase a plane for the war in Korea, Dongya donated yet another plane.[84] Subsequently, in September of 1951 the City of Tianjin decided to build a model steel machinery factory and it asked Tianjin industries to invest. In considering the investment, one Dongya board director objected that the proposed investment was outside of Dongya's area of expertise and moreover, "We have a capital of 15 billion. An investment of 5 billion would be one-third of capital and that would not be appropriate." In spite of this objection, the board eventually decided that investment was "a necessity," but they weakly hoped that the chairman of the board could negotiate with the government the exact amount in the range of three billion to five billion People's Bank Notes.[85] This donation in the construction of a state-owned industrial sector eliminated any possibility that Dongya could make significant investments itself. The second gunny sack factory and any other expansion plans quietly disappeared from company discussions.

In the midst of these events, perhaps seeing the writing of partification of economic life on the wall, in May of 1950 Song Feiqing requested permission to visit Hong Kong once again, ostensibly to further plans for the new gunny sack factory in Tianjin and foreign exchange earnings. He never returned to the PRC. Two months later, his remaining family in Tianjin, his wife and two youngest daughters, surreptitiously went south in the care of a young and loyal Dongya employee. After a long and harrowing journey by train and boat they slipped into Hong Kong through Macao and joined Song Feiqing there.[86] Song Feiqing remained in intermittent contact with Dongya where he pleaded ill health, and the board of directors entreated him to return to Tianjin, but he no longer directed factory affairs.[87]

In Song's absence, the factory in Tianjin fared surprisingly well under the stewardship of his experienced and well-trained middle managers. Throughout the rest of 1950 and 1951, profits remained steady and gunny

---

84. Shareholders' meeting July 29, 1951, Dongya Corp., 2-99-5-01, board of directors meeting of October 20, 1951, Dongya Corp., 2-91-7-16, and board of directors meeting of November 20, 1951, Dongya Corp., 2-91-7-17.

85. Board of directors meeting of September 26, 1951, Dongya Corp., 2-91-7-15.

86. Song and Wang, *Tade meng*, 348–358.

87. Board of directors meeting of July 23,1950, Dongya Corp., 2-91-7-08, and board of directors meeting of October 30, 1950, Dongya Corp., 2-91-7-09. Song's activities in Hong Kong are beyond the scope of this chapter. On this subject, see Brett Sheehan, *Industrial Eden: A Chinese Capitalists Family under Five Authoritarian Regimes* (forthcoming).

sack production soared. Dongya produced 1.2 million gunny sacks in 1949 and more than doubled that in 1950. By the end of 1951, production had increased to almost 3.5 million sacks.[88] At the same time, most arenas requiring strategic vision or entrepreneurship had been slowly cut off by growing government restrictions and partification of economic life.

Finally, in April of 1951 the Dongya board bit the bullet and dealt with Song Feiqing's absence because "criticism in the newspapers and inquiries from the government" had forced the issue. After much discussion, the board removed Song Feiqing from his position as company president.[89] The new president, Yang Tianshou, clearly disturbed about taking on such a responsibility amid the web of controls woven by the party, suggested that Dongya move toward a model of collective decision making. Other board members were less thrilled by the idea and preferred to let Yang shoulder the burden of responsibility for a capitalist enterprise under socialism. They only reluctantly agreed to meet once a month and "continue to discuss the idea of revising the charter to move toward a system of board management."[90] Of course, the board had little to do but try to fulfill government directives. In its public announcement the board performed the expected self-criticism and resolved to do better. "In the past year, directors have not performed their responsibilities well. Starting today the board of directors will face production and take responsibility. In observing land reform and seeing the increase in grain production, gunny sack production will also increase accordingly."[91]

The picture is clear: self-criticism, learning from campaigns, financing a growing state sector, financing the ongoing war in Korea, government control of purchases and sales, dependence on government sources of finance, disciplined and compliant labor, adoption of the rhetoric of revolution, production targets, and production competitions. Well before the Five Anti campaign came to Dongya, the company had become fully integrated in socialist society. Partification of economic life had proceeded without the conversion of private enterprises to state ownership or outright struggle against capitalists.

---

88. Production reports discussed at board of directors meetings, Dongya Corp., 2-91-7-04, 2-91-7-10, and 2-91-7-17.

89. Board of directors meeting of April 11, 1951, Dongya Corp., 2-91-7-19.

90. Ibid..

91. *Jinbu ribao*, April 13, 1951, 2–1.

CONCLUSION

The speed with which the Communists integrated Dongya into a system of government controls and party work methods belies any thought that the party really wanted to take advantage of the managerial and entrepreneurial skills of capitalists such as Song Feiqing. In fact, history shows that middle managers at Dongya proved fully capable of fulfilling party expectations. The question remains: Why did the party try so hard to recruit Song and other capitalists? As Sherman Cochran has shown, the party even convinced Liu Hongsheng to trick his eighth son into coming back to China.[92] Why bother? Why bring back educated and charismatic people who could potentially lead anti-Communist activities? True, the party feared capital flight and the effort to convert capitalists to the cause stemmed the flow to some extent. Song Feiqing even once remarked on the fact that his friend and head of the Renli Woolen Mill in Tianjin had recalled US$400,000 plus on deposit in the United States during the early period of Communist rule to help with national construction.[93] But long after Song Feiqing had gone to Hong Kong and he and his immediate family had all taken up residence outside China and he had little money to bring back, the Chinese government still sent representatives to convince him to come back. Agents kept watch on him and his family; his brother, also in Hong Kong, was afraid to go to work.[94] At that time, the party had virtually taken over Dongya and its productive ability. Why did it want so much for Song Feiqing and other capitalists to return? We may never know for sure, but there is one clue. The Nationalists under Chiang Kai-shek also sent agents to persuade Song to go to Taiwan.[95] Something about the existence of overseas Chinese capitalists' rejection of party orthodoxy, either Communist or Nationalist, was simply untenable to either party's sense of itself, threatening to its own sense of legitimacy. Subsequently, of course, overseas capitalists in Hong Kong and Taiwan played a critical role in the rebirth of the Chinese economy after 1980. Capitalism and communism have come together again in a marriage the final consequences of which will not be clear for a long, long time.

---

92. Cochran, "Capitalists," 382.
93. Song and Wang, *Tade meng*, 353.
94. Ibid., 370–371.
95. Ibid.

Abbreviations

Dongya Corp.	Archives of the Dongya Corporation, Tianjin
History Museum	Copies of Archives of the Dongya Corporation held at the Tianjin History Museum
Li Jingshan	Papers of Li Jingshan (Li family holdings), Tianjin
(Nantes)	Archives of the French Consulate in Tianjin, French National Archives, Nantes
(Paris)	Archives of the French Foreign Ministry, French National Archives, Paris, Asie-Oceanie 1944–1955, file 172
Griffen	Papers of R. Allen Griffen, Hoover Institution, Palo Alto
ECA	United States Economic Cooperation Administration Mission to China, Tianjin Regional Office

This page is intentionally left blank.

3 AVOIDING ISOLATION BY THE REVOLUTION | K.P. Chen's Dealings from Hong Kong with Shanghai and Taipei, 1948–1956

Pui-Tak Lee

The year 1949 is a great divide in modern Chinese history. How Chinese bankers responded to it is an interesting question to answer. Once Chinese capitalists chose to leave Shanghai and settle in the British colony of Hong Kong, could we suppose they were permanently separated from either China or Taiwan? It is generally assumed that once they confined themselves to their new home in Hong Kong or moved on to other locations in Southeast Asia, Australia, the United States, or elsewhere, they immediately severed all ties with China under the Communists and Taiwan under the Nationalists. Such an assumption leaves the impression that their departure from China curtailed their involvement in the People's Republic or the Republic of China in 1949.

It may be true that some emigrant capitalists never looked back, but others remained in touch with their home or company in China either as a result of being contacted by government representatives sent to Hong Kong by the People's Republic and Nationalist Taiwan or because they themselves took the initiative to reach back across the borders to mainland China or Taiwan. From their sanctuary in Hong Kong or elsewhere, how did Chinese capitalists conduct border-crossing relations after 1949? K.P. Chen (Chen Guangfu, 1880–1976) illustrates the techniques that were used in the field of banking.

K.P. CHEN'S DILEMMA

K.P. Chen was considered one of the most successful bankers in China between the 1920s and 1940s. He had abandoned business from Shanghai twice in his life. First in August of 1937 when Japan attacked Shanghai, he followed the Nationalist government in its move to Chongqing where he set up another headquarters. During the war, the Shanghai Commercial and Savings Bank (SCSB) had no remarkable development. Large amounts of deposits had been withdrawn (as much as 30 million yuan in Shanghai), loans were not returned, communications among branches within the Japanese occupied areas were stopped, as most of the branches were either inactive or shut down. The second time Chen abandoned his banking business was in 1949. Just before the Communists liberated Shanghai, Chen left for Hong Kong on an excuse of sickness and never returned. Chen considered his departure from Shanghai in 1937 to be an act of resistance to Japanese rule and made this decision without hesitation. But in 1949 he became deeply troubled by a dilemma—having to choose between communism and capitalism and having to make a decision between returning to Shanghai or remaining in Hong Kong. As he said at the time:

> We are like a ship out on the high seas, unable to see very far ahead and not quite sure of the direction in which we are going. We simply sail along slowly and very cautiously. The sea has been rough, but so far we have managed. We are still afloat— waiting, seeing and hoping. This cannot go on indefinitely. Sooner or later we shall be at a crossroads. The time will soon come, if it has not already, when a decision can be postponed no longer. A course will have to be charted now so that we may steer accordingly this ship of ours. ... We may say that there are two courses open to us. One, to steer our ship clear of Communist influence. Two, to stay within the orbit of Communist rule.[1]

In the above, Chen's reference to "waiting, seeing and hoping" reflects his special situation in Shanghai from 1945 to 1949. After the war, political chaos and economic depression caused him to become disappointed with the Nationalists, who made all business in Shanghai come to a standstill. This gave him a sense of crisis, especially at the time when the Communists were taking over city after city from the Nationalists. Soon Chen would confront a critical choice in what he referred to as "a crossroad," and that was choosing between staying within or outside Communist influence.

---

1. This was originally quoted in KPCPP, box 9, file 8: Notes (June 18, 1949), "We Chart A Course," 1.

In May 1949, before Shanghai was captured by the Communists, K.P. Chen fled to Hong Kong. In his diary, he explained that he chose Hong Kong because he could release himself from ties with the Nationalist government and make new plans for development of his bank, the SCSB. What he wrote was true, but it doesn't reflect the complete story of the dilemma that he had confronted. Why had Chen insisted on staying in Hong Kong? How much was he tempted to return to Shanghai? Based on SCSB archives, personal papers belonging to Chen himself, and other materials such as the records of the Hong Kong government, my research shows that Chen was at the crossroads in the beginning but then gradually reached a decision to remain in Hong Kong during the critical years of 1949–1951.

K.P. CHEN IN 1940s SHANGHAI

K.P. Chen had always been regarded as a supporter of the Nationalist government. He was also one of the prominent successful bankers in Republican China. He founded the SCSB in 1915 with a small capital of CN$50,000. After twenty years, the SCSB became one of the prominent private banks in China. Chen's record at financial entrepreneurship was path-breaking in modern China.[2] Like most Chinese bankers, K.P. Chen was sensitive to market changes. According to him, without a sound business environment, a bank cannot grow.

Chen was opposed to the oppressive rule of China's government as compared with the democratic style of the West. Moreover, he blamed government leaders who were not "men of integrity" for striving only for an impossible unification under "one person" mentioned above, Chiang Kai-shek. He objected to policies such as the gold yuan (*jinyuan quan*) reform, a policy of depreciation of Chinese currency that finally resulted in hyperinflation in the late 1940s.

Even though Chen had been appointed as a member of the Nationalist government's State Council in 1947, he claimed that he was reluctant to take up the post and, furthermore, identified his relationship with the Nationalist government as "sometimes close and sometimes isolated" *(ruoji ruoli)*.[3] At first, Chen suggested a series of government reforms in order to save China's economy from disorder, chaos and depression, but it was never accepted. He proposed methods previously

---

2. Pui-Tak Lee, "Chinese Financial Entrepreneurship: Case of K.P. Chen," in *Journal of Asian Business* 14.1 (July 1997): 23–40.

3. KPCPP, box 7: Notes, "State Council Meetings, 1947–1948."

used in Shanghai: first, to encourage and protect investment as had been done in Hong Kong; second, to keep a reasonable rate of wages; third, to absorb foreign capital and technology; fourth, to free restrictions on foreign exchange; fifth, to keep currency independent and not issue it to cover financial deficits.[4] Chen believed this plan would become effective if carried out within a period of five years.

Chen has always been regarded as closely associated with Chiang Kai-shek for he successfully led two missions from the Republic of China to the United States in order to strengthen the political and economic relations between the two countries. There is no doubt that he won Chiang Kai-shek's admiration. However, the situation changed in 1948 when the government's gold currency reform completely failed, and from then on Chen gradually disassociated himself with the Generalissimo. In the late 1940s, Chen was quite disappointed with the leadership of the Nationalist government for its inefficiency, corruption, and oppressive rule.

In 1948, when China was plagued by a hyperinflation, Chiang Kai-shek's son, Chiang Ching-kuo, came to Shanghai in order to attack speculators and people who had hidden their foreign assets. This was called "*da laohu*" (hunting the tigers),[5] and it marked the point where the Shanghai capitalists disassociated themselves from the Nationalist government. As shown in Table 3.1, banks were forced to surrender their foreign assets to the government.

When Chen learned that the government would not promise to launch his reform, he lost hope for the Nationalist government and began to find an alternate solution. In January 1949, Chen stated, "All that the Gimo [Chiang Kai-shek] was interested in was to fight and to borrow money from America so that he could go on fighting. I can say now that all the talks and plans for industrialization, currency stabilization, transportation development, etc. were mere dreams."[6] No real economic and commercial progress seemed possible as production ceased and inflation continued with revenues unable to meet expenditures and an antiquated tax system.[7]

---

4. KPCPP, box 9, file 8: Diaries (December 12, 1948), 21–22.

5. See Wang Zhangling, *Jiang Jingguo Shanghai "dahu ji": Shanghai jingji guanzhi shimo* (On Chiang Ching-kuo coming to Shanghai to "hunt the tigers": Treatise on the economic control of Shanghai) (Taipei: Zhengzhong shuju, 1999).

6. KPCPP, box 9, file 8: Notes (January 6, 1949), 1.

7. On Chen's political relations with the Nationalist government during the post war years, see Yang Tianshi, "Nanjing zhengfu bengkui shiqi de Chen Guangfu" (K.P. Chen during the period of the collapse of the Nanjing government), in *Jindaishi yanjiu* (Journal of modern history) (1992) 4: 214–243.

**Table 3.1 Confiscation of foreign currencies (cash) and gold
from Shanghai banks dated September 24, 1948***

Names of bank	US$	£**	HK$	Gold (ounces)
Shin Hwa Savings Bank of China	126,871.95	48:15:4	—	957.716
Continental Bank	252,145.76	135:19:6	265.0	—
Chekiang Commercial Bank	130,122.86	—	—	—
SCSB	385,000.00	5,700:0:0	53,688.86	—
China & South Seas Bank	812,674.00	—	72,600.00	—
Chekiang Industrial Bank***	433,436.00	14,000:0:0	337,191.14	2,499.530
Yin Yieh Commercial Bank	—	772:4:11	—	—
Jincheng Bank	223,122.00	—	163,045.00	1,012.140
Others	1,961,105.31	40,513:4:9	682,870.09	5,459.783
Total	4,324,477.88	60,735:4:6	1,309,660.09	9,929.169

Source: Hong Jiaguan, ed., *Zhongyang yinhang shiliao* (Collected materials of the Central Bank of China) (Beijing: Zhongguo jinyong chubanshe, 2006), 1347–1348.
*On securities, see ibid., 1348–1349.
**According to the old sterling standard, 1 pound=20 shillings, 1 shilling=12 pennies.
***In April 1948, this bank was renamed the Chekiang First Commercial Bank.

In early 1949, when Beijing and Tianjin were taken by the Communists, Chen had an idea to explore a new place for business. First, he considered making the SCSB's Hong Kong branch an individual company. Second, he opened a branch of China Travel Service in America.[8] Both required Chen to divert assets out of China to Hong Kong and the United States.

As early as the end of the Sino-Japanese War of 1937–1945, K.P. Chen became concerned about the deterioration of the Shanghai business

---

8. KPCPP, box 9: Zhang Jia'ao, "Chen Guangfu yu Shanghai yinhang," (K.P. Chen and the Shanghai Commercial & Savings Bank), unpublished manuscript, K.P. Chen Papers, Columbia University Library, 22–23.

environment, so he tried to look for an alternative. His chosen target was New York. As Chen wrote in 1947 to E.K. Hsu, his business associate in New York:

> At present the conditions in China, both financial and economic, are such that no important import-export firms are in a position to do much business. I may say that the future control of exchange for imports will be even more restricted than is now. There is current in the thinking of some top-level Central Bank people an idea that we may seek improvements by giving exports a better and more realistic rate of exchange. ... The exchange thus accumulated by the approved banks will be surrendered to the Central Bank. ... I agree with you too that in both services and facilities Irving has an edge over Chemical. ... We have about US$3,000,000 in investments in New York, which is quite a large amount considering the limited financial strength of the Bank. ... If we are to keep this foreign exchange, and if the Government will not interfere as I hope will not, we shall need someone in New York to watch and study the market.[9]

So, according to Chen, "The New York Office has been serving our Head Office in such things as investments and establishment of contact with American business people."[10] From 1945 to 1946, cooperating with Li Ming of Chekiang Industrial Bank and other Chinese capitalists, Chen launched a series of joint projects with American counterparts. Table 3.2 shows that the SCSB raised a total of US$6,025,000 for investing in the four proposed projects. Though the two biggest ones—China Industries, Inc. and Manufacturing Enterprises of China—were not carried out due to reasons of inflation and social instability in China, the SCSB raised a large sum of capital mainly from the bank's reserve funds in America. Chen instructed his office to take the following steps: "Firstly, create and maintain close relationship with American banks and business circles; Secondly, study the investment market and make precise periodical reports on our investments; Thirdly, keep personal contact with the personnel of the new Cathay Insurance Co.; Fourthly, act as a training station for the junior officers of our institutions."[11]

---

9. K.P. Chen to E.K. Hsu, August 6, 1947, SMA#Q275-1-2446, SCSB archives.
10. K.P. Chen to E.K. Hsu, June 5, 1947, SMA#Q275-1-2310, SCSB archives.
11. E.K. Hsu to K.P. Chen, July 2, 1947, SMA#Q275-1-2310, SCSB archives.

Table 3.2 The investment of SCSB in the United States
during 1945–1946 (unit: US$1,000)

Name of Company	Total Capital	US%	SCSB%	Others%
China Industries, Inc.	5,000	40.0	30.0	30.0
Manufacturing				
Enterprises of China	10.000	50.0	40.0	10.0
Cathay Insurance, Co.	2,000	25.0	47.5	27.5
Chrysis Corporation	25	—	100.0	—

Source: KPCPP, Box 7, "Bank's Post War Plans, 1945–1946."

Chen had a strong sense of mission to modernize the banking industry and he also had an identity as a professional banker. He regarded the SCSB as part of his life. In early 1949, Chen anticipated that there would be either nationalization of the bank industry or gradual extinction of private banks through outright liquidation in the mainland, which would make the function of banks as a provider of capital unnecessary and obsolete. Therefore, he decided to find a new place where the SCSB could continue to function and where he could be relatively free from any political controls. Chen left Shanghai in March 1949, two months before Shanghai was liberated.[12]

As Chen expected, private banking in China came to an end. First, private banks were transformed into joint public-private enterprises (*gongsi heying*); second, keen competition came from state-owned national banks; third, labor unions expanded their power; fourth, private properties were confiscated in the form of numerous political contributions during the Three Anti campaign (*sanfan yundong*) and Five Anti campaign (*wufan yundong*) as well as the Korean War. All tended to eliminate individual deposits.[13] In 1952, the name of the SCSB vanished in China, and it was reorganized as part of the People's Bank of China.

---

12. KPCPP, box 9, file 8: Diaries (March 20, 1949), 2.

13. For the background of the anti-bourgeois movement, see Lynn T. White, III, "Bourgeois Radicalism in the 'New Class' of Shanghai, 1949–1969," in James L. Watson, ed., *Class and Social Stratification of Post-revolutionary China* (Cambridge: Cambridge University Press, 1981), 142–174.

WHY HONG KONG WAS CHOSEN

Political chaos in the 1940s and the founding of the People's Republic of China in 1949 led Shanghai's capitalists to seek a safer location for their businesses. Many of them chose to reestablish themselves in Hong Kong where they found a favorable setting for development of modern entrepreneurial activities, but largely for political reasons. Hong Kong was free of political interference, particularly from Communist China and Nationalist Taiwan. Most of the prominent bankers such as Li Ming of Chekiang Industrial Bank,[14] Song Hanzhang of Bank of China, Chang Kia-ngau (Zhang Jia'ao) of Central Bank of China (Zhongyang yinhang), Qian Xinzhi of Bank of Communications, Wu Dingchang of Yien Yieh Commercial Bank, and Zhou Zuomin of Jincheng Banking Corporation (on whom see Parks M. Coble's portrait in chapter 7 of this volume), found Hong Kong a place free of ideological formalities or political restrictions, which had been imposed on them while they were in Shanghai. As early as the Sino-Japanese War, a few Shanghai capitalists had arrived in Hong Kong. In 1938, Rong Zongjing, one of the cofounders of the largest Chinese textile enterprises group, sought refuge in Hong Kong, where he hoped to escape from political instability and government intervention. The anti-capitalist stance of the Communists caused them to transfer their capital out of China.

In the late 1940s why did the Shanghai capitalists flock to Hong Kong rather than to other destinations? Most countries, mainly in Europe and America, had strict immigration controls. Almost all of the governments in Southeast Asia and elsewhere closed their doors in anticipation of a tide of Chinese refugees in the wake of the Nationalist collapse in China, thus making Hong Kong and Taiwan the only places that Chinese could freely enter.[15] An estimated 1,285,000 refugees came to Hong Kong between September 1945 and December 1949. They chose Hong Kong as their sanctuary because of its accessibility, stability, and relative absence of government regulation in economic life.

K.P. Chen regarded Hong Kong as a safer place than Shanghai. As Chen said, "The only place that can hinder the Communist influence is Hong Kong, where I can meet my friends, correspond with my friends in the U.S., and read books and newspapers freely, a high degree of freedom

---

14. Like K.P. Chen, Li had reorganized his bank, transforming the Chekiang Industrial Bank into the Chekiang First Commercial Bank in Hong Kong by 1950.

15. Siu-lun Wong, *Emigrant Entrepreneurs: Shanghai Industrialists in Hong Kong* (Hong Kong: Oxford University Press, 1988), 20–21.

as it was enjoyed in Shanghai's concession of the past."[16] Chen considered not only his personal safety but also the future prospect of the SCSB. As he said, "We are not interested in personal profit. Rather, we want to maintain the life of private enterprise free of government control."[17] By 1948, the total deposit of the SCSB in China amounted to US$500,000, while the branch at Hong Kong had HK$10 million (far more than its parent bank in China).[18] In 1949, the Hong Kong branch made a net profit of HK$900,000 in only the last six months of the year."[19] According to Chen, "With Shanghai going downhill, it is inevitable that Hong Kong will rise in importance. It will be the chief trade and business center of this area."[20] This satisfactory result convinced Chen to base his business in Hong Kong.

The SCSB's Hong Kong branch was established in 1934. Its main aim was to develop the exchange business of Hong Kong-Shanghai-London that was to buy foreign exchange in Hong Kong and sell in Shanghai, making a profit rate at about 0.005 percent. Revenues from foreign exchange business constituted more than half of the total revenues of the SCSB. Even in the early 1940s when Chen served as chairman of the Currency Stabilization Board organized by the Chinese, British, and U.S. governments, he made use of the opportunity of staying in Hong Kong to observe business environment in person, and he said, "I felt more convinced than ever that our forces in Hong Kong were too weak and needed to be augmented if we were to have our roots firmly planted on the soil of Hong Kong."[21]

KEEPING CONNECTIONS WITH SHANGHAI AFTER 1949

Even after Chen had physically moved to Hong Kong, he did not immediately cut off his connections with Shanghai before 1952 when the SCSB was nationalized in China. At the very beginning of his arrival in Hong Kong, Chen thought that the fall of Shanghai had deprived the bank of a principal source of revenue; therefore the hard currency earned in Hong Kong would be important to meet the expenses of branches in

---

16. KPCPP, box 9, file 8: Diaries (December 16, 1948), 28.

17. COH – K.P. Chen: Twenty-fourth interview with K.P. Chen, 7.

18. KPCPP, box 7: *Benhang shengzhang zhi youlai* (The origins and growth of our bank), 6.

19. KPCPP, box 9, file 9: Memos (December 15, 1949), "On 69th Birthday," 3.

20. KPCPP, box 9, file 8: Notes (January 6, 1949), "Hongkong," 2.

21. KPCPP, box 9, file 8: Notes (March 16, 1949), "Cooperation," 2.

such liberated cities as Shanghai, Tianjin, Nanjing, Beijing, and Hankou. However, Chen had to deal with events such as the British government's recognition of the PRC regime, the United Front program launched by the Chinese Communist Party (CCP) in Hong Kong, and the question of the independent status of the SCSB. As a result, he faced a second dilemma over returning to Shanghai or staying in Hong Kong.

The CCP United Front work on Shanghai bankers started long before the Chinese Civil War. Gu Zhun had been praised as "smart" in soliciting the support of the white collar class which consisted of people working in banks, native banks, insurance companies, and department stores. Gu did not use the formal party organization. Instead he used the staff clubs to absorb these people and successfully exert the CCP's influence over them.[22] (See Christopher Leighton's characterization of Gu Zhun in chapter 6 of this book.)

Starting in 1936 when the United Association of Banks of Shanghai (*Shanghai yinlian*) was established, it recruited a large number of members. In the summer of 1938, the CCP set up a general division (*zong zhibu*) for the banking industry and eventually set up sub-branches (*dang zhibu*) in different banks including Bank of China, Jincheng Bank, Continental Bank, Yien Yieh Bank, China & South Seas Bank. So, with help from United Association, the CCP had early successes in reaching into the banking sector.[23] In 1939, the number of CCP members who came from the banking sector increased to a hundred and the total number of CCP members in United Association increased to more than 7,200, scattered throughout a total of 368 banking institutions.[24]

According to the memoir of Li Lixia who had been the vice president of the Central Bank of China, "During that time I was in contact with the CCP underground. I followed their instructions to solicit the support of the staff and successfully retain all the bank's property so that the staff would finally welcome the liberation of Shanghai."[25]

---

22. Iwama Kazuhiro (Yanjian Yihong), "1940 nian qianhou Shanghai zhiyuan jiecen de shenghuo qingkuan" (The current situation of the white collar class living in Shanghai before and after 1940), *Shilin (Journal of Historical Review)*, 4 (2003): 44–45.

23. Zhonggong Shanghaishiwei dangshi ziliao zhengji weiyuanhui (The committee for collecting historical materials on the CCP in Shanghai and the committee for collecting historical materials on the CCP in Shanghai's banking industry), comp., *Shanghai yinlian shisan nian, 1936–1949* (The thirteen years of the Shanghai yinlian, 1936–1949) (Shanghai: Zhonggong Shanghaishiwei dangshi ziliao zhengjiweiyuanhui, 1987), 38.

24. Ibid., 42.

25. Li Lixia, "Liu Gongyun de zuihou zhengzha" (The final struggle of Liu Gongyun), in Shou Congyi and Shou Leying, eds., *Zhongyang yinhang shihua* (Narrative of the history of Central Bank of China) (Beijing: Zhongguo wenshi chubanshe, 1987), 76.

Many of the Shanghai industrialists had regarded Hong Kong as a "paradise," and the CCP underground sought out these industrialists in Hong Kong to recruit them into a United Front with the CCP.[26] In May 1947, the Hong Kong Bureau of the Central CCP (*Zhonggong zhongyang Xianggang fenju*) was established. The purpose of setting up a bureau in Hong Kong was to mobilize resources to support the Communist forces in their war with the Nationalists on the mainland. This bureau was staffed with highly capable cadres such as Zhang Hanfu, Xia Yan, Xu Dixin, Qiao Guanhua, Pan Hannian, and Hu Sheng. Xia Yan and Pan Hannian had been especially active in launching the underground war with the Nationalists during the Sino-Japanese War.

According to recollections of Xia Yan, he was in charge of the United Front work on Du Yuesheng of Chung Wai Bank.[27] Other bankers who were recruited included Zhou Zhuomin of Jincheng Bank, Song Hanzhang of Bank of China, Luo Meihuan of Central Trust of China, Zheng Tieru of Bank of China's Hong Kong Branch.[28] The CCP considered Hong Kong to be "useful" after the end of the Sino-Japanese War, particularly in helping to win the Civil War of 1946–1949 in the mainland and successfully establish the PRC regime.[29] The CCP regarded Song Hanzhang to be a model banker because he had a high reputation in the banking community, knew much about the Bank of China, and supported the struggle for gaining control of the bank's foreign reserves abroad. Since K.P. Chen had disassociated himself from the Nationalist government, the CCP also considered him to be a promising recruit.

After the establishment of the PRC, Beijing soon entrusted the foreign exchange business to the SCSB, the Chekiang Industrial Bank, and the National Commercial Bank in Hong Kong. On September 15, 1949, the SCSB's Hong Kong branch received a remittance order for a

---

26. Yuan Xiaolun, "Zhanhou chuqi Zhonggong liyong Xianggang de celue yunzuo" (The CCP's strategic operation of using Hong Kong during the early post-war period), *Jindaishi yanjiu* 6 (2002): 126.

27. Xia Yan, *Lanxun jiumeng lu* (A recollection of the old dreams) (Beijing: Sanlian shudian, 1986), 585. On the CCP policy of aligning the Chinese capitalists in Hong Kong, see Lee Pui-Tak, "1949-nianqian Zhonggong zai Xianggang de fazhan ji dui bendi huashang de tongzhan" (The development of the Chinese Communist Party in Hong Kong and its United Front policy on local merchants before 1949), in Pui-Tak Lee, ed., *Daguodu: shidai bianju zhong de Zhongguo shangren* (Great transition: Chinese merchants in a period of drastic changes) (Hong Kong: Commercial Press, 2013), 212–232.

28. Yang Shiyi, "Shanghai jinrong dixia dang gongzuo de jidian jingyan" (My few experiences with underground work on the banking industry of Shanghai), in *Shanghai dangshi ziliao tongxun* (Newsletter of the CCP history in Shanghai), 6 (1989): 37.

29. Yuan, "Zhanhou chuqi Zhonggong liyong Xianggang de celue yunzhuo," 121–148.

sum of HK$9,500,000 sent from Shanghai to Hong Kong. However, the telegram from Shanghai to Hong Kong took much more time than ordinarily needed because full confirmation was requested from Hong Kong. Unfortunately on the day after it arrived, the British government declared devaluation of the pound sterling. Beijing pressed the SCSB for redemption through the Bank of China in Hong Kong as the money was urgently needed to pay for government purchases. Disputes arose not only over the arrival time of the telegram but also over the qualification of the assigned payee, the Po Sang Bank. SCSB asked the Po Sang Bank to have a major bank in Hong Kong serve as its guarantor so that the time of payment could be postponed.

Chen assumed the bank was responsible for neither the telegram received nor immediate payment of the remittance according to international practice governing foreign exchange operations. However, he was afraid that the new government in Beijing, founded on October 1, 1949, would take revenge and cancel the SCSB's license of exchange business or confiscate its foreign reserves in the mainland. As Chen recalled, the Communists used this opportunity to request his presence in Beijing to settle the problem. In his words, "The reason was that they wanted me to return to Peking. Chou En-lai [Zhou Enlai] was very polite about the whole thing. He said that since K.P. Chen was involved, they would settle the matter nicely by fining us a sum of HK$60,000 to be turned over to the Bank of China."[30]

In this case, Chen discovered the extent of the Communists' reach from Shanghai into Hong Kong: "My staff wanted me to return to Mainland China. ... When they first entered Shanghai, the Communists wielded a powerful influence. Its weight was felt in Hong Kong."[31] Chen found that he had become a target of the United Front campaign launched by the Communist Party in mainland China.

In 1949, Chen was sensitive to the accusations that he was unpatriotic or undutiful for remaining in Hong Kong while Shanghai was undergoing economic rehabilitation and needed professional advice. As he summarized his dilemma, "All the time, we bear in mind the hardships which our Shanghai people are now going through; all the time, we try to do our utmost to help our people pull through."[32]

In April 1950, Chen received two invitations from the Bank of China, one from the mainland and one from Taiwan, to attend the meetings of

30. COH–K.P. Chen: Twenty-eighth interview with K.P. Chen, 2–3.

31. Ibid., 3.

32. KPCPP, box 9, file 8: Notes (September 14, 1949), 1.

each place's board of directors. The invitation letter from Beijing arrived in Hong Kong earlier than the one from Taipei.[33] Though he had a concern for Shanghai and sympathy toward his colleagues remaining in China, he refused to go to Beijing. He finally accepted the Taipei invitation and became one of the directors of the Bank of China with headquarters in Taipei. The excuse Chen used in declining the invitation from Beijing was his "bad condition of health." In his notes he wrote, "At seventy, I have not and cannot be expected to have either the energy or the interest, much less the ambition, to play an active part in business or other undertakings. I shall have to be satisfied with a passive role. ... Political connections and personal friendship with the government still count, but not so much in the new pattern of things as in the past."[34] He made no mention of why he accepted the offer from Taipei.

Meanwhile the beckoning from Beijing did not stop. Another invitation from Beijing came in October 1950. The letter was sent from Zhou Enlai to ask Chen for assistance in running a newspaper in Hong Kong. Two of Zhou's emissaries approached Chen in person, identified themselves as Zhou's representatives, and asked him a series of questions concerning whether he was willing to go to Beijing.[35] Chen feared that the letter was fake and that the two representatives who presented themselves as agents from Beijing were in fact sent by Taipei to test his loyalty to the Nationalist government.[36] Guo Dihuo who ran the Wing On Textile Manufacturing Company in Shanghai, had a similar experience when he came to Hong Kong in 1963. He received a fake letter from Fei Yimin who was the chief editor of the newspaper *Dagong bao*, asking him not to return to China since China was in the midst of a great famine and severe local riots during that time.[37] As Guo saw it, he was being closely monitored by the Chinese Communist Party in the mainland. Obviously, capitalists like Chen and Guo had to be cautious even while they were in Hong Kong because the two regimes were engaged in great rivalry.

---

33. In the KPCPP, I have found the invitation from Taipei dated April 12, 1950, but no such invitation from the PRC. However, from another invitation from the People's Political Congress in Beijing, it is evident that K.P. Chen was one of those invited by the PRC government.

34. KPCPP, box 9, file 10: Notes (January 29, 1950), "Question of Domicile," 2.

35. KPCPP, box 9, file 9: Diaries (November 11, 1950), 1–4.

36. KPCPP, box 9, file 9: Diaries (November 13, 1950), 1.

37. "Guo Dihuo tan qu Xianggang de yixie qingkuan" (The situation in Hong Kong as told by Guo Dihuo), May 20, 1963, *Guangdong gongshangye lianhehui* (The Guangdong Federation of Industry and Commerce) (1963), 90–93, Guangdong Provincial Archives 248-1-48.

In order to avoid such political entanglements, in April of 1952 Chen decided to resign from the SCSB (which by then had been renamed Shanghai Commercial Bank), and he took a trip abroad. Two years later, he returned to Hong Kong and resumed his position at the bank.

THE NATIONALISTS' AND CCP'S ATTEMPTS TO SEIZE SCSB'S ASSETS

In January 1950, the British government declared its recognition of the Chinese Communist regime. At that time, Chen was confronted with a legal problem. On the one hand, the SCSB in Hong Kong was vulnerable to a takeover by Beijing because it was registered in China, and on the other hand, official protection from the Nationalist government seemed impossible as no private banks were to be permitted in Taiwan. Therefore, Chen planned to seek protection from the local Hong Kong government. He reorganized the SCSB as an independent company with a new registration under the Hong Kong Company Laws. A separate capital of HK$10 million was to be raised from independent sources and not provided by the parent bank. This newly reorganized bank was regarded as an entirely separate unit and named the Shanghai Commercial Bank, Ltd. (SCB). K.P. Chen was elected as the chairman of the SCB's board of directors.

The new SCB commenced business from January 1951. However, just prior to its opening the U.S. government froze the assets and properties owned by the Chinese government and its nationals because China had become involved in the Korean War. The freezing order was valid from December 1950, and thus the SCB appeared on the list as a "Designated National" and was ordered by the Military Control Commission of the U.S. government to suspend its foreign exchange and remittances. Its assets as well as its investment were frozen in America. It was not until 1953, after prolonged negotiations that the U.S. government agreed to transfer the frozen account of SCSB's Hong Kong branch to the SCB. Not until October 1957, with the assistance of the Nationalist government, was the application for unfreezing of the blocked assets finally approved and the "Designated Status" cancelled.[38] The SCB then reopened its business in U.S. dollar exchanges.

Chen understood that to apply for unfreezing the blocked assets, the legal status problem of the SCSB would have to be solved first. Therefore,

---

38. See Yao Songling, *Chen Guangfu de yisheng* (Life and times of K.P. Chen) (Taipei: Zhuanji wenxue chubanshe, 1984), 145–147.

by gaining support from the shareholders meeting, he decided to change the headquarters of the bank from Shanghai to Taipei. After frequent contacts with the Nationalist government in Taiwan, Chen finally got approval to establish the bank's headquarters in Taipei but only under three conditions: first, the headquarters of the SCSB had to be established in Taiwan and registered under the Nationalist government; second, the SCSB had to hold the shares of SCB; and third, once the existing assets in America were unfrozen, half of the amount had to be put into an account in the Nationalist government's New York branch of the Bank of China, and the other half had to be used outside mainland China.[39]

There were a lot of reasons for Chen to accept these conditions: first, to preserve the assets in America; second, to have an official status in order to apply for unfreezing blocked assets and gain the help of the Nationalist government of Taiwan; third, to seek support in case of lack of official protection in Hong Kong; fourth, to preserve the old status for the old shareholders of the SCSB to reclaim ownership; and fifth, to develop business in Taiwan if the political situation in Hong Kong became worse (as it did later, in 1956, when Hong Kong had a local riot). To alleviate American fears about relations with the People's Republic, the Ministry of Foreign Affairs of the Nationalist government assured the U.S. Foreign Assets Control Commission that no connection with the PRC would be allowed.

It is worth noting that as late as 1948 the SCSB conducted business with the Communists in the liberated areas of China. According to K.P. Chen, on the one hand he tried to avoid collaborating with the CCP, but on the other he instructed his bank to do business in the liberated areas. Rather than say Chen had a dilemma, it is better to say that he was "a snake with two heads" (*liangtou she*).[40] One "head" consisted of the previous members of the board who continued to serve on it. The other "head" consisted of two new members of the board, Zeng Ling and Shien Shon-tien, both from the People's Bank of China. The presence of Zeng and Shien on the board indicates that the capitalization of the SCSB had still not become completely separated from the parent bank in the mainland.[41]

---

39. KPCPP, box 9: Zhang, *Chen Guangfu*, 385.

40. Historians have used this term to describe the Catholics who collaborated with both the Ming and the Qing regimes. See Huang Yinong, *Liangtou she: Mingmo Qingchu de diyidai tianzhujiaotu* (The snake with two heads: The first generation of Catholics in the late Ming and early Qing dynasties) (Xinzhu: Guoli qinghua daxue chubanshe, 2005).

41. PRO HKRS113-2-24, Registrar General's Files Relating to Proceedings for the Voluntary Liquidation of Foreign Companies—Shanghai Commercial and Savings Bank, February 21, 1947–April 28, 1952.

In April 1948, quite apart from the SCSB, the Bank of China elected a new board of directors, consisting of twelve members from the commercial sector and thirteen members from the government sector, including prominent figures such as Song Hanzhang (as CEO), K.P. Chen, H.H. Kung, T.V. Soong, and Du Yuesheng.[42] Many of these bankers fled to Hong Kong after the liberation of Shanghai. In Hong Kong the CCP and the Nationalist government competed with each other to seek the help of these bankers as each side sought to secure the Bank of China's assets.

The total assets left by the Nationalists in Hong Kong were about HK$0.243 billion. The amount was calculated from the properties owned by twenty-nine organizations in aviation, navigation, banking, transportation, and trading. Zheng Tieru, who shifted his loyalty to the CCP, successfully prevented the Nationalist government from relocating assets of HK$40 million to Taiwan.[43] On December 31, 1949, a CCP underground member Luo Jingyi made a report to the CCP Central Committee on the recent situation of the Bank of China's Hong Kong Branch and included suggestions for an appropriate policy to be adopted. It read:

> The Hong Kong Head Office of the Bank of China has a net balance of US$20 million. Fifteen million of this is held in New York, being monitored by the New York State Bank. Recently, the reactionary [Nationalist] group tried to withdraw this money but without success. This can be made by obtaining any two signatures from Song Hanzhang, Huo Baoshu, Chen Changtong, and Gao Bochang. Chen and Gao have already resigned and Xu Baiyuan has replaced them so the signing authority rests with Xu, Song, and Huo.
>
> Among all the overseas branches, only London, New York, Canada, and Tokyo have not yet contacted us. Hsia Pin-fang of the London branch is closely connected with T.V. Soong [in

---

42. The other members were: Bei Zuyi, Mo Liucheng, Zhang Jia'ao, Bian Baimei, Li Ming, Xu Jiqing, Jin Runquan, Xu Kan (later resigned, replaced by Xi Demao), Guo Jingkun, Wu Dingchang, Huo Baoshu, Chen Qicai, Wang Xiaolai, Wu Liqing, Chen Zhiding, Xu Qingfu, Li Tiqun, Qing Xinzhi, Ji Jingcheng, Xi Demao (later replaced by Wu Tiecheng).

43. Liu Jingfang, "Jieshou Xianggang Guomindang zhengfu jigou he zichan shulue" (A brief discussion of the takeover of the assets of the Nationalist government's offices in Hong Kong), in *Zhonggong zhongyang dangxiao xuebao* (Journal of the Central Party School), 1 (1997): 94–104.

the Nationalist government]. As suggested by Zheng Tieru, it is likely we can get Hsia [to align with us]. The Singapore branch recently showed they are coming to [align with] us. According to Zheng Tieru's guarantee, he will not give even a penny to the reactionaries [in the Nationalist government]. According to him, the Hong Kong branch has about HK$30 million whereas the Bangkok branch has more than HK$10 million.

We have promised to appoint Zheng Tieru to the position of manager of the Hong Kong branch if he could prevent the bank's assets from being transferred to Taiwan. Zheng is now in a struggle with Xu Baiyuan. ... if there is a struggle between the middle and lower levels of employees of the Hong Kong branch, we may rely on the lower level of employees. Chen Changtong, Huo Baoshu, and Song Hanzhang have not yet declared their support to us.

In anticipation of the diplomatic recognition of PRC by Britain, we suggest that Beijing should be ready to take over the bank. Since the bank has both government and private capital, we have to call a meeting of the board of directors in order to elect new members of the board. Besides taking over the Hong Kong branch, we may also take over the branches at Singapore and London.[44]

According to the report, the most critical point for the CCP was to secure the assets of the Bank of China before the British government made the announcement that it was recognizing the status of the PRC as a nation. Luo's report had confirmed the important position occupied by Song Hanzhang in the Bank of China. It also confirmed that once Zheng Tieru aligned with the PRC, Beijing would appoint him as the head of the Hong Kong branch. In addition, it showed that support from members of the old board of directors was considered important since they would vote for the new members of the board, particularly for those who were now serving on the board.

---

44. "Luo Jingyi guanyu gangzhonghang wenti de baogao" (Luo Jingyi's report on the question of Bank of China's Hong Kong Branch, December 31, 1949, in *Zhonggong zhongyang huanan fenju wenjian huiji* (Collected documents of the South China Branch of the Central CCP), April to December 1949 (Guangzhou: Zhongyang danganguan and Guangdongsheng danganguan, 1989), 420–421.

On January 6, 1950, Britain officially announced its recognition of the PRC. On January 7, 1950, Beijing formally appointed Zheng Tieru to be the manager of Bank of China's Hong Kong branch. According to Yao Songling, who had long served the Bank of China, only then did the Bank of China's London branch finally fall into the hands of the CCP:

> Once the British government made the announcement, the London branch sought legal advice on its status. The London branch continued to conduct business and send reports to the bank's headquarters in Beijing and Taipei. Obviously, the head of the London branch, Hsia Pin-fang, was trying not to offend anyone. However, because of his unclear declaration of his political loyalty, he lost his standing. Before long, the CCP sent people to take over the London branch, and the person who was originally in charge of the branch finally lost his position.[45]

On April 9, 1950, the new board of directors held a meeting in Bei-jing. K.P. Chen, Li Ming, Chang Kia-ngau, Du Yuesheng, and Song Hanzhang sent Zheng Tieru to attend it. On June 8, 1950, a "work team in charge of Hong Kong finances" (*Xianggang jinrong gongzuo tuan*) arrived in Hong Kong and took over all of the former Nationalist financial institutions.

On April 20, 1950, soon after the meeting of the board of the Bank of China in Beijing, another Bank of China's board meeting was held in Taipei. According to the personal diary of Lei Zhen:

> I met Hong Lanyou, and he said to me that Zhang Jia'ao [Chang Kia-ngau], Chen Guangfu [K.P. Chen], Li Ming, and Song Hanzhang have received the invitation to the fake Bank of China's board meeting. They all have asked for leave and signed the leave letter. Du Yuesheng wrote separately and has sought to reach an understanding with Taipei. Nevertheless, the meeting in Taipei has already been held, and the four persons claimed they all have attended the meeting. Du said he will give an explanation to Taipei.[46]

---

45. Yao Songling, *Zhonghang fuwuji* (My memoir of serving in the Bank of China) (Taipei: Zhuanji wenxue chubanshe, 1968), 99. On Hsia Pin-fang, see Elisabeth Köll's characterization in chapter 12 of this volume.

46. Fu Zheng, ed., *Lei Zhen quanji: Diyige shinian, Lei Zhen riji, 1950* (Collected materi-

This meeting in Taipei was held eleven days after the meeting in Beijing. Obviously, the anti–United Front work by Taiwan did not prevent Hong Kong bankers from sending Zheng Tieru as their representative to Beijing. When the U.S. government froze all the China assets in December 1950, Shanghai bankers hesitated to make contacts with the CCP. Since Taiwan had been an ally of the United States in the Korean War, the Nationalist government definitely played a role in helping the bankers to unfreeze those assets.[47]

Table 3.3 Foreign Reserves Held by Bank of China's New York Branch (US$)

Date	Bank of China (A)	Total (B)	A/B %
January 1945	78,137,020.07	944,320,999.66	8.27
July 1945	76,214,635.62	786,339,098.52	9.69
December 1945	88,538,509.89	790,358,685.32	11.20
February 1946	82,801,058.23	751,013,955.85	11.03
July 1946	53,162,915.41	570,192,621.30	9.32
December 1946	33,860,744.14	384,119,661.14	8.82
January 1947	34,708,835.01	333,972,961.92	10.39
February 1947	30,477,624.56	284,268,286.80	10.71
March 1947	37,798,558.00	290,056,653.68	13.03

Source: "Xi Demou cheng Jiang Zhongzheng Zhongguo yinhang liuyue fenhang yewu zhuangkuang" (Letter addressed by Xi Demou to Chiang Kai-shek on the business situation of the Bank of China's New York Branch), April 18, 1947, Geming wenxian, v. 36, no. 66, 259–266, Guoshiguan, Taiwan. **Note:** The Bank of China's total assets (B) include those of Central Bank of China, Agricultural Bank of China, Postal Bureau, Zhongyang Xintuoju, The National Commission of Natural Resources, Bank of China, and Bank of Communications.

---

als of Lei Zhen: The first ten years, Lei Zhen's diary for 1950) (Taipei: Guiguan tushu gufen youxian gongsi, 1989), 88.

47. Pui-Tak Lee, "Toichi sensen to hantoichi sensen: senkyuhyaku yonjunendai matsu kara gojunendai hajime no honkon ni okeru shanhai ginkoka" (The United Front and anti-United Front: The Shanghai bankers in Hong Kong during the late 1940s and early 1950s), in Nihon Shanhaishi kenkyukai (Japanese research association on Shanghai history), ed., *Kenkoku zenko no shanhai* (Shanghai before and after the establishment of the People's Republic of China) (Tokyo: Kenbun shuppan, 2009), 255–285.

CONCLUSION

Like many other Chinese capitalists in the late 1940s, K.P. Chen successfully removed assets from China but not all at once. Instead, he carried out this process in several steps: first, he reorganized the SCSB's Hong Kong branch and turned it into an independent company that was separate from the parent bank in Shanghai; second, he used this Hong Kong company in his appeal to the U.S. government to unfreeze the bank's assets in America; third, he insisted on staying in Hong Kong in order to observe the changes that happened in both the mainland and Taiwan, and he continued to maintain relationships with both places; finally, he moved the headquarters of the SCSB first from Shanghai to Hong Kong and then from Hong Kong to Taipei in 1965.

K.P. Chen thus made strenuous efforts to maintain contact with both the Nationalist government in Taiwan and the People's Republic of China. As he himself claimed, he felt "sometimes close and sometimes isolated" *(ruoji ruoli)* from these two governments. This position between the two political rivals reflects the unstable position of Chinese capitalists like Chen as they tried to respond to the rapid changes that occurred in China dating from the late 1940s. The year 1949 signified the beginning of a new era of Chinese history. However, as the case of the SCSB shows, the process of moving the bank from Shanghai to Hong Kong spanned years both before and after 1949.

It is generally assumed that Shanghai bankers chose Hong Kong because they were not willing to deal with the CCP for political reasons after Shanghai was liberated. However, as has been discussed in this chapter, Shanghai banker K.P. Chen kept contact with Shanghai even after he emigrated. Long after he left Shanghai for the last time, he continued to feel torn. As he aptly expressed his predicament in exile: "I am in Hong Kong, but my heart remains in Shanghai" *(renzai Xianggang, xinzai Shanghai)*.

Abbreviations

COH	Chinese Oral History, Rare Books and Manuscript Library, Columbia University
KPCPP	K.P. Chen Private Papers, Rare Books & Manuscript Library, Columbia University
PRO HKRS	Hong Kong Record Series, Public Record Office, Hong Kong S.A.R. Government
SCSB	Shanghai Commercial & Savings Bank
SMA	Shanghai Municipal Archives

This page is intentionally left blank.

4 THINK IT THROUGH THREE TIMES |
Zhang Jianhui's Decisions in the 1950s
Kai Yiu Chan

In October 1949, the Chinese Communist Party gave itself a mandate to rule China. Unlike many past regimes, this new one claimed to be ideologically different, aiming at establishing a Communist society, which would eventually abolish private property and individual ownership according to its primary leader Mao Zedong.[1] Many residents in the country, especially the Chinese capitalists who were meant to be the target of this ideological attack, had to face a dilemma of how to deal with this new regime. The reactions of the Chinese capitalists, as discussed in this volume and elsewhere, varied. Some stayed, some left, and some first left and then returned.

The reasons behind these different actions were complicated. By leaving China, as suggested by Siu-lun Wong's study of Shanghainese "emigrant entrepreneurs" in Hong Kong, the capitalists had searched for a safe location to avoid social and political unrest since the Second Sino-Japanese War of 1937–1945. In particular, they had left China to escape from what they were afraid of under the newly established anti-capitalist government of Communist China.[2] The explanation for why some stayed, as Maurice Meisner once remarked, is that the capitalists were "nearly ruined by the extralegal exactions of a corrupt bureaucracy and the economic chaos of the civil war … [and] had little to lose. They hardly could have been enthusiastic about a government which proclaimed socialism and communism to be its aims, but they could hope that the new rulers would honor the promise to control but not immediately

---

1. On the political ideology of the Chinese Communists as represented by Mao Zedong, see Stuart Schram, "Mao Tse-tung's Thought to 1949," in John K. Fairbank and Albert Feuerwerker, eds., *The Cambridge History of China, Republican China 1912–1949* (Cambridge: Cambridge University Press, 1986), v. 13, pt. 2, 789–870.
2. Siu-lun Wong, *Emigrant Entrepreneurs: Shanghai Industrialists in Hong Kong* (Hong Kong: Oxford University Press, 1988), 16–20.

eliminate capitalism."[3] Those who first left and then returned in the early years of Communist China, such as Liu Hongsheng and his sons as studied by Sherman Cochran, wanted "to pursue new opportunities there as a family."[4] On the whole, the capitalists made their decisions according to their economic and political position before the Communists came to power and on the basis of their expectations for their future under communism.

Although making calculations from the past to imagine the future might yield a certain amount of truth, it was not the only way. As this paper on the experience of Zhang Jianhui shows, the dilemma of the capitalists was a dynamic one, with decisions based on rapidly shifting circumstances. Zhang made seemingly final decisions about whether to leave China under Communist rule no less than three separate times. At first, as Mao Zedong defeated Chiang Kai-shek in the Civil War of 1946–1949 and announced the establishment of the People's Republic on October 1, 1949, Zhang chose to stay in China. Not until 1951, nearly two years after the new government had been founded, did he reconsider and make a second decision—this time to move from China to Hong Kong. Even then he did not put the possibility of living in China completely out of his mind. In 1957–1958, he returned there for the winter and made a third decision: to keep his residence in Hong Kong rather than move back to China. Zhang's three decisions show that he wrestled repeatedly with the capitalist dilemma not only in 1949 at the founding of the People's Republic but throughout the 1950s.

In Hong Kong in 1992, I met Mr. Zhang Jianhui (1905–1999; also known as T.V. Chang) through the kind introduction of Professor Cho-yun Hsu, who is related to Zhang on his mother's side. Although Zhang spoke only Wuxinese, a dialect of Chinese with which I am not familiar, we could still communicate with each other by writing. In a series of meetings, Mr. Zhang kindly offered to meet with me in his residence on the higher levels (the more expensive part) of Hong Kong Island, and in restaurants and the Hong Kong Jockey Club with his friends. At these meetings, he gave me drafts of his memoirs, together with a commemorative volume dedicated to his mother, which serve as

---

3. Maurice Meisner, *Mao's China and After* (New York: The Free Press, rev. ed., 1986), 87–88.

4. Sherman Cochran, "Capitalists Choosing Communist China: The Liu Family of Shanghai, 1948–56," in Jeremy Brown and Paul G. Pickowicz, eds., *Dilemmas of Victory: The Early Years of the People's Republic of China* (Cambridge: Harvard University Press, 2007), 359–385; for the quotations, see 359, 384.

the principal sources of this essay.[5] Only a small part of his memoirs, notably the section on his activities during the Sino-Japanese War, has been published.[6] These writings, together with other related documents, reveal the complex considerations underlying Zhang's struggles with the capitalist dilemma.

BECOMING A "CAPITALIST"

Zhang Jianhui came from humble origins. Born in 1905 in Wuxi county, he began his career in 1923 as a trainee in Wuhan, entering into the service of Shenxin Cotton Mill No. 4.[7] Located in Wuhan, that mill, together with more than a dozen flour and cotton mills, was under the management and, in most cases, majority ownership of the famous Republican Chinese capitalists, the Rong brothers, Rong Zongjing and Rong Desheng, who hailed from Wuxi county just as Zhang did.[8]

Besides sharing a native-place tie with the Rong brothers, Zhang was also related to the Rongs through his maternal kinsman, Li Guowei, the son-in-law of Rong Desheng and deputy manager of Shenxin No. 4 Mill.[9] By 1929, Zhang had attained the position of "technician" of the

---

5. Zhang Jianhui, *Xueni zaji: Jianhui huiyilu* (Recollections of snowy mud: Memoirs of Zhang Jianhui; hereafter cited as XZJH) (Hong Kong: private printing, 1984–1993), 8 volumes (13 and A–E); Zhang Jianhui, *Xueni zaji: Jianhui huiyilu zhaiji* (Recollections of snowy mud: Abstracts of memoirs of Zhang Jianhui) (Hong Kong: private printing, n.d.); Zhangshi xiongmei (Brothers and sisters of the Zhang family), *Xuantang ji: 1878–1972* (Recollections of our mother Qin Xuanyi) (n.p.: author's private publication, 1992). The pages in Zhang's memoirs are not numbered consistently. I have identified passages by citing sections, subsections, and page numbers within the sections and subsections.

6. Zhang Jianhui, "Xueni zaji: Bazhi huiyilu" (Recollections of snowy mud; Memoirs at the age of 80), Zhongguo jindai fangzhishi bianji weiyuanhui (Compilation committee of the collected materials on modern China's history of textiles), comp., *Zhongguo jindai fangzhishi yanjiu ziliao huibian* (Collected materials on modern China's history of textiles), v. 2 (Shanghai: Zhongguo jindai fangzhishi bianji weiyuanhui, 1988), 8–19. Most of the sections have been typed in simplified characters but a few sections are rendered in traditional characters (implying Zhang's intention to reach an audience outside China), including the ones addressing the decisions that he made in the 1950s.

7. Zhang Jianhui, *Xueni zaji: Jianhui huiyilu zhaiji*, 1.

8. Shanghai Shenxin zongguanlichu (General Management Office of Shenxin in Shanghai) and Shanghai caijing xueyuan (Shanghai Academy of Finance and Economics), comp., *Shenxin xitong qiye shiliao* (Historical documents on the Shenxin enterprise), 2.1 (October 1956), unpublished copy (held by the Research Center for Chinese Business History, Institute of Economic Research, Shanghai Academy of Social Sciences), 87–98.

9. Regarding Li Guowei's position, see Maoxin-Fuxin-Shenxin zonggongsi (Maoxin-Fuxin-Shenxin headquarters company), "Zonggongsi ji gechang zhiyuanlu" (A list of staff

mill.[10] The following year he was promoted to "engineer."[11] Before the outbreak of the Second Sino-Japanese War, he became "works manager" (*changzhang*).[12] In short, Zhang was hardly a full-fledged "capitalist" (capable of investing substantial capital in production) in the pre-war era. At best, he was a salaried technician or manager working for the capitalists.

Zhang's career took a turn for the better when the war between China and Japan broke out in July 1937. Within months, the most populated areas along the coast were under attack and became occupied by Japanese troops, leaving untouched only the foreign concessions, especially the ones in Shanghai and the British colony of Hong Kong. The Nationalist government had to leave its former capital, Nanjing, and moved inland. Its first destination was Wuhan but under attack by the Japanese forces in 1938, it moved further upstream to Chongqing.[13] Many of the Chinese capitalists moved either into Shanghai's foreign concessions or to Hong Kong for temporary protection, and the bosses of Shenxin No. 4, the Rong brothers, were no exception. Rong Zongjing died in Hong Kong in early 1938. Rong Desheng had stayed in Wuhan until late 1937 and then returned to Shanghai the next year to take charge of the business that was previously managed by Rong Zongjing.[14] The managers of the factories, including Li Guowei of Shenxin No. 4 Mill, had fled, leaving their original positions vacant. The flight of these capitalists created a managerial power vacuum in the individual enterprises formerly owned by the Rong brothers. Staying behind in Wuhan, Zhang Jianhui stepped into this vacuum when Li Guowei delegated authority to him.[15] While Zhang remained in Wuhan, he sent some of his children to be under his mother's care in Shanghai's International Concessions.[16]

---

members of the Headquarters Company and each mill), Maoxin-Fuxin-Shenxin zong-gongsi, comp., *Maoxin-Fuxin-Shenxin zonggongsi sanshizhou jiniankan* (Commemorative volume of the thirtieth anniversary of the Maoxin-Fuxin-Shenxin Headquarters Company) (Shanghai: Maoxin-Fuxin-Shenxin zonggongsi, 1929), 15; regarding relationship between Li and Zhang, see XZJH v. 1, sec. 4-1, 1.

10. See Maoxin-Fuxin-Shenxin zonggongsi, "Zonggongsi ji gechang zhiyuanlu," 15.

11. Zhang Jianhui, *Xueni zaji: Jianhui huiyilu zhaiji*, 1.

12. XZJH, v. 1, sec. 4, 1.

13. On the early history of the war, see Lloyd E. Eastman, "Nationalist China during the Sino-Japanese War 1937–1945," in John K. Fairbank and Albert Feuerwerker, eds., *The Cambridge History of China, Vol. 13 Republican China 1912–1949*, pt. 2, 547–608, especially 547–557.

14. Shanghai Shenxin zongguanlichu and Shanghai caijing xueyuan, comp., *Shenxin xitong qiye shiliao*, 6.2 (January 1957): 162–165.

15. XZJH, v. 1, sec. 4, 2.

16. XZJH, v. 1, sec. 2-1, 1; Zhangshi xiongmei, *Xuantang ji: 1878–1972*, 114.

Zhang's first major decision after assuming managerial authority was to dismantle the factory and move inland. This move had originally been proposed by the government in 1938 but without positive response from the Chinese capitalists.[17] In the autumn of 1938, according to Zhang, Madame Chiang Kai-shek paid an unexpected visit to Shenxin No. 4 Mill and asked him when his factory was scheduled to move. In raising this question, she was implicitly putting pressure on Zhang and other factory decision-makers to make up their mind on this issue.[18] Pressure also came directly from Chiang Kai-shek who considered those who disobeyed his order to move to be traitors deserving the death sentence.[19] With the help of the whole managerial team, Zhang was able to relocate Shenxin No. 4 Mill in September.[20]

Zhang's managerial authority extended beyond his original domain of Shenxin No. 4 Mill and came to include another flour mill, the Fuxin Flour Mill No. 5 that was located opposite Shenxin No. 4 Mill in Wuhan. Though producing different commodities, Fuxin No. 5 and Shenxin No. 4 mills shared the same power generator, which was located in the same compound as the mills. To move the cotton mill, Zhang needed to take the generator with him. In the absence of the flour mill's top managers who had all fled, Zhang took the initiative to dismantle the mill and take the power generator.[21] Although he regarded his cousin Li Guowei as his mentor—literally his "leader" (*lingdao*)—Zhang made all these decisions by himself.[22]

To resume factory operations inland, Zhang needed new capital. In November 1938, after moving machines and materials into Sichuan, Zhang began to consider raising funds from new sources. One option was to obtain financial support from Shanghai where in pre-war years the company headquarters (*zonggongsi*) had channeled funds through enterprises bearing the names Shenxin, Fuxin, and Maoxin.[23]

---

17. On the Nationalist government ordering the removal of Chinese-owned factories to the interior, see Lin Jiyong, *Minying changkuang neiqian jilue* (A brief record of the removal of civilian factories and mines to the interior) (Chongqing: Zhongguo gongye jingji yanjiusuo, 1945).

18. XZJH, v. 1, sec. 4, 1–2. See also Mei Xing, "Zhang Jianhui xiansheng yinxiangji" (A note on my impression of Mr. Zhang Jianhui), *Fangzhi zhoukan* (The Textile Weekly), 8.26 (November 10, 1947), unpaginated.

19. XZJH, v. 1, sec. 4, 1–2.

20. Ibid., sec. 4, 2–3.

21. Ibid., sec. 4, 2.

22. XZJH, v. 2, sec. 5, 2.

23. On the functions of the company headquarters, see Kai Yiu Chan, "Cong jiu ge'an, jiu dianfan zhong de xin renshi: Yi Wuxi Rongshi xiongdi suoban fangzhi yu zhifen shiye

However, as the Rongs had not been in favor of the move inland, they only allowed Zhang to lease the machines.[24] Turning to other sources, Zhang first obtained an emergency loan of 500,000 yuan from the Chongqing branch of the Shanghai Commercial and Savings Bank.[25] In addition, he and his team raised capital from new investors in Sichuan, especially from newcomers who had fled from Shanghai and Wuhan.[26] In January 1939, with their backing, he installed the machines of Shenxin No. 4 Mill and operated under the name of "Qingxin Cotton Mill."[27]

Zhang's final step in completing the transfer of factories from Wuhan to Sichuan was to obtain the endorsement from the Rongs. This was particularly important to Li Guowei, Zhang's mentor, who shared responsibility for Zhang's actions. When Qingxin opened, Li Guowei, who was injured and hospitalized in Hong Kong, had ordered Zhang to take a trip from the British colony to Shanghai to seek the Rongs' approval. Following Li's instructions, Zhang took a steamship from Hong Kong to Shanghai and met Rong Desheng in the foreign concessions. After three days of talks, Rong Desheng finally approved Zhang's move inland. Zhang immediately returned to Chongqing and registered Qingxin Cotton Mill as a joint-stock limited company. Fuxin Flour Mill was also reorganized and had its name changed to Qingxin Flour Mill.

"At that point," Zhang recalled in his old age, "I began to become a boss."[28] Although Zhang Jianhui's managerial authority over Shenxin No. 4 and Fuxin No. 5 mills was temporary, it provided the foundation for him to establish his reputation in business circles. In late 1940, after Zhang had moved and reorganized the businesses, he and the Rongs dissolved

---

wei zhongxin (1901–1937)" (New understanding from old cases, old paradigms: with special reference of the cotton-textile and flour milling enterprises of the Rong brothers in Wuxi (1901–1937), paper presented at the conference "New Paradigms of Chinese Business History: Conception and Case Studies," organized by Department of History, Fudan University, August 24–25, 2007.

24. Regarding the Rongs' attitude, see Shanghai shehui kexueyuan jingji yanjiusuo (Institute of Economic Research, Shanghai Academy of Social Sciences), comp., *Rongjia qiye shiliao* (Historical materials of the Rong family business enterprises) (Shanghai: Shanghai renmin chubanshe, 1980), v. 2, 198.

25. XZJH, v. 2, sec. 6, 2.

26. Li Wujiu, "Shenxin sichang ji Fuxin wuchang neiqian Sichuan-Shaan gaikuang" (The brief situation of the removal to the interior by Shenxin No. 4 and Fuxin No. 5 mills), in Zhongguo renmin zhengzhi xieshang huiyi xinan diqu wenshiziliao xiezuo huiyi, comp., *Kangzhan shiqi neiqian xinan de gongshang qiye* (Industrial and business enterprises which moved into the southwest interior during the War of Resistance period) (Kunming: Yunnan renmin chubanshe, 1988), 241–252, particularly, 246.

27. Shanghai shehui kexueyuan jingji yanjiusuo, comp., *Rongjia qiye shiliao*, v. 2, 197.

28. XZJH, v. 2, sec. 6, 2.

Qingxin Cotton and Flour mills and restored their names as Shenxin and Fuxin, and the Rongs permitted Zhang and Qingxin's original investors to become shareholders in these companies.[29] During the rest of the war (1940–1945), under the nominal leadership of Li Guowei, Zhang Jianhui used profits generated from Shenxin No. 4 and Fuxin No. 5 mills to set up a number of factories in Sichuan, Yunnan, Guangxi, and Shaanxi.[30] He also invested in some new shipping and trading companies, and he became known in business circles as an "industrialist."[31]

BETWEEN CAMPS

When the Civil War broke out, Zhang Jianhui was faced with the dilemma of whether to support the Communists or the Nationalists.[32] But even before the outbreak of this war, Zhang already had associates in both camps.

On the Communist side, although he had a personal relationship with some Communists without knowing they were party members, he did not know any leading figures in the party. His second younger sister, Yangfen, had responded positively to the Communist cause. When the war against Japan broke out, she and her husband joined the Communist-led New Fourth Army where she became a medical officer, a position that she held even after the war ended.[33] It is unclear whether Zhang's younger sister served as a liaison between him and the Communists.

On the Nationalist side, during the war, Zhang was one of the industrialists who cooperated with the Chongqing government. He followed the government's instructions to take trips to the interior of northwestern China, seeking opportunities to set up factories and utilize resources there.[34] Zhang also hosted parties and gatherings in his house in a Chongqing suburb, with guests who were not only part of his business circles but who were also active in politics and in the military. Zhang's

---

29. XZJH, v. 2, sec. 7, 3.

30. For these activities, see XZJH, v. 2, sec. 6, 3–4; sec. 7, 4.

31. XZJH, v. 3, sec. 8, 4. He made this impression probably because of an article written by a journalist for the most important publication in his specialty. See Mei Xing, "Zhang Jianhui xiansheng yinxiangji."

32. On the history of the Civil War, see Suzanne Pepper, "The KMT-CCP conflict 1945–1949," John K. Fairbank and Albert Feuerwerker, eds., *The Cambridge History of China, Vol.13 Republican China 1912–1949*, pt. 2, 723–788.

33. Zhang Yangfen, "Jinian qing'ai de muqin" (In remembrance of my beloved mother), in Zhangshi Xiongmei, *Xuantang ji: 1878–1972*, 60–61.

34. XZJH, v. 2, sec. 6-2.

hospitality even included putting up some of his guests in his own home, or using his home as a venue for wedding parties.[35]

Zhang's closest connection with the Nationalist government came after the Japanese surrender. In September 1945, the Minister of Economic Affairs, Weng Wenhao, recruited him to serve as a government agent in reclaiming Chinese property.[36] Returning to Shanghai, Zhang was in charge of taking over mills that had been under Japanese management. During his four months' service as a government agent, he also helped a few Shanghai capitalists who had stayed behind in the occupied areas and who were suspected of being Japanese "collaborators." After completing his mission, Zhang returned to his former position as Operations Manager of Shenxin No. 4 Mill.[37] In a sense, he merely did what he was told. He did not actively show support for the Nationalist camp.

Rather than committing himself to either the Nationalist or the Communist camp, Zhang was most closely allied with a third force, the "democrats." As he later recalled, he considered many of these democrats to be "my good old friends"; these included Huang Yanpei, Shao Lizi, Zhang Fengzhou, and Zhang Naiqi.[38] Of these associates, Huang Yanpei and Zhang Naiqi had focused on economic development in the pre-1937 years and only became politically active as democrats after the war with Japan.[39] Shao Lizi was a member of the pro-Communist Revolutionary Committee of the Chinese Nationalist Party, a group of Nationalists who had denounced Chiang Kai-shek for betraying Sun Yat-sen's revolutionary doctrines.[40] Zhang Fengzhou had been an assistant to a Nationalist general, Feng Yuxiang.[41] These and other democrats were not

---

35. XZJH, v. 2, sec. 6-1.

36. XZJH, v. 3, sec. 8, 1.

37. XZJH, v. 3, sec. 8, 1–3.

38. XZJH, v. 3, sec. 9, 2.

39. On their political activities, see Guchi Guiqing (Kikuchi Takaharu), trans. by Liu Daxiao, *Zhongguo disan shili shilun* (A treatise of China's third power) (Tianjin: Tianjin renmin chubanshe, 1991), 16–39, and particularly the chapter on Huang, 75–111. On Zhang Naiqi's political activities, see Zhou Tiandu and Zhang Lifan, "Zhang Naiqi zhuan" (Biography of Zhang Naiqi), in Zhou Tiandu, ed., *Qijunzi zhuan* (A biograhy of the "Seven Respectable Gentlemen") (Beijing: Zhongguo shehuikexue chubanshe, 1989), 161–305.

40. On history of the "Revolutionary Committee of the Chinese Nationalist Party," see Zhongguo Guomindang geming weiyuanhui zhongyang xuanchuanbu (Central Propaganda Bureau of the Revolutionary Committee of the Chinese Nationalist Party), comp., *Zhongguo Guomindang geming weiyuanhui de lishi daolu* (Historical path of the Revolutionary Committee of the Chinese Nationalist Party) (Changsha: Hunan renmin chubanshe, 1987); on Shao's participation from September 1949 to his death in December 1967, see 81–124.

41. See Tang Ke, "Zheng Fengzhou: Heping laoren bainian chuanqi" (Zhang Fengzhou:

followers of Chiang Kai-shek, and they delivered anti–Civil War speeches long before the outbreak of the Civil War in June 1946.[42]

In July 1946, Zhang was enlisted by the Nationalist government to attend the International Labor Organization conference "as a representative of the employers," and he decided to go. He probably left China to avoid taking sides too early in the Civil War. Having finished his first mission, Zhang immediately accepted another government assignment— this time to attend another conference in Switzerland on the government's behalf. It is not clear how he managed to cover his expenses for these travels. What is clear is that these travels kept him outside China for the first year of the Civil War.[43]

Zhang's initial response to the Civil War was similar to his earlier response to the Sino-Japanese War. Once again he made plans to move both machinery and inventory to another safe haven, but this time it was from Chongqing to Taiwan and Hong Kong.[44] Many Chinese capitalists, including Zhang's mentor Li Guowei, had considered moving or had already started moving their fortunes to Hong Kong or Taiwan. From late 1947 to late 1948, Li and Zhang exchanged letters to discuss moving factories and homes from Chongqing to south China, Hong Kong, and Taiwan. Zhang, in particular, once suggested, "Taiwan is a better option [than Hong Kong]" for relocating the spindles.[45]

The Nationalists' defeat and subsequent retreat to Taiwan in 1949–1950 forced Zhang to face political reality and confront his first dilemma in the Chinese revolution.

THE FIRST MOMENT OF CHOICE

The war that ended in the Communists' "liberation" of China defined Zhang's options. With the defeat of the Nationalist troops in the Battle of Huaihai (late 1948 to early 1949), and the Nationalists' moving

---

The legend of a hundred-year-old man of peace), *Renwu* (Personage), 2003, no. 1, http://www.renwu.com.cn/UserFiles/magazine/article/RW0167_200408021009595796.asp, cited on August 28, 2009.

42. See Zhang Xianwen, ed., *Zhonghua minguo shigang* (A historical sketch of the Republic of China) (Zhengzhou: Henan renmin chubanshe, 1985), 656–661; Roger B. Jeans, *Roads Not Taken: The Struggle of Opposition Parties in Twentieth-Century China* (Boulder: Westview Press, 1992).

43. XZJH, v. 3, sec. 8, 1–3.

44. Ibid., sec. 9, 1.

45. Shanghai Shehui kexueyuan jingji yanjiusuo, comp., *Rongjia qiye shiliao*, v. 2, 664–666; on the quotation, 665.

of their capital from Nanjing to Canton in April 1949, the final demise of their regime seemed obvious. As the southwestern interior was under Communist control in December 1949, Zhang was inclined to accept the *fait accompli.*[46]

While not celebrating this political reality, Zhang, according to his recollections in his old age, raised three points about the Communists' victory that seem to suggest he was not completely pessimistic at the time about the future under communism.

> After unifying the whole country, the Communist Party repeatedly promoted New Democracy in order to consolidate the industrial and commercial capitalists of the whole nation to complete the first phase of building socialism. The party never talked about the communism of class struggle, and thus found that ordinary capitalists were receptive. For example, Liu Hongsheng and Wu Yunchu, the Guos, the Wangs, and Li Zhuchen and Fan Xudong in the north, Sichuan's Lu Zuofu, the Hus and the Lius, all sincerely supported it. They expected the Communist Party to bring peace and prosperity. I made this same observation and had this same hope.[47]

This recollection suggests that Zhang understood the role of Chinese capitalists as a viable and important component in the building of Chinese socialism under Communist leadership.

Zhang's second consideration concerned the Communists' United Front strategy. As he recalled:

> Deng Xiaoping as the director of the Southwestern Military-Administrative Committee, which was in charge of the situation in Southwest China, was resolute and capable in his work. He deeply understood the ancient teaching that one who "takes [power] on horseback cannot rule on horseback." Therefore, Deng was eager to recover civilian control over distribution and the economy. He treated us, the ordinary leaders of industry and commerce, as targets of the United Front strategy, and called me a democratic and enlightened capitalist. I was appointed as a member of the Consultative Committee, the Financial and

---

46. On the final stage of the civil war, see Suzanne Pepper, "The KMT-CCP conflict 1945–1949," 774–784; Maurice Meisner, *Mao's China and After*, 74.

47. XZJH, v. 3, sec. 9, 1.

Economic Committee of the Southwest, and the Industrial and Commercial Association of Chongqing. I also became the Chairman of the Chongqing Textile Manufacturers' Association. Deng often asked me for my opinion. It seemed that I was quite respected by the Communist Party.[48]

Just as Zhang found a way to serve the Nationalist government, so he also found his place in the new government.

The final reason for Zhang to consider staying in Communist China at the time was political.

> In 1950 Beijing held the National Tax Conference and Textile Conference. I was appointed as a representative of Chongqing to attend these conferences in Beijing. There I met many of my good old friends, such as Huang Yanpei, Shao Lizi, Zhang Fengzhou, Zhang Naiqi and Xue Muqiao, who were permitted to meet with the leaders of the Communist Party. This reinforced my inclination to stay in my home country and to serve the people.[49]

In other words, Zhang believed that these democrats (except for Xue Muqiao who was a well-known economist in the Communist government until his last days[50]) might become political patrons of the capitalists. He took comfort in the prospect of his friends and earlier acquaintances exercising their influence on this new regime. With this future in mind, Zhang initially decided to stay and accept Communist rule in China in 1949–1950.

THINK IT THROUGH A SECOND TIME

Zhang's second dilemma came at the outbreak of the Korean War in 1950 and the threat that the remnants of the Nationalists under Chiang Kai-shek's command mounted in Taiwan. Before fighting those from without,

---

48. XZJH, v. 3, sec. 9, 2.

49. Ibid.

50. On the life of Xue Muqiao, see Xue Xiaohe, comp., *Bainian cangsang yidai zongshi: Xue Muqiao shishi yizhounian jinian wenji* (A hundred years of great change, the master of the generation: Collected essays to commemorate the first anniversary of the death of Xue Muqiao) (Beijing: Zhongguo fazhan chubanshe, 2006).

the Communist Party wanted to "cleanse" their potential supporters from within.[51] The primary target was the capitalists, including Zhang.

At this critical juncture, Zhang saw an actual internal document concerning the coming of the new campaign to suppress counter-revolutionaries in late 1950. As he recalled:

> When I returned to Chongqing [from Beijing], I at first actively reorganized my cotton and flour mills and resumed operations. I also often participated in the meetings called by Deng [Xiaoping]. To my surprise, at the end of 1950, the central [party] issued a document for internal discussion of the suppression of counterrevolutionaries. I felt insecure about the future. Meanwhile, in several incidents at occasional social gatherings, I noticed the possible changes.[52]

In Zhang's memoirs, he did not clearly reveal which "internal" document he was referring to and exactly what kind of "incidents" he encountered, but his eldest younger sister, Zhang Yingfen, was accused of being a "special suspect" and a "counterrevolutionary" at the end of the year.[53] According to Zhang Yingfen's own account, she was accused of committing a "crime" because she promoted welfare for workers when she was Zhang's factory personnel manager on labor affairs during the war with Japan.[54] Compared to hearsay about the party's attitude toward capitalists, this charge hit closer to home because it posed a direct threat to Zhang's own sibling. As such, it raised doubts in Zhang's mind about dreams of a Communist future.

The internal document that frightened Zhang was perhaps the one issued on February 21, 1951, called the Regulations Regarding the Punishment of the Counterrevolutionaries (*Zhonghua Renmin Gongheguo chengzhi fangeming tiaoli*), which Mao Zedong himself introduced.[55] Here, the "counterrevolutionaries" included not only those elements who might want to take military action against the new People's Republic but also referred to those who worked as "spies" or "intelligence agents"

51. Maurice Meisner, *Mao's China and After*, 78–80.

52. XZJH, v. 3, sec. 9, 2.

53. Zhang Yingfen, "Yongyuan he muqin zai yiqi" (Be with my mother forever), in Zhangshi Xiongmei, *Xuantang ji: 1878–1972*, 43–56, particularly 51.

54. Zhang Yingfen, "Yongyuan he muqin zai yiqi," 51. On her role in Zhang's management during the war with Japan, see 49–50. See also XZJH, v. 1, sec. 2-2, 4.

55. Gao Kai and Xiong Guangjia, comp., *Xin Zhongguo de licheng* (Historical path of New China) (Beijing: Zhongguo renmin daxue chubanshe, 1989), 31.

for the Nationalists.[56] It also targeted those who had had contact with or worked for the Nationalists in the distant as well as the recent past, people exactly like Zhang Jianhui. As Meisner summarized the aims of the document:

> The purpose of the February decree was somewhat different; it not only extended the scope of political repression by defining more broadly what were deemed to be counterrevolutionary activities, but was also designed to instill an atmosphere of terror in society through public campaigns against all forms of political dissidence.[57]

This decree created an atmosphere that implied a political storm was coming fast and unleashing terror.

Zhang Jianhui's political sensitivity finally pushed him into action. Once the document was issued, he started his move. As he noted:

> In early March 1951, I quickly took a ferry from Chongqing to Wanxian to visit the hemp cloth factory, which was under the management of my brother-in-law, Mi Huasheng. He accompanied me to Hankou via Yichang. From Hankou [I] took a train to Canton. With the help of my relative Fang Yuanmou, I reached Hong Kong through Shenzhen. I was afraid and felt as though I might lose my soul along the way. I could feel myself holding my breath until I arrived at Hong Kong! The psychology of fear was palpable! The preciousness of liberty is an eternal truth in China as it is in foreign countries, in both ancient and modern times.[58]

Pretending to take a business trip, Zhang thus utilized his family connections (and protection) to escape from a country that was now fundamentally changing its political climate and society.

Zhang's escape turned out to be a surprise to some of those in Hong Kong who were considering returning to the mainland. In particular, his former mentor and elder cousin Li Guowei, who had settled temporarily

---

56. Liu Guoxin, comp., *Zhonghua renmin gongheguo lishi changbian* (Compilation of the history of the People's Republic of China) (Nanning: Guangxi renmin chubanshe, 1994), 61–62.

57. Maurice Meisner, *Mao's China and After*, 80–81.

58. XZJH, v. 3, sec. 9, 2.

in the British colony during the Civil War, questioned Zhang about his worries. In an evening meeting with Zhang, Li said that he had left "all his assets in the country" and thus would have to return to China to look after them. Zhang, in reply, argued that "in the future, even a piece of grass or wood would no longer be under the private ownership of capitalists." Ultimately, Zhang failed to convince Li and his wife, who returned later in the same month that Zhang escaped.[59]

In his early months in Hong Kong, some leading Communists in China, including Deng Xiaoping, did not give up on Zhang. They sent him telegrams to convince him to come back. Zhang's friends and relatives, including his mentor Li Guowei and Zhang's former colleagues in Shenxin No. 4 Mill, did the same. Later in the year, the party authorities ordered Zhang's wife to travel to Hong Kong to "bring him back." Obviously, the Communists were desperate to have Zhang back but their plan did not achieve the desired effect, as Zhang's wife not only failed to bring him back but instead stayed with him in the British colony.[60]

Events in China further reinforced Zhang's determination to stay away from China. After his departure, the Communist Party began its mass line strategy of political purge against anti-Communist elements and resorted to violence. In early 1951 it launched thought reform campaigns against "all categories of intellectuals" by conducting a series of "mass meetings, … criticisms and self-criticisms, public humiliations."[61] In 1952, the party launched the famous Three Anti campaign and Five Anti campaign directly against the former Nationalists, the capitalists, and the bureaucrats who were accused of anti-communism, corruption, and embezzlement.[62] In the midst of these political campaigns of mass participation, Zhang's associates were affected. Not only his good friends but his family members also suffered. In particular, his younger sister, Yingfen, was jailed in Hankou as a "special suspect."[63] The more Zhang heard such news, the more he wanted to stay in his new haven under British protection.

In Hong Kong, Zhang had at his side his wife but not his children. Now in their early adulthood, they were still in Shanghai and eager to

---

59. XZJH, v. 3, sec. 9, 3.

60. Ibid.

61. Maurice Meisner, *Mao's China and After*, 95.

62. Ibid., 96–98. On the Wufan Campaign, also see John Gardner, "The Wu-fan Campaign in Shanghai: A Study in the Consolidation of Urban Control," A. Doak Barnett, ed., *Chinese Communist Politics in Action* (Seattle: University of Washington Press, 1969), 477–539.

63. Zhangshi Xiongmei, *Xuentang ji: 1878–1972*, 118.

hear why their father had left China. In explaining his decision to his third son, Zhang described the "fate" of being a "capitalist" under "liberated" China. He noted that at a young age he had not criticized communism, and he expressed sympathy for what had happened to Yingfen, regarding her as "a victim of her times" (*shidai de xisheng*). He doubted the necessity of the "class struggle" strategy in getting rid of "the old, the rotten," and he explained his decision to live abroad as part of the long Chinese tradition of migration, in which the emigrants would not be denigrated as "villains" (*jianmin*) by those in the home country.[64]

Hong Kong became Zhang's new refuge not only because of its proximity to China but also because its attractiveness as a haven favored by other Shanghainese capitalists. Some of them had asked Zhang to help them start new businesses there.[65] As early as 1952, Zhang had used Hong Kong as a base to help his former associates set up textile factories in the British colony, the Philippines, and Thailand. According to Zhang's account, he helped his friends by designing their factory layouts, taking charge of the management during the factories' early operations, and retaining a position of leadership only during the initial stage of the factories' development. Once the transfer of technology was completed, he stepped down. He thus played a role similar to that of other technology advisors among emigrant entrepreneurs in the postwar industrialization of Hong Kong and Southeast Asian countries.[66] Although his jobs on short-term contracts were not as sustainable as the one he had held in Shenxin No. 4 Mill during the pre-1949 period, they were still attractive to Zhang, who had no capital and only his wife by his side.

Throughout the 1950s, Zhang accepted no invitation to visit the Nationalists' last stronghold, Taiwan. In 1951, a senior official in Taiwan, Wang Shijie, sent an invitation to Zhang to offer him opportunities to set up new factories there, but Zhang declined.[67] As early as 1948, Zhang had suggested moving factories to Taiwan, but most of his associates belonged to a faction that opposed the leadership of Chiang Kai-shek who finally moved his troops and government operations to the island in late 1949.[68] After 1949 if Zhang had moved to Taiwan, he might have brought

---

64. XZJH, v. 3, sec. 9, 3–6. There is no date for this letter but it was probably written in the 1950s.

65. Ibid., sec. 9, 3.

66. Ibid., sec. 10.

67. Ibid., sec. 10, 1; Wang was then the secretary of the Presidential Office of the Republic of China. See http://archives.sinica.edu.tw/80th/main/presidents4-1.html, cited on August 29, 2009.

68. See Zhang Xianwen, ed., *Zhonghua minguo shigan*, 761.

suffering on himself as someone affiliated with the democrats and on his family and friends who were still in China under the Communist regime.

Remaining tentative, Zhang and his wife did not buy real estate during their first three decades of sojourning in Hong Kong. As he noted, he "had leased his Hong Kong home beginning in 1951 for the sake of taking refuge. Unexpectedly, [we] stayed there for thirty years." Not until 1974 did Zhang buy a new apartment on Hong Kong island and "settle in" there late in life.[69]

THE THIRD DECISION

Zhang's decision not to buy real estate in Hong Kong in the 1950s and 1960s reflects his unsettled mind and lingering attachment to China. Business was probably the least of his concerns, as he was now well employed with assignments to work in Hong Kong and Southeast Asia for his capitalist friends. It was his family that kept Zhang thinking and rethinking his relationship with his home and country. Settling permanently and definitively in Hong Kong would have prevented him from making a quick decision to leave it if circumstances in China changed or anything happened to his family. In 1957–1958, when circumstances did change, Zhang considered standing once again on Chinese soil.

In 1957–1958, Zhang thought of paying a visit to China because of his mother.[70] In 1951–1952, when he left China, he did not have a chance to say goodbye to his mother because she was visiting his sister in Manchuria. In late 1957, the moment came when he and his siblings planned to celebrate their mother's eightieth birthday in China. He started preparing to attend this event by contacting his former associates who were still in the government. One of his friends, Zhang Fengzhou, was then working as a secretary under Premier Zhou Enlai.[71] In reply to Zhang Jianhui's letter, Zhang Fengzhou wrote, "The government expresses goodwill to you and will allow you to return. It also guarantees that you can then subsequently return to Hong Kong but hopes that you can pay a visit to Beijing after Shanghai."[72]

---

69. XZJH, v. 1, sec. 2-1, 3.

70. Zhangshi Xiongmei, *Xuantang ji: 1878–1972*, 118.

71. On Zhang Fengzhou's career since the formation of the People's Republic of China, see Tang Ke, "Zheng Fengzhou: Heping laoren bainian chuanqi," *Renwu*, 2003, no. 1, http://www.renwu.com.cn/UserFiles/magazine/article/RW0167_200408021009595796.asp, cited on August 28, 2009.

72. XZJH, v. 3, sec. 9, 6.

It is unclear who in the Communist government made the decision to let Zhang return. The party had just completed its First Five-Year Plan and had nationalized private enterprises, which drew criticisms of the single-party dictatorship from intellectuals and democrats during the Hundred Flowers campaign.[73] In approving Zhang's reentry into China, the Communist Party implied that it had a plan for enlisting his services. The arrangement for Zhang's schedule of visits also implies that the Communist Party might have used the family factor as a trump card in its negotiations with Zhang.

On this trip, Zhang saw his mother for the first time since the end of the Civil War. He also had his first family visit with other relatives except for his eldest younger brother, who had been living in the United States since the late 1940s and did not return for the occasion. So, in the winter of 1957, Zhang and his wife returned to China to meet with his other siblings and their children, and Zhang's own children, all as part of their celebration of his mother's birthday.[74] He was very happy to see them, and he did not realize that it would be the last time that he would ever see his mother.[75]

Meanwhile, he deliberated for the third time as to whether he should stay in China. In early 1958, Zhang fulfilled his promise to visit Beijing after his mother's birthday party in Shanghai. During his one-month stay in the capital, he met many of his former associates who almost all attempted to persuade him to remain permanently. His former mentor Li Guowei and his wife met with Zhang and urged him to participate in the nationalization program. Many of Zhang's old friends also asked him to stay and cooperate with the new regime. One of them said, "Judging from your beliefs and behavior, you are very well suited for the conditions under communism, but I am afraid that your life style is different."[76] Zhang, "showing a sense of humor," as he recalled, "replied that Hong Kong will soon be liberated. There will be equal opportunities for me to serve my country in Hong Kong."[77]

In Beijing, family connections once again played a role as to whether Zhang should stay and live under the new regime. His second younger sister and her husband met him in the capital. Since both were party cadres, he might well have expected them to aggressively urge him to stay

---

73. See Maurice Meisner, *Mao's China and After*, 113–137, 167–200.
74. XZJH, v. 3, sec. 9, 6.
75. XZJH, v. 1.
76. XZJH, v. 3, sec. 9, 7.
77. Ibid.

in China. Zhang's sister did make a strong case, but Zhang noticed that his brother-in-law "was quiet" at the meeting. Zhang took this silence to mean that his brother-in-law had doubts about China's future.[78]

While in Beijing, Zhang also noticed some events that left him with the "feeling that it was still best to leave."[79] It is not clear exactly what events he referred to but perhaps one was the fate of his old friends. In late January 1958, democrat Zhang Naiqi, who had become the head of the Ministry of Food, was sacked by Mao Zedong and was denounced as a "rightist."[80]

Before Zhang left China, the Communist authorities sent an official to have a talk with him. This official, who came from Zhang's area of expertise, the textile industry,[81] urged Zhang to serve China. Zhang finally agreed that on his travels abroad, he "would secretly send [to officials in China] information on the foreign textile industry." In addition, Zhang "promised not to express any treasonous opinion or take any treasonous actions."[82] According to Zhang's perception, it seems that he struck a deal with the Communist regime in exchange for permission to return to Hong Kong.

Zhang's tactic of making a deal with the Communist authorities probably saved his life during the last stage of the political purge of the "hidden counterrevolutionary elements" in China that followed his departure. As he recalled, "One month after I arrived in Hong Kong, the number of people who suffered in China from the Campaign to Wipe Out Hidden Counterrevolutionaries (*shufan fengchao*) was enormous—as many as tens of thousands. My third decision of not staying in China allowed me to escape from this disaster!"[83]

78. XZJH, v. 3, sec. 9, 7.

79. Ibid.

80. Gao Kai and Xiong Guangjia, comp., *Xin Zhongguo de licheng*, 131.

81. Regarding Zhang's reports, see a letter from Chen Weiji to Zhang Fengzhou, n.d., but probably before 1960, in XZJH, v. A, 1.

82. XZJH, v. 3, sec. 9, 7. Zhang's memoirs named this official "Deputy Minister Chen" of the Ministry of Textiles but it was actually Chen Weiji who was deputy of the ministry from 1949 to 1982. See internet materials http://www.gmw.cn/content/2006-05/05/content_410726.htm, cited on August 28, 2009.

83. XZJH, v. 3, sec. 9, 7.

CONCLUSION

This chapter shows how Zhang Jianhui was transformed from a silent Chinaman, who passively accepted the regime change, into a subtle objector to the Communist Revolution during the early 1950s, and then into a true emigrant entrepreneur in Hong Kong in the late 1950s. Neither family nor business played the most crucial role in his calculations. It was, above all, his personal freedom that mattered. His intriguing experiences and changes of mind in the 1950s imply that the capitalists' relationship with the Chinese Communists was more complicated and less clear-cut for him than a simple stay-or-leave dichotomy.

The experiences and choices of Zhang Jianhui also suggest that the relationship between Chinese capitalists and the Communist Revolution of 1949 cannot be fully understood without looking at the process of negotiation in the 1950s and beyond. The Communist Revolution of 1949 itself did not have an immediate or decisive impact on the Chinese capitalists. It was those events that followed the revolution, including the terror, the purge, the violence, and so on that gradually pushed some capitalists into the position where they made clear-cut decisions.

During these events, capitalists made various responses: helplessly accepting changes, actively adapting to them, or rejecting them and running away. Zhang was politically sensitive enough in 1950–1951 to envisage the violence and terror of the age. Many others, including Zhang's sister and some of his old friends, suffered from tragedies or even lost their lives. Later they had fewer and fewer choices, and they sometimes resorted to suicide during the Cultural Revolution (1966–1976).[84]

At the same time, the capitalists were probably one of the most resourceful groups in China during the 1950s, and they had room to maneuver because the new Communist regime wanted their help in rebuilding the economy in the aftermath of the war with Japan. The capitalists provided not only capital but also technical know-how. The party authorities therefore undertook negotiations within the framework of the United Front strategy, giving the capitalists time to decide whether to stay in China. As long as the United Front strategy was honored, the party and the capitalists continued to negotiate, and the two continued to dance their tango. Zhang Jianhui's activities in the later years of his life provided evidence of how final his decision was to leave China in

---

84. On those cases related to the suicides and violence during the Cultural Revolution, see Gao Gao and Yan Jiaqi, *"Wenhua dageming" shinianshi 1966–1976* (History of the ten years of the "Great Cultural Revolution") (Tianjin: Tianjin renmin chubanshe, 1986).

1958. In the 1960s, he kept his word and sent secret reports to Chinese officials concerning the development of the international textile industry, but he stayed away from China's soil even when his mother died in early 1972.[85] In the next year, he agreed to visit China once again for the first time in fifteen years.[86] He was not the one to initiate this trip. In fact, he was invited by the new administration under Deng Xiaoping, who had regained his party position through Zhou Enlai's support. As part of Deng's program of economic modernization, Zhang became a kind of advisor, a symbol perhaps, of a Communist state's interest in promoting economic reform.[87]

After his trip of 1973, Zhang visited Beijing almost every year.[88] In 1985, he even stayed longer, traveling not only to the interior in the northwest but he also visited his mother's tomb.[89] The government did not contact him or attempt to keep him in the country. Nor did Zhang consider living in China permanently. In 1986, although he visited his former apartment in Shanghai, he still regarded himself as a "duckweed overseas," a wandering leaf which could spread the species without having roots.[90] He continued to live in Hong Kong and took it as his primary home in his old age.

---

85. Zhangshi Xiongmei, *Xuantang ji: 1878–1972*, 121; XZJH, v. 1, sec. 1, 2; regarding Zhang's reports, see a letter from Chen Weiji to Zhang Fengzhou, n.d., but probably before 1960, in XZJH, v. A, 1.

86. XZJH, v. 3, sec. 9, 7.

87. On Deng's resumption of power in 1973, see Gao Gao and Yan Jiaqi, *"Wenhua Dageming" Shinianshi 1966–1976*, 528–708.

88. XZJH, v. 3, sec. 9, 8.

89. XZJH, v. 3, sec. 9, 7–8; Zhangshi Xiongmei, *Xuantang ji: 1878–1972*, photo of the Zhang siblings at the tomb tablet of their mother, taken in 1985, unpaginated.

90. XZJH, v. 3, sec. 9, 8.

PART TWO

CAPITALISTS WHO STAYED
IN CHINA

This page is intentionally left blank.

5 JANUS-FACED CAPITALISM |
Li Zhuchen and the Jiuda Salt Refinery, 1949-1953

Man Bun Kwan

On July 1, 1952, Jiuda-Yongli became a joint public-private enterprise, making it the first major privately held conglomerate in Tianjin to do so. As the largest chemical industrial complex in the country (whether public or private), it controlled the production capacity of half the country's soda ash, one-sixth of caustic soda, one-seventh in ammonia sulphate, and one-tenth of salt from Changlu Division (Hebei province) in 1949.

Why did Li Zhuchen (1882–1968), Jiuda's general manager and a shareholder with 207 shares to his name, a capitalist who had resisted attempts by the Nationalist government to annex the private company, forge such a "strange alliance" with the Communists?[1] Chen Yun, then head of the central government's Finance and Economics Committee (hereafter CFEC) suggested it was a matter of personal motives.[2] Did Li have a psychological complex that caused him to evolve from enthusiasm to fear and resignation?[3] Or was he reacting to the company's own

---

The author would like to thank ACLS, CSCC, and the Charles Phelps Taft Memorial Fund for their support of the research for this project. All errors are mine.

1. Marie-Claire Bergère, "Shanghai Capitalists and the Transition from Nationalist to Communist regime (1948–1952)," *The Second Conference on Modern Chinese Economic History* (Taipei: Institute of Economics, Academia Sinica, 1989), v. 3, 1037–1058.
2. See CFEC cable dated June 27, 1951, in Zhongguo shehui kexue yuan, et. al., *Zhonghua renmin gongheguo jingji dang'an ziliao xuanbian* (Selected economic archival materials of the People's Republic of China), *Gongshang tizhijuan* (Volume on commerce and industry, hereafter cited as ZJDGS) (Beijing: Zhongguo shehui kexue chubanshe, 1993), 483.
3. Shi Jijin, "1949–1956 nian Zhongguo minzu zichan jieji xinli zhi bianqian" (Change of the national bourgeoisie's psychology, 1949–1956), *Anhui shifan daxue xuebao* (Bulletin of Anhui Normal University) 3 (2004): 30–34. Dong Baoxun, in contrast, characterized the reaction as passive, resigned, and an instinct for survival. See his "Heping shumai yu minzu zichan jieji de shehui xintai" (Peaceful purchase and the social psychology of the national bourgeoisie), *Wenshizhe* (Literature, history, and philosophy) 4 (2004): 61–67.

difficulties?[4] Taking a macro view, political scientists and historians have identified a logic of "objective inevitability" in the Chinese Communist Party's practices of seizing of Nationalist "bureaucratic" enterprises, holding foreign companies "hostage," and persecuting both corrupted cadres and capitalists in the Three Anti and Five Anti campaigns.[5] This "Stalinization" of China's economy has been considered as nothing more than Mao Zedong's radical scheme to effect a quick transition into socialism.[6]

Drawing on government papers and the company's published and unpublished archives, this essay is a case study of the "strange alliance." Part I traces the background of Li Zhuchen—a capitalist who considered profitmaking secondary to national salvation. Part II focuses on the interaction between various levels of the government and Li and shows how Li was squeezed (*"jia,"* to use Chen Yun's apt characterization), by plan or otherwise, into socialism through state control of credit, raw material supply, consolidated state purchases and orders, and planned distribution, culminating in joint public-private ownership as the highest form of organization.[7]

On the other hand, the Chinese Communist Party (CCP) also confronted dilemmas of its own in governing an unsettled country. Its many pressing tasks included stabilizing the economy, taming rampant inflation, and raising enough revenue to cover expenses while blending

---

4. Dong Fuying et al., *Zhonghua Renmin Gongheguo jingjishi* (An economic history of the People's Republic of China) (Beijing: Jingji kexue chubanshe, 1999), v. 1, 191.

5. Yang Kuisong, "Jianguo qianhou Zhongguo gongchandang dui zichan jieji zhengce de yanbian" (Policy change toward capitalists before and after 1949) *Jindaishi yanjiu* (Studies in modern history) 2 (2006): 1–25, esp. 2. For an admiring account of how the Chinese Communists held foreign enterprises "hostage" through taxation, denials of exit visas, and permissions to leave, see Aron Shai, *The Fate of British and French Firms in China, 1949–1954* (London: MacMillan, 1996). See also Thomas Thompson, *China's Nationalization of Foreign Firms: The Politics of Hostage Capitalism, 1949–1957* (Baltimore: School of Law, University of Maryland, 1979); and Zhang Kan, "Jianguo chuqi zaihua waizi qiye ganzhao chutan (1949–1962): Yi Shanghai weili" (Transformation of foreign enterprises in the early years of the republic: The case of Shanghai) *Zhongguo jingjishi yanjiu* (Journal of Chinese economic history) 1 (2004): 99–106.

6. Hua-yu Li, *Mao and the Economic Stalinization of China, 1948–1953* (Lanham: Rowman & Littlefield Publishers, 2006); and Liu Jianhui and Wang Hongxu, "The Origins of the General Line for the Transition Period and of the Acceleration of the Chinese Socialist Transformation in Summer, 1955," *China Quarterly* 187 (August 2006): 724–731.

7. "Tiaozheng gongsi guanxi he zhengdun shuishou" (Adjusting public and private relations and consolidating tax revenue), June 6, 1950, in Chen Yun, *Chen Yun wengao xuanbian, 1949–1956* (Selected writings of Chen Yun) (Beijing: Renmin chubanshe, 1982), 91–97, esp. 92; and Chien Chia-chu (Qian Jiaju), *State Capitalism in China* (New York: Far East Reporter, 1956), 10–13.

together new and inherited institutions. The gabelle was a major source of revenue, salt a daily necessity, and the salt industry (both private and state-owned) an employer of thousands of workers. The CCP had to learn how to deal with "Janus-faced" capitalists of various political persuasions, commercial or industrial, beyond the simple political category of "national bourgeoisie." The alliance might have been strange not only in its bridging of the capitalist-Communist divide. It was also consensual.

A JANUS-FACED CAPITALIST

One simple explanation for the strange alliance, of course, might be that Li was not a capitalist and thus had little to "lose."[8] He came from a farming and inn-keeping family in western Hunan province. Like many of his generation, he aspired to save the country through industry ("shiye jiuguo"). After attaining a first-level degree (*xiucai*) on the traditional civil service examinations in 1900, he studied chemistry at the Asakusa Higher Technical Institute in Tokyo and went to work in China for Fan Xudong, first at Jiuda Salt Refinery and then Yongli Soda Ash Company. Fondly called "Grandpa Li" ("Li laotaiye"), he was one of the architects of an industrial group that prided itself less for being a profit-making machine and more for being a socially responsible enterprise dedicated to national economic development.[9]

Drawing on this public image and close ties with high Nationalist officials such as Wu Dingchang and Zhu Jiahua, Jiuda and Yongli received from the Nationalist government millions of yuan in subsidies, loans, and guarantees to finance their evacuation to and operations in the interior during the Anti-Japanese War of 1937–1945, so much so that the State Department in Washington, D.C., mistook the group as state-owned and opposed Yongli's application for a US$16 million credit facility from the U.S. Export-Import Bank in 1945.[10] Li, as a member of the Nationalist

---

8. Li's speech to staff and workers of Tianjin head office dated January 24, 1949, in Archives of the Jiuda Salt Refinery (hereafter JD), Tianjin Soda Ash Corporation, Tianjin, 800071b.

9. "Ben tuanti xintiao" (Our group's principles), *Haiwang* (Neptune) 7.1 (1934): 25–29. For a history of Jiuda, see my *Beyond Market and Hierarchy: Patriotic Capitalism and the Jiuda Salt Refinery, 1914–1953* (New York: Palgrave Macmillan, 2014).

10. O.C. Lockhart to Emilio (Pete) Collado, January 25, 1945, in State Department China/Japan/Korea Lot Files RG-59, Box 5, National Archives, Washington, D.C. Both Fan and Li had fended off repeated Nationalist attempts to annex the group. All the loans and subsidies were repaid in full by 1949.

Political Council, National Assembly, and the Economic Planning Council, enjoyed personal access to Chiang Kai-shek, although he also questioned, following Fan Xudong, the wisdom of a state-controlled economy in China.[11]

On the other hand, Li Zhuchen also knew, wittingly or otherwise, a few Communists. He counted among his acquaintances party elders Lin Boqu who had been his schoolmate and Xu Teli who had been a friend since 1905. His son, Li Wencai had joined the CCP in 1930. He also befriended Gong Yinbing, a fellow Hunanese from Changsha who once served as the CCP's chief accountant and investment officer.[12] Another colleague, Li Chenggan, who was recruited from the Nationalist No. 21 Arsenal by Hou Debang to be chief of Yongli's Nanjing plant in 1947, had become a secret party member through Li Weihan, yet another Hunanese from Changsha.[13]

In charge of evacuating the industrial group to Sichuan during the war, Li Zhuchen became increasingly active in a range of political activities. He was a charter member of the China Democratic National Construction Association and worked with Xu Dixin and Sha Qianli, both CCP members (although Sha's membership remained secret even after 1949), in the Society for the Promotion of Economic Enterprise in China (Zhongguo jingji shiye cujinhui).[14] When the group launched the Enterprise Construction Bank (Jianye yinhang) in 1943 as its house bank with a capital of ten million yuan, Li served on the bank's board along with Gong Yinbing who represented the CCP's 17 percent initial stake (44 percent in 1945).[15] Under Gong as general manager, the bank

11. Fan's and Li's files in the Personnel Files, Generalissimo's Office, Supreme National Defense Council, held at Academia Historica, Taipei, Taiwan; and Li Zhuchen, *Xibei licheng* (Journey to the northwest), reprint (Yinquan: Ningxia renmin chubanshe, 2000), 131–132.

12. Gong joined the Chinese Communist Party in 1923 and kept the party's central archive and communications through a national network of Wanyuan Hunan embroidery shops. Li frequented the Tianjin branch in the 1930s. See Xu Ying, "Li Zhuchen," *Gongshang jingji shiliao congkan* (Anthology of economic history on industry and commerce) 2 (1983), 41.

13. Hou Debang, general manager of Yongli Chemical Industries, was appointed expert advisor and member of CFEC. See endorsement, April 18, 1950, in Zhonggong zhongyang wenxian yanjiushi et al., eds., *Jianguo yilai Liu Shaoqi wengao* (Writings and drafts by Liu Shaoqi since 1949) (Beijing: Zhongyang wenxian chubanshe, 2005), v. 2, 61. On Li Chenggan, see Zheng Hongquan, "Aiguo binggong zhuanjia Li Chenggan" (Li Chenggan: A patriotic weaponry expert) *Chongqing wenshi ziliao* (Historical materials of Chongqing) 35 (1991): 116–136.

14. Recollection of Li's daughter Yujuan as cited in Feng Jie, *Yan jian dawang Li Zhuchen* (Li Zhuchen: Magnate of salt and soda ash) (Beijing: Jiefangjun chubanshe, 1996), 176, 239; and Hu Juemin, *Hu Juemin huiyilu* (Memoirs of Hu Juemin) (Beijing: Zhongguo wenshi chubanshe, 1994), 78.

15. Chen Juxiang, "Wo suo zhidao de Gong Yinbing yu Jianye yinhang Chengdu fen-

expanded to seven cities, providing loans and guarantees to the group and shared offices.

Li also had contacts with the CCP at the highest level. Beginning in 1943, Zhou Enlai appointed Xu Bing (Xing Xiping) as his liaison with Li. In 1945 while in Chongqing for the peace talks with Chiang Kai-shek, Mao Zedong met Li three times. Impressed by his Hunan compatriot's frank political neutrality and advocacy of private enterprise, Mao wrote Li for help in keeping Tianjin intact during the Civil War and takeover of the city.[16] He nominated Li to the first People's Political Consultative Conference in 1948 as a leading member of the national bourgeoisie. Following the conference, Li served on the Central People's Government Council, the country's highest executive body chaired by Mao.

Li's political allegiance might thus have been neutral, if not conflicted, although his relationship with the Chinese Communist Party, especially Mao, remains opaque.[17]

THE CASE OF JIUDA

Jiuda clearly was in trouble by 1949. The total losses of the group during World War II amounted to over US$27 million.[18] Surviving the interwar years on loans, especially from its house banks, Jiuda had halted work in October 1948 as a result of war, inflation, and brine and coal shortages. Production did not resume until March 23, 1949. Although the new government did not target Jiuda specifically, its monetary reforms, worker mobilization and shifting gabelle policies meant that the company's business would no longer be conducted as usual.

The attempt to stabilize the economy, the regime's first task, did not begin well. Short on hard currency, it missed an opportunity to rein in raging inflation.[19] Speculation fueled by government organizations and

---

hang" (Gong Yinbing and the Chengdu branch of the Jianye Bank that I knew), *Chengdu wenshi ziliao* (Historical materials of Chengdu) 8 (1985): 66–80.

16. Fu Guanqun, "Gandan shangzhao jian zhenqing," *Xiangxi wenshi ziliao* (Literature and historical materials on western Hunan) 42 (1997): 1–10, esp. 2–3.

17. Author's interview with Li Mingzhi, Li's grandson, June 7, 2006.

18. "Kangzhan wen'an" (Files on the war of resistance) 302, *juan* 179-2, Academia Historica.

19. Huabei renmin zhengfu gongshangbu, "Pingjin jiefanghou de siren gongshangye dongtai yu women de gongzuo" (Activities of private capitalists in Tianjin and Beijing after the liberation and our work), March 1949, in *Huabei jiefangqu caizheng jingjishi ziliao xuanji* biansheju, ed., *Huabei jiefangqu caizheng jingjishi ziliao xuanji* (Selected materials on

enterprises further destablized the fragile economy.[20] Following the first wave of speculation in April 1949, all private banks and financial institutions in Tianjin were stress-tested, required to improve their capital-reserve ratios, and forced to deposit their reserves with the People's Bank. On September 19, 1949, after another round of speculation, the surviving banks were grouped into syndicates (*lianhe yintuan*), including the group's house banks Jianye and Jincheng, so that the People's Bank could supervise their lending. In the aftermath of a volatile January 1950 during which prices almost doubled, credit was further tightened by a ban on lending among private banks and long-term financing of capital projects. To limit the amount of money in circulation, bank checks were valid for only three days after issue and, when presented, had to be cleared overnight by cash on deposit with the People's Bank.[21] Three months later, the People's Bank ordered Jianye, with over half of its paid-up capital already state-owned, to convert into a joint public-private operation on April 20, 1950.[22] Jiuda could no longer be assured of its house banks' facilities, and could no longer use its fixed assets as collateral for loans.

Li Zhuchen struggled to keep Jiuda afloat amid difficulties created in part by the new government's monetary policies and politics. Distinguishing the national bourgeoisie as an ally of the party quite apart from private capitalists, Beijing wanted to use both to promote economic development while restricting their growth. As unions mobilized workers against their employers, Tianjin's party leaders would not shake hands

---

fiscal and economic history of the north China liberated area, hereafter cited as HCJZL), (Beijing: Zhongguo caizheng jingji chubanshe, 1996), v. 2, 811–813.

20. "Zhonggong Huabeiju dui jiguan shengchan de jueding," December 1948, and "Zhonggong Huabeiju guanyu chengshi gongzuo he zhengdan gongzuo xiang Mao zhuxi dangzhongyang de baogao," February 5, 1949, in ibid., v. 1, 428–429 and 460–462.

21. Wang Juqing and Zhu Xintian, eds., *Tianjin jinrong shishi'nian* (Forty years of money and banking in Tianjin) (Tianjin: Renmin chubanshe, 1988), 93, 100, 153; and Xuan Yichang, "Tianjin jiefang chuqi lianhe yintuan" (Bank syndicates in recently liberated Tianjin) *Tianjin wenshi ziliao xuanbian* (Historical materials on Tianjin, hereafter cited as TJWSZL) 68 (1995): 62–71. The Municipal Financial and Economics Committee was highly critical of the over-tightening and emphasis on short-term financing by the People's Bank. See rescript of the committee's summary for the first half of 1950, Tianjin Academy of Social Sciences Library.

22. According to Huang Zhaoxing, an infusion of capital from Jiuda, Yongyu, and the Yellow Sea Industrial Chemical Research Institute in 1948 brought the group's stake back to 44 percent. See *Wenshi ziliao xuanbian* 88 (1983): 32–63, esp. 53. The bank was merged into Xinhua Bank on January 1, 1952. Officially, Jincheng, Jiuda's other house bank, became a joint public-private in September 1951, although state directors had been posted to the bank a year earlier.

with capitalists, much less tend to their needs.[23] With a glut of stockpiled crude salt, officials already had their hands full in attempting to persuade peasants to cease production of salt leached from saline soil.[24] Cut off from its main market in central China, Jiuda's products were too expensive for north China's consumers. Li pleaded in vain with Tianjin's Military Commission for a loan of seventy million old renminbi so that he could meet his payroll.[25] But Bo Yibo dismissed Li's claim of hardship. Such a ploy worked under the Nationalists, but the Communists would not be "blackmailed" so easily.[26] Production was hampered by a breakdown in discipline as workers demanded raises and other benefits with the support of their new union. After the removal of "feudal" contractors ("batou," or gang bosses), former temporary workers enjoyed the same salary and benefits as regular employees, including the right not to be laid off without government approval. With a million piculs (approximately 900,000 pounds) of crude salt in inventory and no market or transportation, Li found the company saddled with more workers than it needed and high labor cost.[27] To meet its payroll, the company sold one hundred *mu* of

---

23. Bo Yibo, "Zhongguo jingji goucheng ji jingji jianshe jiben fangzhen" (China's economic structure and guiding principles toward economic construction), 1948, in HCJZL v. 1, 429–436, esp. 430.

24. Bo Yibo, "Guanyu Huabei caijing zhuangkuang xiang Mao zhuxi de zonghe baogao" (General report to Chairman Mao on the fiscal and economic condition of north China), June 16, 1949, in HCJZL v. 1, 652–656.

25. Transcript of meeting, June 28, 1949, in "Jiuda-Yongli Papers," Tianjin Municipal Archives (hereafter TMA). On the mistakes and "leftist" attitude of the Tianjin's party leaders, see "Tianjin shiwei yu rucheng hou suofan cuowu jiantao de jueyi" (Resolution on mistakes made by the Tianjin municipal party committee after entry into the city), February 5, 1949, held at the Tianjin Academy of Social Sciences Library; "Huabei renmin zhengfu dangzu guanyu Ping-Jin jiefanghou de jingji qingkuang xiang Zhonggong Huabeiju bing Zhongyang de baogao" (North China People's Government party committee report to the North China Bureau and the Central Committee on the economic condition of Beiping and Tianjin after liberation), dated February 28, 1949, in HCJZL v. 1, 483–484; and Huang Kecheng's report May 1949 in Tianjinshi dang'anguan, comp., *Jiefang chuqi Tianjin chengshi jingji hongguan guanli* (Macro economic administration of a recently liberated Tianjin) (Tianjin: Tianjinshi dang'anguan, 1995), 29–34.

26. Bo Yibo's report to Mao Zedong, April 9, 1949, in Bo Yibo zhuzuo biansheju, ed., *Bo Yibo shuxinji* (Collected letters of Bo Yibo, hereafter cited as BYBSXJ) (Beijing: Zhonggong dangshi chubanshe, 2009), v. 1, 96–99, esp. 97. Bo cited 90 million as the amount requested.

27. Li's presentation in a meeting with the Military Commission, April 7, 1949. See Tianjinshi dang'anguan et al., eds., *Zhongguo ziben zhuyi gongshangye de shehui zhuyi gaizao: Tianjin juan* (Socialist transformation of capitalism in China: Tianjin; hereafter cited as ZZGZ [Tianjin]) (Beijing: Zhonggong dangshi chubanshe, 1991), 39. On inventory, see minutes of board meeting October 8, 1949, in Zhao Jin et al., eds., *Jiuda jingyan gongsi dang'an huibian zhuanji* (Collected archives of the Jiuda Salt Refinery) (Tianjin: Renmin chubanshe, 2010), v. 2, 825–826 hereafter cited as JDJYZJ, and JD 300405.

land and 2,270 tons of coal while incurring a debt of over twenty million old renminbi to various banks.[28] With attempts to sell salt at Linqing and Wuhu frustrated by local trading companies' defenses of their turf, the company's business was confined to Tianjin, Beijing, and a few other cities in north China. March and April sales averaged only 950 piculs (refined salt) and 15,350 piculs (washed salt), a fraction of the monthly averages of 22,575 and 66,575, respectively, for 1948 (which itself was not a good year). Instead of loans, the state purchased as a favor 22,000 piculs of washed salt and 30,000 piculs of crude salt at prices from 40 to 190 old renminbi per picul to help reduce the company's inventory. Cash flow was improved after the People's Bank advanced 45 million old renminbi against bills of lading ("yahui", or document billing). But Jiuda needed more help, and the constant pleas for more loans led officials to complain about Li's "dependency" on the government to solve his problems.[29]

As a high-ranking member of the central government, Li Zhuchen used what access he had to help his company. Taking advantage of Liu Shaoqi's visit to Tianjin in 1949 to study "urban work," he met with Liu at least three times and peppered him with questions: Why was Jiuda being shut out of the salt market at Linqing by state trade companies?[30] Was the state trying to eradicate private enterprises immediately? He also questioned Mao Zedong's equation of big capitalists with bureaucratic capitalism.[31] Were he and other "big" (but nonbureaucratic) capitalists being targeted by the Communists? Claiming that he only had 800 yuan in capital, he rejected the capitalist "label" and the claim that he

---

28. Letter to Huang Jing, mayor of Tianjin, with a copy to Liu Shaoqi, undated, in "Jiuda-Yongli papers," s-1095, held at TMA.

29. "Tianjinshi renmin zhengfu gongshangju bannianlai gongshang gongzuo zonghe baogao" (General report of six months of work from the Commercial and Industrial Bureau, Tianjin People's Government), August 1949, in HCJZL v. 1, 715–730, esp. 723.

30. Liu arrived in Tianjin on April 10 and left after a tour of Yongli on May 5, 1949. See Huang Xiaotong and Li Wenfang, *Liu Shaoqi yu Tianjin jianghua* (Liu Shaoqi and his Tianjin speeches) (Kaifeng: Henan daxue chubanshe, 1998), 26–27; and "Jiefang shinian lai Tianjinshi fazhanshi" (A decade of economic development of Tianjin since liberation), undated mimeograph manuscript), 2-4-3. See also Kenneth Lieberthal, *Revolution and Tradition in Tientsin, 1949–1952* (Stanford: Stanford University Press, 1980).

31. "Muqian de xingshi yu renwu" (The present situation and our tasks), December 25, 1947, in *Mao Zedong ji* (Annotated writings of Mao Zedong) (Hong Kong: Yishan, n.d.), v. 10, 97–116, esp. 108–110. Subsequent published editions of the speech replaced the term "big capitalist" with "upper capitalist" ("shangceng zichan jieji") without a clear definition or explanation of the change. Perhaps this is an attempt to differentiate between bureaucratic capitalists and non-Nationalist "big" capitalists. This is an example of how Mao's formulation was evolving.

was exploiting workers. When others pointed out that he was merely a "medium-sized" capitalist, Li retorted that there would be no incentive for him to reinvest and become "big."[32]

Liu Shaoqi tried to placate Li in his reply. He instructed Linqing to cease and desist in its opposition to Jiuda's shipments. For the time being, legitimate exploitation of workers was encouraged, "the more the better."[33] Following up on Liu's reassuring speeches, Li, citing a shortage in the central Yangzi provinces, sought and quickly received permission to ship 70,000 piculs of crude salt each month to Henan, Hubei, and Anhui.[34] The company appealed in November directly to the CFEC, and the Changlu Administration Bureau quickly approved a one-month grace period. Otherwise, suspension of document billing by the People's Bank would have left Jiuda with no means to finance its shipments. This was followed by a request for a ten-day extension to settle the transportation bill, and ultimately, permission to ship up to 300,000 piculs of crude salt under these privileged terms. Overruling the municipal government, Beijing also authorized the company to export gabelle-free salt to barter for Japanese equipment needed in its by-product plant.[35] On December 24, 1949, Jiuda received confirmation from the Ministry of Finance that it would have what it had been seeking since 1914: abolition of all administrative divisional boundaries. Once the gabelle was paid, salt could be traded anywhere in the country.[36]

---

32. Li had raised the issues in a meeting with the Tianjin military commission on April 7, 1949. He also challenged officials to define national bourgeois industry ("minzu gongye"). Would "large" enterprises such as Jiuda, Renli, and Dongya qualify as medium or small and thus be under the "national bourgeoisie" or would they be big (and hence considered bureaucratic capital according to Mao's definition)? See transcript of the meeting in ZZGZ (Tianjin), 39. Li was right, as Mao had admitted in his politburo speech on September 8, 1948, that he did not distinguish clearly between bureaucratic capital and national bourgeoisie while writing "New Democracy." See Zhonggong zhongyang wenxian yanjiushi, ed., *Mao Zedong wenji* (Writings of Mao Zedong; hereafter cited as MS) (Beijing: Renmin chubanshe, 1993), v. 5, 140.

33. Liu Shaoqi's speech dated May 2, 1949. He repeated the same argument during his visit to Dongya as reported in TJWSZL 79 (1998), 102–111. During the Cultural Revolution, these speeches became the basis for charges against Liu which he admitted to. See Kenneth Lieberthal, "Mao versus Liu?" *China Quarterly* 47 (1971): 494–520.

34. Application to the Changlu Salt Administration Bureau dated July 6, 1949, in JD 300341-2.

35. Gabelle grace period, November 29, 1949; transport bill for the grace period limited to 300,000 piculs, December 17, 1949; and 1949 annual report in JD 300377, 300413, 300352, 300407. The municipal government raised concerns in minutes of the meeting dated April 28, 1949, held at the Tianjin Academy of Social Sciences Library.

36. JD 300348.

Buoyed by these generous policies, Li Zhuchen executed his plan. Jiuda shipped over 400,000 piculs of crude salt on gabelle extension. Using its salt inventory and soda ash from Yongli as collateral, it raised from Tianjin's People's Bank and the bank syndicate 3.1 billion old renminbi to finance spring salt production, lease seven salt pans, and purchase new equipment needed at the by-product plant to produce magnesium carbonate (for glass manufacturing) and sodium sulfide (for making dye, tanning, and synthetic rubber). These waivers and extensions cost the state an estimated 4.7 billion old renminbi in revenue and lost interest while the company returned a gross profit of 2.4 billion for 1949 (see Appendix 5.1A).[37]

THE SQUEEZE

In delivering a socialist planned economy even Liu Shaoqi found the new government's midwifery wanting. With the country still at war, half of its budget was financed by printing money. Inflation raged, fueled by salt speculators and hoarders in Shanghai and Tianjin. While waging a civil war and consolidating its rule, the new government had to tackle quickly the same contradictions that past regimes had confronted: fiscal needs and consumer welfare, division of revenue and labor between the central and provincial governments, regulation of producers and merchants, and distribution to non–salt-producing regions. Mao reiterated that private enterprises should be promoted if they benefited the country, but salt should be a state monopoly.[38] Despite the party's promise that it would make a revolutionary break from the old, Beijing returned to an ancient institution.[39]

A series of meetings in Beijing began to address the complex prob-

---

37. Li Zhuchen's circular dated April 1, 1950, in JD 300243; balance sheet as of December 31, 1949, in JDJYZJ v. 2, 902; and annual report for 1950 in JD 300407. After paying 257 million in commercial and industrial tax and 2.8 million in property tax, and setting aside 210 million for depreciation, net profit for 1949 was reduced to 1.94 billion old renminbi. See minutes of board meeting dated January 8, 1951, in JD 200060.

38. Mao's written comment, April 1950, in Zhonggong zhongyang wenxian yanjiushi, comp., *Jianguo yilai zhongyao wenxian xuanbian* (Selected important documents since 1949) (Beijing: Zhongyang wenxian chubanshe, 1992), v. 1, 215–216. Zhu De, in contrast, suggested only "considerable" control.

39. See my *The Salt Merchants of Tianjin* (Honolulu: University of Hawaii Press, 2001), chap. 2; and Xu Jiansheng, *Minguo shiqi jingji zhengce de yanxi yu bianyi* (Inherited and shifting economic policies of the republican period) (Fuzhou: Fujian renmin chubanshe, 2006), chap. 6.

lems of state-building and economic planning. At the National Tax Conference, November 24–December 10, 1949, and the Conference on Salt, December 5–16, 1949, it was decided that the entire gabelle belonged under the central government just as it had been under the Nationalists.[40] The in-kind gabelle rate inherited from the base area was raised on January 1, 1950, from 30 *jin* to 100 *jin* of rice or millet per picul of salt, effectively restoring the old rate under the Nationalists. In a division of labor, the Salt Administration under the Ministry of Finance was responsible for salt production and gabelle accounting while the National Salt Corporation (hereafter NSC), established on January 12, 1950, by the Ministry of Trade, handled salt distribution and collection of the gabelle. The NSC recruited a staff of experienced cadres who had operated various base area–run salt companies during World War II, and it planned to deliver some 3.2 billion *jin* of grain or its equivalent in gabelle for the year.[41]

What seemed like a principled division of labor between salt production and distribution to create a stable gabelle flow created new problems. The gabelle's rates fueled rising prices and, in parts of north China where peasants had long leached salt from saline soil, stimulated smuggling which, in turn, required policing. Elsewhere, the poor looted salt depots.[42] As the price of grain varied from region to region, salt prices and the effective gabelle rate also fluctuated, creating disparities that merchants and speculators as well as units of the People's Liberation Army exploited.[43] The NSC soon found itself struggling. Both sales and

---

40. Chi Aiping, *Xin Zhongguo diyinian de Zhongcaiwei yanjiu* (A study of the first year of Central Fiscal and Economic Committee in a new China) (Shanghai: Fudan daxue chubanshe, 2007), 255–256; and Li Hai et al., *Tongyi caijing, wei xin Zhongguo dianji liye* (Financial and economic unity for a new China) (Beijing: Dangdai Zhongguo chubanshe, 2008).

41. "Quanguo yanwu huiyi zonghe baogao" (Summary report of the national conference on salt) in Zhongguo renmin gongheguo guojia jingji maoyi weiyuanhui, comp., *Zhongguo gongye wushinian* (Fifty years of industry in the People's Republic of China) (Beijing: Zhongguo jingji chubanshe, 2000), v. 1, pt. 2, 1230–1231.

42. Liu Shaoqi, "Guanyu tuoshan jiejue Huabei yanwu tongguan hou suo quxian wenti de piyu" (Comments on how to resolve problems pursuant to state monopolization of salt in north China) and "Dui Jiaodong qiangyan shijian de piyu" (Comments on salt looting in Jiaodong) both in Zhonggong zhongyang wenxian yanjiushi et al., eds. (2005), v. 1, 607–608 and v. 2, 212–214.

43. On the ban, March 8, 1950, against the People's Liberation Army and other state organizations from participating in the salt trade, see Dangdai Zhongguo shangye bianjibu, ed., *Zhonghua renmin gongheguo shangye dashiji* (Major events related to commerce in the People's Republic of China, hereafter SDSJ) (Beijing: Zhongguo shangye chubanshe, 1989), 18. Price per picul of packaged refined salt in December prior to the gabelle increase stood

gabelle collection failed to meet the planned target (82.5 and 75 percent, respectively, for the first half of 1950). Moreover, a budgetary shortfall and financing of salt production were not the only problems straining the NSC's meager resources. The NSC favored salt fields convenient to its operation, leaving the Salt Administration with burgeoning inventory at more remote facilities, further aggravating problems of smuggling and policing.[44]

The young government responded decisively. The money supply was tightened further by issuing People's Victory Bonds (included in a basket of commodities) and requiring that all credit extended to salt merchants be reported to the People's Bank Beijing head office beginning February 12, 1950.[45] To prevent interregional arbitration, a windfall profit tax (*guofen lideshui*) was imposed, followed by a national standard gabelle tied to the planned revenue target and fluctuating grain prices.[46] To facilitate production planning, gabelle collection, and administration, the state slightly modified the inherited boundaries of the eight salt divisions to coincide with its new seven major administrative regions.[47]

In an attempt to balance public and private needs (*gongsi jiangu*), the NSC summoned representatives of major salt companies, both state and private, to Beijing for a series of conferences. The aim was to secure state revenue, a reasonable profit to both producers and merchants while ensuring the supply of quality salt at a cheap and stable price to the consumer. From March 28 to April 4, 1950, the Conference of Alimental Salt Dealers discussed how to resolve these issues through planning, resulting in the "Provisional Regulations on Transport-wholesalers of

---

at 45,000 and 95,000 old renminbi in Tianjin and Shanghai, respectively. After tax and transportation, Jiuda had expected a net profit of 20,000 old renminbi per picul before it was caught by the sudden gabelle adjustment. See report of Shanghai office, JD 300388.

44. "Review of 1950," in Bo Yibo's summary of the second national salt conference (April 1951), JD 300153-8.

45. By late 1952, the People's Bank stopped all lending to salt merchants on the grounds that they were competing against the state-owned companies and disrupting the market. See Wang Juqing and Zhu Xintian, eds. (1988), 49, 159.

46. Fang Weizhong et al., comp., *Zhongghua renmin gongheguo jingji dashiji* (A chronological history of major economic events of the People's Republic of China) (Beijing: Shehui kexue chubanshe, 1984), 23–24; *Zhonghua renmin gongheguo jingji dashi dian* (Major economic events in the People's Republic of China) (Changchun: Jilin renmin chubanshe, 1987), 27; and Zhongguo yanye gongsi, ed., *Zhongguo yanyeshi* (A history of the salt industry in China, hereafter cited as ZYYS) (Beijing: Renmin chubanshe, 1997), *Jindai dangdai*, 414.

47. CFEC order, March 11, 1950, in Zhongguo shehui kexue yuan et al., *Zhonghua renmin gongheguo jingji dang'an ziliao xuanbian* (Selected economic archival materials of the People's Republic of China), *Zhonghe* (general, hereafter cited as ZJD [zhonghe]) (Beijing: Zhongguo chengshi jingji shehui chubanshe, 1990), 645–648.

Alimental Salt," promulgated April 5, 1950. The state authorized NSC to register private salt merchants and require them to file monthly and quarterly marketing plans with proof of available capital (exclusive of fixed assets). Approved registration would be valid for three months and nontransferable. With gabelle and other receipts from the People's Bank, registered merchants were to take delivery of salt from a state depot (minimum lot of 297 piculs, or half the capacity of a rail freight car).[48] Private merchants could still participate in interregional salt trade, subject to state approval and divisional production and sales quotas. In effect, stability of salt prices and gabelle revenue through planning were achieved by returning to the autarkic divisional system inherited from the Nationalists and the Qing dynasty.[49]

The NSC's dual roles as a "business" and a regulatory authority created tensions between the public and the private sectors. Combating smuggling and speculation through its national network of wholesalers, retail outlets and local cooperatives, the NSC drove the suggested price (*paijia*) down until there was little difference between wholesale and retail market prices.[50] The merchants, including Jiuda, complained that the NSC had been setting salt prices too low without consulting producers in the industry, leaving them with little, if any, profit. Its agency policy— NSC's local dealers were forbidden to accept supplies from private salt merchants—also had the "unintended" effect of monopolizing the market.[51]

With price stabilization as the paramount goal, the NSC called another meeting, June 10–12, 1950, to rebalance the needs of the public and private sectors.[52] In the meeting, the NSC acknowledged partial responsibility for some of the problems. Collection of excessive profit

---

48. JD 300123-5. NSC's registration regulations for private merchants issued February 1951 required proof of financing at the rate of 60 million old renminbi per rail car of salt. See JD 300457-61.

49. JD 300392.

50. Ibid.; JD 300104 and 300122; and CFEC directives dated March 15 and July 1950, in Fang Weizhong et al., comp. (1984), 17; and Shangyebu shangguanju, comp., *Siying shangye shehui zhuyi gaizhao wenjian xuanbian* (Selected documents on the socialist transformation of private commerce) (Beijing: Shangye chubanshe, 1982), v. 1, 149, respectively. On the high transaction cost of this pricing system, see Xu Jianqing, "Jianguo qianqi de shijia yu paijia" (Market price and suggested price system early in the People's Republic) *Zhongguo jingjishi yanjiu* (Studies on Chinese economic history) 2 (2002): 45–58.

51. JD 300094-97.

52. Report to the Central Committee dated July 6, 1950, in Chen Yun, *Chen Yun wenji* (Collected writings of Chen Yun) (Beijing: Zhongyang wenxian chubanshe, 2005), v. 2, 149–151.

taxes, purchases of People's Victory Bonds, and a stringent registration procedure caused some salt merchants to abandon the business. To help meet the state plan and stabilize prices, NSC overexpanded its distribution network. Henceforth, it promised to reduce the number of exclusive agencies and share its sales data. Weak sales were addressed by halving the gabelle rate on June 1, 1950, refunding the paid gabelle on unsold inventory, and granting a 2.5 percent rebate on gabelle due for wastage during shipment. In return, salt merchants accepted a handling charge of 2.5 percent and a profit of no more than 5 percent of their net cost.

On the other hand, it was also state policy (but unpublicized) to steer private commercial capital toward industrial production instead of speculation.[53] To promote that transition, state-owned retailers and cooperatives enjoyed a cash and carry discount of up to 7 percent on wholesale price, a commission of up to 2 percent of wholesale prices and, for their bank loans, an interest rate 3 percent lower than that charged on private merchants.[54] As a result, the share of the salt market handled by cooperatives grew quickly. By 1952, the public sector (state and cooperatives) had command over 80 percent of the salt trade (see Appendix 5.2). Sales and gabelle collection exceeded the planned targets, beginning in the second half of 1950.[55] Jiuda might not have been targeted, but the days of private salt merchants were numbered.

LI ZHUCHEN'S DILEMMA

Despite Zhou Enlai's claim that 1950 and 1951 were banner years for China's surviving capitalists, these institutional and policy changes affected Jiuda profoundly. The year began with a rainy spring, resulting in a harvest of only 300,000 piculs of crude salt, well short of the 1.2 million target. Gabelle increases and a poor market further reduced the company's shipment to 173,825 piculs for the first half of 1950. For the year, it sold 76,030 piculs of refined salt and 191,555 piculs of washed salt, a fraction of its pre-war business volume.

---

53. Liu Shaoqi's comment on the goal of uniting with industrial capitalists to compete against commercial capitalists, May 2, 1951, in Zhonggong zhongyang wenxian yanjiushi, ed. (2005), v. 3, 294–295. Liu specifically ordered that this comment could only be transmitted by word of mouth to concerned cadres.

54. Order dated October 25, 1950, in SDSJ, 42; and ZYYS, 412–413.

55. ZYYS, 416–417; and resolutions of the conference, June 20, 1950, in JD 300129-138. By 1951, the percentages were further reduced to 2 and 2.5 percent, respectively. See resolution of the Second National Conference on Salt Trade, April 12, 1951, in JD 300179-186.

Then there were bonds, taxes, and more credit-tightening. The company's assigned quota of People's Victory Bonds came to 2.7 billion old renminbi (which took all of 1949's profits and more).[56] Even though the gabelle contributed over 95 percent of the salt price, the company had to pay taxes again on its turnover (at 2 percent) and income (0.008 percent). To prevent unscrupulous merchants from evading these taxes by keeping multiple ledgers, the government instituted a "democratic" system of peer assessment.[57] For Jiuda, a company that prided itself on its meticulous accounting, this new system was not merely an insult. Even officials acknowledged that peer assessment often translated into demands for companies such as Jiuda to be charged higher rates simply because of their presumed ability to pay.[58]

What had once been a privilege became a noose. The grace period for gabelle payments had eased the company's capital shortfall and permitted it to stay in business. However, the government terminated that privilege on March 24, 1950, because of pressing revenue needs, and it demanded immediate payment of 10.6 billion old renminbi. Although the deadline was repeatedly extended on appeal, the increase in the gabelle rate on its unsold inventory and a weak market made settlement impossible. By June 1, 1950, Jiuda owed 5.76 billion old renminbi in overdue gabelle and penalty interest.[59]

Nevertheless, Li and his colleagues appreciated the state's support and respected its need for revenue. Although taxes were many, some perhaps even onerous, every cent went into the public coffers.[60] But the

---

56. JD 200035. Although the bond issue reduced the budget deficit by 40 percent, speculators remained unscathed as local cadres pleaded hardship in fulfilling their quota. See ZJD (zhonghe), 727–730.

57. For a summary of various problems with this tax collection system, including the many inequities, see "Tianjinshi zhengshou 1948 nian xiaoban'nian gongshangye suodeshui gongzuo chubu zongjie" (Preliminary summary on the collection of commercial and industrial income tax of the second half of 1948 in Tianjin Municipality), September 1949 in HCJZL v. 2, 1655–1664, esp. 1661–1662.

58. By the company's estimate, effective rate on turnover tax varied from 4 to 16 percent, at least double the official rate. See JD 300396 and 300409. Chen Yun did not care about the method so long as taxes were collected. See his speech at the National Conference on the United Front, June 11, 1952, in *Zhongguo ziben zhuyi gongshangye de shehui zhuyi gaizao: zhongyang juan* (Socialist transformation of capitalism in China, volume on central government, hereafter cited as ZZGZ [Zhongyang]), v. 1, 327.

59. Termination order in JD 300353; extension to June dated May 15, 1950, and to October dated July 19, 1950, in JD 300356 and 300357, respectively. In Li's report to the company board on May 18, 1950, he cited seven billion old renminbi in total indebtedness. See JD 200031.

60. JD 300692.

company did not have the cash to produce salt, advance the gabelle in full, and finance a distribution system of its own because the state tightened credit even further.[61] Shen Huaqu's warning earlier in the year proved prescient: salt production by private enterprises might continue for two or three more years, but the trade was dead.[62] Despite these dire prospects, Li Zhuchen remained optimistic. There might be several difficult years ahead, but demand for refined salt would recover as the economy improved. He discussed plans to cut costs through vertical integration and pay cuts, and he proposed to raise more capital through a public offering of company stock or an issue to existing shareholders.[63]

However, Li's business plan soon became obsolete because of more policy changes by the government. On June 30, 1950, with the nationalization of salt flats as part of the land reform campaign, the company could no longer rely on its own supply of salt for quality control and economy of scale because these practices were deemed unfair, if not illegal, advantages according to the NSC.[64] The final blow to Jiuda's prospects came on July 29, 1950, when the Ministry of Trade rescinded permission for the company to sell crude salt across divisional boundaries (though the sale of refined salt was still permitted). Officials repeated the same concerns often cited in the past. They feared that interdivisional movements of crude salt would compromise the state plan for salt production and gabelle collection, not to mention the interests of salt producers in other divisions.[65] On November 11, 1950, production of washed salt also ceased because the NSC-set suggested price fell below the company's production costs.[66] What should Li do?

THE STATE'S DILEMMA

Conversion to joint public-private ownership offered a possible solution to Jiuda's problems. However, even had this been part of the

---

61. ZJD (zhonghe), 738.

62. Letter to Li Zhuchen, April 1, 1950, in JD 300208. Shen, a board member, had been in charge of Jiuda's sales office before his posting to Yongyu.

63. Joint board of directors and supervisors meeting, May 18, 1950, in JD 200028.

64. Li had privileges that not even the NSC enjoyed, including the thirty-day grace period for gabelle payment. (NSC had only five days.) See NSC (Tianjin office) memo, March 11, 1950, in "Archives of the Tianjin Municipal Financial and Economics Committee," X77.1801 held at TMA.

65. JD 300368 and final denial, January 18, 1951, in JD 300370.

66. Minutes of transition planning committee meeting dated January 17, 1951, in JD 300288-292.

Communist scheme, the process was neither simple nor straightforward. Li Zhuchen's reputation and "insider" status as a high-ranking member of the new government notwithstanding, he encountered tough negotiations with management, shareholders, workers and staff, as well as the Tianjin Municipal government, and the Ministries of Heavy Industry, Labor, and CFEC, each with its own concerns and priorities. Even worse, a revolutionary proletarian government might be caught between labor and capital.

The Yongli Company, very much straining under similar burdens of limited cash flow, lack of capital, and a poor market, made application to the Ministry of Heavy Industry in June 1950 for conversion.[67] Separately, on July 19, 1950, Li made a personal appeal to Bo Yibo for help in easing Jiuda's credit crunch. The company then owed 7.1 billion old renminbi in gabelle, bank loans, and other short-term obligations. With 4.72 billion in inventory and 3.2 billion invested in production, it did not have the cash flow to service its debts, production, and trading. Li sought Bo's assistance for a loan of seven billion old renminbi from the People's Bank using its shares in Yongli as collateral.[68]

The Ministry of Finance and the CFEC were concerned with the political ramifications of the offer. Bo Yibo advised Li that, as important as his industrial group was to the country's economy, state involvement might send the wrong message domestically and internationally. After Li's further appeals, Bo authorized the People's Bank to proceed with Jiuda's loan request but declined to let him use shares in Yongli as collateral.[69] An undaunted Li assured Bo that the offer was made voluntarily and urged reconsideration.[70] On August 28, 1950, Li and Hou Debang together filed an application to convert the two companies into joint public-private ownership.

Chen Yun reported cautiously to Zhou Enlai on the application, emphasizing the group's initiative and needs. While demand for Yongli's and Jiuda's products would undoubtedly be strong once the economy

---

67. JD 301169. In Jiuda's board meeting on May 18, 1950, Li had asked for instruction on how to vote Jiuda's stake on Yongli's request for either more state loans or conversion to joint enterprise. The board instructed him to vote for the former. See JD 200037.

68. JD 300357.

69. Ministry of Finance approval dated August 8, 1950. By regulation, the People's Bank could offer only up to 70 percent the value of any collateral, forcing Li to appeal again to the CFEC. Finally the bank provided a three billion old renminbi loan secured on Jiuda's physical plant and equipment for six months at a monthly interest of 33 percent. With another three billion it raised, the company finally settled all gabelle due in November 1950. See JD 300364.

70. Minutes of Jiuda joint board meeting dated September 28, 1950, in JD 200038.

improved, their equipment was obsolete. Short of capital and lacking a market for soda ash and ammonium sulphate, Hou Debang had twice raised the possibility of conversion, but he had wavered each time after being advised that the state preferred the group to remain private. Since Hou and Li felt they could not solve their problems in their businesses as private enterprises, the CFEC recommended approval of their applications for conversion of these businesses into joint public-private enterprises. If the conversion were carried out, at least the CFEC would be spared from having to deal with more pleas from Li for loans. One week later, the Central Committee cabled agreement in principle, instructing the Ministry of Heavy Industry to commence negotiations. Zhou Enlai's cable explicitly cautioned the negotiators to prevent the company from "trying" (*shitan*) the state.[71] Xue Xianzhi, Jiuda's sales manager, was assigned by Li to represent the company. Zou Jiayou, assistant chief of the ministry's accounting section, visited Jiuda twice. On October 23, 1950, a memorandum of understanding was signed, and a transition planning committee was formed. Zou headed the committee with Xue as deputy head, an assignment that proved daunting.[72]

SHAREHOLDERS

Xue's first task was to persuade the shareholders to approve the conversion of Jiuda into a joint public-private enterprise. Although Li Zhuchen had discussed the matter with the company's board of directors on September 28, 1950, he had not informed the shareholders about it. Concerned with this oversight, Liu Yousan, deputed from Ministry of Heavy Industry as secretary of the planning committee, suggested an extraordinary meeting to authorize the application, if only retroactively. In a contentious session on November 26, 1950, shareholders questioned Li. With 2.4 billion old renminbi in profits from 1949 and 1.6 billion in liquid assets, was there a need for conversion? Without a thorough audit of the company's assets and investments, some were concerned with the

71. CFEC to Central Committee August 31, 1950, in ZJDGS, 491–492; and reply September 7, 1950, in ZZGZ (Zhongyang) v. 2, 1244; and Zhou's cable to CFEC of the same date on behalf of the Government Administration Council. See Zhongyang dang'anguan et al., eds., *Jianguo yilai Zhou Enlai wengao* (Zhou Enlai's draft writings since 1949) (Beijing: Zhongyang wenxian chubanshe, 2008), v. 3, 259.

72. See JD 300288, although in Xue's memoirs the roles were reversed. See Xue Xianzhi, "Jiuda yanye gongsi shimo" (The beginning and end of Jiuda Salt Industries), *Tanggu wenshi ziliao* (Historical materials of Tanggu) 3 (1992): 69–81, esp. 76.

appraisal procedure, the size of the state's investment, and the danger that the equity belonging to existing shareholders would be diluted. Others raised procedural issues, questioning why Li had initiated the discussion with the state without first receiving authorization from the shareholders.

In his defense, Li acknowledged his managerial shortcomings, but he pointed out that the People's Victory Bond purchase had taken all (and more) of Jiuda's meager profits for 1949, and the three billion old renminbi "profit" for 1950 was calculated according to a revaluation of the company's inventory and raw materials without taking inflation into account. If inflation were taken into account, Jiuda had actually lost over four hundred million for the year. The company had only been kept afloat by loans from the People's Bank and generous tax treatment secured by Li through personal appeals to officials, and he was not sure how long he could bank on that generosity. At Liu's prompting, Xue challenged his fellow shareholders either to take over the company's finance office or consider the only alternative left: a rights issue to the shareholders themselves. After four hours of heated discussion, the shareholders approved the application for conversion "in principle" and authorized the board of directors to work out the details.[73]

WORKERS, STAFF, AND THE STATE

In contrast, Li Zhuchen faced more formidable and tenacious opposition to conversion from workers and staff members in Jiuda's sprawling sales organization. Li Zhuchen's warning of the need for drastic reorganization and his question of why workers under proletarian leadership would still want company shares (making them capitalists) caused an uproar.[74] Led by Fan Xudong's relatives and other senior management at the head office, they challenged Li's assertion that the company, with a few dilapidated buildings and antiquated evaporation pans, was "worthless" (but see Appendix 5.1B), and they questioned Li's view that what was good for the company would also

---

73. Xue Xianzhi (1992), 76–77; and minutes of the shareholder meeting in JD 200045-59.

74. Li's speech at the national sales managers meeting, July 24, 1950, and circular November 7, 1950, in JD 300277. The campaign was allegedly led by Shen Huakui, Fan Xudong's nephews Lin Shougu (manager of Changsha office) and Xu Zhi'an (chief auditor), and Xiang Jianshi (chief accountant). See report of Liu Yousan to the ministry ca. July–August 1951 in JD 301153-1159.

benefit individual workers. They were defending their rights against the company, not the government or the proposal for joint enterprise.[75] The result was an impasse despite the mediation of the Tianjin Municipal Labor Bureau.

Chen Yun and the CFEC intervened after another personal appeal by Li Zhuchen. With debts of over six billion old renminbi and monthly losses of another 500 million, the company would be bankrupt by the end of the year if the impasse continued. Li begged Chen to relieve him of this burden.[76] Five days later, CFEC directive #117 ordered a People's Bank loan of up to eight billion old renminbi to Jiuda. The Tianjin municipal government should find jobs for the company's surplus workers, and the NSC purchased the company's entire output of refined salt and chemical by-products.[77] On June 13, 1951, Jiuda announced closure of all its regional sales offices.

These measures did not satisfy the workers, and their campaign continued. Instructed by CFEC to facilitate a settlement, Liu Yousan and Chen Rong of the Municipal Labor Bureau minced no words in their report on this campaign. Since Jiuda's announcement of the proposed conversion, "reactionary" elements of landlord families and former Nationalist officials led staff and workers in making more and more demands. They wanted severance pay, back pay, and subsidies for 1949, a subsidy to make up for salary reductions under NSC compared to Jiuda, continuation of benefits for those rejected by NSC, a thorough audit of the company's ledgers, half of all net profits through the years, and a share of Jiuda's assets, including its investments in Yongli.[78] Behind these "excessive" demands, they "selfishly" opposed the conversion to preserve their well-paid jobs—among the best paid in the country and far better than those in state-owned enterprise. Their strategy was to wage a protracted fight by insisting on their rights and due process as long as possible to collect more pay. With their union's support, they mounted a campaign of writing letters and sending telegrams criticizing Li and Xue and accusing them of deceit, violations of the law, and attempts to pass their responsibilities on to the state.[79]

---

75. Li's circular, November 7, 1950, and letters and cables from various regional offices October 18 and November 22, 1950, in JD 300266-7; 300284-87.

76. Letter May 10, 1951, in JD 300437-8.

77. CFEC order #117, May 15, 1951, to Tianjin Municipal Government, Ministry of Trade and People's Bank in JD 300300.

78. List of demands June 16 and 21, 1951, in JD 300447-53.

79. "Qing Jiuda zongguanlichu dafu women de wenti" (Questions for Jiuda head office to answer), July 25, 1950, in JD 300462-481.

Fearful that Li Zhuchen would fold under the pressure of a national campaign, Liu and Chen urged better coordination among the ministries, especially the Ministry of Labor and local unions.[80] Xue was assured by Zou and his superiors that, should the joint public-private enterprise proposal fail, he would be reassigned elsewhere by the ministry. For a month Xue negotiated with over twenty representatives of Jiuda's regional sales offices and workers through the Mediation Bureau of the Ministry of Labor in Beijing. Finally, Zou advised a frustrated Xue to apply for arbitration to force a decision, much to the displeasure of the Mediation Bureau.[81] Several days after Xue briefed Mao Qihua, vice minister of labor, a decision was reached. The workers' demands had no legal merit and were dismissed, but the company also acknowledged that it had made procedural errors and offered workers a severance package: one month's salary for every two years of service with the company, and severance pay of two months' salary (including subsidies), which officials deemed excessive in comparison with state-owned enterprises.[82] Caught between labor and capital, an embarassed government sided with the capitalists.

ACCOUNTING PROBLEMS

Determining the value of Jiuda presented challenges of another kind. Notwithstanding Li Zhuchen's assertion that the company was "worthless," officials found that appraising the company was a difficult task. The planning committee scheduled one month to complete the process but vastly underestimated the time needed and difficulties involved: what assets to include (or exclude) and how to assess Japanese and Nationalist "enemy investments."

The Ministry of Heavy Industry's report of 1954 was highly critical of the process, blaming the failures on the inexperience of its representatives in dealing with Jiuda's "capitalist treachery." Mistakes began with attempts to define the assets of the company. Without giving the matter much thought, state representatives permitted the company to exclude from the joint enterprise valuable assets, including its Dapu plant, the People's Victory Bonds, and the holdings of Hengfengtang.[83] At

---

80. Liu Yousan's report to CFEC, ca. July–August 1951, in JD 301153-59.

81. Xue Xianzhi (1992), 77.

82. Ministry of Labor ruling #1587, July 31, 1951, in X77.1691 held at TMA. Severance agreement August 28, 1951, in JD 300482-85. The minister of labor then was Li Lisan.

83. Hengfengtang served as the group's holding company to mask its business involve-

stake was not merely the capitalists' retention of the company's properties but also the loss of assets needed to satisfy workers' claims.[84]

In late 1951 and early 1952, the cadres' assessment of Li's proposal for conversion veered "left" because of two campaigns that the CCP launched at the time. In December of 1951, the CCP started the Three Anti campaign against cadres' corruption, waste, and bureaucratism, and on January 26, 1952, it introduced the Five Anti campaign against tax evasion, bribery, fraud, theft of state property and economic secrets. According to the ministry's report, instead of following the party's policy of acting "fair, reasonable and according to the facts," the guiding principle became "the state must not be wronged." In practice, that meant under-valuation—the less the better in the calculation of Jiuda's assets. The group's centrally located head office building in the former French concession of Tianjin was initially valued at 400 million old renminbi. Upon appeal, it became 600 million and finally 800 million. The more the cadres changed their minds, the more dissatisfied the capitalists became.

Li Zhuchen was also unhappy with the treatment of "enemy investments." In 1946, the Nationalists had demanded that Jiuda turn over to the government the three million weilianbi that the North China Political Council (which was regarded as a puppet front for the Japanese) and the Kahoku engyō kabushiki kaisha [North China Salt Industries, a Japanese-owned company] had "invested" in Jiuda. Li Zhuchen successfully persuaded Chiang Kai-shek that his company did not deserve such a "harsh" treatment because the "investment" in it had been lost through Japanese mismanagement during the war. It deserved more compensation than the 2,055 tons of refined salt and 1,445 tons of washed salt that the Japanese left behind during the war.[85]

The Communists, however, rejected that argument. Other enterprises and the people did not receive such compensation, and Jiuda should not be an exception. The Tianjin Municipal Committee rejected the company's appeal and ruled that the Japanese "investment" should be converted to

ment, circumvent regulations, and evade Nationalist taxes in various investments, including salt pans and Tanggu wharf. See Yu Xiaoqiu's letter to Li Tifu, July 8, 1935, in Yongli Papers, 1048.243, held at Nanjing Municipal Archives.

84. Report, September 9, 1954, in JD 301185-301190.

85. Nationalist Executive Yuan order, July 13, 1946; Li Zhuchen's petition and Wang Yichen's report, November 21, 1946, in Archives of the Ministry of Economic Affairs 18.36a held at the Institute of Modern History, Academia Sinica, Nankang, Taiwan. See also the company's balance sheet as of October 31, 1945, in the Japanese transfer files in Jiuda-Yongli papers, S-75-81 held at TMA.

state shares as of October 1945.[86] On October 28, 1952, before finalizing the audit (and hence confirming the state's share), the Ministry of Heavy Industry gave Jiuda a 10.3 billion old renminbi infusion in return for an 18 percent stake in the company (see Appendix 5.1C).[87] Chen Xiping was deputed from the ministry as plant chief for both Yongli and Jiuda, and Li Zhuchen became the chairman of the new group. Jiuda became profitable again in 1953, while Yongli's profit for 1952 alone amounted to over one trillion old renminbi.[88]

POSTSCRIPT

Jiuda's transformation under Li Zhuchen from a private to joint public-private company under state control was thus the result of a "strange alliance" blurring the capitalist-Communist divide. As a socially responsible capitalist with fiduciary duties to his shareholders, a Janus-faced Li also served the new government in his official capacity, using his access to secure loans and favorable policies to save a company weakened by years of war. Squeezed into socialism by the state's labor mobilization and shifting monetary and gabelle policies, Li volunteered to convert Jiuda and Yongli into a joint public-private company. However, both Li and Hou wavered in their resolve, just as Zhou Enlai, Chen Yun, and Bo Yibo all urged caution in this and other cases. Officials at the Ministry of the Chemical Industry and the municipal government also opposed Jiuda's conversion for a variety of reasons. They did not want responsibility for a company that was a burden yielding few benefits.[89]

Indeed, the case posed dilemmas for capitalists as well as the Communists. Since its inception, the Chinese Communist Party's policy toward private enterprises and the national bourgeoisie had shifted as

---

86. Jiuda appraisal report, 1953 in JD 200088-90. Officials were following the regulations issued by the Private Enterprise Bureau (1950) and the CFEC (February 4, 1951) in ZJDGS, 109–110 and 452–457.

87. JD 300316. 9.6 billion old renminbi immediately went to the People's Bank to repay the 7.4 billion loan with interest. The amount due would have been close to 13 billion had Bo Yibo not intervened again at Li Zhuchen's request.

88. Bo Yibo erred in his letter to Zhu De, November 30, 1951, in saying that Jiuda's profit for the year amounted to 30 billion old renminbi. That was for Yongli. See Bo Yibo, *Bo Yibo wenxuan* (Selected writings of Bo Yibo) (Beijing: Renmin chubanshe, 1992), 163.

89. Bureau of Chemical Industries "Report on Jiuda," October 18, 1950; Tianjin Municipal Finance and Economics Committee memo to Huang Jing, July 7, 1952; and Huang's recommendation to CFEC in "Archives of the Tianjin Municipal Financial and Economics Committee," X77.1691 held at TMA.

priorities and circumstances had changed.[90] The new government could easily have forced Jiuda into liquidation, as it did foreign companies; or, following the example of the Soviet Union under "war communism," it could have seized the company.[91] It did neither, consciously rejecting a timetable for transition into socialism. As it searched for a way to build a new state and economy, it gave both the national bourgeoisie and private capitalists roles to play.

Defining the "roles," however, posed many problems in practice. Despite a poor market, work had to be resumed as quickly as possible, taxes paid, prices kept low, and government bonds purchased. A theoretical unity of labor and the new state notwithstanding, if the state sided with the workers and their own independent unions, it might have jeopardized production, weakened the joint public-private initiative, or even taken an action that could be considered "anti-Marxist."[92] But if the state supported shareholders, it could become accused of a "right" deviation, or worse, succumbing to capitalist "sugar-coated" bullets.[93] From his unique perspective—not even the Ministry of Heavy Industry knew of his secret membership in the party—Li Chenggan reported that his capitalist colleagues intended to use the government to solve the group's labor problems.[94] Dedicated officials at all levels thus had to be vigilant against being "taken in" by capitalists against workers, and they

90. For a concise review of the issue, see Li Qing et al., *Zhongguo gongchandang dui ziben zhuyi he fei gongyou zhi jingji de renshi yu zhengce* (The Chinese Communist Party's understanding and policy toward capitalism and nonpublic ownership) (Beijing: Zhonggong dangshi chubanshe, 2004), passim.

91. On wartime communism, see Silvana Malle, *The Economic Organization of War Communism, 1918-1921* (Cambridge: Cambridge University Press, 2002).

92. Li Lisan was accused of making this mistake. See Li Fuchun, "Zai gonghui gongzuo wentishang de fenqi" (Divergent views on issues related to labor union work), December 20, 1951, in Zhonghua quanguo zhonggonghui bangongting, comp., *Jianguo yilai Zhonggong zhongyang guanyu gongren yundong wenjian xuan bian* (Selected documents of the Chinese Communist Party Central Committee on the labor movement) (Beijing: Gongren chubanshe, 1989), v. 1, 96-116.

93. Bo Yibo soon came under heavy criticisms in 1953. See Bo Yibo, *Ruogan zhongda juice yu shijian de huigu* (Recollecting certain important decisions and events) (Beijing: Zhonggong zhongyang dangxiao chubanshe, 1990), v. 1, 290-291; and Zhou Enlai's conclusions on Bo, August 11, 1953, in Zhongguo renmin jiefangjun guofang daxue dangshi dangjian zhengong jiaoyanshi, comp., *Zhonggong dangshi jiaoxue cankao ziliao* (Reference materials for teaching party history, hereafter ZDJCZ) (Beijing: Guofang daxue chubanshe, 1986), v. 20, 132-143, esp. 136-139.

94. Summary of Li Chenggan's confidential letter to Li Weihan, January 23, 1953, in JD 301180-84. Li Chenggan then represented Yongli's shareholders on the transition planning team. He left in 1954 for the National People's Congress Budget Committee as vice director and concurrently chief of the State Metrology Bureau.

should not pay for buildings and equipment that were worthless and dilapidated (as Li Zhuchen admitted Jiuda's were). For Mao and Zhou Enlai, by 1952 the national bourgeoisie was no longer "neutral." It had given rise to the primary class contradiction in the country and needed to be fundamentally transformed.[95]

Yet, as the Ministry of Heavy Industry observed, Li had to be handled with great care. Unlike Hou Debang or Li Chenggan whom officials could ignore, Li Zhuchen enjoyed access to the highest echelon of authority. In fact, Mao exchanged letters with him and visited him at home. Together they toured the northwest for over a month in 1952.[96] As a member of the Central People's Government Council, Li insisted that a dividend rate of 8 percent for private investors be included in the provisional regulations on investments in private enterprises.[97] In such public forums as the People's Political Consultative Conference, Li took the political high road. He vowed to support the state's policy of "quartering" profits while drawing attention to the ministry's decision to distribute less than 5 percent of the group's net profit. In 1953, an embarassed ministry was forced to raise its recommendation for dividends to 20 percent.[98] The same forum also allowed Li to complain bitterly about the appraisal process. Whereas other private enterprises that had collaborated with and prospered under Japanese occupation remained untouched, Jiuda, despite its losses during the war, had had to "pay" yet again because of "enemy investments."[99] Once more officials were put on the defensive, settling the matter with a 10 percent discount on the appraised 7.3 billion old renminbi of "enemy investment" dating from December 1949 (see Appendix 5.1C).[100]

---

95. Bo Yibo (1992), v. 1, 164–165; Mao's written comment. June 6, 1952, on Li Weihan's report from the Ministry of United Front in MS, v. 5, 55; and Zhou's speech in the National Conference on United Front, June 19, 1952, in ZZGZ (Zhongyang), v. 1, 332–340.

96. Personal communication from Li Mingzhi, February 8, 2009. One source placed Mao's visit in the winter of 1950 and another on December 28, 1951. See http://www.szmgw .com/ReadNews.asp?NewsID =1045. Of Mao's 372 published letters, three were to Li, the earliest dated June 23, 1951.

97. Letter to the Central Committee, July 28, 1950, in BYBSXJ v. 1, 134–135. Subsequently, the regulations were incorporated into the first company law after 1949. On the debate on this and other provisions, see Xue Muqiao's letter of transmittal in ZJDGS, 576–585.

98. Ministry of Heavy Industry report ca. 1954 in JD 301200. This was Li Weihan's principle of "quartering [profits] by four horses." See Li Weihan xuanji bianzhiju, ed., *Li Weihan xuanji* (Beijing: Renmin chubanshe, 1987), 263–267.

99. JD 301203.

100. Industrial Chemicals Bureau to Ministry of Heavy Industry, May 9, 1955, in JD 301201-04.

Much to the displeasure of local cadres, Li continued to uphold shareholders' interests even as he was given more and more official posts.[101] While chairman of the new group, he was also concurrently vice chairman of North China Bureau and a standing committee member of the National People's Congress and the Political Consultative Conference. During the Three Anti and Five Anti campaigns, he was declared inviolable—one of only two Tianjin capitalists to enjoy such a privilege.[102] In its report to Beijing, the Tianjin municipal party committee complained, without naming names, of capitalists who had long feigned cooperation with the party, staying one step ahead to ride the "tide" toward joint public-private enterprise and become officials. These untrustworthy capitalists were accused of caring about only three matters: a "fair" appraisal of their property, control over personnel decisions, and guaranteed dividends for shareholders.[103]

Such distrust did not facilitate a smooth socialist transformation of the group, official historiography notwithstanding.[104] A Ministry of Heavy Industry report on Jiuda in 1954 accused Li of inciting workers to challenge cadres. In particular, it was claimed that Li protected his son, Li Wenming (then assistant plant chief), and other close associates when they did not respect cadres' authority and clashed repeatedly over personnel and other matters.[105] Despite these criticisms, in 1955 Mao again invited Li for a tour of the Yellow River, and in 1956, he appointed Li Minister of Food Industry with responsibility over salt production (subsequently reorganized as Ministry of Light Industry), a portfolio that he held until his death of natural causes in 1968.[106] The alliance between Li as a capitalist and the Communists was strange indeed.

---

101. Ministry of Heavy Industry draft report, May 9, 1955, in JD 301201–1204, esp. 301203. As a result of successive reappraisals, one yuan invested in 1917 in the group was worth 7.55 in 1955, not counting the stock splits and dividends through the years. See capitalization report held at the Archives of Tianjin jianchang.

102. Big character posters and posters assailing Li as a "big tiger" had appeared. See Tianjin Municipal Committee United Front Department classified emergency notice, March 4, 1952, and a report, April 1, 1952.

103. Report of the Tianjin municipal party committee to the Central committee, November 14, 1953, in ZDJCZ, v. 20, 198–199.

104. For a hagiography of Li in the socialist transformation campaign, see, for example, ZZGZ (Tianjin), 1027–1035.

105. JD 301165, 301185–1190.

106. Zhongguo renmin zhengzhi xieshang huiyi Xiangxi wenshi ziliao yanjiu weiyuanhui, ed., *Li Zhuchen ziliao zhuanji* (Special volume of materials on Li Zhuchen) (Jishou, Hunan: Xiangxi wenshi ziliao bianjibu, 1992).

APPENDIX 5.1

A. Jiuda Salt Industries (Tianjin)
Salt Shipped/Net Profits, 1949–1954
(unit=piculs/old renminbi)

Year	Refined	Washed	Crude	Net profit (loss)
1949	36,090	136,102	547,056	2,431,258,234
1950	76,030	241,711	518,418	56,273,484*
1951				(2,900,688,989)
1952				(1,420,450,261)
1953				5,018,320,603
1954				10,375,905,142

*With inventory marked-to-market valuation 3,070,492,625.
See JD 300198 and text for explanation.

Appendix 5.1 continued

B. Jiuda Salt Industries (Tianjin)
Balance Sheet, September 20, 1950
(unit=old renminbi)

Debit		Credit	
Bank loan	7,200,000,000	Crude salt	4,000,000,000
Gabelle due	3,873,760,000	Refined salt	1,100,000,000
Misc. debts	714,414,000	Supplies	2,000,000,000
Accounts payable	3,466,834,700	Inventory	8,473,418,500
		Autumn salt	
		Harvest	980,000,000
		Cash/deposit	539,653,375
Subtotal:	15,258,008,700		17,093,071,875

Fixed / other assets

Equipment/land	18,000,000,000
Yongli shares	150,000,000,000
Yongyu shares	15,000,000,000
Victory Bonds	2,715,000,000
Subtotal:	185,715,000,000

Source: JD 300325-6.

Appendix 5.1 continued

C. Jiuda Salt Industries (Tianjin)
Assets and Liabilities, 1953
(unit=old renminbi)

Assets

Fixed assets (net)	14,741,479,000
Fixed value assets	4,762,933,083
Other	86,720,757,678
Total assets:	106,225,169,761
Liabilities	9,730,751,887
Net asset value:	96,494,417,874
Shareholders' equity:	78,879,056,590
State capital infusion:	10,300,000,000
Japanese/puppet government:	7,315,361,284[#]

Source: JD 200089. [#]Value as of October 1, 1949; value as of October 1, 1945, was appraised at 8,211,717,685 old renminbi. Final appraised value by the State Council in 1955 was 6,780,000,000, reducing the state's stake to 17.7 percent. See JD 200090 and 301201, respectively.

Appendix 5.2
Salt Trade by Sector, 1949–1954

Year	State* %	Cooperative %	Private %	No. of Merchants	Capital million renminbi	Volume handled
1949				519#		
1950	57.82	—	42.18	380	10	1,000,000
1951	58.57	9.82	31.61	346	5.5	765,800
1952	62.36	23.26	14.38	236	3.38	334,500
1953	65.86	24.02	10.12	152	2.51	139,500
1954	78.94	18.59	2.47	51	0.38	

Source: ZYYS, Table 1–11, 418; Table 2–8, 471; Table 2–9, 472; #JD 300087.
*Including joint public-private enterprises.

6 VENTURE COMMUNIST |
Gu Zhun in Shanghai, 1949–1952
Christopher R. Leighton

When the Communists took Shanghai in 1949, they brought
seasoned soldiers, but scarcely an accountant. The victory that they
claimed in the city presented both resources and temptations, including
riches to fund a fledgling regime but also the taint of capitalism. How
would they fight their new battle to control and reform China's financial
heart? For help, they turned to Gu Zhun (1915–1974), an accounting
wunderkind, native Shanghainese, and veteran member of the Chinese
Communist Party (CCP). Over the next three years, he oversaw and
overhauled the city's financial structure from various perches in government, sometimes concurrently heading as many as three municipal
bureaus. He thus shaped many of the dilemmas capitalists confront
elsewhere in this volume. That he sometimes shared as much with
them as with his superiors in the party perhaps only compounded their
predicament.

Gu Zhun's key position afforded him unusual influence. He occupied
not only the bureaucratic extraction point between China's greatest profit
center and its revenue-hungry state, but stood also at a series of other
junctures: between business and government, the party and technical
experts, and revolutionary and bourgeois Shanghai. While such realms
remained in balanced tension, Gu Zhun ably intersected them. Present
at and participating in the creation of a new regime, he pioneered
policies that reverberated beyond Shanghai and echoed down after his
era. Of course, he still operated under constraints. As a local official
he followed orders from superiors, couched his innovations within
the outlines of general policy, chafed at jurisdictional boundaries, and
trimmed to the political weather. Institutional particulars at his different
posts, meanwhile, alternately helped and hobbled him in achieving
his goals. Yet, even within both the prevailing institutional matrix and
the wider political context, Gu Zhun's distinctive character radiated
through, illuminating the course of Shanghai's financial reorganization,

unexpected congruences between cadres and capitalists, and perhaps too the pattern of their eventual collaborations.

An unusual personality in an unlikely context, Gu Zhun confounds some of our assumptions about Communist cadres. Although not a capitalist himself, Gu Zhun had been steeped in the business world. His earliest work and expertise had been in accounting, and he had rented his talents to major Shanghai companies to help shield their profits. In a parallel career he marketed to the urban masses not only textbooks but also the dream of economic self-improvement through education. So while he may have been a cadre, Gu Zhun was also something of an entrepreneur (of economic related ventures more than actual firms, to be sure), conversant with the language and processes of business, and accomplished at introducing novel ways to novice audiences. He was not so different from those he would oversee. His story shows how the categories of cadre and capitalist, and the layers of intellectual, cultural, and sociological givens that those categories have accreted, obscure rather than illuminate. Not all cadres were bent on wiping away Shanghai's past; taxes could be an exciting, modernizing innovation, and within the party some evangelists for economic change imagined a different sort of socialism.

This chapter explores Gu Zhun's brief career in post-revolution Shanghai to show how he bridged business and politics to control and reform Shanghai's capitalist inheritance. His attempts to recruit experienced civilian cadres, rationalize taxes, and create locally owned state enterprises show us an unfamiliar image of the Communist cadre: professional, experimental, and even creative in management. The policies he pioneered and the personal example he presented as the face of finance for the incoming government crucially informed the perceptions and calculations of the capitalists examined elsewhere in this volume. Though ultimately undone by the tensions between centralized control and local autonomy, the pressure of expediency on professionalism, and the personalized politics of the early People's Republic, Gu Zhun nevertheless presents us with an intriguing counterintuitive insight into the unrealized possibilities of the period.

This chapter proceeds through four sections. The first recounts Gu Zhun's past in Shanghai and his return to it to take over the financial system; it demonstrates that Gu Zhun's private and public life in post-liberation Shanghai built on his earlier career there. The second reviews his tax policies and the conflicts that complicated them; it shows that he innovated in producing a professional system for tax collection despite practical difficulty and even some official disapproval. The third describes his cultivation of local industry and fiscal autonomy; it indicates that he conducted an incipient experiment in decentralized socialist enterprise. The fourth narrates his abrupt fall and considers its meaning for his peers and heirs.

RETURNING TO A NEW SHANGHAI

Gu Zhun entered Shanghai just behind the People's Liberation Army (PLA) as part of an elite economic planning team tasked to take over the economy.[1] His work and life would ripen from deep pre-1949 roots in the city. Born in 1915 to a family of modest and declining means, he grew up in the southern Nanshi district, which comprised the old Chinese core of the city around which the modern metropolis developed. Precarious family finances pushed him from school to work as a teenager, when he apprenticed under Pan Xulun, his longtime boss and mentor, under whom he mastered accounting. Pan, a Harvard and Columbia graduate, had founded an eponymous accounting practice in 1927 and the closely related Lixin Academy in 1928, and through them he had become famous as a proponent of Western-style business practices, vocational education, and even a model for the modern-minded in 1930s Shanghai. Gu Zhun was part of it all. As a crucial aide he learned the trade well enough to help Pan run the firm and school that made his reputation. In addition to teaching, he found time to write textbooks and advise capitalists on how to avoid taxes.[2]

While grateful for earnings substantial enough to support his family, Gu Zhun did not necessarily sympathize with his clients. Wide reading, frustration over injustice, and an impulse to act led him to organize

---

1. For descriptions of the economic team and their preparations, see Wang Ruzhen, "Shan yu guo hou bu jian jun, bai hua cong zhong liu xiao rong: Shanghai jiefang qianhou Gu Zhun er san shi" (Through mountain and rain without meeting a gentleman, From among many flowers leaves a smiling face: A few matters about Gu Zhun before and after the liberation of Shanghai), in Chen Minzhi, ed., *Gu Zhun xun si lu* (Contemplating Gu Zhun; hereafter cited as GZXSL) (Beijing: Zuojia, 1989), 331–336; and also Gu Zhun, *Gu Zhun zi shu* (Gu Zhun memoirs) (GZZS) (Beijing: Zhongguo qingnian, 2002), 138–140.

2. For Pan Xulun, the Lixin Academy, and accounting, see Yeh Wen-hsin, *Shanghai Splendor: Economic Sentiments and the Making of Modern China, 1843–1949* (Berkeley: University of California Press, 2007), 198–199; Robert Gardella, "Squaring Accounts: Commercial Bookkeeping Methods and Capitalist Rationalism in Late Qing and Republican China," *Journal of Asian Studies* 51.2 (1992): 317–339; David Strand, *An Unfinished Republic: Leading by Word and Deed in Modern China* (Berkeley: University of California Press, 2011), 162.

like-minded acquaintances into a discussion group. A progression of political commitments culminated in his decision to join the CCP in 1935. Unlikely though it might seem, Gu Zhun's professional alter ego brought out his inner revolutionary. When the danger grew too great, it was the accountant who would find shelter and work at the Bank of China in the foreign concession. Under lingering suspicion, it was the revolutionary who slipped out of Shanghai to journey to Yan'an.[3]

Though it took a conquering army to bring him home and to power, from the first days back Gu Zhun returned to rather than rejected many of the patterns of his native city. His life did not seem so different from those of high officials under the Nationalists—or indeed for Shanghai's capitalists. While PLA soldiers were famously billeted along city streets, he slept above them in the Pacific Hotel on Nanjing Road. At that posh address, he received underground operatives who had worked within the Nationalist government's finance departments[4] and implemented the entire financial takeover by installing just a few key people in each, thereby ensuring continuity in personnel.[5] In the tax sections, where there was a bit more thorough housecleaning, he dismissed dozens while channeling in more than a hundred men who had come south with his takeover team. The most technically complex, exceptional, and ultimately troublesome office, where Gu Zhun assigned five party members but still retained nonparty veterans,[6] was the Direct Tax Bureau, which handled most business taxes. Atop this pile, Gu Zhun formally held simultaneous posts in the Shanghai government as head of the Finance and Direct Tax

---

3. Gu Zhun's early career is recounted in English in Yeh, *Shanghai Splendor*, 196–204, and also GZZS, chs. 1–3.

4. Gao Jianguo, *Chai xia lei gu dang huo ba: Gu Zhun quan zhuan* (Tearing a rib for a torch: Biography of Gu Zhun; hereafter cited as GZQZ) (Shanghai: Shanghai wenyi, 2000), 267–268; Chen Xinhua, "Huiyi di yi ren shuiwu juzhang Gu Zhun" (Remembering the first director of the Tax Department, Gu Zhun), *Caishui zhi sheng*, June 10, 1990.

5. The thicket of agencies under Gu Zhun's control was dense. He took from the Shanghai municipal government its Finance Bureau, Land Administration Bureau, Accounting Office, and Auditing Office; and from the national Ministry of Finance the Shanghai branches of its Commodity Tax Bureau, Direct Tax Bureau, Government Bond Office, and General Office. He had little use for some, and dissolved the Auditing Office, the Government Bond Office, and the General Office in short order; after putting the Land Administration Bureau in trusted hands, he rarely checked back on it.

6. These were on the one hand either capitalists like Zhang Qiweng, a commercial capitalist and relative of Huang Yanpei who had been politically active in the Shanghai Democratic National Construction Association and would go on to work for Gu Zhun in other offices; or so-called holdover personnel like Lu Ruoqian, who had worked for the tax office of the Nationalist government but who had been introduced by underground party members. Details of staffing decisions are in GZZS, 139–142.

Bureaus, and within East China, the regional administration to which Shanghai was subordinate, he was also the assistant head of the Finance Ministry.

Occupying a third floor office in the main municipal building, Gu Zhun played a central role in Shanghai that was both actual and apparent, and his centrality was readily grasped by officials as well as citizens. He participated in the pomp of the formalized handover on May 28, 1949. A few days later he attended the government's five-course reception for courting influential and notionally representative members of Shanghai's various social circles (ostensibly nonpolitical but important occupational groups like industry, commerce, and the arts). Along the way, he mingled with the prominent at a performance by the renowned opera star Mei Lanfang. Thanks to his prolific official bulletins, Gu Zhun soon became familiar even to regular folk; where there were tax notices, there he was too. As one man recalled, "All kinds of tax notifications [were] put up in every street and in the papers" at the time and "signed by the bureau chief," frequently in an official and "eye-catching" red. "Gu Zhun was the head of three bureaus, so his name appeared everywhere and everyone knew it and saw it all the time." Of course, neither new faces nor ubiquitous leafleting necessarily brought about change. As Gu Zhun noted, the very first proclamation of the incoming regime (which he probably authored), ordered people to follow the old laws and keep paying the old taxes. [7]

Pressing as the need for cash was, Gu Zhun and others in the party also knew that building a new China required human as well as financial capital. Rooted in his native place and intimate with its bourgeois world but still loyal to the party, Gu Zhun was a man whose connections could bridge old and new Shanghai, and he tried hard to bring them closer together. He later explained his position: "I was a [native] Shanghainese, but I was also someone returning from the liberated areas to Shanghai." [8] Spanning, or better still, binding the two together required a personal touch and an ability to trade on existing relationships.

Gu Zhun had begun his outreach well before April 1949 when he had written his old mentor, Pan Xulun, and had asked him to remain in

---

7. GZQZ, 273 has the Mei Lanfang anecdote. These are the recollections of Chen Danchen. There was confusion over the number of bureaus Gu Zhun headed. Chen had him heading the Commodity Tax Bureau, but Shanghai gazetteers indicated otherwise. Chen Danchen "Gu Zhun yu Gu Zhun riji" (Gu Zhun and the Gu Zhun diaries), *Suibi* (February 1998). Found through a reference in Luo Yinsheng, *Gu Zhun zuihou ershiwu nian* (Gu Zhun's final twenty-five years; hereafter cited as GZ25) (Beijing: Zhongguo wen-shi, 2005), 28.

8. GZZS, 193.

Shanghai through its imminent fall. Once he himself had returned, Gu Zhun called on Pan at home and invited him to work for the government, leaving the name card of the vice mayor, Pan Hannian, to convey the seriousness of the offer. Wary that his history of service to the Nationalists would cause trouble, Pan demurred, replying, "With my status a 'remarrying widow,' taking public office for the People's government will inevitably cause me extreme grief." Nevertheless, a mutual courtship developed when Pan reciprocated by inviting Gu Zhun for meals and later presented him with small gifts. These meetings reached a culmination of sorts when in August 1949 Pan offered Gu Zhun either the presidency or a trusteeship at Lixin, his alma mater, but this time it was Gu Zhun who declined.[9]

As the two men revived old cultural and professional networks, a relationship took shape that was broad and deep, extending beyond them. Name card in hand, Pan Xulun paid a courtesy call on the vice mayor, Pan Hannian, a fellow native of Yixing county in Jiangsu province and a very distant relation. Though they had not previously met, the elder Pan knew the younger Pan's brother, and could only have been pleased when the vice mayor respectfully addressed him as "uncle." Pan Xulun recalled, "Although I didn't go to work for the party, I was still concerned about the nation's accounting profession, so I urged and recommended and introduced many old colleagues and students for positions at government bodies, businesses, and state-run institutions."[10]

Pan Xulun did not act alone. His school, Lixin, had an institutional interest in cultivating Gu Zhun, and it held a banquet in honor of his return and perhaps to promote its graduates. One of many men with Lixin connections who later found his way into government recalled at that time that when private firms looked like they might close, he almost went out of work, until he tapped that old network: "I had to turn to my alma mater ... With Pan's personal attention and through Gu Zhun's introduction ... [I became] a specialist accounting cadre and have worked in the Jiangsu province ... for more than forty years."[11] Gu Zhun also reached out, telephoning a Lixin professor to explain how education and accounting would be needed in the new China and promising a

9. Pan Xulun, *Pan Xulun huiyilu* (Reminiscences of Pan Xulun) (Beijing: Zhongguo caizheng jingji, 1986), 51–52. At some meals others were present, for example, Nan Hanchen, an executive at the Bank of China, or Wang Liangchen, a future head of the national Federation of Industry and Commerce.

10. Ibid., 52.

11. Evidence of Lixin connections are obvious in the backgrounds of personnel mentioned in GZZS, chs. 16–20. Details of the Lixin banquet and this anecdote are quoted from GZ25, 17.

great future for his students. Within his own administration, Gu Zhun drew together a diverse group that included party members, Lixin alumni, businessmen, and incumbent personnel from the Nationalist government.[12]

Reviving these old ties clearly served multiple interests and the drive to do so came from multiple directions. The emerging state secured the well-trained experts it needed to operate its understaffed bureaucracy. Lixin graduates worked under Gu Zhun in Shanghai to implement his innovations there, but some percolated out into the financial control systems throughout the country and to the capital as accounting experts. At the same time, the accounting profession in general and Lixin as an institution in particular reaffirmed their importance and won recognition and jobs for their members. For Pan and Gu as individuals, reunion bolstered them both, as each gave the other a practically and symbolically valuable contact in the network of the other. Yet their relationship remained fraught and short of a full embrace, as Gu declined to identify himself fully as a trustee of Lixin and Pan avoided a similar entanglement in government service. Benefits might flow from informal contact between them, but formal affiliations were another matter.

Just as Gu Zhun was taking up the reins of government, he was also settling down into life with his family. By 1950 the household grew to seven: Gu Zhun, his wife, their four children, and his mother. They lived well. From the Pacific Hotel, Gu Zhun had relocated with family in tow to a Western garden-style house on Yuyuan Road that had belonged to the national Ministry of Finance. Ample grounds accommodated a front lawn for tennis and a separate two-story carriage house in the rear. Though they did share the estate with two other families, Gu Zhun took the best part. The couple had their own bedroom and his mother and children had theirs together, with two small rooms left for staff, as well as a large reception area for guests, who might also be seen on a spacious balcony.

The perquisites of Gu Zhun's position were considerable. A ration-based salary system for cadres provided not only for him but his wife, mother, and children, who were tended by two nannies. Gu Zhun had even more minders: a chauffeur to drive a reserved black Chrysler Plymouth, a gatekeeper to guard the house, three secretaries for aid, and even two bodyguards and an actual watchdog to protect him. Though

---

12. Li Hongshou "Huiyi Gu Zhun tongzhi er san shi" (Remembering a few matters about Comrade Gu Zhun) in GZXSL, 317. In his own writing Gu Zhun simply calls them capitalists. These were men like Zhang Qiweng or Wang Daifei, mentioned above, particularly the ones serving in the Direct Tax Bureau.

spare in his eating habits, he admitted to attending many banquet meetings during which he would negotiate with capitalists and then dine with them in the Shanghai Mansions. Years later, Gu Zhun would have to defend himself, writing: "The standard of living I described would not be considered 'wasteful' among cadres of my rank at that time." Nor was he particularly targeted on these grounds despite serious subsequent political problems.[13]

The workplace had perks, too. Gu Zhun's office held a cabinet of confiscated goods, including French wine and cognac, American whiskey, and English cigarettes (all of which had supposedly been confiscated because of tax evasion). Even if Gu Zhun himself did not privately indulge, a visit from a prominent businessman, official, or the odd Soviet expert gave cause to entertain. Smitten women wrote him letters, approached him after lectures, or loitered outside his office.[14] As Gu Zhun himself had to admit later in the Cultural Revolution era account that became his autobiography, "This kind of luxurious living reached the level of old Shanghai's big capitalists or great officials."[15] But of course that was more or less what he was; it was just that at the time leading the life of a great official was not so remarkable as it later seemed to have been. Indeed, despite political trouble in the 1950s, Gu Zhun faced no contemporary accusations over his lifestyle, which his enemies could easily have used against him had he behaved in any way out of the ordinary.

TAXING SHANGHAI

At the helm of the Finance and Tax Bureaus, Gu Zhun spent most of his Shanghai career extracting revenue. Far from being a dry affair of audits and accountancy, taxation exposed otherwise submerged tensions and proved controversial in the early People's Republic. The amounts to be extracted pitted not only payers against collectors but also the local interest in husbanding wealth against the national interest in siphoning it off to other areas. At the same time, the techniques deployed to effect extraction precipitated internal party conflicts between proponents of professionally minded change and followers of revolutionary precedents. Gu Zhun stood at the center of the disputes, and though at times he tried to balance them, he often acted as an instigator. While his actions may be

---

13. Ibid.
14. GZQZ, 290, 292.
15. GZZS, 201.

interpreted from multiple perspectives, here the emphasis remains on Gu Zhun as a professional and an innovator.

The drama in the taxing of Shanghai unfolded in two phases. First, from May through December 1949, Gu Zhun revived the old tax bureaucracy, met revenue quotas, and experimented with reform. An interlude followed during the early months of 1950, when central government pressure for funds broke the local bureaucratic routine in favor of quick and massive extraction, even before fiscal pressures brought on by China's decision to enter the Korean War. Second, the period between June 1950 to March 1951 saw the gradual institutionalization and central endorsement of the locally innovated tax system. The ultimate outcome demonstrated Gu Zhun's ability to innovate and change PRC economic practices even against central resistance.

Throughout Gu Zhun's career in Shanghai, the city's unique symbolic role in the country and its preponderant place in the national economy forced him to confront two distinct and at times irreconcilable responsibilities: one to city and the other to nation. During the summer of 1949, his duty to nurture local finances clearly came second to funding a fledgling regime still fighting a civil war. Despite the difficulties Shanghai faced even through that grim time, it provided a quarter of national tax receipts—more than any other region. Shanghai was, as Chen Yun put it, "worth five Tianjins."[16]

To raise more funds, Gu Zhun creatively designed taxes that allowed him to achieve multiple goals, fulfilling the broad thrust of party policy according to his particular expertise. This worked most famously with the land tax, with which he helped remake the map of Shanghai. Gu Zhun considered hangovers of imperialism galling enough, and he noted that foreign-owned properties had enabled Chinese investors to evade taxes because they had hidden behind foreign front-men through layers of registration. After 1949, he decided to maintain the same land tax structure but ratcheted up the rate and improved enforcement. Taxes on many of these commercial properties soon exceeded their incomes, and, as anticipated, owners turned over their deeds as payment. One by one Gu Zhun took back the major landmarks that still define the city, from the Racecourse to the Peace Hotel, palpably reinforcing Chinese authority.[17]

---

16. Chen Yun, "Kefu caizheng jingji de yanzhong kunnan" (Overcoming serious difficulties in finance and the economy) in *Chen Yun wen xuan* (Selected writings of Chen Yun) (Beijing: Renmin, 1985) v. 2, 8.

17. These included the Shanghai Racecourse (present-day People's Square), the Sassoon

While he deployed both the land and the utility tax to great political as well as economic effect, Gu Zhun made a virtue of necessity and scored great gains with marginal tools.[18] Gu Zhun found other taxes more difficult to implement. The regular machinery of tax collection had long been badly broken by war, inflation, and political fragmentation. Direct taxes, which included most business taxes, offered the greatest potential but provided scant precedent for regular, rationalized collection.[19] On these taxes, as simple as his reforms might seem, he actually worked the hardest. He had to engineer anew an entire system.

Business taxes proved especially complex and ultimately bruising. At the dangerous intersection of government and capitalist enterprise, they attracted attention and generated controversy.[20] The party had scant history of implementing them. In recalling precedents, Gu Zhun himself drew on a rough-and-ready version known as "democratic assessment" that had been used in 1948. This method amalgamated excises, earnings, and operations tax into a single quota apportioned in three steps. First, a total revenue quota for an area was set. Second, the city's tax collecting agencies collaborated with its chambers of industry and commerce to apportion the gross quota out to each trade. Third, within each trade, the trade organization allocated the burden to individual firms, through a negotiated process of self-reporting and public discussion.

The rapid pace of the PLA's takeover of Shanghai left little time to formulate new policies, so at first the new government temporarily preserved the Nationalist system of tax collection. To tap businesses as a final source of revenue, Gu Zhun settled on the formula of "self-reporting

---

Mansion (Peace Hotel), Hardoon Gardens (Shanghai Exhibition Center), the Cathay Apartments (Jinjiang Hotel), the French Club (Okura Hotel), and the Canidrome (Culture Square).

18. This tax was as effective but more obscure and was levied within the local political and fiscal context. Historically, the price of electrical power had been unequal across city districts, and was cheapest in the International Settlement where the American-owned Shanghai Electric Company provided it at preferential rates. This promoted residential and industrial development there, and hindered urban planning. To compensate, Gu Zhun devised what amounted to an equalizing tax. He set different tax rates for different districts in order to equalize the price of power to the final consumer. This became an important and lasting source of city revenue, and Gu Zhun heard that when he visited Shanghai in 1962, it was still being collected, even though by then the power company was in state hands and the underlying price structure could have been changed (GZZS, 173). Deleted portions reproduced from the manuscript are in Luo Yinsheng, *Gu Zhun zhuan* (Biography of Gu Zhun, GZZ) (Beijing: Tuanjie, 1999), 254–256.

19. Tuan-sheng Ch'ien, *The Government and Politics of China* (Cambridge: Harvard University Press, 1961), 212–214.

20. The actual term he used was "direct tax," which included the business operations tax on turnover and the earnings tax on profits.

and full payment; light taxes but harsh punishments." As the phrasing made clear, the new business tax merely refined the old by substituting tastier carrots and sharper sticks, but the method suited the limited means available. From June through August of 1949 collections increased, and Shanghai met its revenue obligations. Yet, the very mechanisms that Gu Zhun used to accomplish this feat—audits that verified accounts and downward reappraisals of capital that won businesses' trust—generated the controversies.[21]

The necessity of supervision to compel compliance was well understood, and Gu Zhun's appointment of auditors comported with contemporary practice.[22] During the Republican era, Gu Zhun himself had been an accountant who represented firms and handled their tax payments to the government. Now, the Tax Bureau would select a special group of auditors to fulfill that function. When businesses declared their taxes, these auditors would certify their books, which the government might then verify.[23]

The first controversy came from how these men were chosen. Gu Zhun chose many men from his former profession and specifically from his alma mater. One of the auditors defended the process as meritocratic: "I had no association with Gu Zhun before Shanghai was liberated ... in November 1949 he wrote to invite me to attend a discussion about tax work, and this is how we first became acquainted." The man assumed he had been tapped because of his experience, which mirrored Gu Zhun's: "Before liberation, the two of us both had used connections with the Shanghai Chamber of Commerce, long represented the interests of national capitalists, dealt with the Direct Tax Bureau under the Nationalist government, and had a certain understanding of the old tax system and could draw present lessons from past experiences."

The accounting world welcomed Gu Zhun's interest. As this auditor pointed out, it validated both the person and the profession: "The laurel of being a 'special auditor' definitely drew the interest of more than a few people ... If you could gain the title it was obviously good, but even if

---

21. GZZS, 145, 150–152. Shanghai finances stabilized by October 1949 and the quota increased thereafter. See GZQZ, 279.

22. Wang Shaoguang, "The Construction of State Extractive Capacity: Wuhan, 1949–1953," *Modern China* 27.2 (2001): 229–261.

23. Like the entire self-reporting system, the mechanism of "specially engaged auditors" was the suggestion of a democratic personage, Xu Yongzuo, a contemporary of Pan Xulun who had almost equal eminence in the accounting world. Gu Zhun noted that Xu resided in Shanghai during the Japanese occupation and had close relations with the enemy and with the capitalist class.

you didn't win it, at least it proved that accountants could be of service to socialism."[24] Still, it looked bad when so many of the men chosen were from Gu Zhun's alma mater, Lixin. Later, he admitted that accountants hired as auditors probably did a thriving business: "The Shanghai capitalists knew I was a Lixin old boy, and perhaps [thought] Lixin benefited more than a little by special association. Even though I definitely didn't play favorites, in truth I did create the opportunity for my old colleagues to get rich."[25]

Years later this whiff of cronyism soured into a political stink, and Gu Zhun had to admit in his Cultural Revolution era self-examinations that by bringing in accountants he had entrusted the business of government to former agents of the capitalist class, and thus capitulated in the class struggle. Even if he did not favor friends, he favored a certain kind of person, technically trained and from old Shanghai's bourgeois milieu.

This was not only a question of personnel; an analogous problem arose with his choice of method. Because the earnings tax was collected progressively according to the profit margin on capital, the plummeting value of the currency meant that the registered book value of firms' capital became trivial. Therefore, calculating the profit rate on that basis put all firms into the highest bracket. To Gu Zhun, this was "obviously not logical." By allowing businesses to recalculate their property at present prices and thus amend the book value of their capital, he propitiated capitalists, satisfied his own sense of professionalism, and made somewhat abstract accounting rules seem to conform with reality. But while this was "profoundly welcomed by Shanghai's capitalists, and especially accountants," it drew censure from the center, because the Ministry of Finance thought it "opened a route for Shanghai capitalists to legally evade taxes." On this point Gu Zhun remained forever unrepentant: "If we didn't let private business reappraise capital, the progressive earnings tax rate objectively would not work, so I still think that step was necessary, and had no ill influence ... It was not a political measure, it was nothing more than a necessary technical measure to improve the calculation of economic criteria, nor did it open any legal routes for tax evasion."

For Gu Zhun, the Western-style accounting he had learned under Pan was only a tool. Capitalists might use it to protect profit, but Communists could wield it too, to raise state revenues or even wrest back property and wipe away the stain of imperialism.[26] Not everyone agreed. Critics

---

24. Zhu Shangyi, *Shang Gong za yi* (Miscellaneous pieces by Shang Gong) (Shanghai: Shanghai renmin, 1994) v. 2, 106–107. Found through GZXSL.

25. GZZS, 152–153.

26. Ibid., 153–154. For an example of the approval of accountancy types, see Zhu Shangyi's praise in GZXSL.

viewing it from a class-based standpoint saw it as a weapon wielded by capitalists and considered it inherently political.[27] A new kind of socialist-style of accounting, some suggested, would be needed to suit China's new circumstances.[28]

These criticisms first surfaced in October 1949, when Gu Zhun sensed real trouble: "I became aware that I had committed a serious error in tax collection work, and I ... went to handle it." But before he could get on top of the matter, *People's Daily* published an editorial and reportage from Shanghai critical of its tax system, and the party organization began to attack it.[29]

The party's prescription was clear: implement democratic assessment, the old quota-assigning system. But though Gu Zhun conceded that the tax system needed to change, he dismissed democratic assessment as insufficient. He had a professional's and a perfectionist's sense of objections. Under such a system, "There could only be two possibilities: the amount collected will fall short of the set tax rate and favor capitalists or it will exceed the rate and thus become an appropriation." Moreover, he found in its apparent simplicity a deceptive opaqueness of process. Since the quota would filter through the same trade associations whose members were of disparate size and influence, he expected that larger capitalists would take advantage of the smaller and foist proportionally more onto them. Compounding the problem of implementation, democratic assessment was in conception "necessarily completely separated from tax laws."[30]

Pursuing his own diagnosis, Gu Zhun focused on Shanghai's exceptionalism, not only in scale but heterogeneity. Unlike other Chinese cities, it "had tens of thousands of tax paying companies, among which were great enterprises of near monopoly-capital scale like Shenxin and Wing On, along with countless mom and pop shops." Old Lixin clients like Shenxin and Wing On were among Shanghai's many large firms with sound accounting books, which had long studied "how to wage a

---

27. Xing Zongjiang and Huang Shouchen, "Zenyang jianli xin Zhongguo kuaiji lilun jichu?" (How to establish a theoretical basis for accounting in the New China?) *Xin Kuaiji* 1 (1951): 12–16.

28. This new socialist-style of accounting would eventually be equated with Soviet accounting, which ironically retained many of the techniques of capitalist accounting that Chinese critics objected to. Though focused primarily on the shifts in accounting from the Mao to the Deng era, the best English overview of the earlier debate is in Mahmoud Ezzamel, Jason Zezhong Xiao, and Aixiang Pan, "Political Ideology and Accounting Regulation in China," *Accounting, Organizations, and Society* 32.7 (2007): 669–700.

29. GZZS, 147–148.

30. Ibid., 148, 151, 154.

struggle against the government within the scope of the tax laws." Yet the government's recordkeeping left it with just a light grip on businesses: the sum of its knowledge resided in 12,000 paper cards filed in the main bureau, according to which notices to pay would be sent and receipts recorded.[31]

Just at this time, a tax bureaucrat from a Soviet delegation of experts appeared in Gu Zhun's office. Gu Zhun found many Soviet suggestions "simple ... and of no use at all," but he did learn that the USSR had a system of specialists providing oversight for business taxes, and he wrote a report about it and circulated the report to his superiors. Gu Zhun preferred this "medicine," which proved easier to swallow under the cover of Soviet precedent. It had three key ingredients: specialization, which assigned each tax cadre a fixed stable of firms; verification, which relied on auditing to ensure compliance; and collaboration, which drew the workers at each firm in through their union to aid the tax bureau. This proposal demanded more structure and bureaucracy rather than less— in over twenty municipal and ten suburban districts, newly established branch tax offices would group firms by sector and parcel them out to cadres. Over some internal opposition from subordinates and despite lukewarm support from superiors, Gu Zhun resolved to implement this system.[32]

Extraordinary fiscal and political pressures from the central government in the first half of 1950 later compounded by the need to fund the war in Korea delayed his plans, but once out from under heavy fiscal demands, Gu Zhun devoted himself to building the specialist system of tax collection that ultimately earned national implementation. He acted within a muddled context of general nationally declared political goals, specific economic policy directives, and local supervision that allowed him surprising latitude to reconfigure one of the country's richest revenue-generating systems.

Locally, the Shanghai Party Committee had insinuated itself closely into tax collection during the drive for revenue in early 1950, but, according to Gu Zhun, later it had begun to withdraw. Gu Zhun reasoned

---

31. Ibid. Gu Zhun himself admitted to being a part of this process: "In the 1930s when I revised the book *Earnings Taxes in Principle and Practice*, actually it was to aid capitalists in carrying out this kind of struggle."

32. His system was known as "specialized supervision, account checking, clerk cooperation." Wang Jihua, Wang Liang, and Zhou Xin all had objections to it. Gu Zhun implied that they had these objections because in his scheme he did not make good use of shop clerks as collaborators. The Shanghai party committee gave consent but never issued a formal statement. Perhaps they were taking a wait and see approach. GZZS, 155.

that the Shanghai Party Committee was satisfied that the tax bureau was not committing political errors and turned its attention elsewhere. This gave Gu Zhun room to maneuver, and he assembled his specialist system of tax collection by taking new initiatives and retooling parts of the existing bureaucracy. At the same time, he paid lip service to democratic assessment and sought support for his approach from his superiors. His work fell into three broad thematic areas: organization, supervision, and propaganda.

Organization required more knowledge, so first Gu Zhun completed a detailed survey of taxpayers. According to rough pre-1949 figures, Shanghai had 130,000 tax paying companies and 100,000 street peddlers. Gu Zhun aimed not just to update these figures but to add information by determining where companies were, whether they belonged to a trade association (and if so which one), and what their recent record of tax payment was. More than a thousand cadres assembled and canvassed the city over a month, discovering 21,000 new and unregistered businesses amounting to a total of 107,830 operations across 443 trades, 15 percent in industry and 85 percent in commerce. While he boasted that this accumulation of detailed data provided a firm ground for the negotiated aspect of democratic assessment—the Tax Bureau now knew better how much they might expect to get—Gu Zhun probably realized how a specialist system could easily be built on this basis. Indeed, his establishment of ninety-six specialized tax collection areas and twenty district offices appear to be spadework to that end. [33]

On the basis of the survey, he then ranked the companies in three tiers, from large enterprises to peddlers. Each group got slightly different treatment. Because the first two tiers kept books, they paid according to tax rates and had specialized handlers. Large businesses were grouped and minded at the city level by a special auditing section while small and medium companies were monitored by their district offices. The smallest fry were often itinerant peddlers who could not be made to keep books, and so they paid a kind of set licensing fee collected by the district.

Several control mechanisms made this system work. Most crucially, Gu Zhun leveraged the accumulating paperwork of the PRC's burgeoning bureaucracy as an extra check on tax payment. His investigation teams collected transactions that produced written vouchers—from the customs, the railroad, market duties, freight transport, contracts—and compared

---

33. Ibid., 159–161; GZZ, 244–246.

them with companies' written books. Moreover, he created tax-paying mutual aid groups for taxing small- and medium-sized capitalists. While his rhetoric emphasized their patriotism and contributions to the nation, he clearly tapped into the group members' suspicion and self-interest and encouraged colleagues to inform on each other as well as to love their country. These measures were mostly borrowed from previous examples but were modified to carry out taxation.

The cultural framing of tax payment, for instance, probably owed much to the example of the donations solicited from businesses for the Korean War.

In the realm of propaganda, Gu Zhun made use of his department's *Taxation Newsletter* as a mouthpiece for his vision of professional conduct. With its colophon in the calligraphy of Chen Yi, the newsletter was published every Wednesday and Saturday and went to all members of the staff. Gu Zhun regularly editorialized, urging the staff members to improve communication and share experiences with each other. To him its purpose was to "emphasize professional work, and not give prominence to politics."[34]

Throughout the summer Gu Zhun grafted this system onto the existing one. Even the democratic assessment committees themselves were transformed from consultative groups that fixed revenue quotas into tools of standardization that calculated firms' profits. While the old name was preserved, his specialist system sought to capture more revenue as times became more flush.

That summer, there was an economic upturn thanks to half a year of peace, better transport, a more stable currency, and military procurement for the Korean War. With factories operating at near full capacity, only a rate-based taxation system could keep up with the swift changes in profits. In a rough example, Gu Zhun showed how a hypothetical factory going from one-third to full production would increase profits many times, and only a tax on the profit on capital could easily keep pace with this increase. "If you use the democratic assessment method, even the boldest estimate won't estimate that the tax quota will increase by 16.5 times; moreover, when applying the democratic assessment method, the power over taxation is really left in the hands of the capitalist class."

By August, even the appearance of implementing democratic assessment had worn thin, and with the cornerstones of the specialized system in place, Gu Zhun owned up to his intentions and asked the

---

34. This newsletter, *Shuiwu tongxun,* began its run earlier once the three bureaus merged; it was suspended by Pan Hannian during the Three Anti campaign. GZZS, 162.

local authorities to approve its use for Shanghai. Chen Yi agreed, siding with Gu Zhun against Pan Hannian, who remained "firmly opposed," instructing them to drop democratic assessment.[35]

The new system swung into action by early fall, and it profoundly increased revenue collection. Tax receipts for March 1951 swelled to almost eleven times their level of a year earlier. Critics quieted. Gu Zhun remembered that in March of 1951, an unnamed central government cadre came to Shanghai and expressed approval of the tax collection method, and then from the middle of 1951 after the third national tax meeting, the Ministry of Finance no longer criticized Shanghai's methods in publications, nor did they send more auditors. Finally, in December 1951, Chen Yun opined in a central Party meeting that the "Gu Zhun method" was correct, and he noted that Chairman Mao agreed.[36] Long before the Five Anti campaign and without its tactics or theatre the state had found a way to increase revenue extraction.

This was a great victory. Gu Zhun had taken over the Shanghai tax system and made it work. The revenue he extracted funded national reconstruction and war in Korea, all while keeping the goose alive to lay more golden eggs. Creative and improvised taxes filled the nation's coffers while fulfilling multiple goals that included opposing imperialism and building durable sources of municipal revenue. Of course, Gu Zhun did not achieve this alone. Social and professional connections helped him tap a deep pool of local talent to make his system run. And if he was wonkishly expert, he was also Red enough to be trusted. He had found enough leeway to run his fief in ways that clearly frustrated or came close to contradicting the policies of the central government.

LOCALISM

Gu Zhun's service in Shanghai touched on many areas beyond taxation. He also headed the city's Public Finance Bureau, which involved him in municipal planning. Here too, while budgets and costing might

---

35. Ibid., 162–163, 165–166.

36. Gu Zhun remembered that the tax receipts in March 1951 (which included the earnings tax) were six times greater than in March 1950: 180 million yuan in 1951 compared to 30 million in March 1950. In fact, using the figures from the 1995 edition of the Shanghai Finance and Tax Gazetteer, Luo Yinsheng has shown that the difference was still greater, actually 10.8 times the size. Zhu Ruyan to Chen Minzhi, GZZ, 248; GZZS, 163, 167–168. See also GZZ, 250; and Chen Minzhi, "Wo suo zhidao de Gu Zhun" (What I know of Gu Zhun), *Wenhui bao*, March 31, 1994.

seem like dry subjects, they open up surprising vistas on the early PRC. Rather than copying the Soviet-style centralized command economy, Gu Zhun and other like-minded cadres pursued a different vision: a decentralized, locally based system of socialist enterprises, overseen by regional governments with budgetary independence from the central government. This scheme ultimately failed, but its limited implementation highlights the possibilities for contingencies and negotiations under Chinese socialism, and later it offered a precedent for decentralization and market socialism in the reform era. Gu Zhun began introducing this scheme when he first returned to Shanghai, but he carried it out in two fairly discrete phases. First, from May 1949 through March 1951, as head of the Public Finance Bureau, he pushed for local fiscal autonomy and better fiscal management. Second, from March 1951 through the end of that year, Gu Zhun devoted himself almost exclusively to building up local state-owned industries through the Shanghai Finance Commission.

Purse strings were drawn tightly in the early PRC, and fights broke out over who should control them. Throughout the debates about taxation, Gu Zhun also campaigned for better budgeting. To him, that meant both local fiscal autonomy from the central government and more rigorous financial controls in state-owned enterprises.

His position took shape in response to a national finance meeting in February 1950. Focused on standardizing financial practices, the meeting was concluded by a recommendation that each ministry should disburse budgetary flows. For example, within the East China Bureau—a vast military control region spanning six provinces—the Ministry of Health would devise a general budget, gain approval from the Ministry of Finance, and then itself choose how to divide funds through its subsidiary Health Departments from Fujian to Shandong. This meant that Shanghai or even an entire province "did not have their own income, nor their own budgets ... This amounted to abolishing the financial administration of provinces and cities."

Gu Zhun thought such a system was "obviously wrong." After conferring with fellow municipal bureau chiefs, he convinced them to collectively suggest that Shanghai have a city budget. The Shanghai party committee agreed, and after negotiation with the East China Department, a partial victory was won. Though Shanghai would have its own city-level budget, East China retained final control over how funds should be directed. Gradually, this arrangement gained support. In the beginning of 1951, the central Ministry of Finance held a meeting to reconsider urban finances and invited Gu Zhun to speak. He lectured to Finance Bureau chiefs from China's ten largest cities, detailing Shanghai's experience and showing how he had managed its budgeting independence. Later, the ministry underscored its approval by circulating the text, and moreover it stipulated that central and regional finances should be segregated.[37]

Budgeting, whether to win autonomy or tighten administration, was both an end in itself and a fiscal measure that promoted a decentralized kind of socialism. This latter aim comes most clearly into focus when considered in the context of Gu Zhun's longstanding interest in state enterprises. He had been mulling over the matter for a long time, and he concluded that proper management of state-owned enterprises remained the great unsolved problem of finance. He suggested that the East China Ministry of Finance establish a financial management office for state enterprises, and once it was in place, he ran it from August 1949, recruiting through "personal connections twenty or thirty 'progressive' people [including his wife] who could understand enterprise management and enterprise accounting." He followed the same pattern as in his early recruitment of Lixin graduates as tax collectors, and later, when questioned during the Cultural Revolution, he characterized the personnel in this office as "capitalists, capitalists' representatives, and professors of the capitalist class."[38]

From this office, Gu Zhun cast a sharp eye on Shanghai's financial administration and strove to strengthen fiscal management. Several branches of city government were sprawling empires of subsidiary enterprises. Public Works and Health in particular supervised construction projects, water, hospitals, waste collection, and slaughterhouses. Though these subsidiaries had vast outlays and substantial incomes, Gu Zhun noted that in 1950 "none had implemented enterprise-type accounting." To tighten fiscal control and management he transferred in key cadres who effected what he called "enterprisification" of those areas by running government concerns along business lines. Gu Zhun pioneered the office—the first of its kind in the PRC—but did not stay to pursue its work because he was distracted when his system of tax collection came under heavy criticism. Years later, at the time of the Cultural Revolution, when called to account for his performance, Gu Zhun could only repudiate his approach as "of a capitalist nature."[39]

Gu Zhun had a second chance to pursue these goals in early 1951. At that time, just when he had resolved most of the difficulties and

---

37. GZZS, 174, 175–176.
38. Ibid., 145, 147. These people were Zhang Qiweng, Wang Zaifei, Chen Fuxiang, Hu Shisheng, Liu Shaofu, Li Xiequan, and Zhou Yukang (a friend of Lu Xiuyuan).
39. Ibid., 176–177.

set up the specialist tax system, serendipity landed him in a newly created bureaucracy: the Shanghai Finance Commission. The Finance Commission held a vague but vital portfolio empowering it to develop Shanghai's economy through numerous government bureaus.

At inception, the commission seemed poised to fulfill its mandate mostly by managing relations between the public and private sectors. Pan Hannian, Gu Zhun's civil and party boss, chaired the commission, and as the theoretically nonparty representative in Shanghai government, he had intimate and extensive contact with prominent capitalists. His appointed deputy on the commission, Xu Dixin, was a close associate and veteran of United Front outreach, having honed his skills at countless dinner parties in Hong Kong during 1948 before taking up a formal post in Shanghai. In addition, Xu headed Shanghai's Industry and Commerce Management Bureau, which attended to the details of corralling and collaborating with capitalists and their companies. Through the first two months of the Finance Commission's existence, Xu had taken the primary role in organizing it, and so the complexion of the staff reflected his preferences.

Gu Zhun had earned his spot as vice chair because he headed both finance and tax, but he had paid little attention to the commission during its preparatory phase. He expressed distaste for its emphasis on collaboration with nonparty groups, noting that its "'United Front' flavor was extremely strong." He remembered that "I was not enthusiastic about this organization because it clearly took as its main work managing public-private relations, which did not conform with my ideas."[40]

More than a month after its founding, Gu Zhun still had not paid attention to its work. Eventually, his absence drew notice, and Gu Zhun's superiors directed him to concentrate on the commission. Gu Zhun resisted, and he suggested that rather than cultivating relationships with capitalists and existing banks, trading companies, and industrial enterprises, the commission should foster new socialist enterprises to develop Shanghai's economy. He worried that the city government had "almost become a merely administrative organization" because East China had kept control of most of the state-run enterprises when Shanghai was separated from it. The Shanghai Finance Commission, he proposed, "should set up many state-run enterprises subsidiary to the city," and thus he "did not attach importance to the United Front work of private-public relations" so far as the commission was concerned.[41]

---

40. GZZS, 181, 184.
41. Ibid.

Gu Zhun was granted permission to pursue his own interests on the commission. Yet the commission's purpose remained undefined, and the organization was rife with partisan strife and bureaucratic sniping. With two leaders and two different foci, the commission soon divided into "Gu" and "Xu" factions that prevented it from functioning as a unit, a problem obviously instantiated in its duplicated offices for general affairs, planning, and statistics. Gu Zhun accepted some responsibility, admitting he neither "cared about nor attached importance to" Xu Dixin's projects. The end result was that "encountering resistance from within the commission" Gu Zhun, in his own words, "became an isolated force fighting alone."

Difficult as this predicament may have been for Gu Zhun, it gave him the opportunity to clarify for posterity his decentralized vision of local state-owned enterprises that he now strove to build. He confronted a peculiar bureaucratic inheritance. First, authority over economic planning was shared by two different levels of government with geographically overlapping jurisdictions. East China oversaw state-run companies, even though the majority operated in Shanghai, while the city controlled enterprises subordinate to municipal bureaus, such as the utilities, transport companies, and a grab bag of miscellaneous factories.[42] Shanghai retained direction of policy areas involving state relations with private enterprise. This was less simple than it sounded.[43] Second, despite the theoretical apportionment of state enterprises to East China, Gu Zhun found a welter of quasi-socialized concerns that remained or had grown up under Shanghai's supervision. These included building projects, city commissaries, supply and marketing cooperatives, some retail shops, a transport company, and some private firms in which the government held shares.[44]

Here he found a base for developing socialist enterprises, and he sent his subordinates to manage many of them while he acquired still more. These included textile, chemical, and manufacturing plants.[45] The case of

---

42. Ibid., 177. Many municipal bureaus had factories that produced goods related to their function; for example, the Public Security Bureau owned a firefighting equipment factory.

43. In textiles, the state-run Cotton Company (under East China) handled the sale of cotton to and the purchase of product from private mills, but stipulations of piece contracts and fees fell under the rubric of private sector relations (under Shanghai) and so involved the municipal Bureau of Industry and Commerce.

44. GZZS, 181–183.

45. Examples include the Guangzhong Ranzhichang (later known as the Shanghai Rongbuchang), which had business trouble and needed investment; Yongxin Chemical (now Wujing Synthesized Detergent Factory) and Tianshan Chemical (now Tianshan Plas-

the Xinyu Number One Mill exemplifies how this process of acquisition and development worked. In May or June 1951, Gu Zhun recalled that "one day Pan Hannian told me that the Kincheng [Jincheng] Bank had financial difficulties and was preparing to sell the Xinyu Number One Mill, and that the city government had decided to buy it. Pan asked me to go find the company's general manager, Chow Tso-min [Zhou Zuomin], for a talk. Pan said also that Chow's attitude was very 'enlightened' and he intentionally was taking all of the Kincheng owned companies and one way or another was 'transferring' them to the government."[46]

After the mill was appropriated, Gu Zhun visited it and retained the incumbent manager. Of the episode, Gu Zhun remembered that "adding a city-run mill subordinate to a state-run mill made me extremely happy." He had more interest in acquiring than running the enterprises that he collected, and was usually hands off about management. Often he just assigned one cadre to look in on acquired factories. "Because at the time cadres were sorely lacking," he explained, he "merely sent a public representative, and for a long while did not sufficiently completely smash the capitalist factories' old structure." He also tended to leave negotiations and management of factories to subordinates, which forced him to admit later in the context of the Cultural Revolution that "in the joint operation conditions for each factory, I fear there were more than a few improper places that guarded the interests of capitalists."[47]

Gu Zhun's attention to budgeting and interest in expanding local state industry was not just entrepreneurial but successful as well. By late 1951, fiscal independence and slightly preferential treatment combined to accrue for Shanghai a sizeable surplus—at one point about twenty percent of the annual budget—that he hoped to spend, both to benefit Shanghai and prevent it from being siphoned back to the center. Consequently, he remembered, "I did my utmost to find an outlet for investment." While some cash went to fund several important infrastructure projects, he also tried to expand Shanghai's base of state enterprises. He arranged a meeting with two other regional officials "and went together to look at an interchangeable machines plant ... and negotiated about Shanghai investing to expand the factory." Though this plan did not ultimately

---

tics); the Xiechang Sewing Machine Factory; and the Guanleming Pen Factory. Liu Xiao had invested in the latter during his underground days in Shanghai as a means of obtaining a cover identity as a manager. He turned over his shares to Gu Zhun's office.

46. GZZS, 188. On Zhou Zuomin, see chapter 7 by Parks M. Coble in this volume.

47. Ibid., 189, 191; these are the same so-called capitalist types who keep reappearing: Zhang Qiweng, Chen Fuxiang, and Han Hongchuo.

come to fruition, Gu Zhun in his confessions had to make clear that it was a mistake, as it brought an "evil style to the internal management of socialist enterprises."[48]

Philosophically, Gu Zhun distinguished his idea of locally subordinate state-owned enterprises from sideline production at regular work units to defray expenses.[49] Like democratic assessment, this was a practice that had been adopted in revolutionary base areas and was reimagined for application in the PRC. His own Cultural Revolution era recollection was that he "thought it impossible for a work unit involved in industrial or commercial production to not carry the thick flavor of capitalism."[50] A contemporary remembered him reasoning: "Businesses seek money, and profit is necessary. But for a department of the government or party, or for cadres to directly deal with managing things this way, then the party would not be the party, and the government would not be the government. For cadres on the one hand to be in business and on the other hand to lead the party and government, how outrageous would that be?"[51]

Gu Zhun happened to be on the right side of this particular debate. In the Three Anti campaign that aimed to cleanse cadres of corruption, all sideline production by government offices was stopped, and Chairman Mao even deplored its ill effects. But Gu Zhun had only a limited chance to pursue his plans in this area before being swept up in larger events.

SETTLING ACCOUNTS

The improbity within work unit production represented just one of many forms of corruption that came to light in late 1951. The perception of widespread abuses prompted the central government to launch two interrelated housecleaning campaigns, the Three and Five Anti, which targeted crooked cadres and the supposedly backsliding capitalists who suborned them. Signaled from the center, Shanghai mobilized locally for the Three Anti in late 1951.

As the broom swept through the ranks of Shanghai's top cadres, it brushed Gu Zhun only lightly. He certainly knew all of the early targets

---

48. Ibid., 178–179.
49. See Wang Yonghua, "Zhongguo lishi shang de jiguan shengchan" (Office production in Chinese History), *Dangshi bolan* 8 (2006): 41–43.
50. GZZS, 197.
51. GZQZ, 316.

of criticism, but he had only limited connections with a couple of them. By 1952, the campaign intensified because Shanghai had to deliver its centrally mandated quota of scalps, and it touched a bit closer, when a friend and associate came under investigation.[52] Eventually, Gu Zhun himself made an obligatory self-criticism, citing his advocacy of deficit finance and some personally wasteful habits. But rather than representing real self-censure, his statement was a kind of ritual reprehension, which had a regular place on the resume of any fast-tracked cadre. In making these statements, Gu Zhun implied that he had been cleared in the campaign and could move forward without further consequence. Indeed, the importance of his duties ensured light treatment: East China permitted Shanghai Tax and Finance to temporize over implementing the Three Anti in order to better manage the imminent collection of the annual business earnings' tax that March. Perhaps he really was not guilty of anything at all.[53]

Such even treatment belied significant churning among the leadership in East China and Shanghai that probably affected how the locals were prosecuted in the Three and Five Anti and their aftermath. In fact, Gu Zhun himself had a significant role in running the campaigns locally: "Tan Zhenlin ... wanted me to take temporary responsibility for the [Five Anti] campaign; he transferred ten or twenty cadres ... under me to start gathering suggestions for steps to advance."[54] Gu Zhun received his appointment from the party committee on February 3 and immediately went to work. His role received prominent play in *Liberation Daily*, which depicted him addressing the shopworkers' union about the Five Anti in a photo on February 4 under a picture of Mao, and again in a separate article on the campaign on February 16. Four days later on February 20 at Mayor Chen Yi's elbow, he attended a rally for industrial workers about the campaign. That same night, he met his superiors again at the local party committee to discuss implementation, and even chatted with Bo Yibo, the national leader of the campaigns. A week later, on February 28, as the local leader of the campaign, Gu Zhun gave a speech about the Five Anti that was broadcast across the city.[55]

---

52. Wang Jihua had been a friend of Gu Zhun's since at least 1934, had been an underground cadre in Shanghai engaged in publishing and propaganda, and had been working in various parts of the Shanghai financial system since 1949. His was one of the families that shared Gu Zhun's house on Yuyuan Road.

53. GZZS, 196.

54. Ibid., 197. One of the reasons Gu Zhun's appointment was temporary might have been that the original choice was Xu Dixin, who was fortuitously sick.

55. *Jiefang ribao*, February 2, 1952; Chen Minzhi, ed., *Wo yu Gu Zhun* (Gu Zhun and I; hereafter cited as WYGZ) (Shanghai: Shanghai wenyi, 2003), 22–26.

The next day the party committee called a meeting and denounced him. Gu Zhun remembered the statement, which announced on behalf of the Shanghai party committee that "I had 'grave individualistic heroism, was self-important, opinionated, disregarded organizational discipline, and distorted the party's policy principles' … They decided to strip all my positions within and without the party and ordered me to reflect on my errors."

Tan Zhenlin, formerly supportive, branded him a Menshevik, a dirty insult in contemporary Communist argot.[56] After censure from party members came criticism in the press. A story in *People's Daily* on March 4 branded him an evil element.[57] Further articles specified the crimes of other cadres denounced at the same time, including loaning seed capital for a new business, protecting relatives with suspect class backgrounds, and having a patriarchal work style. But no concrete accusations were made about Gu Zhun. What was the precise nature of his crime?

Such silence, combined with the very abruptness of his fall, prompted speculation. How had he gone from the leader of one half of the campaign to be dismissed as a target of its other half? His family certainly wondered. Gu Zhun had no clear answer. He had heard recently that both Chen Yun and Chairman Mao made statements settling the tax controversy in his favor. Certainly he thought himself in the clear of the Three Anti because he had already been investigated. Stripped of his posts, Gu Zhun found himself in an unusual and distressing enforced idleness at home. He recalled: "I shut the door and stayed home for two or three weeks, and other than writing a report of self-criticism, I didn't do anything. My mind was in turmoil, my mood depressed, and I couldn't get anything done. Often late at night I couldn't sleep."

After a few weeks, the party committee gathered all the high cadres who had been dismissed at a local hotel, but no one arrived to give further orders or organize them in studying. They played chess to pass the time.[58]

In the weeks and years that followed, Gu Zhun had time to contemplate his fall. With the accumulated perspective and experiences of seventeen years, he set out some of the reasons for it in his confessions during the Cultural Revolution era. His writing on the subject is coy, elliptical, and built on unverifiable hearsay. Disentangling his retrospective understanding from his contempo-rary actions is not

---

56. GZZS, 209.
57. *Renmin ribao*, March 4, 1952.
58. GZQZ, 334; also GZ25, 57, quote from Gu Zhun's eldest son, Gu Yidong.

always possible, but he seems to have grappled with how to assimilate the rumors he heard as he formulated his response. He kept his ear to the ground.

He heard encouraging news, suggesting that some regretted his dismissal. While this must have heartened him, Gu Zhun still had to decide how to craft his self-criticism and where to place the blame. He sensed it might be about taxation, but stubbornly refused to give in: "While writing, I was in a really painful state of mind. The party committee decided it wanted me to make a deep self-criticism. [If] I didn't make a self-criticism about democratic assessment, wouldn't that be taking the easy way out? Also, just as I was writing it, I kept hearing that the tax receipts that March reached … ten times that of a year previously, and could democratic assessment have achieved that number?"

But bad news also flowed in. He became the target of "several slanders," including the charge that after being sacked he had gone to churches or temples to pray and burn incense. Another and perhaps even less flattering explanation of Gu Zhun's downfall also circulated: that he was personally ambitious, and worse, gave the appearance of being so. Gu Zhun's unrepentant attitude—even after he understood the precariousness of his position—probably only enhanced his reputation for arrogance.[59]

Evidence suggests that Gu Zhun had some support. After his dismissal, superiors did him good turns, finding him work, securing entrance for his child into the elite Shanghai Party Committee nursery school, and getting him a transfer to the Economics Department of the Central Party School in 1956 over the objections of his own work unit. Nevertheless, two attempts to petition his organizational superiors to revisit the 1952 verdict failed.

Perhaps no written verdict existed to amend. When, eleven years after his death, his family went to handle the formalities attendant to the Central Party Committee's reversal of his case in 1985, no record of his dismissal could be found. Without definitive proof, several theories have been mooted. Gu Zhun eventually decided the tax controversies had tripped him up. Some biographers have suggested that Gu Zhun was a collateral casualty of a larger national factional battle in which Mao

---

59. GZZS, 210, 211. For example, during the Cultural Revolution, when reviewing the reasons behind his condemnation as a rightist in 1957 (opposing the center by appending his rebuttal to the audit report on Shanghai's finances), he refused to admit his error: "Even now I still think my doing this was not wrong. The signed names on this audit report were Zhao Bingqian and Mi Qiuyang. I had clear reservations about the audit report of these two people, and I did not at all oppose the center." GZZS, 167, 168.

removed two men he thought had plotted to take power. Gu Zhun's own brother understood it as a problem of personality.[60]

Gu Zhun's influence grew after his death in 1974, two years before Mao died. Interest in him was carried forward by the people, writings, and reputation he left behind. Many colleagues survived persecution in the Cultural Revolution, and in the post-Mao era found themselves returning to positions of prominence. His subordinates regained positions and served as consultants on Shanghai's tax work in the 1980s, and Pan Xulun spearheaded the revival of the reinvigorated Lixin Academy.[61] One imagines that even a former rival like Xu Dixin, who had his own struggles in the Cultural Revolution, might have pondered how narrowly he avoided his former colleague's fate. Most important, Gu Zhun's brother collected his writings. Reissues of Gu Zhun's accountancy primer appeared in the 1980s, along with his writings on economics, government, and philosophy.[62] By these means, his conception of accounting as a neutral technology that might help develop China gained ground.[63]

Publishing more personal or pointed material still proved difficult. Only in 1987 did his brother find a sympathetic reader at the Shanghai People's Press who appreciated its politics as well as style: "The writing is concrete and clear, the style incisive, and it stirs the heart—you can't put it down ... the author was loyal to the revolution, loved the people, and wrote out of concern for the nation."[64] From there, matters gained momentum. Gu Zhun was an appealing figure, whose journey from youthful idealism to a more nuanced, even jaundiced empiricism mirrored the odyssey of a generation. The acute extremes he experienced combined to make him seem quintessential. Old comrades remembered Gu Zhun and his achievements, while a younger generation discovered him and recorded their emotional and intellectual reactions to his writings in popular journals.[65]

---

60. GZQZ, 330–331; GZZS, 207. Gao, Gu Zhun's biographer, points out that in the summer of 1953 Mao spoke out against Gu in the context of the Gao Gang affair. Under the proposal of Bo Yibo at the Ministry of Finance, the tax system had lightened taxes on businessmen. Mao declared that this was capitalist and benefited capitalism rather than socialism. WYGZ, 37–48.

61. See Li Haibo, *Lixin kuaiji gaodeng zhuanke xuexiao zhi* (Gazetteer of the Lixin Accounting Academy) (Shanghai: Lixin kuaiji, 1998).

62. WYGZ, 71.

63. Ezzamel, Xiao, and Pan, "Political Ideology and Accounting Regulation in China," *Accounting, Organizations, and Society*, 694.

64. WYGZ, 73.

65. Many are usefully collected in GZXSL; these were publications like *Nanfang zhoukan, Dushu, Huanghe*, and *Zhongguo qingnian*.

In most of this eulogizing, Gu Zhun became more symbol than man. The way his surviving peers revere him reveals how they approach and understand their own experience. The violence of their metaphor—one man describes him tearing out a rib to tap his way through a benighted landscape—is striking. How the students, technocrats, and intellectuals of contemporary times relate his struggles to their own shows how they imagine the PRC's past and present, and their own place in it. In both cases, Gu Zhun is a romantic but serious figure; his wonkish grasp of taxes is as essential to his lionization as it was to his disgrace. To many, he presents an alluring counterfactual possibility, about what could have been.

Gu Zhun's brother finally framed the object lesson as a question of personalized power: "According to some leaders' likes and dislikes, or for the sake of controlling individualistic cadres … [they] were able to decide these people's fates as they like." And yet, in the moral Gu Zhun's brother drew from the tale, those in power would pay a price for this too. In his account, an unnamed man with decisive influence over the case had threatened that if Gu Zhun persisted in disobeying superiors, they "would not even give him food to eat." Later, this same man supposedly complained that such a talented man was a rare find: "In this whole district we can't find even a single cadre as good as Gu Zhun." For Gu Zhun's brother, these apparently opposing statements seem to be in conflict, but actually just string them together and think carefully, and you realize that they are completely consistent; what he's actually saying is that he recognizes ability, but you must submit—that is the most basic prerequisite; if you can do it, you'll have everything, but if not, you won't even get food.[66]

In other words, the desire for talent would always be trumped by a distaste for dissent.

For Gu Zhun, unlike others covered in this volume, the dilemma was never to stay or go. However much he had been formed by the bourgeois world of Shanghai, he was not a capitalist. When he borrowed from its playbook—with accounting, old-boy networks, tax strategy, or an acquired portfolio of local enterprises—it was to build socialism, albeit in a different image than would eventually emerge in the 1950s. In his restless activity and agnostic appropriation of business methods he resembled the entrepreneurs he knew so well even if he remained a loyal party member who shared its ultimate goals. He was a venture Communist. As the product, advocate, and exemplar of a kind of

---

66. WYGZ, 37–48. Circumstantial evidence suggests the origin of this version came from Ren Piaozhai, who transmitted it to Wang Bi in 1963. See GZQZ, 336.

bootstrapped professionalization, the meaning of Gu Zhun's life and career had long been derived from values other than pure loyalty. By 1952, he had run out of room to maneuver; his fall was just one early example of the great tide of deprofessionalization that would change China in the years to come. Even the obvious reservoirs of support he retained within the party were not enough to rehabilitate him until the post-Mao era. From the perspective of the fate of capitalists in the 1950s, it was not so much that the new China was difficult for business, but that it became ultimately inhospitable to the style and values that derived from Shanghai's bourgeois world, whether espoused by capitalist or cadre.

This page is intentionally left blank.

PART THREE

CAPITALISTS WHO RETURNED TO CHINA

This page is intentionally left blank.

7 ZHOU ZUOMIN AND THE JINCHENG BANK

Parks M. Coble

When Chairman Mao proclaimed the People's Republic of China in October 1949, Zhou Zuomin (Chou Tso-min), a prominent private banker in Republican China, was residing in Hong Kong. Founder of the Jincheng Banking Corporation (Kincheng Bank), one of the major modern Chinese banks of the first half of the twentieth century in China, Zhou had left for the British colony in 1948 as the Civil War in China reached a climax.[1] In the weeks following the Communist victory, Zhou like many other capitalists had to determine whether or not to return to China.

Despite the policy of "New Democracy," the People's Republic of China would seem to have held little promise for a commercial banker. Yet in 1950, Zhou decided to return and resume leadership of his bank. Zhou was hardly alone. As Sherman Cochran has noted, "in the wake of the Communist revolution of 1949, the overwhelming majority of China's elites who had the means to escape from China did not flee," and in fact, "many chose to return from abroad."[2] But the new People's Republic of China would not long have a place for Zhou. In September 1951 the Jincheng Bank was reorganized as part of the Five Northern Banks, and in December 1952 all banks in China were nationalized.[3]

Why did Zhou choose to work with the new Communist government? To have a clear understanding of Zhou's viewpoint in 1949–1952, one must examine the history of the Jincheng bank and of Zhou's relationship with the previous government of China—the Nationalists under Chiang Kai-shek.

---

1. The English name used by the bank was the Kincheng Banking Corporation. Zhou Zuomin's name often appeared in English as Chow Tso-min.

2. Sherman Cochran, "Capitalists Choosing Communist China: The Liu Family of Shanghai, 1948–1956," in Jeremy Brown and Paul G. Pickowicz, eds. *Dilemmas of Victory: The Early Years of the People's Republic of China* (Cambridge: Harvard University Press, 2007), 359.

3. Zhongguo renmin yinhang, Shanghai shi fenhang, jinrong yanjiu shi, ed., *Jincheng yinhang shiliao* (Historical materials on the Jincheng Bank; hereafter cited as JYSL) (Shanghai: Shanghai renmin chuban she, 1983), 911–913.

THE JINCHENG BANKING CORPORATION

Zhou Zuomin was one of a handful of pioneering commercial bankers in early twentieth century China, along with K.P. Chen, Li Ming, and Bian Baimei. In the late imperial period, China had a long history of important financial institutions that met the needs of China's government, its officials, and its vigorous commercial sector. With the opening of the treaty ports in the nineteenth century and the growth of foreign trade, foreign banks such as the Hong Kong and Shanghai Bank brought a new institutional form to China, the limited liability banking corporation. Chinese institutions called *qianzhuang* (usually translated as "native banks") grew in partnership with the foreign presence, but operated by more traditional methods. Patrons of the banks were normally introduced and loans made on the basis of personal guarantees. Zhou and his fellow modern bankers introduced a Chinese version of the Western bank, usually called modern banks (*yinhang*), which solicited business from the general population and made loans based on collateral rather than personal guarantees.

Zhou founded the Jincheng Banking Corporation in Tianjin in 1917. Although a native of Jiangsu province in the Lower Yangzi region, Zhou had worked in the Beijing government after returning from study in Japan. He served for a time in the Ministry of Finance and then in the Bank of Communications, which along with the Bank of China had been established as a government bank. Zhou's move was a daring venture at a time in which China was experiencing rapid economic and social change against a backdrop of political disorder and collapse. With initial investment of 500,000 yuan from a group of officials in the Beijing government, the bank was a major success. By 1927 its capital had expanded to C\$7 million. The bank thrived despite political upheavals. Although the initial backers had mostly been associated with the Anhui clique of Duan Qirui, Zhou managed to survive the collapse of that faction and find new investors. Zhou brought little personal wealth to the bank. His investment was said to be little more than 1 percent of the bank's capital. Zhou's primary income came from salary and bonuses, not stock holdings.[4]

---

4. Linsun Cheng, *Banking in Modern China: Entrepreneurs, Professional Managers, and the Development of Chinese Banks, 1897–1937* (Cambridge: Cambridge University Press, 2003), 51, 211; Brett Sheehan, *Trust in Troubled Times: Money, Banks, and State-Society Relations in Republican Tianjin* (Cambridge: Harvard University Press, 2003), 78.

Zhou Zuomin became a driving force in the development of modern banking in China. Realizing the vulnerability of commercial banks in a time of political disorder, he helped organize a joint reserve fund of his Jincheng Bank, the Dalu yinhang (Continental Bank), the Yanye yinhang (Salt Bank), and the Zhongnan yinhang (China and South Seas Bank). Usually referred to as the "Four Northern Banks," their cooperation strengthened the stability of all four institutions. Zhou served as general director of the joint operation. Zhou also assumed leadership in the Beiping Bankers' Association and Beiping Chamber of Commerce and played a visible role in representing the interests of modern bankers during times of political crisis.[5]

The early years of the republic were heady days for the new elite of modern bankers. Not only did they pioneer new financial institutions, but in the absence of an effective government, they and their institutions played a very visible public role. Marie-Claire Bergère refers to this as the "golden age of the Chinese bourgeoisie." As she has noted, Zhou, along with Chang Kia-ngau (Zhang Jia'ao) and Wu Dingchang, played a prominent political role. "The Peking Bankers' Association embodied the unity and power of the local banking community. The influence that it wielded in the National Federation of Bankers' Associations balanced that of the Shanghai banks." The national group reached its peak of influence in 1920 when at its first congress held in Shanghai, it "warned the government that if it wanted funds from them it would have to cut down its military expenditure, readjust internal loans and reform the monetary system."[6]

ZHOU ZUOMIN AND THE NATIONALISTS
DURING THE NANJING DECADE, 1928-1937

The creation of the Nationalist government in Nanjing inevitably reduced the independence of the modern bankers, who now had to deal with a government that was relatively effective at least in comparison with the old warlord regimes. The northern banks, such as Jincheng,

---

5. Parks M. Coble, *The Shanghai Capitalists and the Nationalist Government, 1927-1937*, 2nd edition, (Cambridge: Harvard East Asian Monograph Series, 1986), 122-123; Linsun Cheng, *Banking in Modern China*, 49-52; Howard L. Boorman, ed., *Biographical Dictionary of Republican China* (New York: Columbia University Press, 1967), v. 1, 427-428.

6. Marie-Claire Bergère, *The Golden Age of the Chinese Bourgeoisie, 1911-1937* (Cambridge: Cambridge University Press, 1989), 222-223.

also faced the move of the capital from Beijing (renamed Beiping) to the south. Government-connected individuals such as T.V. Soong (Song Ziwen) and H.H. Kung (Kong Xiangxi) assumed greater control over the banking and financial system. Zhou Zuomin, however, was already skilled at adjusting to new political conditions. Over the next few years he would cultivate ties with a group of Nationalist officials informally labeled the "Political Study Clique." At the same time, Jincheng cooperated with the new government by purchasing government bonds that helped cover the large deficits of the Nanjing regime.[7]

The most dramatic change occurred in 1935 with the "banking coup" and currency reform (of the fabi), which greatly strengthened the government's control of the financial sector. Prior to the "banking coup" of 1935, China's two largest banks, the Bank of China and the Bank of Communications, had functioned with relative independence from government under the leadership of Chang Kia-ngau and Hu Zutong. These banks were not completely free of government control, but generally their management used market criteria in making investment and loan decisions. In March 1935 Minister of Finance H.H. Kung suddenly reorganized these banks, replacing their leaders with political appointees. Three months later several smaller private banks were taken over. By the summer of 1936 Kung firmly controlled over 70 percent of the assets in Chinese modern banks, compared with less than 20 percent prior to these actions. This banking "coup" set the stage for China's fabi reform of November 1935, but it also greatly reduced the political independence of China's modern bankers. Increasingly, banking decisions were based on political factors, not market conditions. Commercial banks also lost the right to issue paper currency, which had been a source of income.[8]

For bankers such as Zhou Zuomin, the "banking coup" and fabi reform meant that they and their organizations such as the bankers associations no longer had the degree of autonomy they had enjoyed earlier. Yet most continued to work with the government. After the fabi reform, H.H. Kung established a currency reserve board that was to supervise the issuance of the paper currency and prevent inflation.

---

7. Additional details about the Jincheng Bank's loans can be found in "Benhang zhengfu jiekuan zhi yanjiu" (Research on this bank's government loans), March 26, 1935, Jincheng Bank archives, Tianjin Municipal Archives. The author thanks Kwan Man Bun for making this information available.

8. Parks M. Coble, *The Shanghai Capitalists*, 172–192. Hu was forced to resign in April 1933. See also "Reminiscences of Ch'en Kuang-fu (K. Cheng), as told to Julie Lien-ying How, December 6, 1960 to June 5, 1961," Columbia Oral History Project, 67–69. The author thanks Andrea McElderry for making this source available.

Kung was eager to have prominent bankers join this board in order to secure public confidence in the new currency. Zhou joined along with Chang Kia-ngau, Wu Dingchang, and K.P. Chen.[9] Zhou also joined with T.V. Soong in May 1934 when Soong organized his China Development Finance Corporation (Zhongguo jianshe yin gongsi). Soong invited an array of capitalists, including Zhou, to subscribe to the stock in the enterprise.[10]

Recognizing that the center of Chinese banking had migrated southward, Zhou moved the headquarters of the Jincheng Bank from Tianjin to Shanghai in the spring of 1936 and increasingly worked with the Bank of China, now headed by T.V. Soong.[11] Zhou also joined the board of directors of the China Cotton Company (Zhongguo mianye gongsi) which had been established by Soong in 1936. This enterprise operated textile mills that had been distressed and engaged in commodity trading and speculation.[12]

Zhou's record during the Nanjing years would suggest that he adjusted to the new political situation with some skill. Much as he had transitioned following the earlier collapse of the Duan Qirui group, Zhou adjusted to the new political reality of Nationalist China, even moving his bank headquarters to Shanghai. But the 1930s were not a fruitful time for economic growth in China. The ravages of the Great Depression limited world trade and investment. The most serious issue was the increasing pressure of Japanese imperialism in China. After the seizure of northeast China and the creation of the puppet state of Manchukuo (Manzhouguo), the Japanese continued to push into north China. By 1935 it appeared that the Nationalist government would abandon north China to Japanese control. Indeed, this was one of the factors that led Zhou to move his bank's headquarters from Tianjin to Shanghai.

Zhou found himself thrust into the midst of this issue. In the fall of 1935, when Chiang Kai-shek was attempting to avoid war with the Japanese in order to eliminate the Chinese Communists, he decided to send a high-profile delegation to Japan to discuss economic cooperation. The delegation was headed by Wu Dingchang and included both Zhou Zuomin and fellow banker K.P. Chen. While in Japan the delegation agreed to the organization of the Sino-Japanese Trade Assistance Association (ZhongRi maoyi xiehui) which was to facilitate economic

---

9. Parks M. Coble, *The Shanghai Capitalists*, 194.
10. Ibid., 217.
11. Ibid., 225.
12. Ibid., 228–229.

cooperation. Zhou thus found himself very publicly supporting Chiang Kai-shek's appeasement policy.[13]

Japanese militarists in north China were seeking to detach the area from Nanjing. Still eager to avoid war, Chiang authorized the creation of the Hebei-Chahar Political Council to be chaired by General Song Zheyuan, commander of Chinese forces in the Beiping area. The council was to be a compromise between Japanese demands for complete separation and Chinese desire to retain sovereignty over the area. In December 1935 Zhou was appointed as one of the sixteen members of this council which became the target of student demonstrations.[14] Zhou apparently tried to avoid this very tense environment, departing for Shanghai so as to avoid participating in the council sessions.[15] Still, when the Sino-Japanese War finally erupted in July 1937, Zhou had developed a reputation not only as a successful banker but as a public figure who could work with the Japanese.

WAR WITH JAPAN

The war posed a major crisis for Chinese bankers. Despite at times heroic resistance by Chinese forces, the Japanese were able to capture China's key coastal cities in the early months of the war, forcing Chiang to abandon Nanjing in December 1937 and Wuhan in October 1938. The Nationalist government along with the headquarters of government banks officially relocated to Chongqing. The war between China and Japan was an undeclared war before December 1941, and many of the foreign concessions remained neutral territory. In Shanghai for instance, the International Settlement, home to virtually all of the modern banks, was an "isolated island" from the time of the Chinese retreat until Pearl Harbor when the Japanese finally occupied the area. Banks such as the Jincheng Bank found that their branches were operating under various regimes and currencies.

13. Parks M. Coble, *Facing Japan: Chinese Politics and Japanese Imperialism, 1931–1937* (Cambridge: Harvard East Asian Monograph Series, 1991), 262.

14. Shimada Toshihiko, "Designs on North China, 1933–1937," in James W. Morley, ed., *The China Quagmire: Japan's Expansion on the Asian Continent, 1933–1941* (New York: Columbia University Press, 1983), 155–157.

15. Ji Xiaocun, Yang Guzhi, "Zhou Zuomin yu jincheng yinhang" (Zhou Zuomin and the Jingcheng Bank), *Tianjin wenshi ziliao xuanji* 13 (1981): 131–132; Marjorie Dryburgh, *North China and Japanese Expansion, 1933–1937: Regional Power and the National Interest* (Richmond, Surrey: Curzon, 2000), 85–88.

In north China the Japanese North China Army sponsored a pro-Japanese regime in Beijing under Wang Kemin. This government established the China Reserve Bank (Zhongguo lianhe zhunbei yinhang) in March 1938. In June 1938 the Wang Kemin regime mandated that everyone in its jurisdiction exchange the old fabi notes of the Chiang regime for the new China Reserve Bank notes. In fact, because the bank issued excessive amounts of currency, few wanted these notes. Often they required a 30 percent discount when exchanged in Tianjin.[16] Nationalist authorities forbade any use of the China Reserve currency, placing Chinese banks squarely in the "crossfire" in the north.[17] Japanese officials were much slower to support a new currency in central China, doing so only after the establishment of the Wang Jingwei government in Nanjing in 1940. The Central Reserve Bank (Zhongyang chubei yinhang) was headed by Zhou Fohai and issued its version of fabi notes. Since notes from the Chiang Kai-shek government circulated widely even in occupied areas and in the foreign concessions in Shanghai, bankers found themselves in a three-way currency war. Even the Japanese found fabi useful because the Chiang government maintained the convertibility of its currency, although some restrictions were put in place in March 1938. The Japanese actually exchanged fabi which they collected for American dollars or British pounds with the foreign banks in Shanghai.[18]

Eventually the Chongqing government began to print currency to cover its massive deficit spending, sending the value of fabi tumbling downward. The exchange value of the Chinese yuan fell from $0.29 in July 1937 to only $0.06 in December 1940. By the time of the outbreak of the

---

16. Nakamura Takafusa, "The Yen Bloc, 1931–1941," in Peter Duus, Ramon H. Myers, and Mark R. Peattie, eds., *The Japanese Wartime Empire, 1931–1945* (Princeton: Princeton University Press, 1996), 171–179, 190; Lincoln Li, *The Japanese Army in North China: Problems of Political and Economic Control* (Tokyo: Oxford University Press, 1975), 138–145; Parks M. Coble, "Chinese Bankers in the Crossfire, 1937–1945," in Cindy Yik-Yi Chu and Ricardo K.S. Mak, eds., *China Reconstructs* (Lanham: University Press of America, 2003), 164–165.

17. Chongqing shi dang'an guan, Chongqing shi renmin yinhang jinrong yanjiu, ed., *Silian zhongchu shiliao* (Materials on the history of the Joint Four Banks General Office) (Beijing: Dang'an chubanshe, 1993), v. 1, 410–411.

18. Shou Jinwen, *Zhanshi Zhongguo de yinhang ye* (The banking industry of wartime China; Chongqing: n. pub., 1944), 75–77; Yao Shengxiang, "Wangwei Zhongyang chubei yinhang shimo" (The puppet Wang government's Central Reserve Bank from beginning to end), *Jiangsu wenshi ziliao xuanji* 29 (1989): 240; Hu Xuantong, "Wosuo zhidao de Wang Jingwei Zhongyang chubei yinhang" (The Wang Jingwei puppet Central Reserve Bank that I knew), *Shanghai wenshi ziliao xuanji*, no. 33 (1980): 155; D.K. Lieu, "The Sino-Japanese Currency War," *Pacific Affairs* 12. 4 (December 1939): 419–420; Nakamura Takafusa, "The Yen Bloc," 178–181.

Pacific War in December 1941, the notes of the Central Reserve Bank had largely replaced fabi in north China. The Japanese had won the first round of the currency war.[19] The going was tougher in central China where the currency of the Wang Jingwei bank was not popular. Only after the attack on Pearl Harbor when the Japanese quickly occupied the International Settlement in Shanghai and the British colony in Hong Kong did Nanjing prevail. The Wang government decreed that after July 1, 1942, the old fabi would no longer be considered legal tender in the lower Yangzi area. All notes had to be exchanged with those of the Central Reserve Bank. Nanjing further decreed that the ratio of exchange would be 2:1 in favor of the Central Reserve notes, even though the two currencies had been close to par. In effect, those holding the old notes lost half of their value.[20]

THE JINCHENG BANK AT WAR

The war posed particular problems for the Jincheng Bank. Over half of its branches were in north China where Japanese economic control became strongest. Its headquarters were in "island Shanghai," which remained a fabi zone, while other branches in the lower Yangzi were in areas that fell under Japanese control. Above all, the war was destructive not just to property but to employees. The bank lost three personnel in a bombing near its headquarters in Shanghai on August 14, 1937. All were killed when a Chinese pilot aiming at a Japanese ship in the Huangpu River misjudged and dropped the bomb near the Great World Emporium.[21]

As the fighting intensified, the bank began closing many branches and consolidating them in safer locations. Banks in such cities as Shijiazhuang and Baoding were consolidated in the Beiping office. Many lower Yangzi banks in cities such as Nantong, Suzhou, and Changshu were consolidated in Shanghai, and mid-Yangzi banks were moved to

---

19. Nakamura Takafusa, "The Yen Bloc," 181; Arthur N. Young, *China and the Helping Hand, 1937–1945* (Cambridge: Harvard University Press, 1963), 158; Robert W. Barnett, *Economic Shanghai: Hostage to Politics, 1937–1941* (New York: Institute of Pacific Relations, 1941), 121–125, 133–135.

20. Wang Zhixian, "Shanghai gudao de huobi zhan" (The currency war in solitary island Shanghai), *Shanghai difan shi ziliao* (Materials on the history of Shanghai), v. 1 (1982), 167–169; Shou Jinhua, *Zhanshi Zhongguo de yinhang ye*, 78–79; Arthur N. Young, *China's Wartime Finance and Inflation* (Cambridge: Harvard University Press, 1965), 180; Wang Ke-wen, "Collaborators and Capitalists: The Politics of 'Material Control' in Wartime Shanghai," *Chinese Studies in History* 26.1 (Fall 1992): 47; Eleanor Hinder, *Life and Labour in Shanghai* (New York: International Secretariat, Institute of Pacific Relations, 1944), 46.

21. JYSL, 560–561.

Wuhan and then to Chongqing. In September 1937, when the fighting had escalated in both north and central China, Zhou directed the manager of the Shanghai bank, Wu Yunzhai, to try to coordinate the business of the three major branches in Shanghai, Beiping, and Tianjin. Operating in the midst of a major war was not an easy task, however.[22]

But what of Zhou himself? Zhou was actually in Nanjing for talks with government officials when the fighting erupted in Shanghai in August 1937. Unable to take the train back to Shanghai because of the fighting, Zhou moved inland to Wuhan then took a plane to Hong Kong. Although he made a quick trip back to Shanghai, he eventually settled in the British colony, much as he would do again in 1948. Zhou chose not to retreat with the Nationalist government to Wuhan and to Chongqing. According to a 1960 account by a former associate, Zhou was said to be pessimistic about the outcome of the conflict, and assumed that Chiang Kai-shek would capitulate at some point. By locating in Hong Kong, Zhou could manage the Jincheng enterprises by proxy, ensure his personal security, and gain the freedom to buy and sell currencies.[23]

In a strategy followed by a number of entrepreneurs during the war against Japan, Zhou attempted to spread his risks, operating in occupied and unoccupied China. The hope was to guarantee that no matter what the outcome of the war, the enterprise would survive.[24] For his bank branches in Beijing (as Beiping was renamed by the Wang Kemin regime), Tianjin, and Shanghai, he appointed individuals who had studied in Japan and could work with the Japanese authorities. Most would work with the client regimes established by the Japanese. The Tianjin branch manager, Wang Yiling, served as the head of the Tianjin Bankers Association under the Japanese. The Shanghai manager, Wu Yunzhai, served on the standing committee of the Commerce Control Commission of the Wang Jingwei government. Yang Jicheng, branch manager in Beijing during the war, assisted Wang Shijing, head of Wang Kemin's bank, in organizing the institution. A former manager of the Dalian branch of the Jincheng Bank accepted a position as assistant director of Wang Jingwei's bank.[25]

---

22. JYSL, 560–561; Xu Guomao, Shao Yidu, "Jincheng yinhang jianshe" (A brief history of the Jincheng Bank), *Zhonghua wenshi ziliao wenku*, v. 14, 115.

23. JYSL, 568, 572; Xu Guomao, "Zhou Zuomin," 156; Liu Xuheng, "Zhou Zuomin yu Jincheng yinhang" (Zhou Zuomin and the Jincheng Bank), in Xu Dixin, ed., *Zhongguo qiye jia liezhuan*, v. 3, 105.

24. For examples of this strategy see Parks M. Coble, *Chinese Capitalists in Japan's New Order: The Occupied Lower Yangzi, 1937–1945* (Berkeley: University of California Press, 2003), passim.

25. Ji Xiaocun, Yang Guzhi, "Zhou Zuomin," 129; Zhu Jijia [pseudonymn of Jin Xiong-

While many of his subordinates worked with the Japanese, Zhou avoided most contact. Operating from his base in Hong Kong, he did sometimes travel to Shanghai and on one occasion to Singapore, but before Pearl Harbor he avoided occupied areas. At the same time, he tried to keep up smooth relations with officials of "Free China" under the Nationalists in the interior. Again, this was an approach used by many of the prominent Chinese capitalists, such as the famous Rong brothers (as discussed by Kai Yiu Chan in chapter 4 of this volume). Zhou's major contacts in Chongqing were with officials loosely associated with the Political Study Clique. Key leaders of this group, Huang Fu and Yang Yongtai, were already deceased by this point, so Zhang Qun emerged as the dominant figure. Zhang was a key advisor to Chiang Kai-shek and served in a number of important positions during the war, including vice-president of the Executive Yuan and secretary general of the Supreme National Defense Council.[26]

Zhou Zuomin seems to have performed financial services for leaders of this group from his base in Hong Kong. Zhou was said to have invested funds in Hong Kong for Zhang Qun, for instance. Chang Kia-ngau, also considered a major leader of the Political Study group, apparently received US$20,000 from Zhou when he stopped in Hong Kong on his way to the United States. Other contacts included Wu Dingchang, Xu Xinliu, and Jiang Bocheng. Zhou had sufficient contacts in Chongqing that he was able to operate a branch of the Jincheng Bank in the city. Zhou thus operated in all three major currency zones in wartime China.[27]

Zhou also established ties with a couple of the key business leaders in Free China. Fan Xudong was undoubtedly China's major chemical manufacturer in the period before the war, operating major factories in north China, as well as the Nanjing area. All of these plants were either destroyed or confiscated by the Japanese, but Fan attempted to restart enterprises in the interior. He had a long-term relationship with Zhou dating back to student days in Japan, and he had long relied on the Jincheng Bank for business loans. Fan actually had only limited success in rebuilding his business in the interior, but he continued to have contacts with Zhou and the bank. Lu Zuofu of the Minsheng enterprises was one of the major businessmen in the interior. Prior to the outbreak of the war Lu had already turned to the Jincheng Bank for business loans.

bai], *Wang zhengquan de kaichang yu shouchang* (The beginning and end of the Wang regime) (Hong Kong: Chunqiu zazhi, 1959), v. 2, 133.

26. Boorman, ed., *Biographical Dictionary*, v. 1, 50.

27. JYSL, 571, 610, 625–626.

He continued to work with the bank and would even join the board of directors after the war.[28]

Zhou's activities during the war reveal much about his basic values. He clearly placed the success of his enterprise, the Jincheng Bank, above all else. He was willing to operate in both occupied and Free China, although allowing associates to handle most of the operations with the Japanese. Yet, shrewdly he kept contacts open with officials in Chongqing. Although the war severely limited some activities of the bank and certainly led to great instability, it did provide some new opportunities. The Jincheng Bank seems to have used its wide access to different portions of China to become involved in speculation and hoarding of a number of commodities, including flour, cotton, and cloth. War did open new avenues of profit.[29]

Zhou also made a few moves to get some of his investments out of the China market. As the war dragged on, the prospects of China's economic growth looked bleak. He sent two of his managers, Wu Yunzhai and Xu Guomao, to Manila in 1940 to establish an investment company. That enterprise was derailed by the Japanese occupation of the American colony after Pearl Harbor.[30]

Although Zhou focused on his enterprises during the months after the Marco Polo Bridge Incident of 1937, he was too prominent an individual to remain completely out of the public eye. He found himself thrust into the role of mediator between Tokyo and Chongqing. Not long after the fall of Nanjing, on January 16, 1938, Japanese Prime Minister Konoe issued a statement that Tokyo would have no further dealings with Chiang Kai-shek. Nonetheless, despite Japan's great military success in the war, the conflict became a great quagmire for the Japanese. By the time of the formation of the Second Konoe cabinet in which Matsuoka Yosuke served as foreign minister, Tokyo had decided to open negotiations with Chongqing. Japan's position was quite strong at this point because of the success of its Axis allies in Europe. The Japanese began to look at Qian Yongming (then chair of board of the Bank of Communications) and Zhou Zuomin as possible intermediaries. Zhou agreed to assist in the negotiations. In October 1940 in Hong Kong, Zhou, Japanese officials from the South Manchurian Railway, an advisor to the Shanghai municipal government, and the Japanese consul general in Shanghai met,

---

28. Xu Guomao, "Zhou Zuomin he Jincheng yinhang" (Zhou Zuomin and the Jincheng Bank), in [Shanghai] *Wenshi ziliao xuanji* 23 (1979): 139–145.

29. JYSL, 581–583, 589–590.

30. Ibid., 579, 585–586.

along with Qian Yongming to discuss the negotiations. Qian and Zhou forwarded a report on the negotiations to Chiang Kai-shek's government, using the manager of the Jincheng Bank in Chongqing. Chiang in fact sent a representative to Hong Kong to undertake the negotiations. Nothing came of these as the two sides were far apart and some in Tokyo concluded that Chiang was simply maneuvering to prevent them from recognizing the new Wang Jingwei government. But as Usui Katsumi pointed out, "Any possibility of success was due to the fact that Ch'ien Yung-ming [Qian Yongming] and Chou Tso-min [Zhou Zuomin] were important members of the Chekiang [Zhejiang] financial clique and thus enjoyed in no small degree the right to speak to Chiang Kai-shek directly."[31]

AFTER PEARL HARBOR

Zhou's strategy had been based on the assumption that Hong Kong and the International Settlement (and French Concession) in Shanghai would remain neutral territory. That approach was shattered in December 1941 when Japan attacked the United States and Britain and their possessions in Asia. Both Shanghai and Hong Kong quickly fell, and Zhou found himself in occupied territory. Several key bankers had been in Hong Kong when the Pacific War erupted, including Song Hanzhang and Bei Zuyi. According to Xu Guomao, Chongqing sent an airplane to rescue those who wanted to escape, but Zhou was scheduled for the second flight. That never materialized because the British position collapsed so quickly. The Japanese placed Zhou and other prominent individuals under house arrest in the Hong Kong Hotel in Kowloon for nearly three months. Finally, Zhou was flown back to Shanghai by the Japanese accompanied by Li Sihao, Lin Kanghou, and Tang Shoumin.[32]

The Japanese pressed key financial officials to join agencies and institutions of the new Wang Jingwei government in Nanjing. Figures such as Zhou would bring credibility to these institutions and to the currency of Wang's bank. Zhou in fact met with Wang, Chen Gongbo, and Zhou Fohai but apparently refused to participate in the new government.

---

31. Usui Katsumi, "The Politics of War, 1937–1941," in Morley, ed., *The China Quagmire*, 416–422.

32. Xu Guomao, "Zhou Zuomin," 138; JYSL, 623–624; Xu Guomao, "Xianggang tuoxian ji" (A record of escaping danger in Hong Kong), *Shanghai wenshi ziliao xuanji* 63 (1989): 68–69.

Meanwhile, Zhou's friends in Chongqing tried to persuade Zhou to leave the occupied area and move to Chongqing, or at least Kunming. Bankers Qian Yongming and He Lian sent word in the winter of 1943 that such a move was possible. An intermediary, Xu Zuoliang, traveled between the occupied areas and Free China, and carried the messages. Although Zhou gave some indication that he was contemplating a move, he in fact stayed in occupied Shanghai.[33]

Although Zhou Zuomin never formally participated in the Wang regime, he maintained close ties with Zhou Fohai. His diary mentions numerous meetings with Fohai and other Nanjing officials, especially during the last weeks of the war. Zhou Zuomin appeared a conduit for communications between Fohai and Chongqing authorities, mostly using Xu Caichen, a representative of Du Yuesheng and the Green Gang. Xu transmitted telegrams between Shanghai and Chongqing, sometimes from a secret transmitter in Zuomin's home. Supposedly on August 12, 1945, Xu told Zhou Zuomin that Chongqing wished Zhou Fohai to keep order in Shanghai until the arrival of Allied Forces. Fohai also stated that he had an extensive conversation with Dai Li, head of Chiang Kai-shek's special forces, on September 10, 1945. Dai apparently indicated that the two Zhou's were doing a satisfactory job of keeping order in Shanghai.[34]

RETRIBUTION

The key worry for Zhou Zuomin and the many other businessmen who had remained in coastal China was that they would be labeled *hanjian* (traitors) and face retribution. Most, like Zhou, had assumed they were safe in neutral territory in December 1941, but ended up in Japanese-held areas. In the aftermath of the Japanese surrender many were threatened with prison terms and "fleeced" to prevent arrest. The retaking of the coastal areas by the Nationalist forces turned into a disaster of major proportions. Looting and pillaging were usually short-lived, but the extortion racket continued for some time. That plus the accelerating hyperinflation prevented any real recovery from the war.

---

33. Ji Xiaocun, Yang Guzhi, "Zhou Zuomin," 129–130; JYSL, 626.
34. JYSL, 626–628; Xu Guomao, "Zhou Zuomin," 146–147; Zhu Zijia, *Wang zhengquan*, v. 2, 135; Gu Guanlin, "Zhou Zuomin," in Xu Yu et al., eds., *Zhongguo shi yinhang jia* (Ten Chinese Bankers) (Shanghai: Shanghai renmin chuban she, 1997), 300–305; Brian G. Martin, "Collaboration Within Collaboration: Zhou Fohai's Relations with the Chongqing Government, 1942–1945," *Twentieth-Century China* 34.2 (April 2009): 84–85.

Zhou Zuomin, however, was a skilled political player, and he flew to Chongqing in August 1945 where he met with his political friends Zhang Qun, Chang Kia-ngau, and Qian Yongming. The latter returned with him to Shanghai. Zhou's contacts were primarily with the Political Study Group, but others were not so friendly. Most officials from the Ministry of Finance were aloof.[35] As with other businessmen who had remained in the occupied area, Zhou found himself vulnerable to demands from those claiming to represent the special services of the Chongqing government. Whether these represented legitimate government agencies or not, most of their actions were essentially blackmail. In November 1945, four agents appeared at Zhou's residence to investigate charges of collaboration with the Japanese. They apparently demanded 20,000 ounces of silver to drop charges. Zhou used his connection with Zhang Qun who appealed directly to Chiang Kai-shek to have the charges cleared. Later, individuals said to represent Sun Ke, then head of the Nationalist government's Legislative Yuan, came to "investigate" Zhou.[36]

Zhou could argue that he had rejected overtures from the Wang Jingwei government and, in fact, only been in the occupied area because he was unable to escape from Hong Kong in time. Other personnel of the Jincheng Bank had been operating in the occupied zone well before Pearl Harbor and under the overall management of Zhou. Wang Yiling, the Tianjin bank manager was arrested three times; Yang Jicheng, the Beijing manager, once. The most serious case was Wu Yunzhai, manager of the Shanghai branch, who also worked with the Wang Jingwei officials. Zhou provided money for bribes to help Wu, and he asked fellow banker Xu Xinliu to appeal to T.V. Soong. Because of Zhou's efforts, Wu's original sentence for collaboration which was two years and six months was reduced to one year and three months.[37]

Virtually everyone who worked with the Wang Jingwei government claimed to have secretly been working with Chongqing. Zhou Fohai, who had met frequently with Zhou Zuomin in the last part of the war, claimed to have been dealing directly with Dai Li, head of special services for Chiang. When Dai died in a plane crash on March 17, 1946, Fohai lost his key witness. Zhou Zuomin was much more fortunate. He had not taken

35. Xu Guomao, "Zhou Zuomin," 156–157; Liu Xuheng, "Zhou Zuomin yu Jincheng yinhang" (Zhou Zuomin and the Jincheng Bank), in Xu Dixin, ed., Xie Mu, assistant editor, *Zhongguo qiye jia liezhuan* (Biographies of Chinese entrepreneurs) (Beijing: Jingji ribao chuban she, 1988), v. 3, 107–108.

36. Xu Guomao, "Zhou Zuomin," 157–161; Liu Xuheng, "Zhou Zuomin," 108.

37. Ibid.; Liu Xuheng, "Zhou Zuomin," 108–109.

a public position in the Wang government, and he had many influential friends in the Chiang camp. Ultimately, Zhou concluded that only the blessing of Chiang Kai-shek himself could lift any cloud of collaborator from him. With the effort of Zhang Qun and Wu Dingchang, Zhou was able to meet personally with Chiang in Chongqing on January 12, 1946. Although they met to discuss the economic situation in Shanghai, the meeting created the impression that Zhou had not been a collaborator during the war.[38] When the collaboration issue was firmly settled in October 1946, Zhou invited several of his political friends to a party at the Jincheng Bank in Shanghai. Wu Dingchang, Zhang Qun, and Qian Yongming were among the guests.[39]

In many respects Zhou was lucky, but he was also shrewd enough to have evaded Japanese pressure. One of his fellow passengers on the Japanese airplane back to Shanghai from Hong Kong in 1942 was Tang Shoumin. Tang had accepted a post on the Wang Jingwei government's Commerce Control Commission. Zhou had been pressed to join but apparently declined and recommended Tang. After the war, Tang was imprisoned and continued to blame Zhou for his fate. In an interview in 1960 he leveled many charges at Zhou, claiming he met frequently with both Zhou Fohai and the notorious Japanese spymaster Doihara Kenji.[40]

THE JINCHENG BANK IN THE CIVIL WAR ERA

For all his attention to his personal fate, Zhou was equally concerned about his enterprise. The Jincheng Bank faced grave challenges in the aftermath of war. One immediate difficulty was disposing of the banknotes of the Wang Kemin and Wang Jingwei governments. Zhou worked with Chang Kia-ngau's brother, Zhang Wenxiong, on this issue.[41] But the real challenge would be the hyperinflation that ravaged China following the end of World War II.

Chiang Kai-shek turned to his son, Chiang Ching-kuo (Jiang Jingguo) in a last ditch effort to salvage the Nationalist government's financial system. In August 1948, Chiang's government announced a new

38. Xu Guomao, "Zhou Zuomin," 148–150; Ji Xiaocun, Yang Guzhi, "Zhou Zuomin," 132–133; "Zhou Zuomin riji" (The diary of Zhou Zuomin), pt. 1, Dang'an yu lishi (Archives and history), 1 (2000): 10–11. The author thanks Pui-Tak Lee for making this source available.

39. Xu Guomao, "Zhou Zuomin," 148–150; Ji Xiaocun, Yang Guzhi, "Zhou Zuomin," 132–133; "Zhou Zuomin riji," pt. 3, Dang'an yu lishi 21 (1990): 24–25.

40. JYSL, 625; Xu Guomao, "Zhou Zuomin," 156.

41. JYSL, 625.

currency, the gold yuan, would replace the now virtually worthless fabi. The exchange rate was to be one gold yuan in exchange for three million of the old fabi notes. Chiang dispatched his son, Ching-kuo, to Shanghai to force the business community to cough up their gold, silver, and foreign currency for the new gold yuan. Given extraordinary powers, Ching-kuo arrested and terrorized the wealthy elite of the city who were most reluctant to surrender their valuables. Even the most prominent were arrested, including the son of the gangster Du Yuesheng and one of the leaders of the Rong industrial family. As Pui-Tak Lee notes in chapter 3 of this volume, K.P. Chen became disillusioned with the Nationalists and distanced himself from the government. Many businessmen, including Zhou Zuomin, fled. Zhou first entered a hospital to avoid arrest, and then slipped out of Shanghai for Hong Kong. Once again Zhou chose the safety of the British colony. The gold yuan, meanwhile, quickly became worthless.[42]

From Hong Kong Zhou watched as the Nationalist position on the mainland collapsed. Always one to hedge his political bets, Zhou had maintained some contacts with Communists over the years. During the war of resistance period, he apparently provided some funds to Pan Hannian and the Chinese Communist Party (CCP) underground. He resumed this support in Hong Kong. Zhou also met with Li Jishen, the militarist from southeast China who had joined with Feng Yuxiang in forming a Revolutionary Committee of Nationalists that began working with the CCP. Li served as a liaison between many in Hong Kong and Communist authorities. Li left Hong Kong at the end of 1948 for Communist areas. He continued to correspond with Zhou and would later urge him to return to China from Hong Kong. Communist authorities considered Zhou one of the most vulnerable of Chinese bankers to the CCP's United Front strategy, in part because of his earlier clash with Chiang Ching-kuo.[43]

Looking at Zhou's career during the period before 1949, we can see that his key concern was in developing the Jincheng Bank and finding ways to allow it to survive in rapidly changing and very unfavorable business conditions. Although he had worked closely with T.V. Soong and H.H. Kung during the 1930s and maintained close ties with the Political Study

---

42. Lloyd E. Eastman, *Seeds of Destruction: Nationalist China in War and Revolution, 1937-1949* (Stanford: Stanford University Press, 1984), 185–193; Xu Guomao, "Zhou Zuomin," 170; Liu Xuheng, "Zhou Zuomin," 109.

43. Liu Xuheng, "Zhou Zuomin," 109; Gu Ganlin, "Zhou Zuomin," 310–311. On Li Jishen's role see Carsun Chang, *The Third Force in China* (New York: Bookman Associates, 1952), 261–265; Guomin zhengfu wenguan chu, renshi dengji juan, no. 499, "Zhou Zuomin." The author thanks Man Bun Kwan for making the latter source available.

Clique, Zhou had kept his distance from the Nationalist government. His reluctance to travel to Chongqing during the war indicates a certain distrust of the Chiang government and perhaps a lack of faith in its ability to win the war. Nonetheless, Zhou's record suggests that he would try to find some way to allow for the survival of the Jincheng Bank under the new Communist government. But could that happen?

THE COMMUNIST REVOLUTION AND CHINESE BANKING

When the People's Republic of China was proclaimed in October 1949, China's financial system was in shambles. Hyperinflation had rendered the old fabi virtually worthless. Foreign currency and gold circulated widely in place of the banknotes of the old regime. One of the first acts of the new government was to attempt to stabilize the currency and gain control over the financial situation. As Ezra Vogel noted in his classic study of the Communist takeover of Canton, "The Communists aimed to get control over banks earlier than most parts of the economy because of their conviction that banks played a critical role in controlling the economy."[44] Beijing sought to restrict the operations of private banks and increase the role of the new People's Bank of China, which would have branches throughout the country.

Even without the new initiatives of the Communist government, the economic environment changed drastically for Chinese private bankers. Nationalist forces blocked several eastern ports, including Shanghai, which has been the center for China's international trade. In November 1950, with the eruption of the Korean War, American forces joined the boycott that virtually sealed China's coastal cities from world trade. The following month, the United States froze all Chinese assets, completely stopping commercial interactions between the two nations. For financial institutions, such as the Jincheng Bank, which had developed in many of the old treaty ports, the new economic isolation radically changed business prospects.

The old private banks would have little role in the new China, although this was not entirely clear for some months. In August 1950,

---

44. Ezra Vogel, *Canton Under Communism: Programs and Politics in a Provincial Capital, 1949–1968* (New York: Harper Torchbooks, 1971), 81. See also James Z. Gao, *The Communist Takeover of Hangzhou: The Transformation of City and Cadre, 1949–1954* (Honolulu: University of Hawaii Press, 2004), 92–96.

the Beijing government convened the All-China Financial Institutions' Conference (Quanguo jinrong ye lianxi huiyi) in the capital city to restructure the financial system. The government wanted the People's Bank to assert control over all of the financial institutions of China. Over the next two years the banks began to be reorganized first into joint public-private entities and then state-owned organizations. In the case of the Jincheng Bank, it would first be merged in September 1951 with others into the Five Northern Banks, a joint public-private venture. Finally in December 1952, sixty banks, native banks, and trust companies were merged into one government entity.[45]

After the national financial conference, the People's Bank pressed the private banks to alter their lending policies. Loans were to be made to small industrial and commercial firms, usually through government-controlled federations of commerce. Although these changes in the structure of private banks were significant, for the first months of the new government, it still appeared that private banking and business would have some place in the new China. But in early 1952 Beijing launched the Three Anti and Five Anti campaigns, which Kenneth Lieberthal labeled "a second revolution." For most citizens of Tianjin, he noted, "the revolution came not in 1949, but in early 1952 when the ferocious Three Anti (*sanfan*) and Five Anti (*wufan*) campaigns washed over the city."[46] By the end of 1952, independent private capitalism had essentially been eliminated in China.

ZHOU RETURNS

Zhou Zuomin remained in Hong Kong during the first months of new China, undecided about his personal future. In July 1949, Zhou had written to Jincheng Bank's board of directors, chaired by Qian Yongming, stating that he wished to retire as general manager, citing his more than thirty years of service. He recommended that Xu Guomao, a longtime manager, take over. When Xu began serving as active general manager in November 1949, he frequently communicated with Zhou about the bank's situation. He continually pressed Zhou to return to the mainland and resume his leadership of the bank. In October 1949, the director of the Hankou branch of the Jincheng Bank had made a special trip to

---

45. Kenneth G. Lieberthal, *Revolution and Tradition in Tienstin, 1949–1952* (Stanford: Stanford University Press, 1980), 94; JYSL, 912–913.

46. Lieberthal, *Revolution and Tradition*, 125.

Hong Kong to explain the situation in China and urge Zhou to come back. Officials in the Beijing government also urged him to return. Zhou delayed for a time claiming ill health.[47] At the same time many friends, especially other financiers who had relocated in Hong Kong, urged Zhou to remain there. His close political friend Zhang Qun had gone to Taiwan and also pressed Zhou to avoid the People's Republic.[48]

Efforts by Beijing to persuade Zhou to return were not unique. Indeed, the new government attempted to lure many capitalists and professionals back to help build "new China." In retrospect, it seems almost perverse that such an effort was made when, as Zhou would discover, there would be little place for their talents in the new society. Many who returned from overseas with education and training would find themselves in great difficulty during the anti-rightist movement of the late-1950s. Virtually all would suffer during the Cultural Revolution. Yet none of this was apparent at the time of the revolution. Most involved probably assumed that the "New Democracy" phase would last for some time. Few anticipated the Korean War and its impact on the domestic situation in China. In 1949, Beijing particularly wanted the support of the private bankers not simply for their talents and credibility. As work elsewhere in this volume by Pui-Tak Lee and Elisabeth Köll demonstrates, banking assets were fluid. Many banks had branches in Hong Kong and overseas. Beijing wanted to ensure that assets would come under its control rather than shift to Taiwan. The government therefore made an all-out effort to lure Zhou Zuomin back.

Although undecided, Zhou wanted to keep his options open. He had a long history of adjusting to new political circumstances. From Hong Kong he realized that north China was short of many commodities, including medicine. He directed the Jincheng Bank's subsidiary corporation, the Heng Feng Company, to rent a ship and transport medicine and hardware equipment for sale in Tianjin.[49] In the meantime the new Communist government created a very different business environment. Private banks were encouraged to make loans that would increase industrial production and contribute to the new People's Republic. In July 1950 the Jincheng Bank pledged to help improve industrial production, particularly in chemicals, textiles, and shipping. The bank had earlier relationships with some capitalists such as the late Fan Xudong, and his Yongli chemical enterprises, as well as

---

47. JYSL, 931–932, 950.
48. Xu Guomao, "Zhou Zuomin," 170.
49. Gu Guanlin, "Zhou Zuomin," 311.

Lu Zuofu, the founder of Minsheng Shipping. The bank also invited government participation and assistance.[50]

The Jincheng Bank itself was not faring well in new China. Many of its investments were in businesses that had failed or were operating at partial capacity. At the same time the bank had twenty-three branches and over one thousand employees. Expenses were high. At the time of the spring festival in 1950, the bank had great difficulties, and Xu Guomao admitted in an April 1950 report that Jincheng was facing "unprecedented difficulties."[51] The future of the bank looked precarious.

The All-China Financial Institutions' Conference in Beijing in August 1950 proved a turning point for Zhou who decided he must attend. Qian Yongming, chair of the board of directors of the bank, decided to step down and urged Zhou, who still served as vice chair of the board, to assume leadership. Since Jincheng and the private banks were not faring well, the government pressured them to restructure and become partners with the government in public-private enterprises. Zhou took a ship from Hong Kong to Tianjin in June 1950. Zhou Enlai dispatched a delegation to greet him, and Li Jishen welcomed him as well. At the time he was considered one of the most important capitalists to return to the People's Republic from outside. Nationalist publications in Taiwan, stung by his defection, revived allegations that he had collaborated with the puppet regimes during the war against Japan.[52]

Beijing pressed Jincheng to join with four other northern banks to form a joint enterprise, the Five Northern Banks. Xu Guomao made a second trip to Hong Kong in April and May of 1950 and met with Zhou as well as representatives of the Lianhe (Joint Reserve) Bank and China and South Sea Bank, about the new plan. Two other banks to be involved were the Continental Bank and the Salt Bank but they did not have key officials in Hong Kong. Xu traveled to Shanghai from Hong Kong to consult with officials of these banks. Some resistance to the new plan continued. Wang Shaoxian of the Salt Bank stated that he could not act without consulting the board of directors.[53] By this point, Xu and Zhou Zuomin had concluded that the only option was to reorganize in

---

50. JYSL, 940.

51. Zhang Xuyue, *Shanghai siying jinrong ye yanjiu (1949–1952)* (Research on the Shanghai private financial industry, 1949–1952) (Shanghai: Fudan daxue chuban she, 2006), 143–144.

52. Gu Guanlin, "Zhou Zuomin," 312; Zhan Xiaomou, Hu Jingquan, "Jincheng yinhang Beijing fenfang shiliao pianduan" (A selection of historical materials on the Beijing branch of the Jincheng Bank), *Wenshi ziliao xuanji* 17 (1983): 220; Guomin zhengfu wenguan chu, no. 499.

53. JYSL, 952.

a joint public-private venture. Business losses worsened monthly and restructuring offered a possible way for the bank to survive.[54]

On August 14, 1950, Zhou received a telegram from the manager of the new People's Bank of China outlining the conditions for restructuring. Some stock in the Jincheng Bank belonged to "the enemy," and would be confiscated by the People's government in accordance with the law. This would be given to the government as its holdings in the bank. Accordingly the government would appoint two representatives to the board of directors. These would be Chen Mu and Ceng Ling of the People's Bank. In addition the People's Bank would now develop close ties with the various branches of the Jincheng Bank and assist it with capital and business development.[55] The reorganized board of directors met in Beijing on that day, and Zhou, having returned, presided. In addition to the two public representatives on the board, there were seven private representatives. The board was to meet in Beijing every three months, although the question of moving the bank's headquarters from Shanghai was left unresolved.[56]

After his return to Beijing, Zhou Zuomin devoted much of his time to the consolidation of the Five Northern Banks. He realized that this was not only necessary under the new regime but also emphasized the historic cooperation that these banks had forged in the 1920s. Zhou seemed convinced that the new joint venture, with government participation, would have a meaningful role in the new society. Before leaving Hong Kong he had talked with several other bankers there, including Chang Kia-ngau, Qian Yongming, K.P. Chen, and Li Ming. Even though the range of banking opportunities would be limited, there would still be a role in financing industrial development, he assumed.[57]

A new board of directors was established, with each of the five banks appointing two members. Zhou represented the Jincheng Bank along with Ceng Ling, the government appointee on the Jincheng board. This body met first in November 1950. It would meet five times, with the final meeting on January 26, 1951. The Jincheng Bank would host the meetings, and Zhou served as chair of the new board. Zhou seems to have thrown himself into the merger effort. His diary records numerous meetings with representatives of the other banks as they negotiated all aspects of this merger.

---

54. JYSL, 953.
55. Ibid.
56. Ibid., 954.
57. Ibid., 964–965.

Perhaps one reason for his enthusiasm is that the Jincheng Bank was clearly the senior partner in the arrangement. The group forged a formula for distribution of any surplus by the new bank. The distribution was to be based on the business assets each brought to the bank based on the business period January to June 1951. Jincheng's share of the pie was 45.28 percent; the China and South Sea Bank, 18.27 percent; the Continental Bank, 16.12 percent; the Lianhe Bank, 11.71 percent; and the Salt Bank, 8.62 percent. Perhaps Zhou saw this more as a takeover of the smaller partners than a merger of equals.[58] After the five banks established a united operation as a joint public-private bank, business conditions did not immediately improve. In June and July of 1951 the bank faced liquidity problems so the People's Bank of China invested 5 million yuan.[59]

The consolidation of the Five Northern Banks was not the only such move underway in the early months of the People's Republic. Sixty major banks and native banks were being merged in five groups. These were originally private banks that had been converted to joint public-private institutions in the same way as had the Jincheng Bank. By mid-1952, it became clear that Beijing planned to combine these five groups into a single banking group under the direct control of the People's Bank. The ultimate goal was actually to consolidate all banking activity under the government and eliminate private banking entirely. It seems in retrospect that Zhou Zuomin had initially assumed that some residual role for the Jincheng Bank would remain. When the government's intention became clear, Zhou continued to assist in the consolidation.

In November 1952, the five groups of formerly private banks agreed to form a common body. Zhou was one of the two signers representing the Five Northern Banks. A new board was established which would have 80 to 120 members. Zhou served as one of the five vice chairs of the board. In Shanghai, new general office was established that was to have complete authority over all of the formerly private banks. The final step occurred in December 1952, when the general office was moved to Beijing in order to facilitate the direction of the People's Bank of China over these institutions. Headquarters of the other major banks, the Bank of China and Bank of Communications, were also relocated to the capital. The new People's Bank of China now exercised complete authority over all banking institutions in China. The role for the old private banks such

---

58. Ibid., 966–990.
59. Zhang Xuyue, *Shanghai siying*, 150–151.

as the Jincheng Bank had come to an end. Most of the personnel of the Jincheng Bank were transferred to the People's Bank of China after some retraining.[60]

Zhou did not disappear from public view. He continued to serve in a variety of functions, including on the board of directors of the Bank of China. Yet his personal involvement in Jincheng Bank ended. While visiting Shanghai on business in 1955, Zhou suddenly became ill and died on May 8 at seventy-two years of age.[61]

CONCLUSION

Looking at the entirety of Zhou Zuomin's career, his dedication to his enterprise is apparent. Operating in one of the most turbulent periods of modern Chinese history, Zhou became skilled at adjusting to new political situations in order to secure the bank. When his original warlord backers failed, Zhou switched to new sources of support. He worked with key players in the Chiang Kai-shek government, including H.H. Kung and T. V. Soong, but particularly cultivated the Political Study Clique with which he had close ties. Zhou did not shy away from controversy, working with Japanese on the eve of the war. When the conflict erupted after July 7, 1937, Zhou managed to operate branches of his bank in north, central, and western China—in three different currency zones. Zhou chose the safety of Hong Kong but found himself in Japanese custody in December 1941. Zhou stayed in the occupied zone for the remainder of the war but tried to avoid public contact with the Japanese. Yet he had frequent dealings with those in the Wang Jingwei regime, especially Zhou Fohai. At war's end, Zhou Zuomin found himself in the hot seat because of his wartime actions. Undeterred, Zhou aggressively worked to eliminate any residual aura of "traitor," meeting with Chiang Kai-shek himself. Only the gold yuan reform and the wave of terror instituted by Chiang Ching-kuo would force him to flee once more to Hong Kong.

When the Communists created their new government in Beijing, Zhou undoubtedly had his misgivings about working within the new China. He attempted to resign his position in the bank; many business friends declined to return to People's China. Yet his institution was in the People's Republic, and it seemed that even reorganized into a joint

---

60. JYSL, 992–1001; Zhang Xiaomou, Hu Jingquan, "Jincheng yinhang," 220–221.
61. Liu Xuheng, "Zhou Zuomin," 109.

public-private enterprise, Jincheng Bank had a future. Zhou returned to the mainland and threw himself into organizing the Five Northern Banks. That consolidation proved only a temporary stage toward the elimination of all independent commercial banks. The Chinese Communist Party and Chairman Mao implemented a revolutionary change so sweeping that even a skilled player such as Zhou Zuomin was rendered helpless.

8 WU YUNCHU AND THE FATE OF THE BOURGEOISIE AND BOURGEOIS LIFESTYLES UNDER COMMUNISM

Karl Gerth

In the first half of the twentieth century, the spread of thousands of new consumer goods, the proliferation of discussions about them, and the reorientation of social life around them contributed to the formation of a distinctive consumer culture in urban China. This new culture included nationalistic and anti-imperialist strains that were often in direct opposition to the actual consumption patterns of Chinese. As the notion of nationality was applied to commodities, products became "Chinese" and "foreign," and commodities themselves defined a nationalistic consumer culture. Consumption thus became a politicized act that called into question—and even sanctioned attacks against—"unpatriotic" consumers who knowingly or unwittingly bought imports. Likewise, this nationalistic consumer culture created heroic patriotic producers such as Wu Yunchu, the manufacturer of a food seasoning powder.

This chapter examines what happened to this nationalistic consumer culture and to its patriotic producers after 1949, when "foreign products" (*yanghuo*), especially those from capitalist countries, were largely removed from the market and the Communists could finally impose nationalistic consumption not only in the usual ways—through tariffs, exchange controls, and outright bans—but also through state-sanctioned mass campaigns. It traces how the Chinese Communist Party (CCP) and its new state promoted hostility toward consumption in general and consumerism in particular and how the criticism of what the official rhetoric called "the tendency to seek pleasure" was linked to the CCP's attack on merchants and industrialists in 1952, paving the way for the formal abolition of the capitalist class four years later. Beyond an analysis of short-term CCP policy goals or Communist ideology, it examines how the campaign against capitalists and consumerism represented the fulfillment of a vision toward commodities, markets, and consumption that had begun in the decades before the Communist Revolution. Despite ideological differences between the Nationalist and Communist regimes, they both established the role of the state as the central arbiter of the meaning of consumption, climaxing in the Three Anti, Five Anti campaign (*sanfan wufan yundong*) of 1951–1952. By examining the case of Wu Yunchu, this chapter demonstrates how, in the course of the campaign, the state destroyed the power, absorbed the wealth, and discredited the lifestyles of capitalists, effectively preparing their final elimination as a class a few years later.

The chapter's examination of the expropriation of Chinese capitalists in the early and mid-1950s focuses on contingencies—the legacies of decades of ruinous international and civil war, fears of inflation, social instability, financial crisis caused by the Korean War, and even rank intimidation—that obviously shaped and sustained the state's ideological objectives. Yet it also argues that without a consideration of those longer-term, deeply embedded objectives, focusing on contingencies inadequately explains the speed, thoroughness, and popular acceptance of the state's takeover of private enterprise and the heightened vilification of the legacies of pre-1949 consumerism. In the Communists' attempt to subordinate all merchants and industrialists and politicize all consumption, particularly consumption deemed excessive, their penetration extended the scope of earlier Nationalist attempts to control the owners of large-scale, modern industries and the consumer class created by such production.[1] Yet, at least at this early stage, the differences between the Nationalists and the Communists were more of degree rather than of kind. As the eminent Chinese economic historian Shih Kuo-heng observed on the eve of the Communist takeover in 1949, "If the [Nationalists win], most of the new industries will be owned and dominated by the government or by officials. If the Communists win, probably all major new industries will eventually be nationalized and put under Party control. In either case there would be not much room for independent industrialists to develop."[2]

---

1. William Kirby has succinctly described this phenomenon: "What distinguished the Communist party-state, and indeed ultimately set it apart from its predecessor, was its attempt to take these trends—political, economic, and military—to the most extreme conclusions." William C. Kirby, "The Nationalist Regime and the Chinese Party-State, 1928–1958," in Merle Goldman and Andrew Gordon, eds., *Historical Perspectives on Contemporary East Asia* (Cambridge: Harvard University Press, 2000), 230.

2. Marion J. Levy and Kuo-heng Shih, *The Rise of the Modern Chinese Business Class: Two Introductory Essays* (New York: International Secretariat Institute of Pacific Relations, 1949), 19.

LOSING OR WINNING?

As I have demonstrated in *China Made* (chapter 8), Wu Yunchu was not just any capitalist; he became a hero to Chinese of all political persuasions. In the Republican era, Wu Yunchu, along with dozens of other manufacturers, was heralded as a model for others to follow, a primer for defending China.[3] Wu was a Chinese-educated scientist and entrepreneur whose flavor-enhancing monosodium glutamate (MSG) powder successfully replaced an "enemy product," the Japanese powder Ajinomoto (or Weizhisu, as Chinese consumers knew it), in the Chinese marketplace. That is, in a time of increasing imperialist domination of the Chinese economy, such "patriotic producers," as they became known, demonstrated that the Chinese could combine commercial activity and anti-imperialist national rejuvenation. Although the reality behind these producers' heroism was, of course, more complicated than the myth might indicate, biographers then and now have included Wu in a roster of Chinese entrepreneurs who successfully defended the nation by producing national products and displacing imports. Among these capitalists, Wu Yunchu was, as one contemporary biographer labeled him, "a shining star in the world of national products."[4]

Wu made his name by manufacturing and establishing his brand of MSG in a very competitive market. According to the nationalistic biographies of Wu Yunchu, his brilliance and patriotism lay in identifying the inexhaustible market potential and nationalistic significance of producing a Chinese alternative to a foreign product sold throughout the world.[5] In 1920, Wu noted the virtual monopoly in the Chinese market

---

3. See "Tianchu wei chang jing" (A brief history of the Heaven's Kitchen Factory), in Guohuo shiye chubanshe, ed., *Zhongguo guohuo shiye xianjin shilüe* (Brief histories of model Chinese national product enterprises) (Shanghai: Guohuo shiye chubanshe, 1934), 221; "Tianchu weijing zhizaochang shi" (A history of Heaven's Kitchen), in Kong Xiangxi, ed., *Gongshang bu guohuo chenlieguan kaimu jinian tekan* (Special commemorative volume of the opening of the Ministry of Industry and Commerce's National Products Museum) (Nanjing: Gongshang bu, 1929); and Liu Taotian, "Huaxue gongyejia Wu Yunchu xiansheng zhuanlüe" (A biography of chemical industrialist Mr. Wu Yunchu), *Jiaoyu yu zhiye* 3 (1935): 207.

4. Guohuo shiye chubanshe, ed., *Zhongguo guohuo*, 221.

5. His primary competitor, Suzuki Pharmaceuticals, remains the world's largest producer of L-monosodium glutamate (MSG) and other amino acid products used in pharmaceuticals, foodstuff, and feed additives. For a chronology of the company, see http://www.ajinomoto.com/about/history/index.html Accessed May 14, 2012. National Industrial Investigation, ed., *China Industrial Handbook: Kiangsu* (Shanghai: Ministry of Industry, Bureau of Foreign Trade, 1935), 589–594; Gao Shi, "Tianzihao xitong chanpin yu waihuo de douzheng" (The struggle between the products of the Heaven Conglomerate and

enjoyed by Ajinomoto, one of the many low-priced Japanese consumer goods that had entered the market during and immediately after the war. The sudden spread of these products in China was conspicuous, their advertisements springing up throughout Chinese cities and expanding the visual dominance of imperialism.

Patriotic producers like Wu took advantage of nascent Chinese nationalism, promoting their products in terms of "national salvation" (*jiuguo*). The managers of his company, Heaven's Kitchen (Tianchu), advertised their product as a "completely Chinese product" (*quan guohuo*). But Chinese capitalists frequently had to navigate between their own interests and their stated commitment to economic nationalist principles. For instance, when the boycott called for by the May Thirtieth movement of 1925 crippled Ajinomoto sales, Heaven's Kitchen took advantage of the situation by widely advertising itself as a "national product" (*guohuo*) and urging compatriots to perform their patriotic duty and consume Chinese products. But as sales skyrocketed and orders poured in from throughout the country and from patriotic Chinese communities overseas,[6] Heaven's Kitchen could not keep up with demand and was forced to purchase additional product from Ajinomoto and sell it under its own brand.[7] Manipulating economic nationalism for private ends helped investors in the company make enormous profits, and not for the last time. The boycotts following the September Eighteenth Incident of 1931 and the Shanghai Incident of 1932 again fueled demand for products from Wu's companies, giving him the resources necessary to branch out into new enterprises, including complementary industries such as his Tianyuan Electrochemical Factory, Tiansheng Ceramics Factory, and the Tianli Nitrogen Plant.[8]

---

foreign products), in Pan Junxiang, ed., *Zhongguo jindai guohuo yundong* (China's Modern National Products Movement) (Beijing: Zhongguo wenshi chubanshe, 1996), 118–121.

6. Ibid., 119.

7. Wang Pilai and Wang Yu, "Dongfang weijing dawang Wu Yunchu" (Wu Yunchu, the king of the East's MSG), in Zhao Yunsheng, ed., *Zhongguo da zibenjia zhuan 5: Gongshang dawang juan* (Biographies of major Chinese capitalists, no. 5: Captains of industry) (Chang-chun: Shidai wenyi chubanshe, 1994), 367.

8. By the mid 1930s, Wu's group of enterprises, consisting of four companies, became known as the Heaven Conglomerate (*Tianzehao*) because each company's name began with the character *tian* (heaven). The Tianyuan Electrochemical Factory manufactured hydro-chloric acid (a fundamental ingredient used to make corn syrup and glucose from corn-starch), caustic soda (used in the manufacture of, among other things, paper, rayon, and photographic film), bleach powder (a standard bleaching agent used to whiten or remove natural colors), and other chloride products. In 1932, Heaven's Kitchen itself was reorga-nized and it opened two more MSG factories and two additional plants to produce starch and fructose. In response to tremendous domestic pressure to manufacture its own con-

In addition to repeating and amplifying this nationalistic rhetoric, Wu contributed directly to China's defense. Following the Shanghai Incident of 1932, Wu briefly attempted to manufacture poisonous gas, but dropped these efforts and instead helped arrange the production of gas masks. Wu also purchased several airplanes in 1933–1934 and donated them to the Nationalist army, an act for which he received considerable positive press at the time.[9] According to historian Parks Coble, Wu also fits into what Coble terms the Nationalists' patriotic capitalist narrative because he moved his enterprises to Free China during the war and restarted production there despite numerous obstacles. The financial setbacks of doing this took a toll, however, and in 1943, after years of struggling to maintain his independence, Wu turned to the Nationalist government's National Resources Commission for capital.[10]

During the Civil War, however, Wu and many other capitalists came to despise the Nationalists. Although the Nationalist government tried to tackle both longstanding and new problems, it remained weak at all levels of government, which fostered corruption and incompetence. It also bungled the takeover from the Japanese. Rather than returning wealth and property to its previous owners, Nationalist troops engaged in looting, reinforcing the negative image of the Nationalist government. Furthermore, despite shortages of consumer goods, industry was slow to resume production, though it did not help matters that in addition to the massively destructive war, the Soviets had dismantled numerous factories in Manchuria. Nationalist leaders also attempted to solve the problem of inflation, and indeed often enacted policies that the CCP later adopted successfully. Although the Nationalists tried freezing wages, setting commodity price ceilings, banning private gold trading and hoarding, and prohibiting capital flight to Hong Kong, these efforts had only a limited effect. The ineffectiveness of the Nationalists' policies destroyed the purchasing power of those earning salaries, namely the urban middle

---

tainers, in 1934–1935 the Heaven Conglomerate launched the Tiansheng Ceramics Factory. Finally, in 1935–1936, the conglomerate formed the Tianli Nitrogen Plant to use the by-products of Tianyuan's operations, such as hydrogen and ammonia.

9. Wang Pilai and Wang Yu, "Dongfang weijing dawang Wu Yunchu," 372; Guohuo shiye chubanshe, ed., *Zhongguo guohuo*, 21. Wu also became a member of several important Nationalist committees that managed China's economy, including the National Economic Council (*Quanguo jingji weiyuanhui*), the National Resources Commission (*Ziyuan weiyuanhui*), and the Ministry of Finance's Planning Committee (*Jihua weiyuanhui*).

10. Parks M. Coble, *Chinese Capitalists in Japan's New Order* (Berkeley: University of California Press, 2003), 181–182; Wang Youping, "Wu Yunchu yu jindai Zhongguo minzu huagong gongye de xingqi" (Wu Yunchu and the Rise of the Chinese domestic chemical industry), *Sichuan shifan daxue xuebao* 1 (2008): 120.

classes, and turned the currency itself into a constant material reminder of Nationalist economic incompetence. Between 1937 and 1948, the Nationalists went from having 1.3 billion yuan in circulation to 24.6 quadrillion (i.e., 24 thousand billion). Between the end of the war in 1945 and the effective end of the Civil War in August 1948, prices rose an average of 30 percent each month. The growing worthlessness of the Nationalist currency redounded on the government, which was more of an abstraction to most Chinese than the currency they held in their hands.[11]

But the policy blunder that most alienated Wu was the Nationalists' last, desperate attempt to gain control over the economy by reforming the national currency, the fabi, which had been greatly inflated during the previous years. The situation had grown even worse in the two months preceding the implementation of the reform, when, for instance, prices in Shanghai shot up tenfold. The urban business environment spiraled out of control as businesses could not change prices quickly enough to keep up with the daily inflation rates, an outcome that Wu had predicted. When the Nationalist government announced its currency reform policy, Wu penned a letter to the Executive Yuan expressing his opposition, charging that this "extreme medicine" would not actually change the economic situation but hurt the standard of living of countless Shanghai factory workers and white-collar employees. And when the Nationalists announced the conversion rate for American dollars to the new currency, he wrote another letter arguing that "patriots are hurt and trusting individuals bitterly disappointed by this policy. May I enquire: how does the government intend to repair the people's loss of faith?"[12] It never did.

To persuade families with foreign currency and precious metals to convert their holdings to gold yuan, the Nationalists tried to generate social pressure for compliance through methods later used by the CCP, such as mobilizing student activists to enforce the new currency and deploying trucks with loudspeakers to the doorsteps of wealthy families to publically urge the inhabitants to comply with the new regulations and convert their assets. They also made an example of a major capitalist, arresting the scion of the founder of Tiger Balm on smuggling charges.

---

11. Lloyd E. Eastman, *Seeds of Destruction: Nationalist China in War and Revolution, 1937-1949* (Stanford University Press, 1984), 178–179.

12. Quoted in Chen Zhengqing, "Tianchu weijing chang de liushiwu nian" (Sixty-five years of the Heaven's Kitchen MSG Factory) in Shanghai shi dang'anguan, ed., *Wu Yunchu qiye shiliao: Tianchu weijing chang* (Historical materials on Wu Yunchu's business enterprises: The Heaven's Kitchen MSG Factory) (Shanghai: Dang'an chuban, 1992), 412.

These efforts paid off in the short run: by the end of September, two-thirds of the Nationalists' haul of foreign currency and precious metals came from Shanghai. But they also earned the Nationalists the scorn of not only the wealthy but also of the middle classes who thought, correctly or not, that the wealthiest were escaping the dragnet and further fanned the broad hostility toward economic elites. Indeed, Chiang Ching-kuo, the son of Chiang Kai-shek, who took the lead in this campaign, repeatedly referred to these people as "traitorous merchants" (*jianshang*) in his diary and struck back by arresting thousands of speculators and scores of leading capitalists, including the son of Du Yuesheng, the head of the criminal underground.[13]

These economic policies did not help urban consumers. Nationalist efforts to terrorize merchants into maintaining steady prices ultimately backfired as commodities flowed from Shanghai to the rest of the country, where efforts at price controls had been less unsuccessful. Consumers were left with currency that was worth less every day and with precious little to buy. Within weeks, there were acute shortages of rice, coal, meat, and vegetables. Just when it seemed the situation could not get worse, government measures got more desperate, and on October 2, 1948, the Nationalists allowed prices on a few items like tobacco and alcohol to double, officially permitting inflation for the first time since the start of the Emergency Measures. Panic set in as the population assumed that the prices of everything else would soon also rise quickly, creating a frenzied buying spree as Chinese made a final push to get rid of their currency before it was completely worthless. Shopkeepers compounded the problem by holding back stock, afraid that anything they sold would be more expensive to replace. Soon shops were empty. By the end of the month, as none of Chiang Ching-kuo's additional measures restored faith in the currency, the government had no choice but to lift the price controls and surrender the economy to inflation. A few months later, the gold yuan, like the fabi before it, had become worthless. The Nationalists had lost any semblance of control over the economy.

In the end, the reforms destroyed the savings of tens of millions of Chinese, most notably those of the Nationalists' middle class and upper-class supporters, including Wu Yunchu. Chiang Ching-kuo's contempt for capitalists was now mutual. Moreover, the final years of Nationalist rule further discredited private enterprise and individual-driven consumption. In other words, Nationalist rule challenged China's commitment to the

---

13. Eastman, *Seeds of Destruction*, 188.

central tenets of a market economy. Its policies undermined commitment to savings and stimulated capital flight, hoarding, and speculation rather than capital reinvestment, further discrediting the party-state. The regime's currency had become worthless, twice.

The lionization of patriotic producers of consumer goods such as Wu Yunchu and "Match King" Liu Hongsheng by the Nationalists and Communists diminished throughout the decades leading up to the Civil War as other priorities—including fighting off first the Communists and then the Japanese and finally the Communists again—forced the Nationalists to treat the bourgeoisie less favorably. And, of course, the position of those like Wu Yunchu changed even more dramatically after the 1949 revolution, when the Communists deemphasized and even attacked the production and consumption of consumer goods and sought total control over all industry. In the years leading up to the Communist takeover, Wu remained suspicious of the CCP and hedged his bets by buying land in Canton (where he assumed the Nationalists would remain in control) in anticipation of building a factory there. Putting his son Wu Zhichao in charge of the Shanghai operations of Heaven's Kitchen, at the end of 1948 he left the country for Hong Kong and then the United States to watch events from there. At the liberation of Shanghai (May 27, 1949), Wu phoned his son to learn what had happened to his Shanghai factories, which had ceased production months earlier, and was relieved to learn that none had been destroyed during the takeover. Two of his factories, the Tianyuan Electrochemical Factory and the Tianli Nitrogen Plant, had established their own contingent of guards to protect the factories from marauding Nationalist troops and refugees who had flooded into the city during the lawlessness.[14]

LIBERATION AND SLOW STRANGULATION

"Liberation" by the Communists was not simply a military campaign but an act of political communication, propaganda, or advertising in which the CCP wanted not just to command adherence to its agenda but also to reassure a skittish population, particularly the skilled and wealthy members that it now needed. Nowhere was this rebalancing act truer than in major cities. Although the CCP had admirers among the intellectual class, it was viewed much more ambivalently and anxiously

---

14. Chen Zhengqing, "Tianchu weijingchang de liushiwu nian," 413–414.

by urban "capitalists," the vast population of individuals and families ranging from wealthy industrialists like textile magnate Rong Yiren to countless owner-operators of mom-and-pop shops. If the CCP forced its way in and plundered the cities—as Nationalists had led the populace to fear—they would have a much tougher time controlling the population and winning its support, much less wooing back the talent and financial resources of leading industrialists like Wu, who watched and waited from the safe harbor of British-protected Hong Kong after his return from the United States. These urban coastal capitalists had reasons to worry. Mao, who believed that nobody who passed the Civil War in the cities could be trusted, had a notoriously hostile attitude toward cities and towns in general and the imperialist-dominated treaty ports in particular.[15]

Shanghai, Wu's primary headquarters and the quintessential symbol of Chinese pre-liberation capitalism and modernity, was viewed as a bellwether for Communist policy toward cities and capitalists. For Mao, Shanghai was emblematic of what new Chinese cities would *not* be. As CCP policies in conquered Manchuria began to reveal, he intended to turn consumer-oriented cities into producer-oriented cities that did not consume the nation's resources and sap its ability to build a wealthy and independent China. But as the People's Liberation Army (PLA) advanced southward, the Communist leadership had reason to worry that its ideological antipathy toward cities might backfire, leading to violence and plunder against merchants and landlords, as had already happened in some northern cities. Mao therefore framed the takeover of Shanghai not as a time for retribution but as an opportunity to demonstrate the benefits of Communist rule: order, discipline, frugality, and, above all, shared benefits of "rational" socialist economic development.[16]

Chinese Communist leaders thus saw the takeover as a potentially defining moment, their one chance to win over skeptical segments of the population. Thus, when the PLA's ragtag troops filed into Shanghai, they camped on the streets rather than in confiscated private houses, symbolizing their discipline and connection with the people. As the PLA swept south with surprising speed and ease, Mao announced to his advancing troops that their next decisive challenge would be reversing the PLA's twenty-year emphasis on controlling cities from the countryside to

---

15. Odd Arne Westad, *Decisive Encounters: The Chinese Civil War, 1946–1950* (Stanford: Stanford University Press, 2003), 210.

16. For a very helpful summary of this change in policy toward cities, see Frederic Wakeman Jr., "'Cleanup': The New Order in Shanghai," in Jeremy Brown and Paul G. Pickowicz, eds., *Dilemmas of Victory* (Cambridge: Harvard University Press, 2007).

now controlling the countryside from the cities. Chinese military leaders must therefore "learn how to govern towns and cities"[17] and, unlike the destructive Nationalist government, to preserve property, even that of the rich. In early June, for instance, the PLA returned to their original owners several thousand automobiles that had been confiscated by the Nationalists.[18]

A few weeks before Shanghai's liberation on May 27, the CCP assembled an army of cadres at the small Yangzi river town of Danyang to communicate the critical economic strategy of cultivating the support of "national capitalists," whom it had distinguished from "compradore capitalists" for decades. Without the help of these capitalists in restarting the war-ravaged economy, China's urban problems would be greatly compounded. This position was codified in Communist policy and ideology. Mao Zedong and Zhu De's "Proclamation to the Chinese PLA" at the Party Congress of March 1949—which included Mao's famous line, "Who is our enemy? Who is our friend? This is the revolution's primary question"—declared that it was crucial to enlist the cooperation of "national capitalists," or at least convince them to remain neutral, in the struggle against the real enemies: imperialists, Nationalists, and bureaucrat capitalists.[19] The military leaders who oversaw the liberation of Shanghai got the message. The march was the messenger: how the troops entered the city gave its residents a first impression of the policies to come. This PR campaign was a great success, earning the CCP favorable press coverage at home and abroad,[20] easing the concerns of many capitalists, and helping persuade others like Wu to return.

At the same time, however, the CCP also invoked longstanding tropes of cities as centers of unpatriotic consumption and decadent consumerism. As with the Republican Revolution of 1911, the CCP represented its revolutionary politics through mandated interpretations of material culture. In contrast to the consumption of traditional elites, which set them apart from commoners, consumption now was intended to flatten socioeconomic hierarchies and unite the Chinese through shared mass consumption. The goal was to replace bourgeois urban values with simple, visible rural values of undifferentiated frugality through dress

---

17. Zhonggong zhongyang wenxian yanjiu shi, ed., *Yang Shangkun riji* (The Diary of Yang Shangkun) (Beijing: Zhongyang wexian chubanshe 2001), v. 1, 8–11.

18. Chen Zu'en, Ye Bin, and Li Tiangang, *Shanghai tongshi* (A History of Shanghai) (Shanghai: Renmin chubanshe, 1999), 5.

19. *Mao Zedong xuanji* (Collected works of Mao Zedong), v. 4, 1428.

20. Thomas N. Thompson, *China's Nationalization of Foreign Firms: The Politics of Hostage Capitalism, 1949–57* (Baltimore: School of Law University of Maryland, 1979), 14.

and leisure activities, such as the popularization of the *yangge*, a "short, prancing folk dance supposedly based on the way a coolie walks while carrying a heavy load on his shoulders,"[21] and the loose-fitting Sun Yat-sen–style cadre uniforms adopted even by business elites in prosperous towns like Hangzhou.[22]

Mao Zedong understood that maintaining this ethos of patriotic limits on consumption required both convincing urbanites to embrace proletarian chic and discouraging a desire for material comforts that could destroy the government and party from within. Accordingly, the perhaps most common trope of the first few years of liberation might be described as tales of urban temptation and seduction. Cities, as Mao saw them, were full of "bad elements" lying in wait. He worried that simple PLA soldiers and CCP cadres who had endured years of poverty and now found themselves ruling over cities with restaurants, prostitutes, night life, movie theaters, and endless forms of entertainment available for a price would be corrupted by these influences, especially during the early years when policy explicitly called for compromising with capitalists, many of whom were indeed eager to introduce cadres to sensual pleasures in exchange for access and influence. In subsequent years, as cadres surrendered to such temptations, a common narrative spread by state-sponsored media was that "it was only after they came to the cities that certain cadres fell victims to the sugar-coated cannonballs of unlawful merchants."[23]

Mao's intended strategy of reengineering cities to eliminate the production of such temptations, to transform so-called consumer-cities into "producer-cities,"[24] also appealed to many middle-class urbanites disillusioned by the way cities had become places for former collaborators

---

21. Edward Hunter, *Brain-Washing in Red China: The Calculated Destruction of Men's Minds* (New York: Vanguard Press, 1951), 22.

22. James Z. Gao, *The Communist Takeover of Hangzhou: The Transformation of City and Cadres, 1949–1954* (Honolulu: University of Hawai'i Press, 2004), 74, 79.

23. *Current Background* 166 (March 14, 1952): 21. Less acknowledged was the negative role urban cadres played in transforming new cadres, who were ridiculed as "country bumpkins" for their austerity. *Survey of China Mainland Press* 254: 17. Liu Suinian, Wu Qungan and Cui Jie, *China's Socialist Economy: An Outline History, 1949–1984* (Beijing: Beijing Review, 1986), 67, notes that the Three Anti campaign was largely directed at hold-overs from the Nationalists and "a handful" of cadres.

24. "Report to the Second Plenary Session of the Seventh Central Committee of the Communist Party of China," March 5, 1949. Also in 1948 *Tianjin Daily* published a widely read editorial called, "Transform the Consumer Cities to Productive Ones," which depicted cities as exploiting workers and farmers alike and as conduits for imported industrial products. Cited in Gao, *The Communist Takeover of Hangzhou*, 107.

and outsiders with government connections to enrich themselves and lead lives of decadence and luxury at the expense of the vast majority.[25] In fact, the CCP was happily surprised by the level of support it found among the urban middle class, particularly students.[26]

PRIDE IN PRODUCTION AND
ANTI-CONSUMERIST DISCOURSE

Despite its rhetoric, the CCP is more accurately labeled "anti-consumerist" rather than "anti-urban." Although it had promoted a cult of revolutionary asceticism at least since Yan'an, after liberation its emphasis on the revolution became much more pronounced, particularly following the conquest of China's major cities. In the early 1950s, CCP internal literature and the mass media frequently directed such phrases and warnings as "guard against the tendency to seek pleasure" (*jingti tantu xiangle*) especially but not exclusively at rural cadres now living in the cities. Denunciations of consumerism included attacks on those who "live a debauched lifestyle" (*shenghuo fuhua*) or who were "corrupt" (*fushi*), who "coveted the degenerate" (*tantu fubai*) and "hankered after a life of ease and leisure" (*tantu anyi*). Again and again, this rhetoric called on Chinese to eschew bourgeois appetites and to distrust their senses and the sensual, most frequently described as the seduction of "sugar-coated bullets" (*tangyi paodan* or simply *tangdan*). It excoriated Chinese who tried to profit at the expense of others through "hoarding and speculation" (*tunji juqi*) and attempted to collect "huge profits" (*baoli*) through "profiteering" (*touji daoba*). In contrast, the teleology of the revolution preached a path of sacrificing now to lead to material rewards later.

More generally, the party-state attempted to replace pride in personal consumption as a measure of individual achievement—the foundation of an individualistic market economy—with collective pride in national production. The party sold socialism at home and abroad through media

---

25. See Westad, *Decisive Encounters*, 79, which includes a description of the 1947 film, "Nothing But a Dream" (*Tiantang chumeng*). In the film, the protagonist, a young architect, has to give his newborn son to someone who became wealthy during the Japanese occupation. See also Suzanne Pepper, *Civil War in China: The Political Struggle, 1945–1949* (Lanham: Rowman & Littlefield, 1999), 155–160. On Chiang Ching-kuo's predatory policies and the alienation of Shanghai elites, see Westad, *Decisive Encounters*, 184; and Pepper, *Civil War*, 125.

26. Westad, *Decisive Encounters*, 276–277.

coverage of production increases and exceeded targets, which found its logical culmination in the fabricated production numbers of the late 1950s that led to massive famines. Countless newspaper headlines and publications like *Ten Great Years* attempted to sell "the people" (and their allies abroad) on the economic accomplishments of the new China, which it posed as the antithesis of the vestiges of old China represented by corrupt urban cadres and hedonistic capitalist-consumers.

Yet after conquering China's cities, the Communists did not, as many feared, immediately nationalize the private sector and confiscate the wealth of China's capitalists. The new regime initially sacrificed ideological purity and implemented pragmatic policies to reassure capitalists that they had a place in new China as members of "the people," despite its ideology that clearly called for the eventual transfer of all private capital to the state.[27] Even before the formal declaration of the founding of the People's Republic of China on October 1, 1949, the party laid the legal basis for the continued existence of capitalists during the September Chinese People's Political Consultative Conference (CPPCC), which adopted the Common Program. This document, which served as the new regime's legal charter until the adoption of the first constitution in 1954, reassured capitalists that state and private enterprises were to coexist under the new regime, though its language suggested that the two were neither equal partners nor independent actors in the new economy.[28]

In essence, the Common Program reflected the ideology spelled out in Mao Zedong's *New Democracy* (1940), in which he described the New Democracy period as an important transitional stage between the "semi-feudal, semi-colonial" stage and China's entrance into socialism. During this stage, the Communists would recognize the legitimate existence of four classes in Chinese society: workers, peasants, petty bourgeoisie, and national bourgeoisie. As this scheme suggests, the CCP did not consider capitalists a single, homogeneous group, instead dividing them into two groups: the "national capitalists" with whom it planned to cooperate and the "bureaucratic capitalists," who were allied with rich

---

27. On entering cities soldiers and cadres were instructed not to interfere with private enterprise. For this and other regulations regarding capitalists, see Chen Boda, "Bu yao daluan yuanlai de qiye jigou" (Don't throw into disarray the existing structure of capitalist enterprises), in *Zhongguo renmin jiefang jun rucheng zhengce* (Chinese People's Liberation Army Policies on Taking Cities) (Hankou: Xinhua shudian, 1949), 17–29.

28. For a translation of the Common Program articles addressing the role of private enterprise in the economic objectives of the new government during the period of New Democracy, see Chien Chia-chu, "Private Enterprise Grows," *China Reconstructs* 6 (1952): 13.

peasants (the basis of feudal rule) and foreign imperialists who used the state apparatus to develop their own narrow interests and suppressed the legitimate aspirations of the other classes. Thus enterprises owned by those labeled bureaucrat-capitalists were immediately confiscated after 1949. The Communist view of national capitalists or bourgeoisie, although more accepting, also ascribed to them a "dual character," one side constructive, another destructive,[29] thereby justifying what would become an alternately harsh and conciliatory stance toward them.

In Communist literature, under the Nationalists, the national bourgeoisie had been at a considerable disadvantage compared with the bureaucrat-capitalists, who through their manipulation of the state apparatus secured financial privileges in government loans, tax relief, and monopoly rights to industries such as mining, power, and transportation.[30] To their credit, according to this narrative, national capitalists had responded to this situation by patriotically opposing imperialism, feudalism, and the bureaucrat-capitalist class, demonstrating their potential to contribute to building a wealthy, powerful, and independent China, at least during the period of New Democracy. Nonetheless, the literature warned, the profit motive often ran counter to the material and spiritual needs of the nation, leading national capitalists to base their decisions on fluctuating, "irrational," and "inefficient" market demands, while the Communists wanted to replace the "anarchy" of the market with planned production and the regulation of private enterprise. As state ownership gradually replaced private ownership, they believed, workers and capitalists alike would realize that they were contributing to the general good rather than to private profit, which in turn would increase productivity and national pride.[31]

The Communist regime balanced its immediate need to revive the economy with its desire to create a socialist state by gradually expanding control over private enterprise. This seven-year process occurred in three stages: utilization (1949–1952), restriction (1952–1953), and transformation (1953–1956).[32] The most important changes during this

---

29. Guan Datong, *The Socialist Transformation of Capitalist Industry and Commerce in China* (Beijing: Foreign Languages Press, 1960), 46.

30. This description of the role of capitalists in Chinese Communist literature on New Democracy relies heavily on Chien Chia-chu, *State Capitalism in China* (New York: Far Eastern Reporter, 1954). In the early 1950s, Chien was the Deputy Director of the Bureau of Industry and Commerce.

31. Chi Chao-ting, "Capitalists Cross Over," *China Reconstructs* 5.3 (1956): 2–5; Chen Han-seng, "New Rise of Industry," *China Reconstructs* 1 (1952): 22–23.

32. In fact, the Communists themselves identified the transformation of private enter-

process took place during the Three Anti, Five Anti campaign, the central initiative of the period of restriction. The campaign represented the final assault of the decades-long process of assertion of state control over private enterprise and the vilification of bourgeois lifestyles. Although the state did not achieve outright control over enterprises in this period, the success of its campaign destroyed the basis of capitalist wealth, power, and consumption-derived status, leaving the capitalist class an empty shell that would soon be destroyed.

THE THREE ANTI CAMPAIGN: DEFLECTING "SUGAR-COATED BULLETS"

By December 1951, the party had identified government corruption and waste as the chief obstacles to increased production and thrift and launched the Three Anti campaign against them nationwide.[33] Within a month, preliminary investigations had uncovered 1,670 offenders in twenty-seven central government organs, evidence of widespread corruption and waste that provided the CCP leadership with an excuse to remove untrustworthy cadres from party, government, and military ranks.[34] From the start, however, the campaign also targeted prevalent but unacceptable forms of consumption that exposed ideological impurities. Gao Gang, who launched the original campaign in the northeast, attacked nepotism, corruption, and old bureaucratic practices but also explicitly targeted material manifestations of cadre malfeasance, including all signs of "extravagance" such as the use of official funds for parties, servants, touring, and automobiles.[35] As always, what were seen as the worst offenses involved imports: "The ostentatious use of British and American made cars, notably at Shenyang (Mukden), being instanced as particularly reprehensible."[36] But even the excessive consumption of smaller

---

prise in this way. This schema is enshrined in Article 10 of the 1954 Constitution, which speaks of "using" the good aspects of the capitalists, "restricting" their potential damage, and gradually "transforming" their enterprises to state ownership. *The Constitution of the People's Republic of China* (Beijing: Foreign Languages Press, 1954), 76.

33. According to historian Peter S.H. Tang, the campaign began on August 31, 1951. *Communist China Today* (New York: Praeger, 1957), 339.

34. Theodore H.E. Chen and Wen-hui C. Chen, "The 'Three Anti' and 'Five Anti' Movements in Communist China," *Pacific Affairs* 26.1 (1953): 4–5.

35. *Neibu cankao*, March 10, 1952.

36. FO 371/99233, December 12, 1951, 2. See also the important article by Yang Kuisong, "Mao Zedong yu sanfan yundong" (Mao Zedong and the Three Anti movement), *Shilin* 4 (2006).

items such as cigarettes, alcohol, and feasts—which often began when goods were supplied by the government to cadres in lieu of salary—were now criticized.[37]

At the same time, the party was taking a giant risk by exposing the prevalence of corruption and waste, as it threatened to undermine public confidence in the new regime. To shift the focus away from corruption within its ranks, the party therefore placed the blame for these problems on the corrupting influence of capitalists and their lifestyles, which used their "sugar-coated bullets" to attack party rule. The course of the Three Anti campaign suggests that the government intended all along to gather information to launch a campaign directed specifically at capitalists. In fact, preliminary preparations for a mass movement against capitalists had begun several months before the government officially launched the campaign. By this time, all businessmen and merchants had been forced to join the appropriate trade or industrial association and had been urged to confess their complicity in government corruption, waste, and bureaucratism. In addition, each association divided its membership into "small study" groups that met nightly to examine various documents relating to the Three Anti campaign and socialism, such as a speech by Zhou Enlai that suggested that the Three Anti campaign should be redirected from "corrupt officials" to "law breaking merchants." Other signs suggested the government intended to attack the capitalists as a class early in 1952. The government, rejecting the notion that only a small percentage of capitalists engaged in corrupt practices, supported claims of a capitalist conspiracy and began publishing the results of its investigations into Three Anti crimes. The results that Beijing made public at the end of January 1952, for instance, found that "the corrupt elements not only include a large portion of personnel taken over from the old regime, but more than 80 percent of the corrupt elements have connections with industrialists and merchants." Mao Zedong had already concluded that private businesspeople were engaged in all manner of corrupt business practices, which, he claimed, collectively posed "an ever more dangerous and serious threat than war."[38]

---

37. This type of material compensation seems similar to the sort of welfare demanded by workers depicted by Mark W. Frazier and leads one to wonder if the party was also implying that similar worker demands were bourgeois. Frazier does not discuss this but does provide examples of how the better material conditions (e.g., hot plates and lamps in an office) cast suspicion on supervisors. See Frazier, *The Making of the Chinese Industrial Workplace: State, Revolution, and Labor Management* (New York: Cambridge University Press, 2002), 109, 115.

38. *Jianguo yilai Mao Zedong wengao* (Mao Zedong's manuscripts following the estab-

GENERATING AN ANTI-CAPITALIST
FIVE ANTI CAMPAIGN

In the wake of such reports, the Chinese press began running articles blaming capitalists for corrupting government officials. Under the title "Resist the Attacks of the Bourgeoisie Class, Determinedly Uphold the Leadership of the Working Class," party theoretician You Guanyuan informed readers of the influential theoretical magazine *Xuexi* (Study) that capitalists had launched a "fierce attack" against the working class and the leadership of the CCP. Appealing to patriotic sentiment, he blamed this "attack" for weakening the economy and hence the nation's ability to "resist U.S. imperialism" and wage war in Korea and transferred responsibility for corruption and waste within the government by arguing that fraudulent business practices had sullied the integrity of cadres.[39] In essence, You Guanyuan provided the official justification for expansion of state control over capitalists: under the United Front, the CCP and the capitalists had had an opportunity to cooperate in building China, but capitalists, true to their nature, had opted for personal profits over the national collective good, and now the survival of the revolution required the party and the masses to strike back.

In light of the earlier government actions noted above, You Guan-yuan's recommended five-point strategy to resist capitalist encroachment must be seen not as part of an open debate but rather an early articulation of a policy already adopted by party leadership. In his first point, he identified five activities of capitalists that the government ought to outlaw that eventually became known as the Five Anti (also known as the "five poisons" [*wudu*]): bribery, tax evasion, theft of state assets, failure to conform to contract specifications, and theft of state economic secrets. The breadth and vagueness of the proscribed activities effectively tainted most capitalists. In the second and third points, he called on the party to educate the masses on the capitalist threat and prepare for class "struggle," which by this time labor organizations had already begun to do. His last two points reflected the depth of the changes underway, as he argued for the systematic and comprehensive inspection of the

---

lishment of the People's Republic) (Beijing: Zhongyang wenxian chubanshe, 1991), v. 3, 21–22.

39. See "Kang Kao Summarizes 3-Anti and 5-Anti Movements in Northeast," Xinhua, June 25, 1952; translated in *Current Background* 201 (August 12, 1952), especially 16–17. Indeed, mainland historians still interpret the Five Anti campaign as an essentially *defensive* measure undertaken by the party to thwart the counterrevolutionary intentions of the capitalist class.

accounting records of all capitalists, in effect promoting massive state penetration into the inner workings of individual enterprises. He also called for the organization of the capitalist class into commercial and industrial associations to facilitate the indoctrination of the capitalists; after a period of study, they would sign a "patriotic compact," acknowledge guilt for past wrongdoings, and agree to cooperate with state authorities in the regular inspection and supervision of their enterprises.[40]

"SMASHING" THE CAPITALISTS

Accounts confirm that the Three Anti, Five Anti campaign constituted a second but more profound revolution for Chinese capitalists. The political revolution that culminated in the establishment of the PRC in 1949 appeared to have changed little in the lives of Chinese capitalists who continued to use the same business practices after the revolution. Although government taxes and inflation threatened profits, enterprises routinely kept two sets of books, falsified receipts and orders, converted earnings to gold and foreign currencies, and devised other methods to shelter profits from state agents. The regime was correct in asserting the prevalence of corruption and bribery in Chinese business circles. By the time the government began to crack down on these widely practiced activities in the campaign of 1951–1952, nearly all enterprises had engaged in illegal activities under the new regime. This made them vulnerable, and the Communists now intended to punish them. One Shanghai businessman neatly summarized the CCP logic behind the campaign: "In fact, if you made a decent profit, this meant by definition that you had done something illegal in the eyes of the Communists. You revealed the ways in which you made your profit, and these were your crimes. You then confessed your crimes, and the Communists took away your 'illegal profits' and returned them to the people—or rather to the People's Government whom you were supposed to have cheated when you made the profit."[41]

The regime sought incriminating evidence in every way imaginable. In December, state auditors were dispatched to enterprises big and small. The government was aware of the widespread practice of double

---

40. You Guanyuan, "Resist the Attacks of the Bourgeois Class," *Current Background* 166 (March 14, 1952): 11–12.

41. Doak Barnett, *Communist China: The Early Years, 1949–55* (New York: F.A. Praeger, 1964), 150, quoting a businessman from Shanghai who had recently fled to Hong Kong.

bookkeeping and so used other means to coerce managers and owners to confess. In some cases, friends and relatives were urged to pressure a given capitalist to confess.[42] All of the information and confessions thereby gathered were carefully assembled for later use. Clearly, the regime was not simply after alleged back taxes: it was also seeking a profound change in the status of capitalists.

The government began to isolate capitalists and to exert tremendous psychological pressure upon them, such as putting up posters throughout the city, denouncing capitalists, demanding that they confess, and urging workers to uncover and collect incriminating evidence. More extreme measures were reported in Shanghai, where the government set up loudspeakers on commercial thoroughfares and directed pedestrians to urge shopkeepers to confess, laying the groundwork for mass mobilization.[43] The campaign also heightened class differences in the workplace,[44] and the constant attacks upon and public humiliation of capitalists weakened or severed ties of loyalty between employers and workers. The campaign acted as a social crowbar to pry the capitalists from their privileged positions, undermining their authority and status in both society and the workplace.[45]

The Communists also atomized capitalists by rewarding capitalists who denounced others or helped elicit confessions. Capitalists who not only diverted attention away from themselves but also confessed were assured more lenient treatment.[46] The creation of "Five Anti Merit Achieving Teams" was the clearest manifestation of government attempts to erode capitalist solidarity. In Shanghai alone, more than 1,600 businessmen were mobilized to work on such teams.[47] By late March 1952, the groundwork had been systematically laid for an official

---

42. "5-Anti Movement Victoriously Concluded in Canton," *Nanfang ribao* (June 28, 1952); translated in *Current Background* 201 (August 12, 1952): 29.

43. Barnett, *Communist China*, 145.

44. See Frazier, *The Making of the Chinese Industrial Workplace*.

45. On the Communists' attempts to transfer worker loyalties to the state, see Andrew G. Walder, *Communist Neo-Traditionalism: Work and Authority in Chinese Society* (Berkeley: University of California Press, 1986), 85–113, and Yang Kuisong, "1952 nian Shanghai 'wufan' yundong shimo" (The whole story of Shanghai's 1952 Five Anti Campaign), *Shehui kexue* 4 (2006).

46. "GAC Directive to Conclude 5-Anti Campaign," Xinhua, June 14, 1952; translated in *Current Background* 201 (August 12, 1952): 1–2. For a description of the classification of lawbreaking capitalists, see "Provisions Laid Down by the Economy Practice Investigation Committee of the Central People's Government," Xinhua, March 11, 1952; translated in *Current Background* 168 (March 26, 1952): 4–9.

47. Barnett, *Communist China*, 149.

campaign against capitalists. Confessions had been gathered and capitalists had been divided and demoralized. All that remained was for them to make their confessions public, a humiliating open acceptance of the Communist narrative of "class exploitation." The public phase of the campaign developed rapidly across urban China, following a set pattern of four stages. Although the dates of the campaigns differed by a few days among various cities, Canton followed the typical pattern. In the first week of April, to test its procedures, the government began the campaign by targeting a single "key point" industry, pharmaceutical manufactures and merchants. In "struggle sessions" with Five Anti work teams as well as workers and clerks, capitalists ritualistically confessed to crimes that had been determined during the preceding months. Punishments were meted out and workers and capitalists were in turn absorbed into the campaign. The second stage began with a citywide rally on April 7. Over the following two weeks, the campaign reached ninety more industries and trades, eventually extending to the remaining 127 industries and trades. In the final stage of the campaign, June 1–20, all remaining cases were settled.[48]

To carry out such a massive campaign, the state mobilized hundreds of thousands of Chinese. During the Five Anti campaign in Canton alone, ten thousand individuals entered factories and shops to organize mass denunciations of capitalists.[49] In Shanghai, over 80 percent of workers and shop attendants participated in these "speak bitterness" mass meetings.[50] In this way, the Communist regime generated mass support for the social and financial destruction of the capitalist class.

The campaign extracted cash, hard currency, precious metals, merchandise, and equipment from targeted capitalists. Estimates of the total vary from US$500 million to upwards of US$1.25 billion.[51] In the short run, these resources provided the regime with badly needed

48. "Victoriously Concluded in Canton," translated in *Current Background* 201 (August 12, 1952): 28. For a description of the campaign in Shanghai, see "[Xinhua] Correspondent's Review of Victory of 5-Anti Campaign in Shanghai," Xinhua, June 7, 1952, and translated in *Current Background* 201 (August 12, 1952): 23–24; and John Garver, "The Wu-Fan Campaign in Shanghai: A Study in the Consolidation of Urban Control," in A. Doak Barnett, ed., *Chinese Communist Politics in Action* (Seattle: University of Washington Press, 1969).

49. "Victoriously Concluded in Canton," translated in *Current Background* 201 (August 12, 1952): 28.

50. "5-Anti Campaign in Shanghai," in *Current Background* 201 (August 12, 1952): 23.

51. Barnett, *Communist China*, 160; *Weekly Bulletin*, Chinese News Service, New York, June 3, 1952 (Republic of China Publication); Chen and Chen, "The 'Three Anti' and 'Five Anti' Movements in Communist China," *Pacific Affairs* 26.1 (March, 1953): 3–23, 18.

revenue to wage war in Korea.[52] This extraction also had long-term implications. During the campaign, capitalists were routinely pressured to overstate their crimes, and consequently, the amount of back taxes and fines they owed. To survive, they often had to liquidate assets. As a whole, the campaign absorbed the liquid capital of capitalists, further weakening their ability to resist further state penetration.

Moreover, over the course of the Three Anti, Five Anti campaign, capitalists like Wu Yunchu gradually surrendered control over their enterprises. Through the use of regulations and internal monitoring by workers, the regime destroyed the already crumbling wall separating public and private enterprises. The state now involved itself in all aspects of operations, from the hiring of workers to the fixing of prices. In 1952, the state was not prepared to exercise outright control over enterprises, and in fact, according to regime literature, private enterprise existed in China until 1956.[53] But these enterprises were "private" only in name. Capitalists' interest in management largely disappeared once they lost control. After the campaign, for instance, Wu adhered to all policies, regulations, and laws even when he knew them to be misguided. One can imagine the sense of resignation of the hundreds of thousands of Shanghai merchants and industrialists who joined in "celebrating" their final demise in 1956, given that they had had nearly four years to anticipate their formal end as a class.

OUSTING A PATRIOTIC PRODUCER FROM HIS PLANT

As noted above, at the time of liberation, the CCP's economic policy was to divide capitalists into those deemed "national," who were allowed to continue operating as before, and those labeled "bureaucratic," who faced extra scrutiny, supervision, and even expropriation. Fortunately for Wu, two of his factories, the Tianli Nitrogen Plant and Heaven's

---

52. According to Mao, the money raised during the campaign could "see [China] through another eighteen months of war." Mao Zedong, *Selected Works* (Beijing: Foreign Language Press, 1977), v. 5, 80.

53. By early June of 1952, economic pragmatism returned to Communist domestic policies vis-à-vis the capitalists. The campaign damaged the country's economy and the state sought to revive private enterprise by extending loans, reducing back taxes owed, and giving state contracts to these businesses. For more information on these policies, see "GAC Directive," in *Current Background* 201 (August 12, 1952): 4–5; and "3-Anti, 5-Anti Movements Victoriously Concluded in Tientsin," Xinhua, June 14, 1952, and translated in *Current Background* 201 (August 12, 1952): 14–15. See also Yang Kuisong, "1952 nian Shanghai 'wufan' yundong shimo."

Kitchen, were deemed "national capitalist enterprises." Heaven's Kitchen resumed operations within days after liberation, but Tianli, which lacked raw materials and faced uncertain market conditions, remained idle. The situation at the Tianyuan Electrochemical Factory was more complicated because the Nationalist government's National Resources Commission had owned part of the enterprise during the war, and thus the CCP determined the factory possessed "bureaucratic capital." The new government confiscated the shares previously owned by the National Resources Commission and ordered Tianyuan to provide detailed information on every aspect of its operations, especially its ownership. The Office of Heavy Industry also dispatched two representatives to the factory to protect the state's interests, although it promised minimum oversight as long as the company maintained its previous employment levels, salaries, and structure. By mid-June, Tianyuan was back in operation.[54] Before liberation, although Wu had jointly owned Tianyuan with the National Resources Commission, he had effectively run things however he saw fit. The official policy of the new government was for workers to participate in management, and thus his two deputies (his son and Assistant General Manager Li Shi'an) now had to have all their decisions approved by the representatives of the workers, effectively shifting control to them. The new power structure also created problems on the ground in small but important symbolic ways. One day in September, for instance, an office administrator forgot his coat and asked a worker to retrieve it, a request that would have been commonplace before liberation. But now the worker refused. After being surrounded by factory workers who berated him for asking a fellow worker to handle a private matter, the administrator admitted his error and publicly apologized.[55]

In the months immediately following the takeover of Shanghai, Wu remained abroad, suspicious of the Communists and how they might treat him, even though he had reason to believe they would accept him. He had, after all, met and received a gift from Mao Zedong, had several positive exchanges with Zhou Enlai, and received CCP literature from its underground agents, but that had been when the CCP was weak and needed him more than he needed them. Yet he had also had extensive contact with Chiang Kai-shek and the Nationalists right up through the war and thus was uncertain about what to do next. So in the fall of 1949,

---

54. Wang Daliang, *Weijing dawang Wu Yunchu* (The MSG king: Wu Yunchu) (Beijing: Jiefangjun chubanshe, 1995).

55. Ibid.

he relocated from the United States to Hong Kong, where he reevaluated the situation. There he met with Xu Dixin, who was now a member of the Shanghai Military Affairs office handling economic policy. During the war, Wu had escorted Xu around his factories in Sichuan, and now Wu wanted Xu to help him better understand the Communists' intentions. Xu had been dispatched to Hong Kong for just that purpose, to try to explain CCP policy to capitalists and convince them to return and participate in building a New China, one of many such efforts at outreach.[56] The following month, Premier Zhou Enlai himself led a delegation to Hong Kong that included Zhang Shijian and Huang Shao to meet with the capitalists and explain the concept of New Democracy.

Wu also continued to receive letters from his son reassuring him that everything was fine. These letters, along with the encouragement of party officials and friends, convinced him to return at the end of October 1949, the same month Mao officially declared the establishment of a new state, the People's Republic of China. After taking a boat to Tianjin, he first traveled to Beijing, where he was met at the station by the head of the United Front, the organization charged with building alliances with nonproletarian social elements, and put up at the Beijing Hotel. He was later taken to the residential quarter for high officials, Zhongnanhai, where he met with Zhou Enlai, who welcomed the "MSG king" home. There he was given a blue Sun Yat-sen cotton suit (later known as a Mao suit), a new marker of status closely associated with party cadres. The party next sent him and another patriotic national products manufacturer, "Match King" Liu Hongsheng, who had returned from Hong Kong around the same time, on an inspection tour of Manchuria. The tour included a visit to Shenyang's Ajinomoto MSG plant, Heaven's Kitchen's Japanese archrival, which had already been nationalized. Wu was impressed with Ajinomoto's operations and the other heavy industry he saw. At the end of November, he finally returned home to Shanghai, where the workers threw him a welcoming party.[57]

As this reception indicated, the CCP was eager to win over Wu and other leading "national capitalists" and to give them formal (if not always actual) avenues for policy input and implementation while also undermining capitalist control over private enterprise (a term that was quickly losing any meaningful definition).[58] At the end of 1950, for

---

56. Sherman Cochran, "Capitalists Choosing Communist China: The Liu Family of Shanghai, 1948–1956," in Brown and Pickowicz, eds., *Dilemmas of Victory*, 369.

57. Wang Daliang, *Weijing dawang Wu Yunchu*, 253.

58. For numerous examples of capitalists treated in this way, see Shou Tongyi, Shou

instance, Wu was named to the East China Military Affairs and to the city government and made the associate head of the Shanghai Municipal Association of Industry and Commerce. But within his factory, Wu soon had problems with his new partner—the state—and its representatives, who subverted his control.

Wu also saw some of his control over his enterprises move to his workers, who were now officially charged with helping to manage the factory. He immediately noticed a change in workers, who now exuded a sense of control that was formalized in their new labor union and workers' meetings and manifest in a growing number of small and large confrontations. When Wu returned to Heaven's Kitchen, for instance, he expected to reoccupy his residence at the top of the factory, and meeting with no objections from the front office workers, he moved back in. The factory had two elevators, one for workers and staff and the other for Wu and his family, and because Wu had not been in residence at liberation, the employees had begun to use his elevator. After he returned, the office staff resumed their preliberation practice, essentially giving Wu—who lived alone because his wife remained in Hong Kong—his own elevator. But the workers objected, arguing not only that there was no longer a difference between "workers" and "capitalists" but also that it was wasteful to provide one person with a private elevator. Furthermore, the workers argued, granting one person an entire floor of the factory for his personal use was a capitalist extravagance, a holdover from a bygone era. Although his son understood the symbolic significance of the private residence, he initially had a difficult time convincing his father to move out.[59] Wu's alienation from his workforce only grew worse in the following years, particularly during the 1952 discussions among workers across Shanghai, the "factory workers' democratic reform movement" regarding "who's supporting whom," and the offensive body searches of female employees, a practice that survived surprisingly far into the Communist era, that taught workers that rather than relying on their employer for their livelihoods, employers relied on them.[60]

Some of the direct tension that developed between Wu and the military representative at the Tianyuan Electrochemical Factory was removed in June of 1951 when, after direct requests from Wu, Wang Daohan, the head of the East China Industrial Bureau, sent to the factory

Heiying, and Shou Leying, eds., *Zou zai shehuizhuyi dadao shang* (Going down the socialist road) (Beijing: Zhongguo wenshi chubanshe, 1988).

59. Wang Daliang, *Weijing dawang Wu Yunchu*, 254–255.

60. Chen Zhengqing, "Tianchu weijingchang de liushiwu nian," 415.

thirty-year-old Yang Zhifu as the new government agent, nominally the "deputy manager." Unlike his predecessors, Yang had experience managing enterprises in Manchuria, and soon Wu found he had lost most of his remaining power and much of his authority over the day-to-day decision making. For instance, Yang abolished Wu's small executive committee, which he had created to maintain effective control over the factory, and replaced it with a much larger committee that included eleven worker representatives and a party member. In January of 1952, just as the Five Anti campaign was starting, Wu was in Hong Kong, where he went to bring his wife back to Shanghai for cancer treatment. He arrived home just in time to experience the height of the campaign. On February 13, Wu spoke to a meeting of the Chemical Supply Association, urging his colleagues to cooperate with the campaign.

The Tianyuan Electrochemical Factory held a struggle session in which the workers accused Wu of living off their labor. Although this situation so distressed his wife that she abruptly returned to Hong Kong, Wu had not lost the favor of the party. In March, Wu was sent to Moscow for an International Economic Conference with the official delegation from the PRC, where he wrote a letter to his daughter sharing his impressions of the Soviet Union, which, despite twenty years of international travel, Wu had only visited once. According to his letter, he was very impressed with the material conditions there—the abundance of food, automobiles, and shop windows full of beautiful items—and concluded that "it was impossible to differentiate between socialist and capitalist cities." Although one might interpret such observations as simply reflecting the party line, Wu also warned that, although the Soviet Union was well on its way to becoming an industrialized nation, China was still experiencing its birthing pains. Speaking at a conference upon his return, he bluntly informed the audience that the Soviet Union's model held limited applicability to China.

Wu's actions following the Five Anti campaign reveal a similarly ambivalent attitude toward his future in China. On the one hand, by the time he returned from the Soviet Union, his enterprises had already been designated "law abiding" (*shoufa hu*), and his responses to questions from an American-based periodical about the Five Anti campaign that summer reflected the official party position. In his written reply, Wu said that despite what Western newspapers reported, the aim of the campaign was "absolutely not the extermination of private enterprise" but rather "the elimination of the Five Evils carried over from Old Society," and that capitalists, as one of four large social classes in China, still had an important place in Chinese society. He argued as well that land reform was good not only for China but for business, stating that his enterprises were now shipping many more products to the countryside. The proof, he said, lay in production numbers, which were doubling at Heaven's Kitchen, tripling at the Tianyuan Electrochemical Factory, and rising eight-fold at the Tianli Nitrogen Plant.[61] On the other hand, despite his claims of new business opportunities and a meaningful place for capitalists, Wu decided there was not much for him to do in Shanghai any more, and by the time of his death from diabetes on October 15, 1953, he had already informed Shanghai's mayor Chen Yi that he wished to sell his conglomerate to the state so that he could do something more than be a figurehead. On the day before Wu's death, Chen Yi visited him in the hospital and informed him that Mao had agreed to let Wu move to Beijing and work with the ministry charged with developing China's chemical industry. On October 18, the city held a memorial for him, Zhou Enlai sent a wreath, and Vice Mayor Pan Hannian eulogized Wu for the huge contribution he had made to the development of China's industry.

CONCLUSION

The accumulated historic legacies of the Nanjing decade, World War II, and Civil War had pressed both the Nationalists and CCP into subordinating their broader ideological agendas to economic and political necessity, which had produced an ambiguous ideological terrain by 1949. Following its victory, the CCP was at first hesitant to act on its ideology. The regime's decision to cooperate with certain capitalists and to maintain a supportive public posture toward private ownership of the means of production was a pragmatic one. The Communist government recognized that it could not simultaneously create a socialist society and revitalize China's war-ravaged economy. Yet this decision to temporarily subordinate its socialist ideological agenda to economic imperatives created several tensions. By sanctioning the continued existence of a capitalist class, the Communists allowed the initial tacit sanctioning of consumerism and a consuming class whose consumption visibly symbolized continued inequality and the fragility of the revolution.[62]

---

61. Wang Daliang, *Weijing dawang Wu Yunchu*, 263–265.

62. On attempts by labor to capitalize on the revolution and Mao's subsequent backpedaling on his revolutionary promises, see Elizabeth J. Perry, "Masters of the Country? Shanghai Workers in the Early People's Republic," in Brown and Pickowicz, eds., *Dilemmas of Victory*.

The Communists understood these risks and, as we have seen, sought to eliminate them through the gradual absorption of private capital and the delegitimization of consumerism, processes that were simultaneous and mutually reinforcing. In other words, Wu Yunchu and similar "national capitalists" made their decisions about whether to stay and cooperate with the new regime in a rapidly changing environment that originally not only permitted them to maintain ownership of their enterprises but also allowed them to maintain their lifestyles. But by the end of 1951, the CCP's ideological and mobilizational needs pushed their policies in favor of more radical, anti-capitalist ones, although their need to move to the left quickly was slowed by accumulated legacies such as the creation of "patriotic" and "national" capitalists like Wu Yunchu. Because of the ideological muddle, various social forces, including those "national capitalists," had a palette of options, discursive as well as tactical, available to them. This chapter has sought to describe and contextualize one individual's deployment of those various options in response to the rapidly shifting conditions in China circa 1949.

This page is intentionally left blank.

9 THE HONG KONG-SOUTH CHINA FINANCIAL NEXUS | Ma Xuchao and His Remittance Agency

Tomoko Shiroyama

At the time of the founding of the People's Republic of China (PRC) in October 1949, reorganizing the financial and monetary system was one of the most urgent problems to be solved. As the newly established People's Bank of China pointed out in August of 1949, "Once we liberate the cities, clearing the financial market and establishing renminbi as the single legal tender is our critical mission in order to found the new economic order, restore production, and secure supply."[1] Against the background of China's wartime economy, the new government's anxiety was readily understandable.

A decade earlier in October 1938, the Nationalist government re-treated to the interior province of Sichuan. From then on, military expenditures increased, and government outlays, financed through a monetary expansion, increased steadily. The Chinese economy succumbed to this inflationary pressure.[2] By the end of 1945, prices were reported to be 1,632 times higher than their prewar levels. Even after the Sino–Japanese War concluded in August 1945 the Nationalist government failed to halt rampant inflation; on the contrary, it exacerbated it. The rapid expansion in government spending increased the supply of money. The flight of capital not only pushed up the market rate of foreign exchange but also worsened the runaway inflation by restricting the use of foreign exchange for imports. The more restrictive the government's allocations of foreign exchange became, the more importers hoarded their goods to profit from

---

1. Zhongguo renmin yinhang zonghang (Head office of the People's Bank of China), "Liu, qi yue fen zonghe baogao, 1949 nian 8 yue 5 ri" (The general report of June and July, August 5, 1949), *Jianguo yilai zhongyao wenxian xuan bian* (The collection of the important documents since the founding of the People's Republic of China) (Beijing: Zhongyang wenxian chubanshe, 1992), 173.

2. Kia-Ngau Chang, *Inflationary Spiral: The Experience in China, 1939–1950* (New York: John Wiley & Sons, 1958), 98–100.

the continuous rise in prices. The resulting hyperinflation undermined the Nationalist government's political legitimacy.[3] The Communist regime needed to tackle the inherited problem of hyperinflation by funneling money into tightly controlled channels.

Furthermore, basing the monetary system solely on the national currency, renminbi, was crucial in establishing the PRC as a modern nation state. Before the nineteenth century, it was commonplace for multiple currencies to circulate within or between political jurisdictions. States rarely expected to monopolize the supply of currencies within their frontiers. In the mid-nineteenth century, however, states started to control both the creation and the management of money inside their territories.[4] Control of money was an important part of the process of nation building. National governments sought to build up the nation as a unified economic and political unit led by a strong central authority. Governments consolidated and unified the domestic monetary order. Ultimate authority over the supply of money was limited to a government-sponsored central bank. Moreover, the free circulation of foreign currencies was banned in most countries. Foreign coins that had served as legal tender were withdrawn from circulation. At the same time, the currency that could be used to pay taxes or other contractual obligations to the state was limited to domestic money. In the West, toward the end of the nineteenth century, each currency's territory came to coincide with a political jurisdiction.[5]

Unlike countries in the West, China did not have a single national currency issued by a central bank until the currency reform in November 1935; instead, different types of money including coins, notes, and silver tael issued by a variety of authorities circulated throughout the country. Although by its 1935 currency reform the Nanjing Nationalist government succeeded in making the notes issued by the three government banks the only legal tender, the unity of the monetary system did not last long.[6] As the Nationalist government, Japanese forces and their allies, and the Chinese Communist Party battled over territories during the Sino-Japanese War (1937–1945), the competition among their currencies also intensified. At the same time, metals such as gold and silver, as well as foreign currencies including the U.S. dollar, were more highly trusted by

---

3. Ibid., 304.

4. Benjamin Cohen, *Geography of Money* (Ithaca: Cornell University Press, 1998), 6.

5. Ibid., 11, 32–34.

6. For the traditional monetary order in China and the 1935 currency reform, see Tomoko Shiroyama, *China during the Great Depression: Market, State, and the World Economy, 1929–1937* (Cambridge: Harvard University Press Asia Center, 2008), chs. 1 and 6.

the Chinese public and circulated widely well into the Civil War years (1946–1949) in spite of the government's efforts to ban black markets.[7] The PRC government needed to bring the monetary and financial situation under its control not only out of concern for the economy but also to consolidate its political power.

Although the PRC government was determined to unify the monetary system and strictly control financial transactions, the Chinese economy, particularly that of south China, did not fit into the government's agenda of nationalization. Historically, the southern province of Guangdong was independent with its own language, literature, music, and customs, and thus had a strong sense of identity. Until BC 111 when the northerners of the Han dynasty conquered Guangdong, the area had been settled by aboriginal tribes like the Miao, Li, and Yao, and the ethnic groups to the west like the Yue. As the northern Han assimilated with these ethnic groups, the local culture that would evolve into contemporary Cantonese culture emerged.[8] In recent centuries, elements from abroad had significant impacts on Guangdong society. Since at least the sixteenth century, during the Ming dynasty, merchants and artisans of the coastal areas of Guangdong and Fujian provinces traveled beyond China, mainly to Southeast Asia, and set up bases at ports, mines, and trading cities. Dating from 1850 the number of people leaving China to live and work abroad significantly increased. The gold rushes in North America and Australia and the development of plantation economies in Southeast Asia created new demands for Chinese laborers, while better and easier transportation facilitated the long-distance movement of people.

The increasing number of Chinese living abroad regularly sent money home to China. At the micro level, the remittance was integral to the household economy of the migrant's family. Without the money remitted by the male family members who had traveled overseas, agricultural production would not have sustained the livelihood of their wives, children, and parents at home.[9] At the macro level, remittances

---

7. Teruhiko Iwatake, *Kindai chūgoku tsūka tōitsu shi: Jūgonen sensōki ni okeru tsūka tōsō* (The unification of the monetary system in modern China: The currency war during the Sino-Japanese War) (Tokyo: Misuzu shobō, 1990); and Edward Kann et al., translated by Masateru Morisawa, *Senjika shina no bōeki to kinyū* (Chinese trade and finance during the War) (Tokyo: Keio shobo, 1938).

8. Ezra F. Vogel, *Canton under Communism: Programs and Politics in a Provincial Capital, 1949–1968*, 2nd ed. (Cambridge: Harvard University Press, 1980), 12–13.

9. There are a number of articles and monographs on Chinese migrant households, including Ta Chen's classic, *Emigrant Communities in South China: A Study of Overseas Migration and Its Influence on Standard of Living and Social Change* (New York: Institute of Pacific Relations, 1940).

were crucial for the Chinese international balance of payments; the money sent by overseas Chinese provided the largest single source of funds to pay for China's imports when they exceeded exports.[10]

The founding of a nationalistic PRC government and the legacy of regionally oriented societies in south China give rise to key questions: Did the historically established financial ties connecting Chinese abroad with Chinese at home survive the initial period of nation building in the PRC, and if so, how? This chapter investigates these issues with reference to the case of a Hong Kong entrepreneur, Ma Xuchao (1878–1959) and his associates in his native place, Taishan, Guangdong. From the mid-nineteenth century, Hong Kong and south China were closely linked through trade, the movement of people, and financial flows. Among other services, Hong Kong served as the hub of overseas remittances to homeland villages. Ma Xuchao was one of the businessmen who provided this banking service to his countrymen. The Hong Kong–south China financial ties were critically tested at the time of the Communist Revolution in 1949. On the one hand, the PRC government transformed the monetary system and the regulation of foreign exchange. On the other hand, in the early 1950s, countries in the West started to restrict financial transactions with mainland China. How did the financial institutions in Hong Kong and in south China cope with the domestic and international risks involved in cross-border financial transactions? And in what ways did they succeed or fail in maintaining financial flows crucial to the local economies in the region? Exploring these questions, this chapter uncovers how the financial institutions in the Hong Kong–south China area negotiated the politics surrounding national borders and what changes made it more difficult for them to send money home in the latter half of the 1950s.

MA XUCHAO'S REMITTANCE AGENCY BEFORE 1949

Ma Xuchao, born in 1878 in Taishan county, Guangdong province, moved to Hong Kong and became successful in the early twentieth

---

10. C.F. Remer, *Foreign Investment in China* (New York: Macmillan, 1933), 149–150. According to the estimates of China's international balance of payments, the ratio of total remittances to the trade deficit was 168 percent in 1903, 98 percent in 1909, 39 percent in 1912, 47 percent in 1913, 41 percent in 1920–1923, and 105 percent in 1928. Possibly because of the 1911 Revolution, remittances dropped in 1912 and 1913, and this lowered the ratio in terms of the trade deficit. Still, remittances were obviously crucial in China's international balance of payments. See Liang-lin Hsiao, *China's Foreign Trade Statistics, 1864–1949* (Cambridge: Harvard University Press, 1974), 128–129.

century.[11] Besides his main enterprise, Gong You Yuan (Kung Yau Yuen), an import-export company that dealt in fabrics, especially silks, Ma engaged in various businesses including banking, insurance, and shipping, and he also invested in a railroad project in Guangdong. Ma handled remittances to members of his clan, relatives, and villagers who had migrated overseas to the United States, Canada, and South America as shown in Ma's archives, which includes letters from family members overseas and from their families in towns and villages in Guangdong. His account books record transfers of money via Hong Kong and shed light on the internal workings of a remittance agency.[12]

Taishan county lay on the southern coast of Guangdong. In spite of its proximity to the ocean and past experience with foreign contact, Taishan did not develop into a trade center as did the nearby cities of Canton, Macao, and later, Hong Kong. The transport of goods by land was difficult because of the hilly terrain. Water transport was also inconvenient because no rivers went through the county. Constrained by its natural endowments, the people of Taishan made agriculture the center of their economy. Thus, when population pressures because of insufficient land emerged in the eighteenth century, residents began to look outside their homeland. To supplement their earnings they first sought work in the nearby cities during the slack winter months. Then, despite strictures against leaving China during the Qing dynasty (1644–1912), many Taishan people migrated to Southeast Asia. The tide of migration changed after the Opium War (1839–1842), and Taishan people, weary of economic hardship and conflicts with minorities, chose the United States and Australia as their major destinations.[13]

Ma's relatives were typical in terms of their migrant destinations. In Canada, they located in Athabasca, Camrose, Lacombe, and South Edmonton in Alberta; Toronto in Ontario; Vancouver and Victoria in British Columbia. In the United States, they settled in Bakersfield, Fresno, King City, Salinas, San Jose, San Francisco, and Walnut Grove in California; New York City; Pittsburgh in Pennsylvania; Portland in

---

11. On Ma's business, see K.C. Fok, "Lineage Ties and Business Partnership: A Hong Kong Commercial Network," in Shinya Sugiyama and Linda Grove, eds., *Commercial Networks in Modern Asia* (Richmond: Curzon, 2001), 159–170.

12. Ma Xuchao's archive, collected by James Hayes, is stored in a special collection at the University of Hong Kong Library. It consists of a large quantity of correspondence, amounting to over seven hundred letters, receipts, contracts, account books, and so on. A brief introduction to the archive can be found in James Hayes, "Collecting Shops and Business Papers in Hong Kong," Working Paper, University of Hong Kong, Centre of Asian Studies, 1982.

13. Madeline Hsu, *Dreaming of Gold, Dreaming of Home: Transnationalism and Migration between the United States and China, 1882–1943* (Stanford: Stanford University Press, 2000), 18–29.

Oregon; and Shelby in Mississippi. In Latin America, they were in Chihuahua and Mexico City, Mexico; Trujillo, Peru; and Port of Spain in Trinidad and Tobago in the southern Caribbean. During the fifteen years from 1926 to 1940, 207 people remitted money through Ma in Hong Kong to Taishan in Guangdong. Many of them were Ma's kin and their spouses. Ma married three women, surnamed Liang, Situ, and Yu. Although the first two wives died young, their relatives continued to use the financial services of Ma's remittance agency.

Although the local terms for these agencies varied from place to place—in Fujian they were known as private postal exchanges (*xinju*), in Swatow as order agencies (*piguan*), and in Canton as remittance and exchange bureaus (*huiduiju*), the main operations of all these remittance agencies served the same purposes: to transfer money and deliver letters.[14] These two operations were closely related to each other. Figure 9.1 charts the flows of money and letters.

If a sender in Southeast Asia wished to remit money to his hometown in the hinterland of Xiamen (Amoy), Fujian province, he first paid for the remittance in local currency at the nearby private postal exchange. The postal exchange converted the money into Chinese yuan and issued a receipt in triplicate: one was given to the sender, one was retained, and one was sent to the handler at the destination. The payment was then dispatched with a letter from the sender to a private postal exchange office in China. Although the letter might contain a personal message, the most important information was the payment amount. The envelope bore the sender's name, address, and the amount of the remittance for verification purposes.

When private postal exchanges in Southeast Asia had accumulated several hundred or even thousands of letters, they sent them to their corresponding agencies in China. At the same time, they transferred money, mainly through foreign banks. Because their counterparts in China lacked adequate funds to cash the received orders, they had to purchase remittance drafts from foreign banks. In addition, by sending money via Hong Kong, they profited from an exchange rate that was more advantageous to them than it would have been if they had sent remittances directly to Xiamen, where the demand for Southeast Asian remittance drafts was much lower. For this reason, they sent remittances by telegraphic transfer to their Hong Kong brokers, and they arranged for the brokers to issue Hong Kong drafts to their correspondents in China.

---

14. Bank of Taiwan, *Overseas Chinese Remittances in the 1910s* (originally published in Japanese in 1914, translated and included in George L. Hicks, *Overseas Chinese Remittances from Southeast Asia 1910–1940*) (Singapore: Select Books, 1993), 69.

Figure 9.1 Chart of Flows of Money and Letters

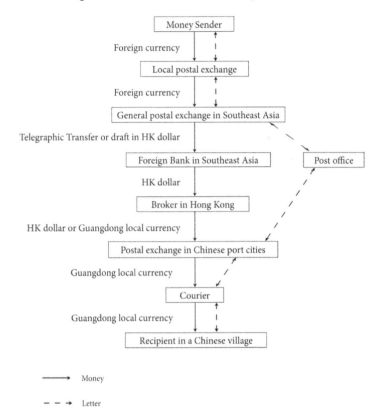

The postal exchange in China sold the drafts to foreign banks or to local Chinese-style banks in Xiamen to get Chinese yuan to hand over to the remittance recipients.[15]

When private postal exchanges in China received notices of remittance transfers from Southeast Asia, they recorded them and arranged for local couriers to come when a ship arrived. The day before the ship arrived, they exchanged the drafts that their counterparts in Southeast Asia had converted into local currency. When the orders arrived, the

---

15. Ibid., 72–73.

postal exchanges checked them against their records and dispersed monies to the appropriate destinations, sending their couriers to rural villages and mountainous regions. When the recipients received the orders, they signed or stamped the receipts for return to the senders. The private postal exchange then collected all receipts, matched them with the remittance orders, recorded their delivery, and sent them as "return orders" to Southeast Asia. When the private postal exchanges in Southeast Asia received the return orders, they checked them against their records and then stamped them "return" before sending them back to the senders of the remittances.[16]

For migrant workers bound for the West, the counterparts to the private post offices in Southeast Asia were the Gold Mountain firms (*jinshan zhuang*) in Hong Kong. Gold Mountain firms started as trading companies based in Hong Kong around the 1850s. They had close links to Chinese businesses abroad, which were often run by kinsmen or people from the same village. Responding to the demand from overseas Chinese for Chinese goods, including Chinese books and magazines, herbal medicines, fruit, and groceries, managers of Gold Mountain firms took orders and arranged for their shipment. They subsequently entered the overseas Chinese remittance business, partly taking the place of couriers. To reach places without banks and post offices in the late nineteenth and the early twentieth centuries, Gold Mountain firms established connections with Chinatown businesses around the world and with local agencies in Guangdong province, where the majority of migrants to the West originated. By 1922, there were 116 Gold Mountain firms based in Hong Kong dealing with North American firms. By 1930, the number had more than doubled to 290.[17]

Sending money and letters home through Gold Mountain firms was done in a similar way to the method used by private postal exchanges in Southeast Asia. However, without organized local agencies on their side of the Pacific, Chinese remittance senders tended to deal with American financial institutions. In the United States, a Chinese worker bought a cashier's check for the required amount from a local bank, wrote a letter with instructions about destination and recipient, and sent both via registered mail to the Gold Mountain firm of choice in Hong Kong. Alternatively, the worker could avoid dealing with American banks by asking a trusted proprietor to send the money and instructions. Once a number of such remittances had accumulated, the proprietor

---

16. Ibid., 72.

17. Hsu, *Dreaming of Gold*, 34–36. Jin Liu, ed., *Taishan yinxin* (The remittance letters to Taishan) (Beijing: Zhongguo huaqiao chubanshe, 2007), 56–57.

would purchase a single cashier's check for the total to be sent with the instructions for each individual. When the money arrived in Hong Kong, the accountant of the Gold Mountain firm cashed the check at a bank, exchanged it for silver or Hong Kong dollars, calculated the amounts to be sent to the destinations, which were mainly in Guangdong, and arranged for local couriers to deliver the money to the recipients.[18]

Ma Xuchao served as the Hong Kong–based remittance agency for his clients. His account books recorded the dates on which he received remittances, from whom, how much, and in what currencies, annually from 1926 to 1940.

Ma usually sent remittance money to the recipient designated by the sender shortly after the money arrived in Hong Kong. If the customer requested, Ma also offered a savings deposit account and an administered savings plan that paid interest. The interest rate from the savings account was 0.4 percent per week. The savings account made the financing of remittance money more flexible and safer in various ways. First, sojourners abroad and their families in Guangdong could keep their Hong Kong dollars until they were needed. Whenever they wanted, they could write to Ma to request any amount from within their accounts. Second, the sender remitted money at an exchange rate that he found favorable and could request that Ma send an amount of money regularly from the fund. Third, for depositors, Ma bought securities or bonds for investment. For example, Liang Zhenyou in Port of Spain in Trinidad and Tobago received 767.43 Hong Kong dollars as the interest for his savings on December 31, 1928, and put in 2,000 Hong Kong dollars for his family's use on March 17, 1931. Before the Sino-Japanese War broke out in 1937, Liang paid for a subscription to the newspaper *Xunhuang bao* (on December 7, 1928, December 11, 1929, September 24, 1930, and October 15, 1931) and for Chinese herbal medicine (on December 29, 1929). The savings were used, along with 397.34 Hong Kong dollars that he sent on November 19, 1938, for his son, Liang Guanghong, to cover living expenses in 1939 until Guanghong left for Port of Spain in 1939.[19]

People's savings were advantageous for Ma Xuchao too, as the foreign exchange could be used to finance his import–export business until the money was sent home. In this way, Ma and many of the remittance agencies engaging in trade could profit not only from their formal commissions but also from benefits on the side.[20]

---

18. Hsu, *Dreaming of Gold*, 37; Jin Liu, ed., *Taishan yinxin*, 57–63.
19. Liang Zhenyou's transaction record, guests' account book, Ma Archives.
20. Jin Liu, ed., *Taishan yinxin*, 38–43.

Ma Xuchao established the route for sending money from abroad to rural Guangdong and dealt with foreign banks as well as local Chinese financial institutions. In this way he could transfer money quickly and safely, enable customers to take advantage of favorable exchange rates, and provide a flexible way of financing savings. The senders' currency had to be changed into the local currencies used in rural Guangdong. Ma's clients looked for the most advantageous way to remit money, and he had to meet their requests. As several currencies circulated both in Hong Kong and in rural Guangdong, Ma and his clients had various options.

When sending money home, Ma's clan members abroad primarily purchased Hong Kong drafts from foreign banks. The number of remittances sent in Hong Kong dollars included 44 remittances out of the total of 66 (67 percent) in 1928; 22 out of 26 (85 percent) in 1933; and 31 out of 43 (72 percent) in 1939. The foreign banks included British banks such as the Hong Kong and Shanghai Bank and the Chartered Bank, the American banks First National City Bank and American Express, the Dutch banks Netherlands India Commercial Bank and the Netherlands Trading Society, the Canadian Commercial Bank of Canada, and Yokohama Specie Bank of Japan. Remitters sometimes used Chinese banks such as the Bank of East Asia (Dongya yinhang) and the Bank of Guangdong. If they did not buy a Hong Kong draft, they sent drafts in foreign currencies, either U.S. dollars or pounds sterling, or checks in foreign currencies. Since not only drafts but also checks in foreign currencies circulated in the Hong Kong foreign exchange, Ma could sell them on the market in exchange for Hong Kong dollars.[21]

In transferring funds from Hong Kong to Guangdong, Ma either converted Hong Kong dollars into the local currency of Guangdong, the Canton subsidiary coin, or directly sent cash or drafts. Guangdong was independent in terms of its monetary system and, the Canton subsidiary coin was widely used instead of the Chinese yuan among the populace. Before 1933, from 40 to 70 percent of the remitted money was changed into the Canton subsidiary coin.[22] From 1934 on, the Canton subsidiary coin was seldom used for transfers, and Hong Kong dollars were sent to China. The financial crisis that arose in 1934–1935, partly caused by the

---

21. Yao Qiqin, *Xianggang jinrong* (Hong Kong money market) rev. ed. (Hong Kong: Times Library, 1962), 104.

22. During the eight years from 1926 to 1933, the percentage each year was 64.5, 69.7, 49.3, 60.2, 48.0, 22.7, 43.2, and 55.1. The amount invested in 1931 was proportionately small because a large amount of the remittance was invested in a share of the Dahua Company.

Great Depression, and the consequent currency reform of 1935, under which China abandoned the silver standard monetary system, obviously influenced decisions to change the currency used for remittances. It is noteworthy that after the currency reform, China's national currency, the yuan, was not used, and the Hong Kong dollar became the dominant currency for Ma's transactions. After the currency reform, the central government tried unsuccessfully to abolish the Canton subsidiary coin and enforce the circulation of legal tender notes issued by the government bank. The popular preference for the Hong Kong dollar increased after the outbreak of the Sino–Japanese War in 1937. One of the recipients of remittances in Guangdong asked Ma to send Hong Kong dollars, saying, "The confusion of financial markets is severe and the rise of prices is steep. Please remit money in Hong Kong dollars but do not change them into Chinese yuan or Canton subsidiary coins, so that I can avoid the loss from inflation."[23]

The method used to remit money to recipients in Guangdong also changed after the mid-1930s. Before 1935, Ma often sent money to rural areas through the local financial agency, Wuzhou and Hongfeng, which his agent, Ma Lianlun, managed; through the Guofeng agency, which his brother-in-law, Liang Shiyang, owned; and through two other agencies, Richang and Changfeng. However, as the demand for Hong Kong dollars increased, he had to hire a courier to travel between Hong Kong and Guangdong instead of using financial agencies. In 1939 the percentage of couriered transactions reached 45.7 percent of remittances compared to only 5.8 percent in 1935. As shown below, dealing with couriers put an extra burden on Ma's remittance business in the 1940s and 1950s.

BORDERS CLOSING

From its inception in 1949, the PRC government under the Chinese Communist Party (CCP) decided to take control and restore order in the foreign exchange market and in widely circulated gold, silver, and foreign currencies in the domestic monetary system.[24] At the same time, the PRC government recognized that remittances were an important source of foreign exchange and a vital source of income for Chinese households

---

23. Bangzhou's mother to Ma Xuchao, September 13, 1939, Ma Archives.

24. Guangzhoushi junshi guanzhi weiyuanhui (The military control committee of Guangzhou), "Yanjin shiyong jinyin waibi" (Strict prohibition of the usage of gold, silver, and foreign currencies), *Nanfang ribao*, November 18, 1949.

with family members overseas. Thus the government tried to control the remittance organizations to accommodate the overseas Chinese in the early 1950s. However, as Western governments' confrontations with Communist regimes heightened in the early 1950s, some of them, including those of the United States and Canada, restricted financial transactions with China and imposed increasing government regulation with which Ma had to cope in the 1950s.

During the Civil War years from 1945 to 1949, the Guangdong populace's preference for the Hong Kong dollar persisted. Ma's clients were no exception. When Liang Xicun, Ma Xuchao's nephew in Trinidad and Tobago, sent drafts in British pound sterling, Ma changed them into Hong Kong dollars and sent them as cash to Guangdong.[25]

In 1949, after the Communists' victory over the Nationalists in the Civil War, the local government in south China tightened control over foreign exchange transactions. In October 1949, while raising the official exchange rate of renminbi to compete with the black market, the government closed the local banks that it suspected of engaging in illegal transactions of foreign exchange.[26] On February 10, 1950, the regime moved to outlaw the circulation of all foreign currency, whether for payment of salaries, purchase of goods, or foreign exchange. Ma's customers in Taishan complained that, because government inspections were rigorous, they could not change the remitted money into renminbi. They did not want to change the money at the official rate for renminbi, which was much lower than the black-market rate, so they sent the remittance drafts back to Hong Kong or kept them while awaiting a change of circumstances.[27] Since Hong Kong dollars in particular had been widely used in south China, the local government recognized that it would be difficult to eliminate this currency completely in the short term.[28] The activities of Ma's remittance agency confirmed the government's concern. According to the archives, Hong Kong dollars, cash, and foreign checks crossed the border frequently in the early 1950s.

25. Liang Xicun's transaction record, guests' account book, Ma Archives.

26. Cai Fusheng, "Yinianlai huanan dui gangbi de toucheng 1950 nian 10 yue 1 ri" (A year of war against the Hong Kong dollar in south China, October 1, 1950), *Jianguo yilai*, 202–205.

27. Liang Chuanwei to Ma Xuchao, October 19, 1950; Ma Jueqing to Ma Xuchao, November 27, 1950, both in Ma Archives.

28. Zhongcaiwei, "Huadong hanan xiqu suqing gangbi de fangzhen" (September 13, 1949), *Jianguo yilai*, 184.

Once the government tightened its control, transactions were not easy and couriers rather than formal financial institutions played the crucial role in transmission during these turbulent years. For more than a decade, from 1939 to 1951, hiring couriers was the main way of transferring goods, money, and information.[29] During this tumultuous period in China, covering the Sino–Japanese War, World War II, the Civil War, and the initial period of the PRC regime, professional couriers commuted between Hong Kong and localities in south China. Sociopolitical confusion and the country's financial chaos significantly deepened. Courier missions were risky, but, at the same time, they could earn large profits from scarce goods and financial resources. Under these circumstances, controlling couriers was very difficult.

Ma recruited fellow Taishan natives as couriers (*shuike*). When hiring them to carry money to Guangdong, he required them to keep records of transactions. Whenever couriers received money, they had to issue receipts stating the amount and the date. Once the recipient received the money, he had to sign the document as proof. Despite local ties and strict tracking of the flow of money, "Couriers became less trustworthy,"[30] as Ma Jueqing, a daughter of Ma Xuchao's niece residing in Taishan, stated in November 1950. Families of overseas Chinese, who had long depended on their family members abroad to cover most of their living expenses, could not live without remittances. They were annoyed with delays and the failure of couriers to deliver money. For example, Ma Zhoucheng, Ma Xuchao's nephew in Toronto, Canada, sent 400 Hong Kong dollars through Ma in Hong Kong to his son, Ma Guochuan, in Taishan in October 1950. However, in December, Ma Guochuan complained that Ma Rongnian, the hired courier, had not delivered the money. Ma Rongnian apparently was not trustworthy. Ma Junlun in Vancouver, Canada, also complained that his check for 1,000 Hong Kong dollars sent to his wife in Baisha, Taishan, was not delivered in full by Ma Rongnian; he handed over only 270 Hong Kong dollars while the remainder, 730 Hong Kong dollars, had not been given to Junlun's wife by March 7, 1951.[31] Wondering which village in Taishan Ma Rongnian came from, Ma Zhoucheng and other fellow clansmen insisted that

---

29. Especially during the war, couriers seem to have been popular among financial institutions. Guangdong Provincial Bank, for example, contracted 280 couriers to offer transfer services with lower rates. See *Nanpō gunsei sōkanbu chōsabu, Marai kakyō no sōkin ni tsuite* (Remittances by overseas Chinese in Malaya) (n.p.: n.pub., 1943), 58.

30. Ma Jueqing to Ma Xuchao, November 27, 1950, Ma Archives.

31. Ma Junlun to Ma Xuchao, March 7, 1951, Ma Archives.

Ma Xuchao, as the center of the native-place network, should force Ma Rongnian to return 400 Hong Kong dollars to Ma Zhoucheng's family.[32] They pointed out, "Otherwise, many overseas Chinese will be shocked by the unreliability." When the money had not been delivered to Ma Zhoucheng's family by early April 1951, Ma Zhoucheng claimed that Ma Xuchao should take responsibility for this failure. Otherwise, as Ma Zhoucheng warned Ma Xuchao, he would go to the foreign bank through which he had purchased the remittance draft and notify them that the draft had gone missing during the transaction. This would have seriously damaged Ma Xuchao's reputation in Hong Kong.[33]

It is not clear how the case of Ma Zhongcheng was resolved, but Ma Junlun and Ma Xuchao were reconciled over the incident of Ma Rongnian, possibly with Ma Xuchao paying compensation.[34] As social disturbances deepened and the black market for goods and foreign currencies thrived during and after the war, the local ties that had traditionally sustained the network obviously were severely strained. Because remittances were indispensable for these Chinese families, there were always demands for transmissions from their overseas members, and thus opportunities for couriers to take advantage of them for their own profit. In fact, it was common for many couriers to use their customer's money to purchase merchandise and sell it on their way to a local village and then to cover the payment out of their profits from the sales. From this kind of transaction the courier could earn an extra profit out of remittance, in addition to the commission, so it became known as "borrow a hen and make it lay an egg" (*jieji shengdan*).[35] Still, once the commodity market turned against a courier, he might not have been able to pay back the amount that his customers gave him. Despite these risks and pressures, remitters continued to make monetary transactions that depended on the local ties connecting people on either side of the border.

---

32. Ma Zhoucheng to Ma Xuchao, February 5, 1951, Ma Archives.

33. Ma Zhoucheng to Ma Xuchao, April 8, 1951, Ma Archives.

34. Ma Junlun to Ma Xuchao, March 7, 1954, Ma Archives.

35. Ceng Tao, "Guangdong de shuike yu qiaopi ye" (Couriers and remittance agencies in Guangdong) in Guangdong sheng zhengxie wenshi ziliao yanjiuhui weiyuanhui and Zhongguo renmin yinhang Guangdong sheng fenhang jinrong yanjiusuo, Guangdong wenshi ziliao (The committee for studying the history of Guangdong province's Political Consultative Conference and the financial research Institute of the People's Bank of China, Guangdong Provincial Branch), *Guangdong wenshi ziliao* 69 (Guangzhou: Guangdong renmin chubanshe, 1992), 68–69.

Traditionally, trade with and remittance to China through Hong Kong was oriented toward the economic advantages provided by Hong Kong, the entrepôt where goods and money in different currencies met. In the 1950s, remitting money via Hong Kong became more political. Money from abroad often took an indirect route, particularly through Hong Kong, because governments controlled foreign exchange in the countries where overseas settlements were located, most notably in the United States.

On December 16, 1950, the United States government issued an order to freeze all Chinese-owned U.S. dollar assets and required all transactions in Chinese names to be investigated for Communist connections. Although the freezing order did not target overseas Chinese, it had a considerable impact on them. On January 10, 1951, Ma Guocong, Ma Xuchao's nephew who was living in Shelby, Mississippi, sent a check for US$100 to Ma Xuchao. Guocong complained that, because the United States government did not allow goods and bank drafts to be sent to mainland China, banks either refused to issue checks or limited the transaction amounts. The banks also declared that if a bank draft used in Hong Kong or Macao reached mainland China, went missing, or was frozen, the bank would not take responsibility. Given these circumstances, Ma Guocong asked Ma Xuchao to change the bank draft into Hong Kong dollars. Initially, Ma Xuchao found it difficult to send the draft to China.[36] On January 28, Ma Fulun, Ma Xuchao's elder brother's son in California, asked Ma Xuchao to send money home. Ma Fulun also expressed his concern about the United States regulations, and decided to send money from his account to meet family members' and relatives' year-end needs; this consisted of five hundred Hong Kong dollars for his son, Wenwei, fifty Hong Kong dollars for his nephew, Jiqun, twenty Hong Kong dollars for his sister, Nugui, and twenty Hong Kong dollars for his niece, Shuzhen.[37]

The foreign governments' policies toward China as well as the Chinese government's tight control over foreign exchange transactions might have affected remittances from abroad, as drops in the financial records of Ma Licheng in Camrose, Alberta, Canada and Ma Fulun in King City, California, suggest. However, the remittances never ceased, as shown by the records of Yu Guojun, in Vancouver, Canada; Liang Yinghong in Port of Spain, Trinidad and Tobago; and Liang Xichao,

---

36. Ma Guocong to Ma Xuchao, January 10, 1951, Ma Archives.
37. Ma Fulun to Ma Xuchao, January 28, 1951, Ma Archives.

in New York.[38] For the remitters, the presence of Ma Xuchao in Hong Kong was the cornerstone of their survival strategy. They could report to the United States government Ma Xuchao's Hong Kong resident ID number as the recipient, so that he could send money from there to villages in inland China. Remitters usually bought bankers' drafts from the Hong Kong and Shanghai Bank or Chartered Bank in New York, San Francisco, or other financial centers, which were then mailed to Hong Kong and sold on the free market.[39] Between 1949 and 1957, at least thirty clients of Ma Xuchao requested this kind of transaction on 108 different occasions.[40]

The remittance agencies in Hong Kong, including Ma Xuchao's, were used because of the technical difficulties of sending foreign exchange directly to China. This special position of Hong Kong became even more crucial toward the mid-1950s.

PRESSURE FROM LOCAL SOCIETY IN THE MID-1950S

In 1952, as the PRC government succeeded in absorbing foreign currencies and metals in exchange for renminbi, it increased its control over China's monetary system. At the same time, it tried to take a tighter grip on the financial system. Its control over overseas Chinese remittances was no exception. The PRC government was well aware of the importance of the overseas Chinese remittances in terms of the micro-level household and the macro-level international balance of payments. As the Guangdong branch of Bank of China estimated, of the province's 30 million people, 6.4 million were out of the country and another 10 million were related to these overseas Chinese. The annual remittance of US$70 million was crucial for the regional economy of south China.[41] From the government's standpoint, the overseas Chinese remittances were most significant as a source of foreign exchange for the national economy. The People's Bank of China noted that the government needed

---

38. Transaction records for Ma Licheng, Ma Fulun, Yu Guojun, Liang Yinghong, and Liang Xichao, guests' account book, Ma Archives.

39. Catherine R. Schenk, *Hong Kong as an International Financial Centre: Emergence and Development 1945–65* (London and New York: Routledge, 2001), 74.

40. The envelopes of remitters record how much they sent, in which currency, through which bank, from where, and when. Envelope collection in Ma Archives.

41. "Huanan waihui gongzuo baogao, Zhongguo yinhang Guangzhou fenhang" (A report on the foreign exchange in south China by Guangdong branch of Bank of China) (September 25, 1951), Guangdong Provincial Archives, 302-1-10.

to fight for this resource, the amount of which was almost equivalent to the total income of Shanxi province.[42] Overseas Chinese remittances in the years 1929 to 1941 had averaged between US$80 million and US$100 million annually, and even in the postwar period had ranged from US$66 to US$130 million.[43] This infusion of funds was timely because the new Chinese government's prospects for obtaining substantial foreign aid were limited to what could be extracted from the Soviet Union, and under a Sino-Soviet agreement of February 1950, this amounted to no more than US$300 million in five annual installments.[44] Provided that the family remittances reached China through official channels, they had the effect of a direct grant of foreign exchange that, unlike the Soviet Union's, did not have to be repaid.

The key aim for the government in securing foreign exchange was to ensure that remittances went through official financial institutions. Beginning in 1951, the government gradually began to establish a routine for sending money to China. From October of that year the Bank of China required that all remittances be handed over to it in the places from which the remittances had been sent. Trust in the government bank rose through time, as several of Ma Xuchao's clients instructed him to send money to the Bank of China or the People's Bank of China. The government tried to collectivize the remittance agencies in the country into various new institutions: joint management offices (*lianying chu*) were established in 1955 and joint sending offices (*lianhe paisong chu*) in 1957.

However, the private remittance agencies in China were not totally eliminated even in the latter half of the 1950s. In 1951, the proportion of overseas Chinese remittances handled by the remittance agencies in Guangdong was 44 percent; more important, in the hometowns of overseas Chinese, remittance agencies were dominant, handling 81 percent in Shantou, 91 percent in Hainan, and 60–65 percent in Taishan. As his clients requested, Ma Xuchao sent money through the Bank of China and the People's Bank of China beginning in the mid-1950s.[45] To the government's regret, the private remittance agencies survived alongside these banks well into the latter half of the 1950s.[46]

42. Renmin yinhang zonghang (The head office of the People's Bank of China), "Di yi jie quanguo jinrong huiyi conghe jilu" (The general record of the first national financial meeting) (March 15, 1950), *Jianguo yilai*, 809–810.

43. *Renmin ribao*, April 21, 1950.

44. Alexander Eckstein, *Communist China's Economic Growth and Foreign Trade* (New York: McGraw Hill, 1966), 154–159.

45. Grandmother of Ma Shaoxiong to Ma Xuchao on September 10, 1954, Ma Archives.

46. Ma Zhilun to Ma Xuchao, December 29, 1954, Ma Archives.

The government intended to control, and late in 1956 to collectivize, the private remittance agencies, but this process turned out to be very complicated. Since each agency was independent and had little sense of solidarity with any other agency, the government had only a fragmented basis for exercising official control. Because the remittance agencies engaged in other business, especially trade, it was not clear how to categorize them in the first place.[47]

Apart from repeated efforts at persuasion, the government could not put much pressure on the remittance agencies since it had to avoid raising fears among overseas Chinese about sending money home.[48] In fact, pressure on the recipients of remittances came from local society rather than the government in Guangdong. Because families receiving remittances lacked their male members, who worked abroad, they often rented their farmland to neighbors. During the land reform campaign, they were criticized for being landlords, even though the piece of land that they possessed was not large.[49] They were also criticized for having greater incomes than others in their villages. By their nature, remittance recipients did not fit the categorization of landlord, rich farmer, or poor peasant. The families of overseas Chinese also suffered because CCP cadres tried to speed up the land reform process by seizing remitted money from these families.[50] Under official slogans such as "Foreign exchange for public benefit, but profit for private benefit" (*Waihui guigong, liyi guise*) and "Make remittance easy, and serve the overseas Chinese well" (*Bianli qiaohui, fuwu qiaobao*), the PRC government attempted to prevent cadres' "mistreatment" of recipients of overseas Chinese remittances, but this

---

47. Zhongguo yinhang Guangzhou fenhang xing jingli, "Guanyu qiaohui wenti de baogao" (Report on overseas Chinese remittances) (July 15, 1953), Guangdong Provincial Archives, 204-1-81-130.

48. "Pizhuan Yuezhong qu dangwei tongzhanbu guanyu Yuezhong qu chengqu wending he fazhan qiaohui huiyi de zongjie baogao" (The final report of the meeting on stabilization and cultivation of overseas Chinese remittances in central Guangdong) (October 30, 1954), Guangdong Provincial Archives, 204-1-111-087. "Ganche dangde 'bianli qiaohui fuwu qiaobao' zhengce zuzhi qiaohui zhichi guojia shehui zhuyi jianshe: Taishan xian zhihang qiaohui gongzuo qingkuang" (Carrying out the party's policy of "easing overseas Chinese remittances and serving for overseas Chinese," institutionalizing overseas Chinese remittances, and supporting to found socialist state: Works related to overseas Chinese remittances by the Taishan country branch) (September 1959), Guangdong Provincial Archives, 222-2-245-26.

49. Ma Weiyu's wife to Ma Xuchao, n.d., Ma Archives.

50. "Zai nongmin yundong zhong youguan huaqiao yu qiaohui chuli de jige wenti de zhishi" (Some problems in dealing with overseas Chinese and their remittances during peasant movements) (August 31, 1951), Guangdong Provincial Archives, 236-1-3-26.

rhetoric did not ease the recipients' fears.[51] Ironically, during this period, the families of overseas Chinese desperately needed money to pay for the compensation that local government organizations requested.[52] To cover these costs, overseas Chinese withheld their money in Hong Kong until the family in need requested that the money be sent home.[53]

The records of Ma's clients confirm the government's assessment of the situation in the mid-1950s. According to his savings account book, twelve clients remitted money between 1951 and 1959. Their transactions took place regularly. For example, Yu Guojun, Ma Xuchao's brother-in-law, who resided in Vancouver, Canada, sent a total of 17,347.10 Hong Kong dollars in eighty-four separate transfers between March 1952 and December 1958. The money received by Ma was sent through the Bank of China to his wife in Guangdong. Liang Yinghong, Ma's former wife's nephew in Port of Spain, Trinidad and Tobago, sent one thousand pounds sterling by telegraphic transfer through the Chartered Bank on July 12, 1956. This sum was changed into Hong Kong dollars and sent to his family in Guangdong in eighteen separate amounts between July 17, 1956, and July 29, 1958. Liang Xichao, another nephew in New York, sent twenty-one US$150 drafts in thirty-six transfers from September 1953 to March 1959. The money was sent through the Bank of China to his wife and mother to finance their daily expenses.[54]

Because Hong Kong and south China were tightly integrated in terms of their economies but politically separated, the remittance agencies in the British colony of Hong Kong, including Ma Xuchao's, served as the intermediaries for overseas Chinese to transmit their assets untouched by government intervention in mainland China. In other words, without the connection with Hong Kong, the families of overseas Chinese could not have received the means of survival nor could the Chinese government have received the foreign exchange that it needed.

Based in Hong Kong, Ma's organization succeeded in coping with the government regulations on both sides of the Pacific. However, during the Great Leap Forward, overseas Chinese became fearful that the People's communes would confiscate their remittances. As the purchasable com-

---

51. Renmin yinhang zonghang, "Di yi jie quanguo jinrong huiyi," *Jianguo yilai*, 808–809.

52. Ma Weiyu's wife to Ma Xuchao, n.d.; Ma Xiaoling to Ma Xuchao, October 11, 1951, both in Ma Archives.

53. "Ganche dangde 'bianli qiaohui fuwu qiaobao' zhengce" (Carrying out the policy "easing overseas Chinese remittances and serving overseas Chinese"), Guangdong Provincial Archives, 222-2-245-26.

54. Transaction records for Yu Guojun, Liang Yinghong, and Liang Xichao, guests' account book, Ma Archives.

modities disappeared under the disorder of the national economy, some Chinese abroad chose to send their family daily necessities including grain, oil, and fertilizer instead of money. The value of overseas Chinese remittances gradually declined in 1960.

Coincidentally or not, Ma Xuchao's archives, with its final traceable remittance by Yu Guojun dated July 13, 1957, have no records from the 1960s.[55]

In order to encourage overseas Chinese to resume remitting money home, the government started to issue an overseas Chinese remittance certificate (*qiaohui zheng*) so that the families of overseas Chinese would enjoy advantages for purchasing commodities. In 1966, under the autarky of the Cultural Revolution, these overseas Chinese remittance certificates were banned.[56] In Taishan, the amount of remittance may have increased during the period partly because the income of overseas Chinese generally increased.[57] Still, it became more risky for their families to receive money in the face of public attacks on such "bourgeois" activities.

CONCLUSION

In this chapter, I have examined transnationality in a Chinese remittance agency during the key transitional era of the early PRC. To conclude, I summarize the theoretical implications of the findings in terms of the internal dynamics of business networks and of the cross-border business transactions in mid-twentieth century Asia.

As previous studies have pointed out, local ties determined the routes for overseas Chinese remittances. Remittance agencies, such as private postal exchanges, reached out to immigrant workers and sojourning traders and offered to connect them with their fellow villagers and

---

55. Ma Xuchao's death in June 1959 might be another reason for the discontinuity, although the other businesses, such as real estate, seem to have been inherited by his descendants.

56. Guangdong sheng tezhong shangpin gongying gongsi (The Guangdong provincial corporation for supplying special goods), "Guanyu dangqian qiaohui shangpin gongying qingkuang he youguan jigou deng wenti de baogao" (Report of the current supply of merchandise for overseas Chinese remittances and the related organization) (September 16, 1966), Guangdong Provincial Archives, 296-1-263-124.

57. During the decade from June 1966 to June 1976, the average amount of remittance reached US$14,690,000, 1.75 times larger than the average per year from 1959 to 1962. Taishan xian difangzhi bianzuan weiyuan hui (The editorial board of the Taishan county gazetteer), *Taishan xianzhi* (The gazetteer of Taishan) (Guangdong: Guangdong renmin chubanshe, 1998), 407.

townsmen in China. Trust based upon local ties was obviously crucial for the network of remittance agencies to carry out exchanges between workers abroad and their families at home. Nevertheless, it is worth noting that each transaction was carefully checked through written records, such as receipts from recipients, contracts with hired couriers, certificates of bank drafts, and so on. Even if long-term personal relationships were the critical factor in the way Chinese businessmen organized their businesses, an important question concerns whether, or to what extent, written contracts and records provided an institutional basis for enhancing the stability of business networks.

The case of Ma Xuchao's enterprise indicates that the network-based remittance business came under severe strains from changes in the business environment between the early 1940s and the mid-1950s. During and after the war, as carrying money became more risky and the black market spread, hired couriers became more tempted to betray personal trust and sometimes abscond with the money. Networks based exclusively on shared values such as kinship and local ties could not formally enforce regulations. So businessmen and their clients resorted to using written records to track down problems and sort them out, and they had a measure of success even if they could not completely eliminate opportunism among couriers and other workers. In light of the weak level of enforcement of international contracts worldwide and the asymmetrical information about trading opportunities commonly observed in international trade and transactions, the business networks' regulatory power in this case is rather impressive.

When the Civil War ended, the formation of the PRC as a nation state and its international ideological confrontations made remitting money to China more difficult. Ironically, the conflict between West and East provided Ma Xuchao with a new business opportunity. Because the remittance system was firmly embedded in the rural household economy in south China, the strong demand for transmission of money had long existed. Taking advantage of his base in Hong Kong, Ma sustained the monetary flow into China from abroad. Although transaction amounts declined by 1960, his remittance business continued at least until then.

The story of Ma's remittance agency and its clients reveals how they negotiated with nation states across national borders. As the policies toward international trade and financial flows changed along with the governments' policy targets, the remittance agencies' activities were sometimes denounced as smuggling or as illegal transactions. Nevertheless, Chinese households in south China remained heavily dependent on remittances from abroad even after China's borders began to close in the 1950s. Aware of households' need for the remitted money from abroad and recognizing its importance as a source of foreign exchange, the PRC government had to compromise with private remittance agencies even while it made efforts to take a firm grip on the monetary and financial system.

The tension between the remittance agencies and the government over the cross-border transactions was one of the most important dimensions in the formation of the national economy during the early period of the PRC. Traditionally China, particularly south China, was closely integrated with the world economy. Remittance agencies met the special demand for international transactions from ordinary Chinese workers abroad. However, throughout World War II and the postwar rise of nation states, governments tightened their grip on the economy, especially cross-border transactions, and they continued to do so at least until the period of deregulation dating from the 1980s. On the important and unexplored question of how business networks have survived the rise of official regulation, the case of Ma Xuchao's remittance agency is more than a mere historical episode. It gives us a point of departure for viewing China's 1949 Revolution in a long-term perspective.

PART FOUR

CAPITALISTS WHO REMAINED ABROAD

This page is intentionally left blank.

10   WITHSTANDING COMMUNISM |
The Ho Tung Family of Hong Kong, 1946–1956
Siu-lun Wong and Victor Zheng

How did "China's richest man" cope with the Chinese Communist Revolution? Did he take flight, like T.V. Soong, to seek refuge abroad? Or did he choose to return to the mainland, like Liu Hongsheng to live with communism?[1] He did neither. He stood his ground. He stayed in Hong Kong with most of his family members. He stared the Chinese Communists in the eye and held his nerve. This man was Sir Robert Ho Tung (1862–1956).

In an interview published in 1933, Sir Robert Ho Tung said, "I am supposed to be the richest man in China. I have already made plans for the disposal of my money when I die."[2] It might not be an exaggeration to designate him as the richest man in China at that time. Just a few years later, when Britain was gearing up for World War II, then governor of Hong Kong, Sir Geoffrey Northcote, wrote to Ho Tung to thank him for his "scrupulous observance of the regulations governing the surrender of foreign exchange." In that letter of May 28, 1941, Northcote referred to Ho Tung as "the largest foreign currency holder in the Colony." He highlighted the fact that "the sums you have so willingly transferred to His Majesty's Government at unfavorable rates represent a really considerable share in this Colony's total monetary

---

We wish to thank other members of our research team, Dr. Sun Wen-bin, Dr. Ho Tsai-man and Dr. Cheng Chi-wai for their support and contributions. We are also indebted to Dr. Wong Sau-ngan for suggestions on important sources, and to Miss Jocko Yuen and Miss Viola Cheung for their research assistance. The research for this paper was partially supported financially by the Hong Kong Research Grants Council for the project on "Entrepreneurial Families: The Rong, Gu and Ho Tung Business Dynasties" (HKU 7468/05H). Subsequent research is funded by the Chiang Ching-kuo Foundation for the project on "Chinese Family Business and Stock Market" (Project Ref. No. RG012-P-10).

1. Sherman Cochran, "Capitalists Choosing Communist China: The Liu Family of Shanghai, 1948–1956," in Jeremy Brown and Paul G. Pickowicz, eds., *Dilemmas of Victory: The Early Years of The People's Republic of China* (Cambridge: Harvard University Press, 2007), 359–385.

2. *South China Morning Post* (hereafter cited as SCMP), July 17, 1933.

assistance to the war effort."[3] So it seems that the financial standing of Ho Tung as the richest man in Hong Kong before World War II was quite certain.

But whether he was the richest man in the whole of China is more difficult to ascertain. Yet we know Ho Tung personally donated 100,000 dollars in 1936 to purchase a war plane to celebrate the fiftieth birthday of Chiang Kai-shek and to strengthen China's air force.[4] In order to acknowledge these donations throughout the country to assist in the purchase of war planes, the Chinese Nationalist government awarded gold medals in 1937 to the top nine donors. Ho Tung came first on the list.[5]

On the eve of the Chinese Communist victory, Ho Tung was in Britain. He was already eighty-seven years old. He had a long interview with Creech Jones, secretary of state for the Colonies on May 27, 1949. On the next day, he told the correspondent of the *South China Morning Post* in London that "Hong Kong is safe." He predicted that there would be "no Communist attack." He expressed regret that he could not do more as a peacemaker to avert the crisis of the Civil War:

> It is a national calamity that the Nationalist Government and the People's Army cannot come to some satisfactory terms ... I believe the Nationalist and the People's Army could have come to a satisfactory agreement two years ago and at that time I was willing to offer my services as mediator because I had a strong feeling that I would have been able to bring the two parties together because I am neither an official nor a politician and I have no other motive than to prevent heavy losses of life and destruction of property but now, of course, it is too late.[6]

Then in late October 1949, soon after the establishment of the People's Republic of China, he made another public statement in Europe. He was received by the French president, M. Vincent Auriol, in the Élysée Palace on October 25. Before seeing M. Auriol, he spoke to reporters to allay fears that the Chinese Communists might attack Hong Kong:

---

3. Hong Kong Public Records Office (hereafter cited as HKPRO), Sir Robert Ho Tung: Confidential Correspondence (HKRS 5022-45), 1946, 1.2.

4. *Xianggang gongshang ribao* (Hong Kong Kung Sheung Jih Pao; hereafter cited as XGGSRB), October 12, 1936.

5. XGGSRB, June 20, 1937.

6. SCMP, May 30, 1949.

I have strong reasons to believe in the good judgment of Mao Tse-tung [Mao Zedong] and Chou En-lai [Zhou Enlai] (Foreign Minister of the Peiping regime) in not taking any steps to attack Hong Kong ... I have not met either of them but I have carefully studied the remarks made by General [George C.] Marshall that both of them are very sincere and honest ... I have also read carefully the autobiography of General Mao written in Chinese, from which I note he went through a very hard life and, in my opinion, when men have gone through such hard lives they will invariably act with wisdom. There is no reason to believe that they will attack Hong Kong, because the population there is about 90 per cent Chinese and in any such attack the Chinese community would be the greatest sufferers.[7]

He further indicated that "in any case he intended to return to Hong Kong to share its future with the territory's residents." This he did. It turned out that his prognosis on the future of Hong Kong was remarkably accurate.

CUTTING LOSSES

Nonetheless, the Chinese Communist victory is a momentous event. As a rich man confronting this tidal wave of communism, Ho Tung would be expected to suffer heavy losses. He was a leading investor in real estate throughout China. He held substantial tracts of land and housing properties in Shanghai, Qingdao, and other ports in the Yangzi delta and northern China, not to mention his extensive land holdings in Hong Kong and Macao. He had dispatched his son, Edward Ho Sai-kim, to be stationed in Shanghai before the Anti-Japanese War to look after his properties in China. Even though Edward had lost both of his legs during a Japanese bombing while seeking shelter in Hong Kong during the war, he returned to Shanghai to resume his business duties for the family after the Japanese had surrendered. When Irene, his sister, left Tangshan to return to Hong Kong in 1946, she told us that she "sailed from the port of Chinwangdao [Qinhuangdao] for Shanghai and again stayed with Eddie and his family in Father's house [in Shanghai] for ten days" before continuing her trip further south to Hong Kong.[8] Before the

---

7. *The China Mail*, October 27, 1949.

8. Irene Cheng, *International Reminiscences* (Hong Kong: David C. Lam Institute for East-West Studies, Hong Kong Baptist University, 1997), 289.

Chinese Communists entered Shanghai in 1949, Edward too returned to Hong Kong. Ho Tung's landed properties on the Chinese mainland were taken over by the new Communist government.

Another big loss for Ho Tung was the termination of the compradore system. As the British "princely *hongs*" were driven out of the Chinese mainland, they had to abandon the huge China trade market. During the first half of the twentieth century, Ho Tung and his brothers had built up one of the largest compradore networks anchored in Hong Kong. In his study of the compradores of the Hong Kong and Shanghai Bank, the historian Carl Smith has identified Ho Sai Wing as the Fifth Compradore of the Bank from 1912–1946. According to Smith, Ho Sai Wing began his career as a compradore of E.D. Sassoon and Company. He became compradore of the Hong Kong Bank in 1912 with security provided by his adopted father, Ho Tung, for $300,000. Smith gave a concise description of the compradore network spun by the Ho Tung family:

> The first generation of the Ho family were compradores for Jardines. The second generation spread itself into other firms. Ho Sai Wing was at the Bank, his brother Ho Sai Iu was compradore of the Mercantile Bank, another brother Ho Sai Kwong, succeeded Ho Sai Wing as compradore at E.D. Sassoon and Company, and yet another brother Ho Sai Leung was a compradore at Jardines. These were all sons of Ho Fuk, though Ho Sai Wing, of course had been adopted by his uncle, Ho Tung. Ho Sai Ki, another son of Ho Fuk, became compradore for Arnhold and Company. Ho Sai Wa, a cousin, was an assistant compradore in the Mercantile Bank.[9]

This sketch only captured the core of the network. If we were to include the in-laws and other relatives by marriage of the Ho Tung brothers, then we would see a more intricate web with compradorial linkages connecting up more firms such as Hong Kong and Kowloon Wharves and Go-downs, A.S. Watson & Co., Banco Nacional Ultramarine, and Nippon Yusen Kaisha. A full list of the compradorial positions occupied by members of the Ho Tung family is shown in Table 10.1. With the Chinese Communist onslaught, this network crumbled.

---

9. Carl T. Smith, "Compradores of the Hongkong Bank," in Frank H.H. King, ed., *Eastern Banking Essays in the History of the Hongkong and Shanghai Banking Corporation* (London: The Athlone Press, 1983), 110.

Jardine Matheson abolished its compradore system in 1950.[10] The Hong Kong and Shanghai Bank removed the title of compradore in 1960, announcing that the term was "an anachronism" and would no longer be used.[11]

Ho Tung had created a family dynasty of compradores. The collapse of the system was undoubtedly a big setback for him. Yet this was perhaps less heavy a blow than the one that nearly shattered his political ambitions for his son, General Ho Shai-lai (1906–1998; also known as Ho Sai Lai). Ho Shai-lai was the son that would not follow in his father's footsteps. He chose a military career for himself. After failing to dissuade his son initially from that choice, Ho Tung threw his weight behind his son by mobilizing high level political connections at his disposal to get Ho Shai-lai admitted to the top British and French military academies for training. He then arranged for his son to be appointed an aide to Zhang Xueliang in northeast China. In 1933, Ho Shai-lai went to the United States for further military training at the U.S. Army Command and General Staff School at Fort Leavenworth. Subsequently, tainted by the Xi'an incident that had been initiated by Zhang Xueliang in 1936, his military career in the Nationalist army stalled. In order to get his son back into Chiang Kai-shek's favor, Ho Tung donated a war plane to celebrate Chiang's birthday. He also took the lead in buying national bonds to assist in the war effort against Japan. Later in life, he told his good friend and consultant, Jack Braga, "he reckoned that if he had not, to please his son Robert [Shai-lai], invested in Chinese Bonds his fortune would have been worth at least twice more."[12]

---

10. Eric Peter Ho, *Times of Change: A Memoir of Hong Kong's Governance 1950–1991* (Hong Kong: Hong Kong University Press, 2005), 9.

11. Smith, "Compradores of the Hongkong Bank," 99.

12. Jack Braga, "Ho Tung (Sir Robert) 21 Dec., 1863 [sic]–26 April, 1956," handwritten manuscript, Braga Collection, National Library of Australia, Canberra, Australia, n.d.

Table 10.1 Ho Tung's Compradorial Network

Name	Relationship with Ho Tung	Name of Firm	Post Held
Ho Tung	—	JM	head compradore
Ho Fook	brother	JM	head compradore
Ho Kom Tong	brother	JM	head compradore
Ho Sai Wing	adopted son	HSBC	asst. compradore
Ho Sai Kim	son	HSBC	compradore
Ho Sai Kwong	nephew	EDS	compradore
Ho Sai Kit	nephew	EDS	compradore
Ho Sai Ki	nephew	AC	compradore
Ho Sai Iu	nephew	MBI	compradore
Ho Sai Leung	nephew	JM	compradore
Ho Sai Wa	nephew	MBI	asst. compradore
Ho Hung Pong	grandson	HSBC	compradore
Choy Sing Nam	brother-in-law	JM	asst. compradore
Cheung Pui Kai	nephew-in-law	JM	asst. compradore
Lo Cheung Shiu	brother-in-law	JM	asst. compradore
Lo Cheung Yip	brother-in-law	JM	asst. compradore
Wong Kam Fook	brother-in-law	HKWG	compradore
Tse Yat	cousin-in-law	BNU	compradore
Tse Kar Po	nephew-in-law	NYK	compradore
Choa Lap Chee	cousin-in-law	JM	compradore
Choa Po Yew	nephew-in-law	DB	compradore

Source: Zheng Wan-tai and Wong Siu-lun, *Xianggang dalao: He Dong* (The grand old man of Hong Kong: Ho Tung) (Hong Kong: Joint Publishing [Hong Kong], 2007), 219.

Abbreviations:

AC	Arnhold & Co.
BNU	Banco Nacional Ultramarino.
DB	Deutsche Bank.
EDS	E.D. Sassoon & Co.
HKWG	Hong Kong & Kowloon Wharves & Go-downs.
HSBC	Hong Kong & Shanghai Banking Corporation.
JM	Jardine, Matheson & Co.
MBI	Mercantile Bank.
NYK	Nippon Yusen Kaisha.

Ho Tung's effort in supporting his son paid off when the United States took part in World War II. Ho's military career began to flourish with the appointment of General Albert C. Wedemeyer, a classmate of Ho Shai-lai at Fort Leavenworth, as U.S. Commander in the China Theatre. Ho rose rapidly to the top ranks of the Nationalist army as the key coordinator for U.S. military aid. When the Japanese surrendered in 1945, Ho Shai-lai was the first Nationalist army general to lead his troops to enter Canton to restore order. Rumors were rife at that time that the Chinese Nationalists would claim Hong Kong and that Ho Shai Lai "would ride a white charger to receive the Japanese surrender."[13] Yet this was not to be. The British government was one step ahead in the scramble for Hong Kong's sovereignty. Before the Nationalists could stake their claim, Admiral Harcourt sailed into Hong Kong to reinstall British rule. Ho Tung's high hopes for his son to become the first Chinese governor of Hong Kong were dashed.

When the Chinese Civil War broke out soon after the Japanese surrender, Ho Shai-lai was appointed military commander in charge of logistics and troop deployment at Qinhuangdao and Huludao in north China. By all accounts, he discharged his duties with distinction.[14] But this was little comfort when the entire Nationalist camp began to disintegrate rapidly. By 1949, the outcome of the Civil War was becoming clear. Ho Shai-lai was on the losing side. Ho Tung had no reason to welcome such a quick and decisive Communist landslide. He did not have any significant links with Chinese Communist leaders, even though he had cultivated high-level political contacts throughout the world. The Chinese Communist bloc was the glaring gap in his political web. It was a "structural hole" that he could not bridge with ease.

However, he saw the looming catastrophe with clarity. He was extremely well informed, not least because Ho Shai-lai had been in charge of Nationalist intelligence in Hong Kong before the Japanese invasion. At that time, Ho Tung left Hong Kong in a hurry to seek refuge in Macao just four days before the Japanese attack. This time when Chinese Communist forces swept through the mainland, he knew they were going to be the winners. But there was little he could do about that. He and his son had cast their lots squarely with the Nationalists. He could only try to minimize his losses to the best of his ability. Yet he hated to be

---

13. Catherine Joyce Symons, *Looking at the Stars: Memoirs of Catherine Joyce Symons* (Hong Kong: Pegasus Books, 1996), 29.

14. Zheng Wan-tai and Wong Siu-lun, *Xianggang jiangjun: He Shili* (The General from Hong Kong: Ho Shai-lai) (Hong Kong: Joint Publishing [Hong Kong], 2008), 180–199.

a loser. He had once said with pride, "I have made mistakes, but I have never failed." He said further, "There are many men who have a good idea. That is not enough. A man should have two good ideas in case one fails ... An army training is good for any businessman. I plan all my business deals on military lines. I arrange my attack and my defence."[15] Even before the Chinese Communist victory had become a certainty, Ho Tung was already working on another idea. He was making an alternate plan. He would build new bridges, in case the existing ones might collapse. At the same time, he had to strengthen the foundation of his defense walls.

BOLSTERING DEFENSES

Between 1945 and 1949, Ho Tung made three moves to bolster his defenses. First, he sought to reassure the British authorities of his unshaken loyalty. Second, he brushed up his cherished image as a mediator and a broker for peace. Third, he consolidated his rear by fortifying his ties with Macao.

In August 1945, the Japanese surrendered. The British government immediately dispatched units of the British Pacific Fleet under Rear-Admiral Sir Cecil Harcourt to rush to Hong Kong to accept the surrender and to resume British rule. Harcourt's units were one step ahead of the Chinese Nationalists. But still, the resumption of British rule did not go unchallenged. Chiang Kai-shek protested. Harcourt had to accept the Japanese surrender in Hong Kong on behalf of both the British and Chinese governments. "Tenseness was caused," according to the historian G.B. Endacott, "by the movement of Chinese troops to Kowloon to board ships to service in Manchuria, because it was suspected that they had been sent to take over the colony."[16] These Chinese troops were under the command of Lieutenant General Ho Shai-lai, who held the position of General in charge of commoditizing Chinese service of supplies for Guangdong province at that time.[17]

As Harcourt was the first to reach Hong Kong, Ho Shai-lai had missed his chance. His golden opportunity for power and glory in Hong Kong was gone. Yet this near miss must have aroused suspicion on the

---

15. SCMP, July 17, 1933.

16. G.B. Endacott, *A History of Hong Kong*, rev. ed. (Hong Kong: Oxford University Press, 1973), 303.

17. *South China Morning Post & The Hong Kong Telegraph*, December 28, 1945.

British side about his ambition and further intentions. Ho Tung moved with great speed to dispel that suspicion. In a small news item with the heading of "Sir Robert Returns" published on the bottom of the page of the *South China Morning Post & The Hong Kong Telegraph* on December 24, 1945, it was reported:

> Sir Robert Ho Tung, after an absence of over three years, returned to Hong Kong from Macao yesterday afternoon, together with His Excellency the Commander-in-Chief, Rear-Admiral Sir Cecil Harcourt, in the C.-in-C.'s launch. Sir Robert was accompanied by his two grandchildren. On arrival they were met by Mr. and Mrs. M.K. Lo, Mr. and Mrs. Ho Sai Wing, Mrs. Ho Sai-lai, Madame Chang Fah-kwei (wife of Canton's Commander-in-Chief) and members of Sir Robert's staff. Sir Robert and Madame Chang proceeded from Queen's Pier in the Governor's car to Idlewild, Sir Robert's residence, where Madame Chang is now staying.

In Ho Tung's own account given in a confidential memorandum to the Hong Kong government in 1946, he stated that "I returned to Hong Kong on the 23rd December 1945 together with Admiral Sir Cecil Harcourt who kindly gave me permission to travel on his ship." It would appear that Ho Tung himself had made the request to travel together with Harcourt, presumably to show symbolically that they were in the same boat. In that memo, just before making the above statement, Ho Tung declared that during his stay in Macao, "[the] Japanese used every effort alternately to threaten or to tempt me with material gain so as to secure my active co-operation, but I have the satisfaction and gratification to say that I remained a loyal British subject."[18]

Just one month after his return to Hong Kong, he made an appointment on January 23, 1946, to call on Lieutenant Colonel C.B. Burgess at the Headquarters of the Civil Affairs Administration to discuss several personal matters. This included the return of the loan of GBP10,000, which he made to the British government in 1941, the granting of a permit to import some medical capsules for his own use, and the return of his motor car which was under requisition. However, the real purpose of his visit, according to Burgess, was to seek some further honors for himself and some posthumous honor for his wife:

---

18. HKPRO, "Sir Robert Ho Tung," memo 1.

What he is after is a baronetcy, or failing that a KCMG [Knight Commander of St. Michael and St. George], or failing that a KBE [Knight of the Most Excellent Order of the British Empire]. He suggested that one or other of the two latter honors had virtually been promised to him in 1925 or 1926, but that since this was so long ago and since his behavior during the Japanese Occupation had been so exemplary and since he had heard that Chungking [Chongqing] was anxious that he should receive some further honors, he thought that a baronetcy should not now be entirely out of the question. He produced a vague sort of letter which he has just received from Earl Baldwin and another from a lady whom he described as a "member of the Chinese Parliament," in which it was suggested that some important personage was endeavoring to obtain some high honor for him.[19]

Why was Ho Tung so anxious to seek these further honors? He knew that the Hong Kong government had just resumed its rule under a temporary military administration. He knew that the administration was preoccupied with the frantic task of post-occupation rehabilitation. He told Burgess that "the urgency with which he wished his claim to be considered was dictated to a large extent by his expectation of life. The New Year's List of 1947 might be a little late."[20] This might well be true to some extent. But it could hardly explain the extraordinary sense of urgency contained in his seemingly vain or even trivial claim. The exasperation expressed by Burgess in his confidential memo might provide a clue to the puzzle. Burgess stated that "I found this subject a very awkward one to deal with and I explained to him that such matters were not normally dealt with except on the highest level."[21] Ho Tung was apparently aware of that. He was most probably seeking to have his request noted at the highest levels of the Hong Kong and British governments so as to reaffirm his allegiance as a "loyal British subject" most attached to the British honors system.

Soon after Ho Tung had made his request for honors, Ho Shai-lai arrived in Hong Kong at the end of February 1946 in his capacity as deputy commander-in-chief for commoditization and supplies of the Chinese Nationalist army. He was responsible for the transportation of

---

19. Ibid., 1.
20. Ibid., 3.
21. Ibid., 1.

the Thirteenth Army, the Eighth Army, and the New First Army, totaling several tens of thousands of troops, to go north via Hong Kong. He made a public statement in the colony to thank Governor Harcourt and other members of the British military administration for providing him with special assistance to facilitate such massive troop movements. He praised them for their vision and their spirit in "promoting Sino-British relationship."[22] He was probably reinforcing his father's message that neither of them had any intention to challenge British rule.

The repeated reassurance given to the British authorities seemed to have borne fruit. On May 1, 1946, the temporary military rule in Hong Kong came to an end. Sir Mark Young returned to resume his interrupted governorship and to reinstall a normal civil administration. On that important occasion, Ho Tung was invited to be the representative of the Chinese inhabitants of Hong Kong and to deliver the speech welcoming the return of Governor Young and the resumption of British civil rule, although he held no official position within the Hong Kong government.[23] However, other members of his family were quickly elevated to high positions. His son-in-law, M.K. Lo, was appointed a member of the Executive Council at the apex of the colonial government in the same year. Two years later, M.K. was knighted, the second British knight in the Ho Tung family. Ho Tung's other son-in-law, K.C. Yeo, was appointed deputy director of the Medical and Health Department in 1948. Yeo was further promoted in 1952 to be director of that department, being the first ethnic Chinese to reach the top echelon of the colonial administration dominated by British expatriate officers.[24] Ho Tung had thus greatly strengthened the political wing of his family dynasty in Hong Kong, even though the compradorial wing was being torn to tatters by the Chinese Communists.

When Ho Tung called on Lieutenant Colonel Burgess in January 1946 to "make application" for further honors, he raised one other request that Burgess nearly overlooked. Ho Tung said that he had heard that Mr. Taggart had been appointed Industrial Adviser to the Administration. He felt that he also was qualified for some similar post and suggested that the simple title of "Adviser" would be adequately vague and comprehensive.[25] Burgess apparently missed the significance

22. XGGSRB, March 1, 1946.

23. C.O. 129.595.54325, 1946. Arrival of Government in Hong Kong: Resumption of Duty (various dates).

24. Zheng Wan-tai and Wong Siu-lun, *Xianggang dalao: He Dong* (The grand old man of Hong Kong: Ho Tung) (Hong Kong: Joint Publishing [Hong Kong], 2007), 277–278.

25. HKPRO, "Sir Robert Ho Tung," 1.

of this request because he was probably not aware of an earlier suggestion made by Ho Tung to appoint himself as the "special agent" to be sent privately by the British government to China.

Ho Tung had made the earlier suggestion during the Peking Conference of 1925 at which the Chinese Nationalist government was negotiating with the Western Powers for tariff autonomy and the abolition of extraterritoriality. On that occasion, Ho Tung had urged the British government "to devise means of stopping the anti-British agitation in the South." He had suggested that a special agent be sent to China "for the purpose of getting in touch with the leaders of the Nationalist party [the party in power in Canton] and ascertaining their true aims" so as to at least settle "the differences between Hong Kong and Canton." He had elaborated on the qualities required for this agent in a confidential memorandum submitted to the British Foreign Secretary in which he had stated as follows:

> Such an agent should in my opinion be a British subject of Chinese race: a man whose reputation, character, and integrity are respected not only by the Cantonese but also by the Northern Chinese, so that he can mix with them without raising suspicion.
>
> He should also be a man of wealth, so that the Chinese would know that he was not working for any selfish ends but only in the interest of peace and good fellowship. He must also enjoy the respect and confidence of the British, and should assume the character of a private unofficial tourist or observer: a friend to all parties but bound to none. He would then be in a position to act as a mediator when the proper moment arrived.[26]

In other words, the ideal representative of Hong Kong should be a person very closely resembling Ho Tung himself.

Ho Tung knew what a unique role that "man of wealth" like himself could play in the power game between China and the West. He was propelling himself to be a broker for peace. But it was not just wealth that would recommend him for that role. Another important qualification, which he left unstated, was his mixed parentage as a Eurasian born in Hong Kong, a Eurasian who assumed a meticulously cultivated Chinese persona. With this fusion of mixed blood and Chinese presentation

---

26. C.O. 129, 491, 1925, 93.

of self, he could gain the confidence of the British who were always suspicious of the double allegiance of the ethnic Chinese in the British colony of Hong Kong.

Ho Tung's offer to act as special agent in 1925 was apparently not taken up by the British government at that time. The Under Secretary of State of the British Foreign Office told his counterpart at the Colonial Office that "Sir Robert Hotung has been verbally informed that the present moment is not considered a suitable one to send a special agent to China for the purposes indicated."[27] But Ho Tung had already planted the idea firmly at the top of the British officialdom that he was ready to be of service in such a role should "the proper moment" arrive.

Had that moment arrived before the Chinese Communist victory? Was he acting as an unofficial emissary for the British or Hong Kong authorities when he toured Europe and met with both British and Scandinavian royal families, the former British prime minister Winston Churchill, the French president, and other high officials in Brussels during May and November 1949? During that tour, he arrived in Stockholm on October 2, 1949, just one day after Mao Zedong had declared the establishment of the People's Republic of China. He was met by the "Chinese Ambassador" at the airport. The next day, the British embassy there hosted a dinner for him.[28] He did not seem to be traveling for pleasure.

When he made the public statement while in London that he believed the Chinese Nationalists and the Communists could have come to a satisfactory agreement "two years ago" and that he was willing to offer his "services as mediator" at that time, to whom did he actually offer his services?[29] There were hints that he might have offered them to the leaders of the United States, as he referred to General Marshall's remarks on Mao Zedong and Zhou Enlai in a later public statement.[30] We shall return to such a possibility later.

Meanwhile, Ho Tung also took steps to renew his ties with Macao. In January 1949 he made a donation of 250,000 dollars to the Macao government to promote Chinese and Portuguese cultures. The Macao authorities decided to use the funds to build a Sino-Portuguese school for Chinese students and add a Chinese wing to the new Macao Public Library, both to be named after Ho Tung. Then on March 8, 1949, Ho Tung traveled to Macao.

---

27. Ibid., 98.
28. XGGSRB, October 7, 1949.
29. SCMP, May 30, 1949.
30. *The China Mail*, October 27, 1949.

The governor of Macao sent his aide to welcome him at the pier.[31] The next day, accompanied by his private secretary and friend, Jack Braga, he paid a visit to the governor at Government House.[32] The governor held a big cocktail reception for him on March 11. Among the crowd of attendees was the Chinese Commissioner for Foreign Affairs in Macao. Ho Tung was invited to give a speech after the governor had welcomed and thanked him for his donation.[33] Before he returned to Hong Kong on March 17, he attended another big reception in his honor, which was hosted by the five major Chinese associations in Macao.[34] About a month later, on April 24, the governor of Macao and his wife paid him a return visit at Idlewild, Ho Tung's residence in Hong Kong.[35]

We know that Ho Tung was about to go on his six-month tour of Europe in May. Why did he make an extended trip to Macao before his European tour? Did he not run the risk of overtaxing his health at the advanced age of eighty-seven? He must have had more on his mind than making donations to build schools and libraries. Was he going there to touch base in person in case he needed to seek refuge again, just as he had done during the Japanese occupation of Hong Kong? We learn from his grandnephew Stanley Ho (born 1921; also known as Ho Hung Sun) that Macao was regarded as "paradise" during the war.

> [The] Japanese honoured the neutrality of Macao and they didn't interfere with the administration in any way. Their only involvement was in supplying food to Macao. In those days, if you have money, you could enjoy the best kind of cigarettes, American, British, right up to the end of the war. If you had money, you could carry on using motorcars and motorbikes all through the war—gasoline was available. And you could have excellent food—if you had the money. I had big parties almost every night. Bird's nest, roast pork.[36]

Ho Tung had money. He also had influence in the Portuguese colony. Stanley Ho told us that he went to Macao soon after the Japanese invaded Hong Kong. He joined the biggest company in Macao during the war,

---

31. XGGSRB, March 9, 1949.

32. Ibid., March 10, 1949.

33. Ibid., March 13, 1949.

34. Ibid., March 16, 1949.

35. Ibid., April 25, 1949.

36. Jill McGivering, *Macao Remembers* (Oxford and New York: Oxford University Press, 1999), 108.

the Macau Cooperative Company Limited. "It was one-third owned by Dr. Lobo, the director of economics, one-third owned by the wealthiest families of Macao, and one-third owned by the Japanese army. I became its secretary because of my knowledge of chemistry, and because they knew I could be trusted, being the grand-nephew of Sir Robert Ho Tung."[37]

He told us a further story:

> I became the teacher of the most important Japanese man in Macao during the war. There was a Japanese Special Branch in Macao, which was even more important than the Japanese Consul General. The head of it, a man called Colonel Sawa, went to see the governor one day and told him he wanted to learn English—but he needed a reliable person who mustn't murder him. The governor thought about it and said: "What do you think of the grand-nephew of Sir Robert Hotung? You were such good friends with Sir Robert—would you trust a member of his family?" Colonel Sawa accepted immediately.[38]

Macao was obviously a safe haven for Ho Tung and his family. They had built up a strong base of goodwill in the Portuguese enclave over a long period of time. In early 1949, Ho Tung went there again to enhance the goodwill and to fortify the protective walls of this base camp in case there was an emergency. While securing his defenses, he was already making his forward moves.

BUILDING BRIDGES

Two years before he traveled to Macao and Europe, Ho Tung undertook his first transatlantic flight to the United States on a Pan American four-engine propeller-driven plane. He had made four previous trips to the United States, but all by sea. The expressed purpose of this long air journey for him was to seek medical care for his ear and teeth ailments. Yet these ailments did not seem to be of a very serious nature, as he was reported to be in good form and feeling very happy about his forthcoming trip on the day of his departure

---

37. Ibid., 107.
38. Ibid., 108.

from Hong Kong on October 16, 1947.[39] His son and daughter-in-law, General and Mrs. Ho Shai-lai, were in Kai Tak Airport together with other friends and relatives to see him off. Ho Shai-lai had just completed his military command at Qinhuangdao and Huludao. He was in Hong Kong on one month's leave before returning to the mainland for other duties. Just six days before seeing his father off at Kai Tak, Ho Shai-lai attended the Chinese Nationalist National Day celebrations in Hong Kong as a senior Nationalist official and exchanged the toast with Governor Grantham.

What was the real purpose of Ho Tung's visit to North America? There was little press coverage of his trip in the United States. We only know that he stayed there for six months and returned to Hong Kong on April 11, 1948. He was reported to be looking very well with a wide smile when he stepped off the plane, showing clearly the new set of false teeth that his American dentist had installed for him.[40] Whom did he meet, other than his dentist and his doctors, when he was in the United States? We know that he was well connected with American politicians. When the vice-president of the United States passed through Hong Kong in 1935 with a big delegation of senators and congressmen to attend the ceremony in Manila for the independence of the Philippines, Ho Tung hosted a reception for the entire American delegation at his residence on the Peak because he was "an old friend" of the vice-president.[41] We also know that General Albert C. Wedemeyer, who had worked closely with Ho Shai-lai during World War II, was back in China on a fact-finding mission in July and August 1947, just two months before Ho Tung embarked on his U.S. journey.[42] Wedemeyer was sent on his "last mission to China" by General Marshall, then U.S. secretary of state, with the directive "to appraise the political, economic, psychological, and military situations—current and projected—in both China and Korea."[43]

When Ho Tung reached the United States, Wedemeyer was already back in Washington writing his "Report on China." Wedemeyer had decided "to recommend to President [Harry S.] Truman that immediate aid be given to China, including military as well as material and moral

---

39. XGGSRB, October 17, 1947.

40. *Dagong bao* (Ta Kung Pao; hereafter cited as DGB), April 12, 1948.

41. XGGSRB, November 6, 1935.

42. Albert C. Wedemeyer, *Wedemeyer Reports!* (New York: Henry Holt and Company, 1958), 384–390.

43. Ibid., 384.

support" in order to "block the spread of Communism." He was well aware that he had a double task: to convince the Chinese [Nationalists] that they must produce proof that American aid would not be wasted; and to convince Washington that such aid must be given.[44] He later recalled in his memoir:

> I had no doubt that my recommendations would be accepted and implemented. My fundamental mistake was due to my anxiety that the American people should realize that I had not been namby-pamby in my examination of the situation in China. In other words, that I had not been biased or influenced by friendships or close relationships of wartime in the area—had not been taken in, so to speak. My eyes were fixed on America, upon whom the fate of China depended.[45]

It turned out that his report to President Truman and Secretary of State Marshall was "suppressed and ignored."[46] Instead of supporting Wedemeyer's recommendation of increasing aid to the Chinese Nationalists, Marshall proceeded to push for a policy designed to establish a coalition government in China. Ho Tung arrived in the United States at this juncture. Like Wedemeyer, his eyes were also fixed on America, "upon whom the fate of China depended." Did he talk to Wedemeyer, so as to renew the wartime bond between the General and his son, Ho Shai-lai, and to affirm their common belief that American aid would not be wasted? Did he meet Secretary of State Marshall, and offer his service as a mediator between the Chinese Nationalists and Communists in order to bring about a coalition government? We have not yet found any records pointing to such meetings, but they remain intriguing possibilities given the timing of events and curious coincidences.

It is reasonable to assume that one of the goals of Ho Tung's American trip was to build new political bridges for his son, Ho Shai-lai. Ho Tung apparently knew that America was of crucial importance in shaping the future development of China and other parts of Asia after World War II. It was thus his top priority to enhance his contacts there in person, and to draw high level attention to his son's qualifications and accomplishments that might help to mitigate the "maladministration, corruption, and lethargy" that Wedemeyer had found within the Chinese Nationalist

---

44. Ibid., 388.
45. Ibid., 391.
46. Ibid.

government.[47] He clearly knew that his son was already too committed to the Nationalist camp. Ho Shai-lai could not change course at that time. He either had to abandon camp, or he must push on regardless of the risk of total failure.

When the entire Nationalist camp crashed on the Chinese mainland in 1949, Ho Shai-lai was in Hong Kong amid the great exodus of Nationalist troops to Taiwan. His superior in the Nationalist army, General Chen Cheng, who had arrived in Taiwan earlier, telegraphed him urgently to join ranks there so as to salvage the Nationalist cause. According to Chen Cheng, Ho Shai-lai was advised by many family members and relatives not to go on such a foolhardy and perhaps suicidal mission.[48] But his elder sister, Eva Ho, strongly urged him to do so, saying that he should answer the call to duty when the country was in such mortal danger, and that he should uphold his loyalty to Chen Cheng as a close friend since for a man of honor, friendship was even dearer than life. Chen Cheng said he was greatly moved and felt eternally indebted to Eva for her critical role in fortifying Ho Shai-lai's resolve to go to Taiwan.

Ho Tung might not have been as vocal as Eva in urging Ho Shai-lai to go but it is quite unlikely that he would have wanted his son to abandon the Nationalist camp. He had already built new bridges for Ho Shai-lai on the American side. His son had a lot to recommend himself as a key link for the Americans should they still wish to come to the rescue of the Chinese Nationalists. Ho Shai-lai had received advanced military training in the United States. He was bilingual and bicultural, given his Eurasian origin. He might be less corruptible as he came from such a wealthy family. He was quite unique among the Nationalist military leadership, a man that the Americans could trust.

But could he gain the full confidence of Generalissimo Chiang Kai-shek and his heir apparent Chiang Ching-kuo? After experiencing innumerable desertions and betrayals accompanying the Nationalist collapse on the mainland, Chiang and his son must have been extremely edgy and highly suspicious of those around them as they arrived in Taiwan. Even though Ho Shai-lai had a strong endorsement from Chen Cheng, Chiang and his son might still have had lingering doubts about him. After all, Ho had served under Zhang Xueliang before. He was educated in Hong Kong with a British colonial upbringing and strong British linkages. He came from a prominent family of compradores, which was presumably

---

47. Ibid., 388.

48. Cheng Chen, *Chen Cheng xiansheng huiyilu—Jianshe Taiwan* (The memoirs of Mr. Chen Cheng: Building Taiwan) (Taipei: Guoshi guan, 2005), v. 1, 476.

not quite to the taste of Chiang Ching-kuo who detested compradores and big capitalists. Ho Tung and Ho Shai-lai had to try hard to remove such doubts. New bridges must be built to cross these troughs of mistrust in order to make Ho Shai-lai's mission to Taiwan a worthwhile one. They were to make an audacious move to accomplish that aim.

Early on the morning of April 2, 1950, seven aircrafts were blown up at Kai Tak Airport. They were part of the fleet of seventy-one aircrafts belonging to the China National Aviation Corporation (CNAC) and the Central Air Transport Corporation (CATC), both being Chinese Nationalist state concerns with substantial American holdings. Since Britain had recognized the newly established People's Republic of China, the new Chinese government was laying claims on these planes that were stranded in Hong Kong. According to the recollection of Sir Alexander Grantham, governor of Hong Kong at that time, the Americans also asked for the planes to be released to them. As he reported:

> To this we replied that, since there were two claimants, the issue as to the ownership would have to be settled in the courts. Action proceeded accordingly: the best counsel being engaged on both sides. In addition, the Americans sent over lawyers from the States, the most prominent of whom was General Donovan, "Big Bill Donovan," who had been the war-time director of O.S.S. [Office of Strategic Services], the American equivalent of the British S.O.E. [Secret Operations Executive], whose function was to sabotage the enemy's effort. He came to see me, and thumping the table, metaphorically if not physically, insisted that the planes be handed to him without further ado, for, he said, if it had not been for the United States Britain would have lost the war. Moreover, he added, if I did not do as he demanded he would make it hot for me with the authorities in London. I remain unmoved: the matter must be settled in the courts.[49]

But the Nationalists' secret agents in Hong Kong were ordered by the Executive Yuan in Taiwan not to wait for the settlement in the courts. One of the leading agents, Sung Hsiang-yun (Song Xiangyun), took action. The aircrafts were under tight security at a secluded area to the north of Kai Tak Airport. It was later revealed that Sung was driven

---

49. Alexander Grantham, *Via Ports: From Hong Kong to Hong Kong* (Hong Kong: Hong Kong University Press, 1965), 162.

into the airport on March 31, 1950, by the chief executive of Central Air Transport Corporation, Tai An-kuo (Dai Anguo), "in Sir Robert Ho Tung's motor car."[50] Sung then sneaked past the police guards and planted bombs that blew up seven of the planes in the early morning hours of April 2. Sung returned to Taiwan in 1954 and was received by Chiang Kai-shek. Together with the group of 378 employees of the CNAC and CATC who went to Taiwan with him, he was given a hero's welcome in a three-day celebration at the military sports ground.[51]

Ho Tung was instrumental in Sung's successful mission of sabotage. His motorcar with an unlettered number plate carried great prestige and would have gained Sung privileged access to the airport, but lending his car to facilitate such a daring act of sabotage was very risky for Ho Tung. Such an act would not have been welcomed by the Hong Kong and British authorities, given Governor Grantham's strong views on the aircraft controversy. Moreover, Ho Tung would have incurred the full fury of the new Chinese Communist government if his role became known. But it seems that his involvement in the matter was not known to either the Hong Kong British or the Chinese Communist sides at that time. At least there was no public reference to this during the aftermath of the sabotage. On the other hand, the contribution made by Ho Tung in this mission must have reached the top of the Nationalist leadership and been noted by Chiang Kai-shek and Chiang Ching-kuo who was in charge of military intelligence in Taiwan.

After Ho Shai-lai made this audacious act to affirm his loyalty to the Nationalist cause, his military career soared. In the fall of 1949, he arrived in Taiwan and took up the post of Commander of Supplies for the Southeast Region. He was responsible for the livelihood and resettlement of 600,000 Nationalist troops relocated to the island. In early 1950, he was made executive deputy minister at the Ministry of Defense. There were rumors that he might be appointed to the important position as Chief of the Chinese Mission in Japan to be responsible for liaison with the Allied Army Headquarters in Tokyo. And this appointment was confirmed only in June 1950, two months after the CNAC and CATC aircrafts were blown up in Hong Kong. When Ho Shai-lai was received by Chiang Kai-shek before he went to Tokyo to take up his new position,

---

50. Guoshi guan, "Song Xiangyun xiansheng shilue" (A brief biography of Mr. Song Xiangyun [Sung Hsiang-yun]), in *Guoshi guan xian cang Minguo renwu zhuanji shiliao huibian* (Collection of historical materials on the biographies of personalities in the Republican period held at Academia Historica) (Taipei: Guoshi guan, 2000), v. 20, 114.

51. Ibid., 115.

he told Chiang about his diffidence as he had no previous diplomatic experience. According to Ho, Chiang reassured him that "as long as he did not take bribes and did not turn Communist, and tried his best to accomplish the liaison work, he would not be held responsible for any possible failures."[52]

About ten days after Ho Shai-lai took up his post in Tokyo, the Korean War broke out. This inaugurated the Cold War and inadvertently stabilized Taiwan. President Truman declared that the United States would not permit a military solution to the Taiwan problem and ordered the Seventh Fleet to enter the ports of Keelung and Kaohsiung via the Taiwan Strait. At this critical juncture, Ho Shai-lai maintained close contact with General Douglas MacArthur in the Allied Headquarters in Tokyo. MacArthur told Ho at a confidential meeting in early July 1950 that he regarded Ho as his sole contact with Chiang Kai-shek.[53] Ho was the only non-American person invited by MacArthur to participate in his strategic meetings with American generals.[54] He was the key liaison man who arranged for MacArthur's surprise visit to Taiwan on July 31, 1950, which served to strengthen American military ties with Taiwan and to calm the jittery nerves on the island.[55]

Ho subsequently negotiated the peace treaty with Japan on behalf of the Republic of China in 1951. Two years later, he was appointed Chief Representative of the Chinese Delegation to the United Nations Military Staff Committee.[56] With this appointment, he reached the pinnacle of his career. He was to play a key role in the United Nations, with an international stature that surpassed the top position which he narrowly missed in Hong Kong eight years earlier, even though that high honor was not openly celebrated in the British colony from which he came.

Ho Tung had reasons to be pleased with his son's achievements. Against great odds, he and his son had accomplished what would at first have appeared to have been the impossible. They had turned an impending failure into a resounding success. That success was not just confined to his son's political advancement. Ho Tung's economic fortunes also grew. With the huge influx of refugees into Hong Kong after the

---

52. *Lianhe bao*, April 15, 1975; cited in Zheng and Wong, *Xianggang jiangjun*, 228.

53. Chiang Kai-shek correspondence July 4, 1950: 002080106056002; cited in Zheng and Wong, *Xianggang jiangjun*, 230–231.

54. Guoshi guan, "He Shili xiansheng shilue" (A brief biography of Mr. He Shili [Ho Shai-lai]) in *Guoshi guan xian cang Minguo renwu zhuanji shiliao huibian*, v. 20, 64.

55. Zheng and Wong, *Xianggang jiangjun*, 236–242.

56. Ibid., 272.

Chinese Communist victory, there was an acute housing shortage.[57] Land prices skyrocketed, and Ho Tung was one of the biggest landowners in the territory. By all indications, he could readily retain the claim to be "the richest man in China," even though the main part of China had already turned Communist.

LAST STAND

Ho Tung died in 1956 at the advanced age of ninety-four. A year before his death, Queen Elizabeth II conferred on him a second knighthood that he had earlier requested: Knight Commander of the British Empire, KBE. This was a singular honor. He was the only person from Hong Kong who had received two knighthoods in his own lifetime. At his death, numerous letters of condolences were received by his family, including those from Chiang Kai-shek and Chen Cheng as president and vice-president of the Republic of China. At his funeral, Governor Grantham and his wife paid their respects together with all members of the Executive, Legislative, and Urban Councils as well as other senior government officials. Flags flew at half-mast at the Hong Kong and Shanghai Bank, University of Hong Kong, Jardine and Matheson Company, Tung Wah Hospital, Po Leung Kuk (Society of the Protection of Women and Children), Queen's College, and many other organizations.[58] Even *Ta Kung Pao (Dagong bao)*, a pro-Communist newspaper in Hong Kong, carried reports on his death and funeral.[59]

In an attachment to his will, which was very detailed and meticulous, Ho Tung had made provisions for the creation of "the North China Fund" and "the South China Fund" to provide for the prevention and relief related to floods in any part of China. He stated that "having made a careful survey and study of the principles of the Carnegie Trust, the Rockefeller Foundation, and the Alfred Noble Foundation I had conceived plans for a Foundation to operate on broadly similar principles, which would under the old conditions operating in China have brought great benefits to the people of China and indirectly to humanity in general." But since the old conditions operating in China had already changed, he further stipulated that "if at the expiration of ten years from my death no part of the North China Fund or the South China Fund

---

57. Siu-lun Wong, *Emigrant Entrepreneurs: Shanghai Industrialists in Hong Kong* (Hong Kong: Oxford University Press, 1988), 20–25.

58. Zheng and Wong, *Xianggang dalao*, 303–308.

59. DGB, April 27–28, 1956.

or the income thereof shall have been applied towards the foregoing purposes, the trust hereinbefore declared for the North China Fund and the South China Fund shall cease."[60]

Even on the eve of his death, he was making plans for the future. He seemed to be anticipating some fundamental change in the situation in China in ten years' time. That change did not come about, but he had already thought about an alternative arrangement. The two China funds would cease to operate and the assets were to revert to the Sir Robert Ho Tung Charitable Fund and his residuary estate. He had withstood the tide of communism quite successfully in Hong Kong. He clearly wished his offspring to follow his example, to bide their time, and to "attempt the impossible."[61]

---

60. Will no. 49/56, Supreme Court of Hong Kong, grant no. 174/56, first codicil, 2–3.

61. Zheng and Wong, *Xianggang dalao*, 351.

This page is intentionally left blank.

11 DECIDING WHETHER TO RETURN TO TAIWAN | Koo Chen-fu, 1945–1952

Tsai-man Ho

As other chapters in this volume have shown, Chinese capitalists fled from China to Hong Kong during the late 1940s and lived there while they decided whether to return to China or settle permanently in Hong Kong or migrate elsewhere. This chapter describes a young Chinese capitalist, Koo Chen-fu (1917–2005), who fled at this same time not from China but from Taiwan to Hong Kong. While he lived in Hong Kong from 1949 to 1952, he did not consider moving to China. Instead, he debated whether to return to Taiwan, stay in Hong Kong, or move elsewhere. As a member of one of the three biggest land-owning families in Taiwan, he was a prime candidate for leadership of programs for land reform and industrialization as proposed by Chiang Kai-shek's Nationalist government in Taiwan at this time. So why was he reluctant to return to the place where he and his ancestors had been born and raised? Koo hesitated to return to Taiwan because of the Nationalist government's accusations against his family for at least three alleged offenses: his father's reputation as a traitor for collaborating with Japan in Taiwan before the Sino-Japanese War of 1937–1945; his family's investments and financial contributions in support of Japanese colonial rule during the war; and his own record as a critic of Nationalist rule since the war.

This chapter draws on a variety of sources: biographies;[1] transcripts

---

The research for this essay was funded by the National Science Council for the project on "Business Dynasties—Comparing the Koos of Taiwan and the Lis of Hong Kong" (NSC101-2410-H-033-051-MY2).

1. Koo Hsien-jung's biography (published in 1939) was done by a committee mainly organized by the Japanese, in order to commemorate Koo Hsien-jung's life. Thanks to Koo Hsien-jung's limited ability regarding Japanese language, all of his communications with Japanese had to go through interpreters, and that has fortunately left us a number of his personal records. As to the biography of Koo Chen-fu published in 2005, it was actually authorized by the Koo Foundation, through which Koo family members took initiatives to

of my interviews with some members and relatives of the Koo family;[2] Taiwan's National Archives, Academia Historica, the Sotokufu (Taiwan Governor-General Office) archive preserved in Taiwan; and a collection about affairs at the end of World War II originally from Japan's National Institute for Defense Studies and from the Ministry of Foreign Affairs of Japan. On this basis I aim to explore the basis for Koo Chen-fu's attachment to Taiwan, his flight from it to Hong Kong in 1949, and his return to it in 1952. After a series of attacks against the major figures of the Koo family, Koo Chen-fu's exit option reveals his feelings about the Nationalist-government regime. Koo, before pledging his loyalty, had to stand in the right position in order to play a role well in a power transition society.[3]

MEDIATION BETWEEN JAPAN AND PREWAR TAIWAN BY KOO CHEN-FU'S FATHER

Koo Chen-fu's father, the founder of the Koo business dynasty, Koo Hsien-jung (1866–1937), is a controversial figure in history. When Taiwan was ceded as a colony to Japan in 1895 because of the Sino-Japanese Shimonoseki Treaty, it was Koo Hsien-jung who guided Japanese troops into Taipei. His willingness to step forward opened the door for his relationships with Japan. For a quarter century, Koo prospered in close cooperation with the Japanese colonial government. His collaboration made him wealthy as the recipient of many monopoly privileges in the salt and camphor wholesale businesses. He won Japanese recognition and even became a member of the Governor's Advisory Council (Hyōgi-Kai) when it was founded in 1921. In 1934 at the height of his power, he was selected as a member of the National Diet. From then on, Koo Hsien-jung devoted himself entirely to the role of peace negotiator between Japan and China until his death in 1937.

---

request two appointed authors to carry out the task. Huang Tiancai and Huang Zhaoxing, *Jin han mei xiang: Gu Zhenfu rensheng jishi* (The life of Koo Chen-fu) (Taipei: Lien-ching, 2005).

2. I had opportunities to interview Koo Kwan-min; Huang Tian-heng, the brother of Koo Chen-fu's first wife; and Vivien Ku (Gu Huaiqun), Koo Chen-fu's first daughter.

3. As I have noted near the end of this chapter, my interpretation has benefited from the insights of Albert O. Hirschman in his *Exit, Voice, and Loyalty: Responses to Decline in Firms, Organizations, and States* (Cambridge: Harvard University Press, 1970).

Like his father, Koo Chen-fu had close relations with the Japanese authorities in colonial Taiwan. In a book published by a Japanese journalist, Itō Kinjirō in 1948, Koo Chen-fu was described as follows: "Trim and courtly, with an aristocratic bearing, Koo Chen-fu from his kindergarten age onward has been educated and socialized in the Japanese system. When interacting with others, his graceful manner and attitude are full of charm. He plays an indispensable role in a Japanese official- and military-centered community. If Japan had not lost the war, he would have had a great future."[4] Although Koo Chen-fu's father only had very limited education in his era, with farsightedness he had his children not only educated in Japanese, but also had them learn English and Mandarin. Koo Hsien-jung had six wives, and among them, one was Japanese. Two of Koo's sons married Japanese. Koo Chen-fu's mother was Chinese. However, from a family letter Koo Chen-fu wrote to his mother when he lived in Tokyo, one could see that the language they used among themselves was Japanese. Koo Chen-fu grew up in two eras as designated by Japanese imperial reigns: Taishō (1912–1926) and Shōwa (1926–1960). The Taishō period was considered the time of the liberal movement known as Taishō democracy in Japan. By the end of the Taishō period, Koo Chen-fu was only eight or nine years old. In his childhood, he witnessed two impressive events. In 1923, due to the Taishō emperor's health, the Crown Prince Hirohito on behalf of the Taishō emperor, went on an inspection tour in Taiwan and visited the elementary school where Koo Chen-fu was studying. Koo Chen-fu was chosen to give a recitation in front of the prince. As late as 1922, the Japanese government agreed to allow only a very few Taiwanese to attend Japanese elementary school. In 1926, Koo transferred from the public elementary school of the Taiwanese to another elementary school exclusively for the Japanese.

Koo Chen-fu's father, Koo Hsien-jung, leaned politically toward Japan, not simply to gain the benefits from the colonial government for himself, but also more importantly, to bring about the outcome of modernization in Taiwan. When helping Japan against Taiwan's resistance movement, he criticized an association of Taiwanese for preserving "traditional Formosan values that would retard the process of becoming Japanese." As a consequence, Koo Hsien-jung was labelled "traitor" (*hanjian*) by his nationalistic critics. In 1925, in a statement to the Taiwan Culture Association, he defended himself against this

---

4. Itō Kinjirō, *Taiwan buke qi ji* (Taiwan cannot be bullied), translated from Japanese into Chinese by Nihon Bunkyo Kikinkai (Taipei: Wenyingtang chubanshe, 2000 reprint from 1948), 177.

accusation by saying, "It was the Emperor of China himself who cast off the Formosans, betraying them in 1895." Koo Hsien-jung was committed primarily to Taiwan rather than China. In the words of his Japanese biographer, Ozaki Shiyushin

> [A]s a Formosan, he [Koo Hsien-jung] no longer owed allegiance to China or the Chinese, but on the contrary, as a Japanese subject, it was his duty to be loyal to the government in Tokyo ... the great material benefit was obvious. To speak fairly, the Formosans had only to compare their present situation to the conditions in war-torn and backward China ... Even though the Republic of China was established, the country was divided by warlords who were corrupt and thus helped to ruin the whole country. They coerced the people for big loans; people suffered from heavy taxes ... Under these circumstances, peace would never come to the people, and consequently, industries had less chance to develop, so the whole nation turned into an impoverished place. By contrast, if we turn our eyes to Taiwan, the economy here has grown almost one hundred times larger than during the Qing dynasty. The living standard also has been enhanced.[5]

The Republic of China in Koo Hsien-jung's eyes was part of a backward world compared with Japan's advanced one. In fact, even for the activists of the Taiwan Home Rule movement, there was little reason to look across the strait to chaotic China.

Right after Koo Chen-fu graduated from Taipei Imperial University (Taihoku teikoku daigaku), he went to Tokyo to strengthen the Japanese networks he had inherited from his father rather than to pursue his studies at Tokyo University. During his stay in Tokyo, he met his future wife, Ms. Huang Zhaohua, a Taiwanese student at Tokyo Art College. Their matchmaker was a Japanese, Kodama Tomoō, who once served as Taiwan's Military Commander from 1937 to 1939.[6] They married in 1940,

---

5. Part of the translation (from the first to the sixth lines) was excerpted from George Kerr, *Formosa: Licensed Revolution and the Home Rule Movement 1895–1945* (Honolulu: University Press of Hawaii, 1974), 131; the rest is my own translation from Ozaki Shiyushin, ed., *Ko Ken Ei ou den* (The Biography of Koo Hsien-jung) (Taipei: Editorial Board for the Biography of Koo Hsien-jung, 1939), 343–345.

6. Kodama Tomoō is the son of the fourth Taiwan governor, Kodama Gentarō, who was in office from 1898 to 1906.

and the wedding was held at Tokyo's Hibiya Hotel.[7] Huang Zhaohua was the niece of a Taiwanese member of the Taiwan Governor's Advisory Council, Huang Xin. The couple stayed in Japan until the winter of 1943.

Evidently Koo Hsien-jung and his children were key mediators between Japan and prewar Taiwan. Even before Koo Chen-fu reached adulthood and launched his career, he had reason to fear retribution from Chiang Kai-shek and the Nationalist government insofar as they considered the Koos' mediation between Japanese colonial authorities and Taiwan to be "traitorous" and held that Koo Chen-fu played a part in his family's treason.

THE KOOS' SUPPORT FOR JAPANESE COLONIAL RULE IN WARTIME TAIWAN

The Nationalist government of China had some basis for accusing the Koo family of making investments and other financial contributions to Japanese colonial rule. During the Sino-Japanese War of 1937–1945, the Taiwanese people, their roles, and even their "enemies" were exactly the opposite as compared to the situation of those living in the mainland. To stay or leave appeared not to be a concern of Taiwanese capitalists. In other words, unlike the Chinese capitalists in China, they were not cast in a "passive role" under the Japanese invaders or forced to flee. Many local businessmen from Taiwan opened new enterprises during the war. The Koo family fits this characterization. Their newly established businesses are shown in Table 11.1. While opening these businesses in Taiwan, they also set up their business branches outside Taiwan in the Chinese cities of Shanghai and Dalian.

When Japan began to suffer wartime losses in China, the Koo family, by asking for the Japanese military's help, was able to move their investment, which was worth three and a half million yen, from China back to Taiwan. This was a situation in which the property was obviously threatened; the capitalists wanted to escape from the danger in China as quickly as possible. They moved their assets to Taiwan, and such a move at that time indicates that the capitalists had no premonition that Japan would ever be compelled to give up the island.

---

7. *Taiwan nichinichi shinpōsha* (Taiwan Daily News), October 30, 1940, Taihoku, 3.

Table 11.1 The Koo Businesses Established during the Sino-Japanese War

Name of company	Time of start-up	Person in charge	Position title	Note
Jidacheng Wood Co.	1938	Koo Wei-fu	On the Board and chief executive	Wood trade
Dayu Tea Co.	1938	Koo Chen-fu	On the Board and chief executive	Tea industry and trade; branches also set up in China at Dalian and Suzhou
Xianming Co.	1939	Koo Bin-fu	On the Board and chief executive	Bond trade
Taiwan Burlap Co.	1939	Koo Yen Pi-hsia	On the Board	
Tianran Cement	1940	Koo Wei-fu	On the Board	Joint venture with Japanese capital
Taiwan Plant Fiber	1941	Koo Bin-fu	On the Board	Joint venture with Japanese capital
Dahe Property	1942	Koo Chen-fu	Director	Agriculture, wood industry
Youbang Industrial Co.	1943	Koo Bin-fu	Director	Wood, fiber industry

Source: Tu Zhaoyan, *Riben diguozhuyi xia de Taiwan* (Taiwan under Japanese imperialism), translation of *Nihon teikoku shugi ka no Taiwan* from Japanese into Chinese by Lee Ming-chun (Taipei: Renjian chubanshe, 1992), 436–445.

Starting from April 1942, Japan implemented the policy of "Special Army Volunteers" to recruit Taiwanese into its military forces. The first quota was for 1,000 men, but by the end, 425,921 Taiwanese in total were processed for registration. In the three-year period of 1942–1944, about 6,000 volunteers were sent to the front. In August 1943, about 3,000 men were recruited as "Navy Special Volunteers." When the tide of war turned against Japan after May 1944, more than 8,000 Taiwanese were sent into the Marine Corps. In September 1944, after the war had resulted in a great number of Japanese casualties, conscription finally began in Taiwan, and 22,000 men were drafted.[8]

Koo Chen-fu expressed his support for this Japanese policy by donating ten thousand yen to the war effort.[9] Meanwhile, Koo Kwan-min, the eighth son of Koo Hsien-jung, was drafted.[10] Some of the Taiwanese capitalists discovered that during an all-out war an individual's influence under colonial rule was worth nothing; all were destined to be dragged into the war under the ultimate command of the colonial state.

Koo Chen-fu, like many other social elites from the upper class, had the obligation to join the Public Service Association of Imperial Subjects (Kōminhokokai),[11] and to carry out many orders from above. In an article entitled "War, Society, and School," which he published in April 1943, he expressed the belief that to make progress toward "becoming Japanese" (kōminka),[12] the discrimination between Japanese and Taiwanese should be eliminated so that other Taiwanese would share the happy memories of his learning experiences in a Japanese elementary school.[13] In June 1943, a special seminar on "Navy Special Volunteers" was given. Besides participants from the General Staff of the navy and army, representatives from law, business, and the literary field

---

8. Li Xiaofeng, *Taiwan shi jian dashi* (One Hundred significant events in the history of Taiwan) (Taipei: Yushanshe, 1999).

9. *Taiwan nichinichi shinpōsha*, October 3, 1943, 2.

10. The author's personal interview with Koo Kwan-min, April 30, 2009. K20090430.

11. *Kōminhokokai*, which literally means "The Public Service Association of Imperial Subjects," was organized and designed to recruit both Taiwanese and Japanese living in Taiwan to achieve a wide range of goals through social mobilization.

12. Leo Ching distinguishes the subtle yet significant difference between *dōka* (assimilation) and *kōminka* (imperialization). He argues that *kōminka* is not an extension of "*dōka*," nor is it the final stage of "*dōka*." He has cited what journalist Takeuchi Kiyoshi stressed in 1938: "*kōminka* means to become Japanese, but since the people of this island were already Japanese some forty-three years ago, there has to be more. How to become 'good' Japanese and to complete that process is what the *kōminka* movement is all about." Leo Ching, *Becoming Japanese: Colonial Taiwan and the Politics of Identity Formation* (Berkeley: University of California Press, 2001), 93.

13. *Taiwan jiho*, April, date is not clear, 1943, 35.

attended the seminar. As a representative of entrepreneurs, Koo Chen-fu stressed that the youth of the island of Taiwan, living surrounded by sea, were physically qualified to serve in the navy and were able to devote themselves to the Japanese-led Greater East-Asia Co-prosperity Sphere (Dai Tōa kyōeiken).[14] Both he and Lin Xiongxiang of the Lin family from Pan-ch'iao, captained Taipei's "Nation Protection Team" at separate times, and they later coauthored an article in *Taiwan jiho* (Taiwan Times Newspaper) about their experiences.[15] In their article, they not only expressed their gratitude toward the government for granting Taiwanese the opportunity to gain discipline through military training, but they also encouraged all Japanese and Taiwanese to protect the island from enemy attacks. At a later stage of the war, the Japanese governor Andō Rikichi was frequently accompanied by Koo Chen-fu on his inspection tours. As a contemporary observer later recalled, "Koo Chen-fu was almost like Andō's secretary."[16]

The war cut short the lives of many Taiwanese. When the Allied military started bombing the island, people were obliged to evacuate to safer places. There were shortages of everything, including access to medical treatment and supplies. Koo Chen-fu's wife became very ill; she probably had intestinal tuberculosis. As wealthy as the Koos were, they were still not able to obtain the services of a doctor, nor were they able to get any medicine. On May 6, 1945, Koo Chen-fu's beloved wife died, causing him to lapse into a state of helplessness and great sorrow. Buying no coffin at that time, he buried his wife with his own hands as the war was coming to an end.

On August 15, 1945, thousands of radios carried Emperor Hirohito's voice to Taiwan announcing Japan's surrender to the Allied forces. Nonetheless, people of the island had no clue at all about their fate in conjunction with Japan's defeat. The status of the colonized had already been stated in the Treaty of Shimonoseki in 1895, and the treaty also said that Taiwan was ceded to Japan permanently. Though defeated, the administrative units in Taiwan—including the general-governor's office—were still in operation, and great numbers of Japanese troops remained stationed in Taiwan. Because many things were controlled and regulated by the colonial state during wartime, including freedom of the press, only

---

14. *Taiwan jiho*, June, date is not clear, 1944, 1–10.

15. *Taiwan jiho*, August 9, 1944, 71–76.

16. He Fengjiao and Chen Meirong (interviewers), "Guyuan huangjia: Huang Tianheng xiansheng fangtan lu" (The reminiscences of Mr. Huang Tianheng) (Taipei: Academia Historica, 2008), 178.

a very small number of elites had access to radios and anticipated Japan's defeat. Others in Taiwan had not heard Allied broadcasts about the "Cairo Declaration" of November 1943 and the "Potsdam Declaration" of July 1945 that would have given them an inkling that Japan might be losing the war. On August 16, 1945, Koo Kwan-min left the army and returned to his home after more than eight months in military service. Only upon entering his home did he learn the news of Japan's defeat. One of his brothers, Koo Wei-fu (the sixth son of Koo Hsien-jung), was not at home; he had flown to Tokyo with some Japanese officers on Japanese military transport.[17]

Even after the war ended in Japan's defeat, there was no concrete evidence that the Koos opted for Taiwan independence. In a diary written by a Japanese military official, Shunji Shiomi, we learn that he together with Koo Wei-fu and other important officers made several visits to the gendarmerie, metropolitan police, prefectural police commissioner, and chief of the radicalism section in Japan. Shiomi recorded on August 27 and 29, 1945, that the purpose of Koo Wei-fu's trip was to explore further Japan's plans for postwar revival. However, Koo Wei-fu was disappointed by what he saw in Japan. He concluded that Japan should correct its mistakes and change its attitude toward China and Asia. He expected both Japan and China to cooperate well with each other and to build Taiwan into an ideal place with an Asian style.[18]

So right up to the end of the war and the beginning of the postwar period, while Koo Chen-fu made some criticisms of Japan, he continued to cooperate with Japanese military authorities and assume that he would mediate between Japan and Taiwan. He fully expected to be a leader of Taiwan but in the context of close relations with Japan and China—not to the exclusion of either one of them.

SAVED BY BEING JAILED AS A "WAR CRIMINAL"

In October 1945, Chen Yi, Chiang Kai-shek's appointee as the chief administrator of Taiwan province, arrived in Taipei from China.

---

17. The author's personal interview with Koo Kwan-min on April 30, 2009. K20094030.

18. Shunji Shiomi (1907–1980) graduated from Tokyo Imperial University in 1930 and served in the Finance Bureau of the Taiwan Governor's house in 1931. In 1943, he became the chief comptroller. In 1979, he published a book: *Hiroku shusen chokugo no Taiwan watashi no shusen nikki* (My personal diary at the end of World War II), translated from Japanese into Chinese as *Milu, zhongzhan qianhou de Taiwan* by Nihon Bunkyo Kikinkai (Taipei: Wenyingtang, 2001), 16–17.

In January 1946, he announced the "Traitors Punishment Act" and launched a campaign to encourage reporting of pro-Japanese traitors and war criminals in Taiwan. Two months later, in March 1946, a young Chinese officer visited Koo Chen-fu in Taipei. He introduced himself by presenting the business card of Lin Xiantang, a renowned advocate of Taiwanese interests under Japanese colonial rule who had pledged his loyalty to Chiang Kai-shek's Nationalist government in 1945 as soon as Japan had been defeated and Taiwan had reverted from Japan to China. The officer offered to accompany Koo to a meeting with Lin, but Koo was suspicious because it seemed that Lin was out of town. After hesitating for a second, Koo decided to follow the officer without informing other family members. Once the Nationalist government apprehended Koo, he was arrested and punished along with other men involved in the so-called Taiwan Independence Plot: Lin Xiongxiang, Xu Bing, Lin Xiantang, Chen Xin,[19] and other alleged "traitors" and "war criminals." Lin Xiantang and Chen Xin were not prosecuted and were released afterward. On July 29, 1945, the others were sentenced to imprisonment ranging from one year to two years and two months. Koo Chen-fu was imprisoned for nineteen months until January 1948; in prison he was known as "number 226."

It is odd that the original file of this case is now missing; the only documents that can be found are the court verdict and other related, subsequent documents.[20] However, the original file is not that important because the sequence of events can be reconstructed based on various narratives. Curiously, if the Japanese were the initiators of the plot, the case was short of any testimony from the Japanese side, but the convicted Taiwanese participants were nevertheless sentenced. Later, Yoshio Makisawa, a former major in the Japanese army, told a Japanese interviewer, Shiego Suzuki, that he was never interrogated by anyone from the government about this case.[21] In contrast to some of the Taiwanese accounts, various sources offering the Japanese version—mainly from the Sotokufu archive and Japan's National Institute for Defense Studies—recorded that the Taiwanese gentry took the initiative to hatch this plan

---

19. Chen Xin (1893–1947) studied at Keiyo University in Japan, and later graduated from Columbia University in the United States. Appointed by Chiang Kai-shek, he was also one of the members of the group that attended Nanjing's formal surrender ceremony on September 9, 1945. His specialty was finance, and he took responsibility for organizing the committee for welcoming the Nationalist government to Taiwan.

20. Taiwan's National Archive, document no. B375018771_0000081100006.

21. Su Yaochong, ed., *Zuihou de Taiwan zongdu fu: 1944–1946 zhongzhan ziliao ji* (The last Japanese Governor-general's office in Taiwan: Collection of materials at the end of the war, 1944–1946) (Taichung: Chenxing chubanshe, 2004), 13.

for self-government.[22] Probably in order to protect people, some of the names of the Taiwanese involved were redacted in the official documents.

In an article on June 10, 1946, *Time* magazine reported on Taiwan's deterioration after eight months of China's rule. The article concluded by saying: "Most foreign observers in Formosa agreed that if a referendum were taken today Formosans would vote for U.S. rule. Second choice—Japan."[23] Three months earlier, the same observation was reported on the front page headline in *The Washington Daily News*: "Chinese Exploit Formosa Worse Than JAPS Did."[24] In light of the evidence and the historical background, the Nationalist government seemed to play down the voice of pro-independence and to gain international support by laying blame on the Japanese.

After the war, the Nationalist regime took over in Taiwan all government offices and properties that originally belonged to the colonial government, and the Garrison Command was given all the facilities that were originally under the control of the Japanese army. Based on the ruling structure of the previous colonial government, the Nationalist government was easily able to set up its ruling regime.

During the colonial period, the Taiwanese economy had been linked to Japan; after that era ended, it was subject to the Chinese economy, which was in tatters after the prolonged Sino-Japanese War, followed by the Civil War between the Nationalist and the Chinese Communists in the late 1940s. As a result, Taiwan suffered. Rice, sugar, and related commodities for the people's livelihood were rerouted to China. The Taiwanese yen from the Japanese period was replaced with the yuan as the Taiwan currency; in addition, a fixed rate was also used between the Taiwan yuan and Chinese currency. In short order, the vicious inflation in China spread to Taiwan through trade and the exchange of currency.

The livelihood of the Taiwanese was severely threatened by the deteriorating economy. As early as the beginning of 1946, Taiwan suffered from both a shortage of goods and inflation. Even worse, the Nationalist government, in response, tried to tackle the problems by issuing more paper money. The total amount of currency issued in September 1945 was 1.93 million yuan. This increased to 29.43 billion in May 1946, then to 53.3 billion at the end of same year, and to 171.33 billion at the end of 1947. The collapse of the economy and the corruption within the

---

22. Ibid., 138–148.
23. http://www.time.com/time/magazine/article/0,9171,792979,00.html.
24. Shi-Shan Henry Tsai, *Lee Teng-hui and Taiwan's Quest for Identity* (New York: Palgrave Macmillan, 2005), 62.

government eventually led to discontentment among the Taiwanese, and this in turn culminated in a massive clash and bloody subjugation known as the "228 [February 28] incident" of 1947.

The February 28 incident started with a small instance of brutal law enforcement regarding unauthorized cigarettes, and ended in an island-wide uprising. On March 7, the "February 28 Incident Settlement Committee" submitted the "Outline of Settlement" to Governor Chen Yi for suggestions regarding political reform. However, things took a turn for the worse. On the afternoon of March 8, two thousand troops of the Fifth Military Police Corps and over 10,000 troops of the Twenty-first Army Division landed at the port of Keelung in northern Taiwan and at the port of Kaohsiung in the south. Upon learning of these landings, Chen Yi immediately denounced the Settlement Committee as an illegal organization and ordered it to be dissolved.

In the aftermath of the February 28 incident, massacres and purges swept over the island. On a number of occasions, Chen Yi contended that former Kōminhokokai members had provoked the violence.[25] Many leaders in society and numerous intellectuals, including councilmen, professors, lawyers, doctors, journalists, and teachers, were arrested. Among those elites, Chen Xin, who had once been detained together with Koo Chen-fu regarding the Taiwan Independence plot (for which Koo was convicted in July 1946), did not escape from Chen Yi this time in 1947, and after that he was never seen again.

On March 9, 1947, the Garrison Command declared martial law in Taiwan. The next day, Chiang Kai-shek gave an address at the Nationalist government's capital in Nanjing in which he responded to the March massacre by saying,

> I hope that every Taiwanese will fully recognize his duty to our fatherland and strictly observe discipline so as not to be utilized by treacherous gangs and laughed at by the Japanese. I hope Taiwanese will refrain from rash and thoughtless acts that will be harmful not only to our country but also to themselves. I hope they will be thoroughly determined to discriminate between loyalty and treason, and to discern between advantage and disadvantage; and that they will voluntarily cancel their

---

25. Xu Xueji, "Kominhokokai de yanjiu: yi Lin Xiantang de canyu weili" (The Kōminhokokai in Taiwan during the Second World War: A case study of Lin Xiantang's involvement), *Zhongyang yanjiuyuan jindaishi yanjiusuo jikan* (Bulletin of the Institute of Modern History, Academia Sinica), 31 (June 1999): 167–211.

illegal organizations and recover public peace and order, so that every Taiwanese can lead a peaceful and happy life as soon as possible, and thus complete the construction of the new Taiwan. Thus only can Taiwanese be free from the debt they owe to the entire nation which has undergone so many sacrifices and bitter struggles for the last fifty years in order to recover Taiwan.[26]

In effect the Chiang regime had created a dichotomy among the people regarding loyalty or treason. Those who did not pledge their loyalty would be categorized as "Communists" or "traitors." In fact, during the colonial period, the Communist activity in Taiwan was actually more associated with the Japanese Communist Party (JCP), and the forces within the Taiwanese Communist Party (TCP) were divided and influenced by power struggles among Comintern, the JCP, and the CCP. That situation had led to the TCP's destruction as early as 1931; the Japanese police force also had had a hand in this destruction.[27] As a consequence, after the Sino-Japanese War, there were fewer than fifty self-declared Communists on Formosa in a population exceeding six million. Nevertheless, in the period during the aftermath of the 228 incident, it is estimated that more than 8,000 people were sentenced to death for crimes said to be "treason" or said to be related to "Communist" activities.

The so-called White Terror became a tool for the Nationalist government to silence its citizens: many schemes were implemented to reeducate Taiwanese who had once been imperial subjects in the Japanese period. One example was the language policy that was meant to infuse "Chinese blood" into the Taiwanese. In an editorial comment in a newspaper, the Nationalist government expressed hope that the Taiwanese would completely eliminate Japanese influence on them. In one instance, they asked the Taiwanese to change their Japanese-style architecture into other forms, either Chinese- or Western-style. The commercial signboard, the business card, the way Taiwanese addressed one another, etc., should be corrected as soon as possible.[28] In the same newspaper in another article published in 1947, the editor again emphasized the following: "The Chinese culture in Taiwan has become

---

26. Chiang Kai-shek, addressing the weekly memorial services at Nanjing on March 10, 1947. Quoted by George Kerr, *Formosa Betrayed* (Boston: Houghton Mifflin, 1966), 307–309. Kerr worked in intelligence regarding Taiwan during the war, and after the war, he served as vice consul at the U.S. consulate.

27. Frank Hsiao and Lawrence Sullivan, "A Political History of the Taiwanese Communist Party, 1928–1931," *Journal of Asian Studies* 42.2 (February 1983): 269–289.

28. *Taiwan xinsheng bao* (Taiwan Shin Sheng Daily), November 20, 1945.

very thin. Currently, Taiwan is ill with cultural anemia, and thus more mainland scholars are needed here to give blood transfusions."[29]

The tragedy that struck Chen Xin during the troubles connected with the 228 incident left Koo Chen-fu with mixed feelings. In his biography, Koo Chen-fu was shown to be reflective but reluctant to comment further on the incident. He concluded that his imprisonment helped him make a narrow escape from a worse fate.[30] It was Koo Chen-fu's misfortune to have been imprisoned by the Nationalist government in Taiwan. Nonetheless, he would have suffered an even worse fate if he had not been in prison when the incident of February 28 occurred.

THE DECISION NOT TO RETURN TO TAIWAN, 1949–1952

After being in prison for nineteen months (July 1947–November 1948), Koo Chen-fu was released. As soon as he emerged from confinement in November 1948, Koo Chen-fu, a widower, remarried—this time to Yan Zhuoyun (a.k.a. Cecilia, 1925–). Yan had been born in China in Fujian province (directly across the Taiwan Strait), and she was the granddaughter of Yan Fu who was famous for his translation of Adam Smith's *The Wealth of Nations* and for introducing many Western ideas to China. Yan Zhuoyun's mother Lin Mulan was from Taiwan's Lin family of Pan-ch'iao before she married into the Yan family in Fujian. Because her brother Lin Xiongzheng had passed away in 1946, Lin Mulan came to Taiwan from Shanghai with her four children for the funeral. At that time her other brother Lin Xiongxiang had already been detained, so she paid a few visits to him in jail—sometimes with her daughters. Koo's and Lin's cases were tried under an international military court, and Yan Zhuoyun had opportunities to attend the hearings, where she met Koo Chen-fu. She was introduced to him by her uncle. Their marriage proved to be a turning point in Koo Chen-fu's life.

In 1949, Koo and his bride fled Taiwan and took refuge in Hong Kong. His brother Koo Kwan-min had been studying in China for more than a year. Li Zeyi advised Kwan-min to go to Beijing but Kwan-min knew that the railroad line from Shanghai to Beijing had come under the control of the CCP. He thought that even if he were able to make it to Beijing, it was very likely that the way back to Taiwan would be blocked.

---

29. *Taiwan xinsheng bao*, August 7, 1947.
30. Huang and Huang, *Gu Zhenfu rensheng jishi*, 103–104.

With that in mind, in 1948 he returned directly to Taiwan and continued his study at National Taiwan University. While at the university he was elected to be chairman of the Student University Association.

Both fortunately and unfortunately for Koo Kwan-min the "April 6 incident" and a student movement occurred in 1949 in Taiwan while he was on a trip to Hong Kong and staying in Koo Chen-fu's house.[31] The incident started on March 20 when a policeman beat up two students who were stopped for riding a single bicycle together, in violation of the traffic laws. Student demonstrations soon occurred on the campuses of the universities. Once again hundreds were jailed and several were killed. Many military policemen made a raid searching for Koo Kwan-min since he was the chairman of the student association. Koo Wei-fu contacted his brothers in Hong Kong, telling Koo Kwan-min not to return to Taiwan.

Meanwhile, in the final stages of the Civil War between the Nationalist government and the Communist forces, the Communists crossed an important river near Shanghai and quickly took the city. Cai Guoyi, who was a young Shanghai woman with whom Koo Kwan-min had fallen in love when he studied in Shanghai, fled to Taiwan first and then went on to meet Koo Kwan-min in Hong Kong. In 1950, Koo Kwan-min decided to marry Cai Guoyi. Shortly thereafter he left Hong Kong for Japan and did not return to Taiwan until 1972.

Another member of the Koo family, Koo Yen Pi-hsia, the wife of Koo Hsien-jung's first son, was also in danger. Because of a small loan she had made to a troubled young man named Lu Heruo,[32] Koo Yen Pi-hsia was arrested in 1950. All her property (an iron foundry, a sugar factory, her house and land) was confiscated. She was jailed by the Nationalist government for five years.

What did Koo Chen-fu think about the Nationalist government after this series of strikes against him, his brother, other family members, and the Taiwanese in general? He continued to consider Taiwan as his home, and he took a keen interest in influences exerted on it by the outcome of the Civil War in China and the attitude of the United States toward the Nationalist government. On October 1, 1949, the Chinese Communists

---

31. The author's personal interview with Koo Kwan-min, November 1, 2007.

32. Koo Yen Pi-hsia (1914–1999) married Koo Yueh-fu (1911–1936), the first biological son of Koo Hsien-jung. Koo Yueh-fu died young in 1936 and left his wife with three children. In August 1949, the *Guangming bao* (Guangming news) was accused of allegedly being the CCP's publication. The publication's editor, Lu Heruo, was blacklisted. He happened to be the piano teacher of Koo Yen Pi-hsia's daughter, and asked for a 2,000 yuan loan from Koo Yen Pi-hsia.

declared the establishment of the People's Republic of China. In December, the Nationalist government withdrew to Taipei. On January 5, 1950, President Harry Truman announced that the United States would not get involved in the dispute across the Taiwan Strait and that the United States would not intervene if the Chinese Communists were to attack Taiwan.

At this critical moment, the Korean War broke out. This then caused President Truman to react immediately by declaring the neutralization of the Straits of Formosa on June 27. He sent the Seventh Fleet to the Straits with an order to prevent any attack on Taiwan by Chinese Communist forces and any attack on China by the Nationalists. Following the outbreak of the Korean War, the Chiang Kai-shek government responded very quickly and declared that Taiwan was in a "state of emergency," and in order to suppress the "Communist rebellion," a law that superseded the constitution was required. Consequently, the so-called Temporary Provisions went into effect in Taiwan, and were enforced for forty-three years. By means of these laws, for the sake of national security, the government tried to do away with the Communists, those who were against the Nationalists, and the pro-Taiwan independence activists.

The turmoil resulting from the Civil War made Hong Kong, as a British colony, a buffer zone for many. There are not many records about Koo Chen-fu's life in Hong Kong. In his autobiography, Koo Chen-fu mentioned that the Chinese Communists tried to draw him to their side by means of various connections. It is not clear what connections he was referring to. The only clue was Cecilia's father. But when considering how effective this connection would have been, one must handle it with caution. In many places, Cecilia Koo emphasized her closeness to her grandfather Yan Fu, rather than to her father Yan Hu. In fact, while her mother went to Taiwan with Cecilia and her siblings, her father decided to stay in China. In 1947, Yan Hu joined the Chinese Democratic League, and in 1951 under Communist rule, he was elected as a member of the Fujian branch of the Chinese People's Political Consultative Conference, as well as deputy mayor of Fuzhou. His holding of this last office ended when he was "taken" for being a "rightist" in 1957. Yan Hu died in 1962. In China the "mistaken" accusation of "rightist" was not corrected until 1979, and since then, he has been honored as a "patriot."[33]

---

33. Shi Jianguo, *Zhongguo gongchandang Fuzhou difang zuzhi zhi* (The regional organization of Chinese Communists in Fuzhou) (Beijing: Zhongguo da baike quanshu chubanshe, 1998).

Koo Chen-fu was not tempted to migrate to China in order to use his wife's family connections to fight against the Nationalists. He felt no commitment to China, but his conscience told him that he had to leave Hong Kong. "Hong Kong, after all, is a strange land for me."[34] Koo Chen-fu himself explained that he returned to Taiwan because his mother got homesick, and because Cecilia's mother, who was living in Taiwan, missed her daughter.

BETWEEN BEIJING AND TAIWAN, 1952:
ONLY IN THE RIGHT PLACE IS THE ACTOR ABLE
TO PLAY A ROLE WELL

After three years in Hong Kong, what changed Koo Chen-fu's mind? His family played a key role in his decision making. His mother, who was homesick and in ill health, pleaded with him to return to Taiwan. His father had passed away fifteen years earlier in 1937, but his father's networks, which Koo Chen-fu had inherited and expanded, were still in place. How could he make use of these networks? Most of the Koos' property, particularly the land and real estate, were rooted in Taiwan. Before the end of the war, the Koo family had already become one of Taiwan's top three landlords. Even though the Koos had accumulated their wealth as intermediaries between the Japanese and the Taiwanese, the investments that the Koos had made during the war were retained by the family and not confiscated by the Nationalists after the war. Moreover the Nationalist government appealed to landlords for cooperation as it carried out land reform in Taiwan. But from Hong Kong how could Koo Chen-fu take advantage of these opportunities?

It was Koo Chen-fu's brother-in-law, Ye Mingxun, the husband of Cecilia's sister, who played the decisive role in helping Koo not only to return to Taiwan but also to enhance his position in many respects.[35] Ye at that time was head of the Central News Agency for the Nationalist government. He cautiously asked General Peng Mengji, the garrison commander, about the possibility of Koo Chen-fu coming back safely. Permitted to reenter with a letter of guarantee signed by Chiang Kai-shek, Koo Chen-fu returned to Taiwan at the age of thirty-five in 1952.

Through Ye Mingxun again, Koo became acquainted with Huang Shaogu, the Secretary of the Executive Yuan, and Zhang Zikai, the

---

34. Huang and Huang, *Gu Zhenfu rensheng jishi*, 121.
35. Ye Mingxun married Cecilia's sister in 1949.

Minister of Economic Affairs. In 1953, the Nationalists began to execute their land reform program, which initially was not welcomed by most of the landlords. Koo Chen-fu was then hired as a consultant to the Ministry of Economic Affairs, specifically to be in charge of this program.[36] At last, he successfully helped the government enact the land reform. While he rose within the government, his wife Cecilia Koo joined the National Women's League of the R.O.C. (NWL) in 1966, which had been established by Soong Mei-ling, Chiang Kai-shek's wife, in 1950. One goal of the NWL was to provide daily necessities to families of soldiers and to organize visits to encourage the soldiers at the front line. In 1977, Cecilia was recommended by other members for an appointment to the Standing Committee, and in 1981, with Madame Chiang's approval, she was placed on it. Ten years later, Cecilia was appointed by Madame Chiang to be the secretary-general of the NWL.[37] From then on, she regularly reported to Madame Chiang about the latest developments in Taiwan and led delegations to celebrate Madame Chiang's birthday in New York. She became Madame Chiang's closest aide.[38] In 2001, when Zhang Xueliang died in Hawaii, Cecilia went there in person to express condolences on behalf of Madame Chiang.

After Koo became active in economic planning in Taiwan, he joined the Nationalist party. Many of those who escaped the massacre and the February 28 incident chose to join the Nationalist party afterward. For them, it was an amulet, a pass allowing entry at many points. Their actions may be aptly described in the words of Albert O. Hirschman: "Exit, Voice, and Loyalty." Once Koo Chen-fu made his decision to reenter Taiwan, he felt the need to speak up and pledge his allegiance to the Nationalist party.

In making his peace with the Nationalist government and pledging his allegiance to it, Koo Chen-fu was representative of some but not all Taiwanese capitalists. At the opposite extreme, Lin Xiantang, who had been a pro-Taiwanese critic of Japanese rule during the colonial era and had become a national hero in the Nationalist government's eyes

---

36. Ho Tsai-man C. and Sun Wenbin, "Entrepreneurship and Risk: The Becoming of the Koo Business Dynasty," *Social Transformations in Chinese Societies* (Leiden: Brill, 2007), v. 3, 161.

37. Koo Yen Cho-yun, ed., *Fujian wushi nian* (The fiftieth anniversary of the National Women's League) (Taipei: National Women's League of the R.O.C., 2000).

38. In a personal interview with Vivien H.C. Ku (Gu Huaiqun), Koo Chen-fu's first daughter, she told the author that Madame Chiang's *qipao* (*cheongsam*, traditional dress for women) were always delivered to Cecilia for tailor's alteration since Cecilia dressed in a *qipao* very often and knew where to find appropriate tailors. The author's personal interview with Vivien Ku, May 9, 2008.

because of his anti-colonial stance, was disappointed with the Nationalist government. In politics, he aspired to become Assembly Speaker but was forced by the government to withdraw his candidacy. In the Taiwan economy, his family's financial base suffered from severe losses as a result of the government's land reform program and rice-harvest levies by the Nationalist military command. When the Nationalist government retreated to Taiwan, Lin Xiantang left for Japan, citing his need for medical treatment as the excuse for his trip. Ironically Lin Xiantang ended up staying in Tokyo for the rest of his life despite the Nationalist government's repeated efforts to lure him back. On the issue of whether to return to Taiwan, he stated his position clearly in his diary: "One should not enter a dangerous country, nor stay in a chaotic one."[39]

CONCLUSION

As an émigré in Hong Kong, 1949–1952, Koo Chen-fu both resembled and differed from Chinese capitalists who had fled there from China. On the one hand, like many of them, he considered Hong Kong to be a temporary stop, and he was preoccupied with his family and his family's immovable assets at home. As shown in the first two parts of this chapter, his family became prominent in Taiwan during its early years as a Japanese colony, 1895–1937, and even wealthier during the Sino-Japanese War of 1937–1945. On the other hand, unlike the capitalists from China, he had fled from rule under the Chinese Nationalist government, not the Communist state, and he was afraid to return home because of charges against him for wartime and postwar treason, not capitalist exploitation.

In Koo's case, he had concrete reasons for fearing that he would suffer if he returned home because he had already served a nineteen-month jail term—a painful experience that had precipitated his flight from Taiwan to Hong Kong in the first place. But he also had cause for hope for a successful return to Taiwan because of his family's influence, especially because of the intervention of his brother-in-law, Ye Mingxun, head of the Nationalist government's Central News Agency. Through Ye, Koo received assurances that the Nationalist government would set aside his criminal record, protect his rights to his family's property, and open the way for him to shift his land use from agriculture to industry.

---

39. Huang Fusan, *Lin Xiantang zhuan* (The biography of Lin Xiantang) (Nantou: Guoshiguan Taiwan wenxian guan, 2004), 222.

In 1952, with these assurances in hand, Koo returned from Hong Kong to Taiwan, and subsequently he found that the Nationalist government made good on its promises. In the 1950s, as Taiwan industrialized, he prospered, and ultimately he rose to the position of head of the Taiwan Cement Corporation.

Koo never seems to have considered any place other than Taiwan to be his home or to have doubted that he would eventually find a way to live his life there. But in an era of Taiwan's tumultuous transformation from a Japanese colony to a base for the Nationalist government, how had Koo known when and where to relocate to his best advantage first from Taiwan to Hong Kong in 1949 and then from Hong Kong back to Taiwan in 1952? Perhaps a clue to his success at choosing the right place at the right time may be found in his observations about his favorite avocation, Peking opera. He was introduced to it as a child, and he began to study it seriously after he moved to Hong Kong, taking classes from the renowned teacher, Meng Xiaodong. When he returned to Taiwan, he had his debut on stage at the age of thirty-nine. Later he wrote about the significance of how an actor positions himself in Peking opera in words that might also have guided him as he made his decisions whether to live and do business in Hong Kong or Taiwan. "The process of moving and taking steps on stage demands discipline," Koo noted. "Where to stand is also important. Only in the right place is the actor able to play a role well."

12 PROFESSIONAL MANAGERS AT POLITICAL CROSSROADS |
Hsia Pin-fang at the Bank of China in New York and London, 1939–1951
Elisabeth Köll

The fate of famous capitalists such as Liu Hongsheng, Wu Yunchu, or K.P. Chen in China's post-1949 transition to a socialist society and economy illustrates the difficulty of choosing political sides with serious personal and economic consequences. The "Dilemmas of Victory,"[1] a term aptly coined by Paul Pickowicz and Jeremy Brown, caused a wide range of reactions to the Communist takeover from Chinese elites hoping to save their livelihood, assets, and families. Some gave the new government a chance by returning from overseas, some expressed their support by staying in the country, while others left China, sooner or later, to escape the politics of the new regime altogether.

Not only major capitalists but also professional managers with highly specialized expertise were courted by the Chinese Communist Party (CCP) and had to choose political sides in the aftermath of 1949. After seizing power in the countryside, the CCP began to eliminate quickly the rural elite both in terms of their economic and political power. However, without sufficient expertise and personnel to control Chinese cities and their economies efficiently, the CCP used the more indirect method of co-opting the urban elite, especially business and professional elites, in order to gain control over the cities and move China eventually toward a command economy.[2]

---

1. See Jeremy Brown and Paul G. Pickowicz, eds., *Dilemmas of Victory: The Early Years of the People's Republic of China* (Cambridge: Harvard University Press, 2007).

2. Ramon H. Myers, "Revolution and Economic Life in Republican China: From World War I until 1949," and Marie-Claire Bergère, "China in the Wake of the Communist Revolution: Social Transformations, 1949–1966," both in Werner Draguhn and David S. Goodman, eds., *China's Communist Revolutions: Fifty Years of the People's Republic of China* (London, New York: Routledge, 2002), 1–11 and 98–123. In contrast to the Russian Revolu-

The professional career of Hsia Pin-fang (1902–1970), the central figure of this chapter, and his public role and private opinions provide us with a unique lens to explore the response of China's foremost financial institution, the Bank of China (Zhongguo yinhang), and its overseas branches during the Communist Revolution. As manager of the New York and London branches between 1939 and 1951, Hsia spent most of his professional life in North America and Europe looking after government investments and the interests of the bank's private shareholders, driven by strong professional ethics and identity as a banker. My analysis in this chapter combines a biographical approach to Hsia Pin-fang's career with an institutional perspective on his interaction and changing relationship with the Bank of China and Chinese government authorities during years of constant national and economic crisis. This approach is possible due to access to Hsia's personal archive containing hundreds of private letters, business correspondence, reports, and memoranda covering the years between 1939 and 1951.[3] The documents allow us insights into the complex, growing responsibilities of this New York and London branch manager that went far beyond managerial and financial control of banking matters and always carried a political dimension.

Hsia Pin-fang's political, professional, and personal dilemmas in China's transition to communism were not unique, as recent studies by Joseph Esherick and Sherman Cochran have shown.[4] Many highly educated professionals, entrepreneurs, and intellectuals faced the difficult choice between giving the new Communist government a chance to prove itself, leaving for Taiwan and Hong Kong, or becoming part of the global overseas Chinese diaspora. However, this chapter argues that the increasingly strained relationship between the Bank of China headquarters in Chongqing and overseas branches, factional fights over promotions and key positions within the bank at large, and the difficulty of keeping up with

---

tion, civil society did not come under attack immediately and Chinese elites had to define their roles in the transition process. See Nara Dillon, "New Democracy and the Demise of Private Charity in Shanghai," in Brown and Pickowicz, eds., *Dilemmas of Victory*, 80–102, especially 85, 101–102; and Toru Kubo, "China's Economic Development and the International Order of Asia, 1930s–1950s," in Shigeru Akita and Nicholas J. White, eds., *The International Order of Asia in the 1930s and 1950s* (London: Ashgate, 2010), 233–253.

3. Manuscripts Mss., 781, Hsia Pin-fang Papers, 1930–1951 (hereafter cited as HPF Papers), Baker Business Historical Collections, Harvard Business School. I would like to thank especially Dr. Laura Linard, Director of the Baker Historical Collections, for drawing my attention to this substantial collection, which amounts to six linear feet, sixteen volumes, and four cases.

4. See Joseph Esherick, "The Ye Family in New China," and Sherman Cochran, "Capitalists Choosing Communist China: The Liu Family of Shanghai, 1948–56," both in Brown and Pickowicz, eds., *Dilemmas of Victory*, 311–336 and 359–385.

frequent management changes during wartime alienated Hsia from his institutional employer long before the Communist takeover in 1949.

Hsia Pin-fang's case also demonstrates the careful tactics of the new Chinese government aimed at convincing him to stay with the Bank of China after 1949. The methods ranged from attempted persuasion, promises of generous compensation, and appeals to his patriotism to more direct pressure via "inspectors" sent from headquarters. It becomes evident that a shrewd and initially patient new management under the leadership of the CCP was not willing to give up easily on Hsia's valuable human capital of excellent professional and social skills.

Arguably, Hsia Pin-fang's decision making was foremost guided by professional and personal values, not by dogmatic political convictions. During the war years he acted as a Chinese "patriot" who was keenly aware of the weaknesses of the Nationalist regime and cautiously watched the rise of the Communist movement and the Civil War leading to the 1949 revolution. Motivated by a strong sense of professional responsibility combined with sound patriotic sentiments, Hsia continued to serve the Bank of China until the spring of 1951. In the end, he refused to yield to the demands of the new management under the leadership of the Communist regime in Beijing; at the same time he also decided against joining the Nationalists, including several of his former colleagues, in Taiwan who sought his professional expertise for setting up their own banking system. Having arrived at a political crossroads, he opted out, as we will see, from both political and professional commitments.

THE CAREER PATH OF A PROFESSIONAL MANAGER IN REPUBLICAN CHINA

Hsia Pin-fang was born on December 2, 1902, as the second son and third of three children in Anjing, Anhui province.[5] His grandfather was a scholar who after passing the imperial exams had served as tutor to Governor-General Li Hongzhang's family during the late Qing dynasty (1644–1911). Hsia's father, Xia Zhongqian, also received training as a classical scholar but in the wake of the late Qing reforms became one of the first candidates to enroll in the Provincial Law College in Anjing. After graduation he advanced to the position of judge at the provincial

---

5. The biographical sketch is based on "Brief Resume of Personal Background and Career of Pinfang Hsia" by his son Y.L. Hsia, April 1977, found in "Hsia Pin-fang, material about," case 4, HPF Papers.

high court in charge of civil cases for Anhui province until his retirement in 1930. According to his autobiographical notes, Hsia Pin-fang took the national entrance exam to Tsinghua University in Beijing in 1916. He passed as one of the youngest applicants and was awarded one of six provincial scholarships the university offered that year. He graduated from Tsinghua in 1924 with a scholarship that allowed him to continue his studies in the United States. First he enrolled at Colorado College in Colorado Springs where he quickly graduated with a B.A. in 1925 with honors in economics and business administration. He then moved east and was accepted as a graduate student at Harvard Business School where he graduated with an MBA and a concentration in investment banking in 1927.[6] During his stay in North America, Hsia met his future wife, Liu Shuting, who had earned a Ph.D. in mathematics from the University of Michigan. The two married in December 1929 and then returned to Shanghai where Hsia started working for the Bank of China in the international department.

The core of the Hsia Pin-fang collection, donated in 1977 to Baker Library at the Harvard Business School by his son, Dr. Edward Hsia, includes papers and correspondence for the period starting in 1939 when he was appointed manager of the New York agency of the Bank of China until his resignation from the bank's London branch in 1951. As a result, we know relatively little about his work during the Shanghai years. Apart from his duties in the international business department, he also worked at the bank's trust department, and apparently his work schedule still allowed him to pursue his interests in teaching and academic research. In 1930–1931 Hsia taught at the Shanghai Industry School (also known as Hujiang University) as an associate professor,[7] and in 1932 he published a paper on "The Future of China's Finance" in the journal *Pacific Affairs*. In this article he proposed foreign investment in railroad construction, basic industries, and government loans as a remedy for the budgetary problems of the Chinese government at the time.[8]

---

6. Harvard Business School, Alumni database, Univ. 3673-J. During his time at HBS, Hsia Pin-fang lived at 349 Harvard Street, Cambridge.

7. I thank Prof. Feng Xiaocai, Department of History, East China Normal University, Shanghai, for this information.

8. Hsia Pin-fang, "The Future of China's Finance," *Pacific Affairs* 5.1 (January 1932): 35–41.

His overseas career began in 1939 when Hsia Pin-fang was transferred to New York and remained at the branch until 1944. During the years of World War II, he was responsible for the day-to-day running of the branch, including both investment management and the remittance business. His portfolio also included the preparation of regular reports for the bank's central office on national and international economic, political, and military developments in his capacity as an observer abroad. In 1944 he was appointed Resident Representative of the Bank of China in Canada and entrusted with the task to build up a branch in Ottawa from where he wrote monthly reports for the Head Office in Shanghai.

After the end of World War II, Hsia Pin-fang was appointed to the special committee in charge of reorganizing the Shanghai Stock Exchange which involved drafting new regulations and procedures for its operation. During his visit to Shanghai in 1946, at the request of the Central Bank of China (Zhongyang yinhang), he also served on the special committee for investigating the United Nations Relief and Rehabilitation Administration (UNRRA) operations in China.[9] However, Hsia's most challenging assignment was his appointment to manager of the Bank of China's London branch in 1946. This branch was responsible for the bank's activities and operations in the United Kingdom, Europe, and Africa during the economic recovery phase following World War II. He held that position until February of 1951 when he resigned after a long and complicated decision-making process.[10]

MANAGING REMITTANCES AND PATRIOTIC RESPONSIBILITIES: THE NEW YORK YEARS, 1939–1945

When Hsia Pin-fang assumed his post as director of the Bank of China's New York agency in 1939, large parts of China were already under Japanese occupation, imposing serious constraints on China's economic and financial operations both at home and abroad. At the outbreak of the Sino-Japanese War in 1937 China's banking system was dominated by four government banks whereas provincial and local banks, private Chinese banks, Chinese native banks, and the foreign banks occupied the

---

9. Hsia Pin-fang in Shanghai to T.Y. Lee in London, August 10, 1946, case 4, HPF Papers.

10. Hsia Pin-fang passed away in New York on December 22, 1970, survived by his widow and two children. Dr. Yujen Edward Hsia became a physician at the University of Hawaii; at the time, his daughter Lucia was the wife of Dr. Ewing Chinn, associate professor of philosophy of science at Trinity College in San Antonio, Texas.

margins of China's financial sector.[11] In early 1935 the government had taken over control of the Bank of China, which had been established in 1912 and, together with the Bank of Communications (Jiaotong yinhang), had long been the leading private bank. The Central Bank of China did little commercial business, whereas the Agricultural Bank of China (Zhongguo nongmin yinhang) established in 1933 under government auspices, operated mostly in the interior and focused on rural credit. As a group these four banks held well over two-thirds of all financial resources of modern-style Chinese banks in 1937.[12] The foreign banks numbered about twenty-five in 1937 and were under American, British, Dutch, French, German, Italian, and Japanese control. They handled primarily foreign trade and sometimes also foreign loans and investments in China.

Although the foreign banks dominated the foreign exchange market at the time, Chinese banks, notably the Bank of China, were becoming increasingly active in that market segment during the 1930s.[13] Under the managerial leadership of Bei Zuyi, Bank of China branches in treaty ports and commercial ports began to engage in foreign exchange transactions, and the steadily increasing foreign reserves allowed the Bank of China to open new branches and agencies abroad.[14] For the purpose of remittance transactions, the bank expanded its branch network. While retaining its four existing locations in London, Osaka, Singapore, and New York, it opened new offices in Jakarta (Batavia), Penang, Kuala Lumpur, Haiphong, Hanoi, Karachi, Chittagong, Rangoon, Calcutta, Bombay,

11. On the banking sector in China during the Republican period see Linsun Cheng, *Banking in Modern China: Entrepreneurs, Professional Managers, and the Development of Chinese Banks, 1897–1937* (Cambridge: Cambridge University Press, 2003); Brett Sheehan, *Trust in Troubled Times: Money, Banks, and State-Society Relations in Republican Tianjin* (Cambridge: Harvard University Press, 2003); Wu Jingping, *Shanghai jinrongye yu guomin zhengfu guanxi yanjiu, 1927–1937* (Research on Shanghai's financial world and its relationship with the Nationalist government, 1927–1937) (Shanghai: Shanghai Caijing daxue chubanshe, 2002); Li Yixiang, *Jindai zhongguo yinhang yu qiye de guanxi, 1897–1945* (China's modern banks and their relationship with enterprises, 1897–1945) (Taipei: Dongda tushu gongsi, 1997); on British banks in China see Niv Horesh, *Shanghai's Bund and Beyond: British Banks, Banknote Issuance, and Monetary Policy in China, 1842–1937* (New Haven: Yale University Press, 2009).

12. Arthur N. Young, *China's Wartime Finance and Inflation, 1937–45* (Cambridge: Harvard University Press, 1965), 134.

13. Ibid., 135.

14. Howard L. Boorman, ed., *Biographical Dictionary of Republican China* (New York: Columbia University Press, 1967–1979). See entry on Pei Tsu-yi (Bei Zuyi), v. 3, 65–69. Among the Bank of China bankers, Bei Zuyi specialized in arbitrage and developed the bank's foreign exchange business.

Sydney, Liverpool, and Havana.[15] In 1940 the total sum of remittances from overseas Chinese through the Bank of China amounted to 222.3 million yuan, with the lion's share channeled through the Singapore branch (160.9 million yuan) and 57.1 million yuan through the New York branch.[16]

As head of the New York agency Hsia Pin-fang was in charge of the bank's business within the entire Western hemisphere with remittances as the emerging core business. Foreign exchange transactions were placed with the New York branch in American and Canadian dollars, and except for the freezing order of 1941, banking transactions were not subject to rigid control regulations. As Hsia pointed out in his letters, a large Chinese population in the United States and the neighboring countries brought tremendous volume of immigrant remittance business for the bank. In his usual frank manner he remarked that not all remittances originated from altruistic, patriotic motivations but were "stimulated partly by the desire to take advantage of the Chinese currency situation during World War II and partly by the necessity of giving financial support to families and relatives in China."[17] Compared to the London operations during the war years, the banking resources accumulating in New York were much larger and allowed for investment operations on a much bigger and more active scale. Most of these transactions were performed by cable under a system by which over 100,000 regular remitters were registered and each assigned a code number to save cable charges.[18]

According to Hsia Pin-fang's business and private correspondence from the early 1940s, the remittance business became the biggest challenge for the New York agency's human resources as it faced the political and military developments impacting the physical operation of the remittance business on the Chinese mainland. In a letter to a Chinese friend from December 5, 1942, Hsia responded to the question of how to send money safely to Ningbo, then a city in occupied territory: "Officially and legally, remittance to Ningpo [Ningbo] is not possible because of the restrictions of United States Treasury General Ruling No. 11, which prohibits any transaction with enemy occupied areas. ... Two ways are possible: (1) Place money with our Chungking [Chongqing] office

---

15. The Editorial Committee on the History of the Bank of China, *A History of the Bank of China, 1912–1949* (Beijing: Sinolingua, 1999), 140.

16. Zhongguo yinhang zonghang, Zhongguo di'er lishi dang'anguan, eds., *Zhongguo yinhang hangshi ziliao huibian* (Documentary collection of the banking history of the Bank of China) (Nanjing: Dang'an chubanshe, 1991–1995), v. 3, 2258.

17. Business Record of Hsia Pin-fang, no date (1960?), case 4, HPF Papers.

18. Ibid.

on a deposit basis and (2) Remit funds to someone in Chungking whom they can trust and who may undertake the responsibility of forwarding the remittance to Ningpo through such institutions as the Shanghai Commercial and Savings Bank."[19]

Besides channeling regular remittances through the bank's counters in New York or via cable, Hsia received requests from friends and influential officials to arrange their personal remittances and deposits, often through intermediaries from other Bank of China branches. The sheer number of these personal requests impacted the efficiency of the New York remittance operations which by 1943 had become an overloaded system. That year, the New York office handled 400–500 remittance transactions per day, which were directed by mail and required cumbersome dealings with personal checks, incomplete addresses, and insufficient balances.

On the Chinese side, the problems were equally challenging: banks suffered from shortages of actual currency notes to meet the payments, the shipping of currency notes was difficult, and Hsia Pin-fang received complaints that payments to recipients were made in depreciated notes issued by the Bank of Communications and the Agricultural Bank. When mail had to be temporarily rerouted through the Indian mail route after the fall of Hong Kong and Burma to the Japanese, the interminable delays and even return of remittances caused a public relations disaster for the bank. Disgruntled Chinese clients complained, and their angry letters to T.V. Soong, then the bank's chairman of the board, were published in Chinese newspapers all over the United States, blaming the New York office for inefficient service.[20] As a result, the Bank of China's wartime head office in Chongqing sent a Mr. Yu to New York with the task to investigate the problem. Although it appears that indeed external circumstances rather than managerial inefficiency were responsible for the situation, the issue eventually led to Hsia Pin-fang's demotion and transfer to the London office—a move that supposedly calmed down angry overseas communities and customers in North America.

Apart from Hsia's dealings with the challenges of a booming remittance business, he devoted a lot of his time as a professional manager to human resource management and the gathering of financial and political intelligence. In order to meet wartime needs, particularly

---

19. Hsia Pin-fang to Dorothy Yu, December 5, 1942, case 4, HPF Papers.
20. Report on remittance business by Hsia Pin-fang, March 17, 1943, case 4, HPF Papers. For a short biography of T.V. Soong, see Boorman, ed., *Biographical Dictionary of Republican China*, v. 3, 149–153.

with respect to financial transactions between the United States and China, the organization of the New York agency expanded from about 40 employees in 1939 to about 140 in 1944. The management of the bank's staff, the recruitment and training of both female and male employees—Chinese and American—was a task that Hsia Pin-fang undertook with great personal interest and dedication. In terms of investment, he personally managed a portfolio of over 100 million dollars invested in U.S. government bonds, Canadian government bonds, American preferred and common stocks, bills and commercial papers.[21] He successfully conducted negotiations with Washington authorities in connection with general licenses involving Chinese assets and transactions under the freezing order in effect during World War II; he also negotiated with the Canadian exchange control in order to facilitate the handling of Chinese remittances by the Canadian chartered banks.

Reading through Hsia Pin-fang's correspondence, it is striking what unreliable information he received from colleagues and friends about the volatile political and economic situation in China. For example, by the early 1940s a large number of concerned letters personally addressed to Hsia sought his opinion on the possibility that Chinese assets would be confiscated by the U.S. government. In a letter to a colleague in November 1940 he considered it highly unlikely that conflict between the United States and Japan would lead to the freezing of Chinese accounts in the United States, unless the Chinese resistance collapsed and the Japanese invasion completely succeeded.[22]

As the war went on, more and more legal questions crossed his desk. For example, the Bank of China's Shanghai headquarters approached Hsia Pin-fang in New York to help with legal advice on the creation of a pseudo-partnership with an American bank in order to protect Bank of China property. Due to the legal protection of foreign businesses in Shanghai's International Settlement until December 1941, many businesses in China in the lower Yangzi area tried to keep their assets intact through foreign registration or a move into the settlement.[23] Hsia responded with great hesitation and warned Bei Zuyi, then acting general manager at the Hong Kong branch, that any registration for partnership would have to be done

---

21. Description of Hsia Pin-fang's business portfolio, no date, personal folder, case 4, HPF Papers.

22. Hsia Pin-fang to Fisher (Yu) at the Bank of China in Shanghai, November 19, 1940, 3, case 4, HPF Papers.

23. For foreign registration in Shanghai during wartime see Parks M. Coble, *Chinese Capitalists in Japan's New Order: The Occupied Lower Yangzi, 1937–1945* (Berkeley: University of California Press, 2003).

properly: "... in regard to our present plan of organizing an American company to protect our properties in Shanghai [and] your suggested scheme to negotiate with American banks and utilities companies instead of exporters. ... We have come to the conclusion that it is very difficult for the American banks to lend us any substantial assistance, because under the American law it has to be backed up by a genuine loan. No fictitious transfer will be permissible."[24] Hsia Pin-fang always insisted on playing by the rules, knowing that legal irregularities would damage the bank's reputation in the United States and jeopardize future financial and political cooperation between the two allies. The Bank of China headquarters, however, often interpreted his straightforward decisions as indications that he lacked flexibility and loyalty.

In the early 1940s his overall judgment of the war situation in China was cautiously optimistic but never enthusiastic. Yet, as head of the New York agency Hsia was obliged to take on a key role in the organization of fundraising and patriotic activities in the United States. In fact, in 1939 the campaign for patriotic contributions through bond purchases and donations grew so large and successful that it attracted the suspicious attention of the Security Exchange Commission (SEC) which began an investigation into the matter.[25] The whole issue came to light when the U.S. postal authorities noticed that huge bulky parcels with large quantities of Chinese government bonds were being mailed to China's U.S. consulates, which functioned as intermediaries and passed on the bonds to Chinese individuals either as reward for their contributions or as a delivery for bond sales made to them under the remittance system. As a result, Hsia Pin-fang and the bank's attorney, James Burke, were interviewed by the SEC. This incident triggered copious legal correspondence and negotiations with the American authorities as well as with the Bank of China headquarters whom Hsia assured that "this agency has been extremely careful in handling patriotic contributions and bond purchases from the very beginning and every step has been taken to keep our procedure in strict accord with the understanding established with the SEC."[26] As in the case of the remittances, the patriotic bond issue led to conflict with the local overseas Chinese Patriotic Associations,

---

24. Bei Zuyi from the Head Office in Hong Kong to Hsia Pin-fang, April 26, 1940, case 3, HPF Papers.

25. Confidential letter from Bank of China's New York agency to Head Office—Trust Department in Hong Kong, signed by Hsia Pin-fang, September 26, 1939, case 3, HPF Papers.

26. Confidential letter from Bank of China New York agency to Head Office in Hong Kong, September 26, 1939, case 3, HPF Papers.

which did not understand the legal implications and criticized the careful and diplomatic approach that the bank took with the U.S. authorities as lack of cooperation for a good cause.[27]

As head of the Bank of China New York agency, an institution under heavy government control, Hsia Pin-fang also had the task of receiving and entertaining Chinese political emissaries, diplomats, and government officials who visited the United States in the early 1940s to drum up political and especially financial support for China in the war against Japan.[28] Hsia accompanied T.V. Soong, the chairman of the Bank of China, during his trip in June 1940 and kept in communication with the Chinese ambassador, Dr. Hu Shih.[29] Hsia Pin-fang had enjoyed T.V. Soong's support during his early years at the Bank of China in Shanghai and accompanied his boss during the weeks of loan negotiations with the U.S. government. At the end of Soong's visit in 1940, Hsia was relieved to inform Bei Zuyi at the Hong Kong branch that the New York agency would take care of crediting a US$25 million government loan to the account of the Central Bank of China through the Bank of China.[30]

The public and social responsibilities of Hsia Pin-fang as an informal representative of the Chinese government and visible anchor of patriotic activities in the United States were exhausting and included appearances on stage with Soong Mei-ling, commonly referred to as Madame Chiang Kai-shek, during her pro-China rallies in New York or serving as patron for "the bowl-of-rice party" at the Waldorf Astoria in November 1940 on invitation of Colonel Theodore Roosevelt, Jr., national chairman of the American Bureau for Medical Aid to China.[31] As manager of the New York branch, Hsia had no choice but to fulfill his obligations to

---

27. Hsia Pin-fang to Head Office in Hong Kong, November 26, 1939, case 3, HPF Papers. This letter describes the impending "draft bill to revise neutrality act": "… if the Act is passed as drafted, the Patriotic Chinese contribution of funds (except those for medical and civilian relief) and purchase of bonds may at any time become unlawful, as soon as a proclamation is made by U.S. government on existence of a state of war between China and Japan."

28. See, for example, the Stabilization Board of China. Holding resources of nearly US$100 million, it was constituted in the summer of 1941 with five members: Bei Zuyi (Bank of China), Xi Demao (Central Bank), K.P. Chen (chairman), A. Manuel Fox, nominated by the American Treasury, and Sir Edmund Hall-Patch, nominated by the British treasury. Young, *China's Wartime Finance and Inflation*, 249.

29. Hsia Pin-fang to T.V. Soong, Chairman, Bank of China, June 22, 1940, case 3, HPF Papers.

30. Hsia Pin-fang to Bei Zuyi, Assistant General Manager, Bank of China, Hong Kong, November 20, 1940, case 3, HPF Papers.

31. Unidentified newspaper photograph, photographs, case 3, HPF Papers; Hsia Pin-fang to Colonel Theodore Roosevelt, Jr., November 1, 1940, case 3, HPF Papers.

raise funds and shape public opinion in the Western world in favor of China's fight against Japan. In a letter to a colleague marked private and confidential from 1942 he complained that the increasingly large Chinese "refugee population" arriving in New York after the beginning of the Pacific War included many acquaintances from his own social circles, furthering the need to socialize for the sake of networking and fulfilling patriotic obligations.[32]

The sources documenting Hsia Pin-fang's devotion to hard work in New York on behalf of the Bank of China, the Chinese government, the overseas Chinese community, and the war effort in general let one to easily forget that, although his wife and two children lived with him in the United States, he also had family left behind in occupied China. It is touching to read his letter to the Shanghai office in 1940 alerting the bank that his father planned to go to the Chongqing office in unoccupied China to withdraw funds from Hsia Pin-fang's Chinese dollar current account with the Shanghai branch every three or four months.[33] Although his business and personal letters expressed worry and also frustration with the weak Nationalist war effort, he remained cautiously optimistic about the outcome of the war through the early 1940s. As his correspondence files show, in late 1943 and through 1944 he began to compile lists and make contacts in U.S. industries for future projects in a free, post-war China. He established contacts with firms in the chemical industry, manufacturing, and the textile industry, which he considered vital for China's industrial reconstruction after the end of World War II.[34] At that time, he clearly envisioned a better future for China.

REORGANIZATION, TRANSITIONS, AND PREMONITIONS: THE LONDON YEARS, 1946–1949

During Hsia Pin-fang's tenure in London, 1946–1949, which coincided with the years of the Civil War in China, he faced many personnel changes and managerial conflicts spilling over from the

32. Hsia Pin-fang to Bei Zuyi at the Bank of China, London, August 11, 1942, case 3, HPF Papers.

33. Hsia Pin-fang to M.H. Cheng, sub-manager, Bank of China, Shanghai, October 19, 1940, case 3, HPF Papers.

34. See Hsia Pin-fang's correspondence with Howard G. Godfrey & Co. Inc., Chinese silk export trade. Hsia Pin-fang states: "Mr. Godfrey is very much interested in the future development of the American market for Chinese silk." Hsia Pin-fang to Godfrey & Co., December 29, 1943, case 3, HPF Papers.

bank's headquarters and China locations into the branches and agencies overseas. Prior to his posting in London, Hsia was de facto demoted to the lower rank of bank representative with the charge to explore new business opportunities in Canada, and he was replaced by Xi Demao as head of the New York office.[35] This decision by H.H. Kung, the new chairman of the bank, came as quite a shock to Hsia Pin-fang. In a number of letters his colleague and friend Bei Zuyi tried to explain the strategic motivations behind the bank's decision and console Hsia at the same time:

> Ever since the resignation of Dr. T.V. Soong from the Chairmanship of Bank of China, I had been under the impression that such a change was inevitable and that the change was intended to bring about a closer collaboration between our bank and Central Bank of China. As you are undoubtedly aware, the bulk of our foreign exchange assets and investments are now with our New York Agency, which has long been the focus of attention of the higher authorities. It was most unfortunate that coincidentally a certain section of overseas Chinese in America had made direct attack against you to the generalissimo [Chiang Kai-shek]. These facts naturally made your position somewhat untenable. Thus about a fortnight ago, I was told by Dr. H.H. Kung that he would like to recall you and to appoint Mr. T.M. Hsi [Xi Demao] as your successor. In spite of my defense for you, it seemed obvious that Dr. Kung was determined to effect this change in order to comply with the wishes of the generalissimo. ... Please do not feel too depressed by the sudden change over which we really have no control.[36]

Obviously, the complaints about the remittance disaster from overseas Chinese in North America, many of them with family roots in southern China, Chiang Kai-shek's native region, had fallen upon open ears. However, Bei Zuyi's remarks also point to internal patronage net-works within the bank and their vulnerability during personnel changes. Since the

---

35. Bei Zuyi to Hsia Pin-fang, May 2, 1944, folder "Relinquishment of N.Y. Agency," case 4, HPF Papers.

36. Bei Zuyi to Hsia Pin-fang, May 2, 1944, folder "Relinquishment of N.Y. Agency," case 4, HPF Papers. T.V. Soong had resigned in 1944 and had been replaced by H.H. Kung as chairman of the Bank of China. For a detailed chronology of events see Zhongguo yinhang zonghang et al., *Zhongguo yinhang hangshi ziliao huibian*, especially v. 3.

late 1930s, T.V. Soong had worked closely with Bei Zuyi, then the director of the Shanghai branch and the bank's foreign exchange department, on various projects.[37] Hsia Pin-fang had been T.V. Soong's protégé during his early years in Shanghai and was close to Bei Zuyi, who had become the acting general manager of the Bank of China since 1941. However, when Soong resigned, nobody with that high level of authority and stature was left to defend Hsia against charges from Chiang Kai-shek.

Sympathetic letters from former classmates and colleagues such as Chen Changtong, then manager at the Bank of China office in Chongqing, address another issue, namely, the increasing alienation between headquarters and overseas branches due to war and the lack of personal contact in dealing with problems on each side. As Chen wrote to Hsia Pin-fang:

> At first, the order from the High Quarters was to recall you to China. But thanks to Mr. Pei's [i.e., Bei Zuyi's] skillful maneuvering Dr. Kung finally agreed to send you to Canada to investigate the possibility of opening an office there ... Meanwhile, as a good friend of yours, may I venture to suggest or to offer you an advice. In the course of further development, it may be necessary for Mr. Pei to send for you to come to Chungking to report in person of your observations in Canada. If so, I would advise you to come promptly without any hesitation. The trip would benefit you in more than one way. First of all, you will have a chance to reestablish your contact with all the colleagues in the Head Office here. Secondly, you will have a chance to meet the new directors of our bank. After all, personal contact means a great deal and will pave the way for Mr. Pei to smooth over your difficulties. Last but not the least, it may also be well for you to come home for a short period to see the actual conditions at home and particularly in the war time capital in the light of our present economic conditions.[38]

Chen's advice suggests that besides losing T.V. Soong's protection, Hsia Pin-fang had lost vital contact with old and new colleagues at the wartime headquarters and was not as much "in the picture" as necessary.

---

37. Parks M. Coble, *The Shanghai Capitalists and the Nationalist Government, 1927–1937* (Cambridge: Harvard University Asia Center, 1986), 213.

38. Chen Changtong, Bank of China Head Office, Chongqing, to Hsia Pin-fang, May 11, 1944, case 3, HPF Papers.

To succeed at the bank professionally, Hsia would have to actively seek out his colleagues in China and rebuild his network in the postwar reorganization of the bank. His refusal to do so contributed to his alienation and loss of interest in office politics back at home.

After two years of representing the interests of the Bank of China in Canada, Hsia Pin-fang was sent to take charge of the London office founded in 1929. In the wake of the postwar reorganization of the Bank of China in 1946, the London office (together with the New York office) was elevated to regular branch status instead of holding its prior designation as an agency. The London branch answered to the headquarters directly and controlled only the office established in Liverpool.[39] Lou Fuqing was appointed submanager of the London branch; like Hsia, he had graduated from Tsinghua University in Beijing and had spent most of the wartime years at the Bank of China's Batavia office. The London office's principal lines of business included the handling of deposit accounts in sterling and other currencies, the issuing of letters of credit on behalf of British, European, and other importers to finance their purchases from China and other parts of the world, and the daily transferring of sterling and other funds—sometimes up to 20 million British pounds of daily turnover—for accounts of branches and correspondents using the London bank as their clearing house.

During the war years, the London branch had stood clearly in the shadow of the New York branch and other Bank of China offices. For example, the London branch transferred remittances worth only 727,000 yuan in 1940, a trifle compared to the volume generated in the Singapore and New York branches.[40] However, Hsia Pin-fang approached his appointment with renewed energy—perhaps he saw it as another chance to prove himself—and did not shy away from introducing major managerial and personnel changes to an office that had lacked attention from the bank's headquarters. Hsia embraced the new beginning as an opportunity to build a banking business able to compete in the international arena.[41]

In his approach to investment, Hsia Pin-fang considered "the cardinal principle of investment being to obtain the maximum income

---

39. Hsia Pin-fang to F.W. Gray, Aug. 30, 1946, folder "Shanghai 1946," case 3, HPF Papers.
40. Zhongguo yinhang zonghang et al., *Zhongguo yinhang hangshi ziliao huibian*, especially v. 3, 2258.
41. Hsia Pin-fang to T.Y. Lee, Manager, Bank of China, New York, 40 Wall Street, January 14, 1947, case 3, HPF Papers.

consistent with a high degree of liquidity."[42] In his correspondence he repeatedly referred to the investment operations as the determinant of success or failure for the bank in the future. Whereas his time in New York had been almost completely dedicated to risk management and many quasi-diplomatic responsibilities, the London post allowed him to focus on the core responsibilities of a professional bank manager. In his autobiographical account, Hsia considered his managerial leadership in the London office a substantial achievement of his banking career resulting in "a clear-cut allocation of work and responsibility, proper placement of officers and clerks according to qualifications and aptitude and a general increase in the efficiency of the office."[43] By 1951 the London branch had grown to fourteen officers and twenty-three staff working in a functional organization divided into secretarial, accounting, cashiers, inward bills, outward bills, and general affairs divisions. He also arranged the move to new office premises in order to improve working conditions and morale of the staff and enhance the public image of the bank.[44]

Hsia Pin-fang's entrepreneurial activities as branch manager would have been bold at the best of times, but the frequent turnover in the bank's China offices during the Civil War years intensified the growing gap in communication and trust issues between the London branch and headquarters. One problem that Hsia Pin-fang was painfully aware of but that did not receive much response from the headquarters was getting good Chinese graduates to work in the London branch as they had many options upon their return to China.[45] The war in Europe had also taken a large toll on the local labor supply, causing Hsia Pin-fang to examine new hires and the compensation packages for his employees with renewed attention. When his proposed pension scheme for English staff and insurance benefits for the Chinese staff received less than enthusiastic support from the headquarters in China, he complained to a colleague in a rare case of serious frustration:

> I am sure that you will tell the Head Office that it is not possible for everything to be completely covered in inter-office letters, and that unless the Head Office is prepared to have

---

42. Business Record of Hsia Pin-fang, no date (1960?), case 4, HPF Papers.

43. Ibid.

44. Another major step was Hsia Pin-fang's introduction of new policies to manage the working funds of the bank, which increased the average rate of return from 0.75 percent to over 1.5 percent per annum. He also replaced "incompetent" public auditors and engaged the firm of Price, Waterhouse, & Co. as auditors of the bank instead. Ibid.

45. T.Y. Lee, Bank of China, London, to Hsia Pin-fang, May 3, 1940, case 3, HPF Papers.

full confidence in their managers to take whatever actions are in their best judgment, in the interest of the Bank, the only other alternative is for a senior officer to come out and look into the affairs of the overseas offices himself and collect all the information at first hand. Our Head Office colleagues, of course, have their difficulties and problems, and at the same time there's probably more truth than fiction in the statement that quite often the Head Office are not as adequately informed as they should be on matters affecting the business operations and personnel problems of the overseas offices.[46]

Just at the time when the head office struggled to reorganize and gain control over all its operations, Hsia Pin-fang demanded more trust in and autonomy for branch managers. For that purpose he tried to gauge the micro-climate and developments at the bank at home through correspondence with colleagues in other overseas branches or those who had just recently returned from visiting China offices. On a daily basis he worried about leadership changes that were motivated by factional politics or frustration about the Civil War situation as a whole and news about the eroding currency exchange rate and inflation in China.[47]

Of course, the more the drama of the Civil War unfolded, the more Hsia Pin-fang was drawn into the financial and political developments in China. In May 1947 Bei Zuyi, who had just been appointed chairman of the Central Bank of China, approached Hsia and suggested that he accept an appointment as general manager of the Bank of Taiwan.[48] In a hasty telegram Hsia refused the offer, trying hard not to burn bridges in this professionally important relationship.[49] He also assured Wei Daoming, then governor of Taiwan's provincial government, in an exceedingly polite letter, that his decision was not so much a political one but that of a professional and personal choice.[50]

---

46. Hsia Pin-fang to Yao Songling, Bank of China, New York, May 15, 1947, case 3, HPF Papers.

47. Hsia Pin-fang to M.H. Cheng, Assistant Chief Secretary, Bank of China, Head Office, Shanghai, on October 16, 1947, case 3, HPF Papers. Hsia lamented, "I notice that since August 18th the exchange rates for sterling have gone up over 30%, and I have heard that the same rates for U.S. dollars have gone up somewhat more. The rates in the so-called Black Market have become even worse, and I was told only yesterday that U.S. dollars are rumoured to be selling at close to 80,000 to one."

48. Bei Zuyi's confidential telegram, May 2, 1947, case 3, HPF Papers.

49. Hsia Pin-fang's confidential telegram to Bei Zuyi in Shanghai, May 5, 1947, case 3, HPF Papers.

50. Hsia Pin-fang to His Excellency Dr. Wei Daoming, Governor, Taiwan Provincial Government, Taipei, Taiwan, China, May 22, 1947, case 3, HPF Papers.

In light of these developments, a handwritten laundry list compiled by Hsia Pin-fang in 1947 offers us unique insights into his analysis of the future of the Bank of China and what certain political developments might mean for his branch and his professional (and ultimately personal) future. On a sheet of paper he listed questions such as "How strongly do Hong Kong people think about early British recognition and about American recognition? What moves and plans have other banks and people made? Can Chungking [Chongqing] be taken too and what then? What will be instructions regarding staff maintenance in London and their eventual return to China? What are conditions in Shanghai like? Would the Communists attack Hong Kong in the near future?"[51] Clearly, as early as 1947, Hsia Pin-fang saw the writing on the wall and was preparing himself and the London branch for a revolutionary takeover in China.

POLITICAL PRESSURE FROM ALL SIDES:
THE LONDON YEARS, 1949–1951

In the wake of the victory of the Communist forces over the Nationalists and the founding of the People's Republic of China (PRC) in Beijing on October 1, 1949, the Bank of China, representing a financial institution of crucial importance to the national economy with strong ties to the discredited former Nationalist regime, came immediately under new government control.[52] Many leading employees of the Bank of China speculated about changes in leadership and their future careers at the bank. Hsia Pin-fang's friend and former diplomat Guo Bingwen tried to be positive in his letter of January 1950: "I am inclined to think that the new regime would welcome your service if you are prepared to render it, because they do not have enough experienced people to go around. Besides, you have not been interested in politics and have made a very fine record. In case you decide to make a change, I hope you will co-operate with me in promoting some business."[53]

---

51. The list, including twenty questions, is included in the folder "Cheng Moo-Hau," 1947, case 3, HPF Papers.

52. The Shanghai Bank of China headquarters came under the control of the People's Liberation Army on May 28, 1949, three days after the takeover of the city. See Zhongguo yinhang zonghang et al., *Zhongguo yinhang hangshi ziliao huibian*, v. 3, 2373.

53. Guo Bingwen from Washington, D.C., to Hsia Pin-fang, January 5, 1950, in folder "Misc. 1950 Friends," case 3, HPF Papers.

As soon as Britain announced its recognition of the new Communist regime in Beijing, the status of the London branch of the Bank of China became a big headache for Hsia Pin-fang. Whom should the branch answer to as its head office? Both Shanghai and Taipei laid claims to being the official headquarters with the authority of bestowing power of attorney. On January 12, 1950, after being bombarded with questions, Hsia Pin-fang replied, "As to the status of our Bank in London, the matter is in the hands of our solicitors and Counsel who have been studying the situation for the past few days, and who have not yet given us a definite reply as to which office we now operate under—whether the one in Taipeh or the one in Peking. I shall be guided by their final decision, and in the meantime do my best to keep the door open and to minimize and ignore any anxiety that may exist among the staff."[54]

It is hard for us to gauge the power of the rumors spreading in the first weeks of the year 1950 among the Bank of China managers, causing panic and frustration among the staff. Contradictory information was constantly flying back and forth among the branches around the globe, leading people to admit that "Nowadays it is difficult to believe what is true and what is not true."[55] Hsia Pin-fang exchanged numerous letters with managers and colleagues at other branches to find out the most recent news about reappointments and departures. Most of it was pure speculation or wishful thinking. Conveying some hopeful news, Guo Bingwen informed Hsia on January 20, 1950, that "There is a rumour here that the manager of the Bank of China in Hongkong is being asked to remain at his post. If this is true, it suggests the possibility of the banking authorities under the new regime wishing the managers of other branches to continue in service."[56] Hsia told Guo that he was getting more and more depressed,[57] and Guo assured him that "While in New York I heard from several sources that you have been asked by the new regime to remain at your post. If this is true I am glad as it gives you further opportunity to render service to the bank and to our people."[58]

In his personal correspondence, Hsia Pin-fang did not direct his dissatisfaction toward the Communist government as a new political regime (perhaps because he was worried about censorship) but toward bad leadership at the bank and the postwar circumstances in general.

---

54. Hsia Pin-fang to Guo Bingwen, January 12, 1950, HPF Papers.
55. Guo Bingwen to Hsia Pin-fang, March 8, 1950, HPF Papers.
56. Guo Bingwen to Hsia Pin-fang, January 20, 1950, HPF Papers.
57. Hsia Pin-fang to Guo Bingwen, January 27, 1950, HPF Papers.
58. Guo Bingwen to Hsia Pin-fang, February 6, 1950, HPF Papers.

However, he began to plan his eventual departure by sending his wife and daughter to New York in late 1950 even though it imposed a considerable financial and emotional burden on the whole family.[59] Meanwhile, Hsia's so-called trouble with Peking began to develop in the London office. In an autobiographical note from 1960, he described the events unfolding in 1950 as a struggle for political authority, but even more so as a fight about access to bank assets:

> Cables were now coming in thick and fast. Peking claimed that the Bank's Head Office had moved there and therefore was in control of the London branch which, by the way, was the bank's clearing house for all import and export business with the British Commonwealth countries as well as the continents of Europe and Africa. The head office in Taipei, struggling to protect its position, also cabled instructions to show its authority to London. It was like a divorce case with both sides claiming for custody of the child, except that in this situation the child was an important and profitable branch bank with assets worth millions of pounds in the financial center of London. In the face of the crisis my chief concern was that the London Branch must at all cost be kept in continuous operation. We must never close our doors. However, the situation was so uncertain and critical that I had to be extremely careful and I was determined not to be the manager to preside over the burial of the branch.[60]

To make things worse, when the new Beijing government cabled the Midland Bank with an inquiry about Bank of China accounts held there, the Midland Bank froze the London branch's accounts in order to protect itself legally. This crisis crippled the London operations and was only solved after lengthy negotiations with Beijing.[61] In addition, the U.S. State Department suspended all existing visas for Chinese nationals in October of 1950, meaning that Hsia Pin-fang would no longer be able to simply enter the United States and reunite with his family should the situation deteriorate.[62] This policy created anxiety among Chinese nationals overseas who had publicly rejected the new Communist government in

---

59. Ibid.

60. "I refused to be a Communist banker," Hsia Pin-fang's personal statement, February 6, 1960, case 4, HPF Papers.

61. Hsia Pin-fang to Guo Bingwen, February 11, 1950, case 4, HPF Papers.

62. Hsia Pin-fang to Guo Bingwen, October 17, 1950, case 4, HPF Papers.

one way or another and were now stranded as they attempted to reach the United States. With heightened feelings of mistrust Hsia was careful to keep his distance from the Chinese community in London: "I try to steer away from them because I cannot tell the intensity of their newly acquired colour."[63]

Echoing these sentiments, the correspondence between Hsia Pin-fang and managers in other overseas branches of the Bank of China gives evidence of their fundamental belief in the professional ethics and responsibilities of bankers during crisis and their disgust with political interference in their professional lives. For example, Alfred Kwok, manager of the Bank of China at the Penang branch, poured his heart out to Hsia: "Much has happened since we last corresponded. My guiding principle has been devotion to duty as a banker regardless of political developments. I suppose you remember the difficult situation I had to face when I first arrived at Penang ... It is almost unbelievable that this office lost more than $0.5 million since the liberation. I don't know whose fault it is, but I certainly have been given a lot of dirty work."[64]

Hsia Pin-fang replied to Kwok expressing his deep disappointment with human nature in the face of political and financial uncertainty:

> Your experience must have been generally the same in nature as mine since the change-over in the control of the bank, but our problems may have varied in the degree of difficulty which they have entailed ... There are so few people in this world who are loyal and sincere and have the courage to stand by sound principles. Most of the troubles here still persist and the outlook remains confusing. I am glad that your operating results have become better. We have witnessed the same tendency here, especially after recent transfers of substantial funds from Hong Kong and other sources. Commercial credit business with China has expanded but to the extent imports exceed exports China must face a loss in foreign exchange.[65]

Other managers like S.C. Lu, head of the Bank of China in Singapore, contacted Hsia for help requesting the extension of an overdraft of 380,000 British pounds for his branch. Like so many branches in the immediate postwar period Singapore suffered from an acute lack of liquidity.

---

63. Hsia Pin-fang to Guo Bingwen, September 22, 1950, case 4, HPF Papers.
64. Albert Kwok to Hsia Pin-fang, Penang, August 17, 1950, case 3, HPF Papers.
65. Hsia Pin-fang to Albert Kwok, Penang, September 19, 1950, case 3, HPF Papers.

Although it still held two million dollars of government bonds, in 1950 there was no investor market to speak of, and without the existence of a government bank, there was no way to deposit these bonds for overdraft facilities. The bonds, in fact, had become "frozen assets."[66]

The new Bank of China headquarters in Beijing was not oblivious to these challenges and began to send inspectors with the mission to evaluate the business situation and "loyalty" of the local branch management to the new bank leadership. The inspections and methods of ensuring loyalty appear to have had a rather clandestine character. For example, in January 1950 S.C. Lu told Hsia that at his Singapore branch

> [a] man just came from Canton and Hongkong. He belonged to the new Government and he told my friend that both you and I were known at home to be very straightforward and businesslike in our dealings. I haven't met the man yet, but he seems to have a good opinion of us. It shows that our way of doing things have been watched. Fortunately we have done nothing unbusinesslike. ... PS: After writing the last page, I was introduced to the man and had a long chat with him. He told me that people at home had a very high opinion of you and had been expecting some kind of expression of attitude from you before cabling you [and] reappointing you London Manager. ... Regarding us here, I consulted lawyers and prepared for the announcement of British recognition. Immediately the latter became official, we cabled Peking and issued a written statement to the papers. That's why my reappointment came so soon. My object has always been that we must keep the Bank going, that we must act according to our past traditions during the past 40 years irrespective of change of political parties at home.[67]

Since 1947 Hsia Pin-fang had turned down several invitations to visit the Bank of China headquarters back at home. It had been easy to turn down written requests with excuses such as health issues, which indeed bothered Hsia at the time. However, when four inspectors from the headquarters showed up at the London office in January of 1951, it was more difficult to decline the invitation.[68] Hsia was wary of a return

---

66. S.C. Lu to Hsia Pin-fang, January 19, 1950, case 3, HPF Papers.
67. S.C. Lu to Hsia Pin-fang, January 20, 1950, case 3, HPF Papers.
68. Hsia Pin-fang to Cheng Moo-Hau, Bank of China, Hong Kong, January 16, 1951, case 4, HPF Papers.

to China for fear that he would be unable to maintain his professional ethics and that his visit would be interpreted as an official endorsement of the new government in China. His wife, Liu Shuting, envisioned immediate danger and tried through her letters to dissuade him from going to China in no uncertain terms.[69] Apart from showing greater distrust of the new regime than her husband, she also argued reasonably that although the bank authorities had approved his stay in London after the recognition, the government might now question why he had stayed there for such a long time without ever returning even once to the mainland offices.[70]

The diplomatic struggle for recognition impacted Hsia Pin-fang personally as well as professionally. His personal bank account in the United States, a remainder from his days as New York office head, was blocked due to his position representing the Bank of China, which the U.S. government then considered an instrument of the new PRC government. It took the intervention of several old banker friends from his New York days to intervene and unfreeze his accounts.[71] Incidents like these created a scenario for Hsia where his position came under attack from all sides: from the PRC government for disloyalty, from the U.S. government for suspicious affiliation with a PRC financial institution, and from the Nationalists who tried aggressively to recruit him. As a result, Hsia began to realize that he would have to leave London relatively soon and return to the United States or Canada because he did not want to throw in his lot with the Nationalist government in Taipei. On a sheet of paper he compiled a list of "Alternatives" and began to contact firms with which he had interacted in the past as head of the New York agency about potential employment.[72]

By February 1, 1951, Hsia Pin-fang had finally decided on resignation from the bank, certainly helped by the fact that he was able to obtain a Canadian reentry permit and then a U.S. visitor's permit sponsored by James B. Burke, his former attorney in New York who over the years had become a close friend.[73] At the same time he was increasingly incensed

---

69. Hsia Pin-fang's wife Liu Shuting to Hsia Pin-fang, January 24, 1951, folder "Resignation and Visa," case 3, HPF Papers.

70. Ibid. Hsia Pin-fang's wife Liu Shuting to Hsia Pin-fang, January 23, 1951, and February 26, 1951.

71. Howard J. Rogers, vice president of the Bank of the Manhattan Company on Wall Street, to Hsia Pin-fang, January 29, 1951, case 4, HPF Papers.

72. Hsia Pin-fang made a list of "Alternatives" in 1951 for his future job hunt, included in case 3, HPF Papers.

73. Hsia Pin-fang to James Burke, February 1, 1951, case 4, HPF Papers.

about the presence of the four "visitors" from the Beijing headquarters and their long visitation in his London office: "At first it appeared to be an inspection but it turned out that their mission was definitely designed to undermine my position. This trick cannot be considered to be altogether unexpected but it is the last straw to break the camel's back. It is clear that they have no intention of doing banking business in an honest and regular way, and it makes me feel that I have no more obligation to anyone, old or new, to continue in London and get more involved. The time has come for me to quit with a clear conscience."[74]

Hsia Pin-fang's resignation from the Bank of China triggered two interesting reactions. On the bank's side, the Beijing office and government authorities suddenly tried very hard to retain Hsia and argued for his "indispensability." Once he had sent off his resignation cable and gone to Canada, the bank authorities offered him a long paid leave of absence and told him that he could take his time with his return. Hsia was still on the payroll through 1951, and various leaders in the bank personally lobbied him to return to his post. The head office in Beijing offered him the position of auditor or special envoy, but he refused. Entitled to a payment of 4,380 British pounds from the London branch's Chinese Staff Provident Fund, he obtained the sum from the Bank's Trust by the end of 1951 after much negotiation through the law office of Sanderson, Lee & Co.[75] Hsia Pin-fang replied from Canada that "I have no apology to anyone and hold malice towards none. Confidentially two of the visitors have said to me quote I understand I probably would reach same decision unquote kindest regards."[76]

Hsia Pin-fang's postwar experience also indicates that the Nationalists did not refrain from playing dirty in their effort to draw a top bank manager and financial expert into their ranks. The Bank of China Taiwan headquarters not only tried to convince Hsia to join their office in Taipei with enticing promises but at the same time actively tried to sabotage his admission to Canada so that he would be forced to cooperate with them.[77] After Hsia reached Ottawa on March 3, he still needed to get an American visa. As he later found out, the Taipei Foreign Ministry had

---

74. Hsia Pin-fang to Dr. Wei Daoming in Rio de Janeiro, February 5, 1951, case 3, HPF Papers.

75. See, for example, his correspondence with Sanderson, Lee & Co., March 5, 1951, case 4, HPF Papers.

76. Hsia Pin-fang's cable to S.J. Chen and Cheng Moo-hau in Hong Kong, February 14, 1951, case 4, HPF Papers.

77. Chen Changtong, Bank of China, Formosa, to Dr. Liu Chieh, Chinese Embassy (Embassy of the Republic of China) in Ottawa, February 20, 1951, case 4, HPF Papers.

advised the U.S. embassy in Canada not to issue any documents without their prior approval.[78] Fortunately, Hsia managed to obtain a visa to the United States through private connections and arrived in New York, as he recalled in his 1960 autobiographical note, "by train from Canada on March 15th, the income tax day. Thus ended my nightmare. A friend later gave me a job in a field entirely new to me, and I have been paying U.S. income tax ever since. Peking never converted me into a Communist banker."[79]

CONCLUSION

Was Hsia Pin-fang an apolitical person? On February 6, 1960, in his autobiographical statement, "I refused to be a Communist Banker," he set out his moral and professional convictions, justifying his choice: "The memories of 1950–1951 still haunt me at times, but I have the peace of mind that I did the only right thing and fulfilled my obligations in the most honorable way possible. I gave up not only a position of prestige but a profession in which I had worked and lived for over twenty years."[80] Considering the relatively strong anti-Communist tenor of this document, I suggest that we need to interpret it in the context of the political climate prevalent during the McCarthy era in the late 1950s as this is Hsia Pin-fang's only direct assessment of the Communist Revolution and government and his past life in and outside China. The archival records make it clear that he bore no ideological grudge against communism per se and was not driven by strong patriotic sentiments, but he hated any compromise of his professional standards and ethics.

When the British government extended de facto recognition to the Communist government of China in 1950, Hsia Pin-fang was caught in a power struggle between the rival claims of the head offices of the Bank of China in Shanghai and in Taipei, each claiming authority over the bank's assets and operations in the name of the Communist or Nationalist government, respectively. He managed to steer the London branch successfully to a legal resolution of these claims without loss of the bank's accreditation, an imminent danger at the time. It is obvious that Hsia's prominent family background, training at Chinese and American

---

78. "I refused to be a Communist banker," personal statement dated and signed February 6, 1960, case 4, HPF Papers.

79. Ibid.

80. Ibid.

elite academic institutions, perfect bilingual language capabilities, and influential social networks, often overlapping with his professional relationships, made him a most desirable asset for the future of the banking business on either side of the ideological divide.

It is an indirect tribute to Hsia Pin-fang's managerial excellence that the official history of the Bank of China compiled in 1999 did not contain any more condemning words about his person and tenure at the bank than a relatively accurate statement that "using the legal procedures as an excuse, Hsia Ping-fang, Manager, balked at pledging allegiance to the Head Office in Beijing."[81] At the same time, he felt betrayed by the actions of the bank's Taipei headquarters, which in turn considered him disloyal. Maybe we should consider Hsia Pin-fang a career professional who tried to fulfill his obligations as a banker first before considering political attachments. This healthy attitude prevented him from siding with either of the extreme authoritarian regimes in the transition period because their priorities did not reflect his professional goals. As Hsia's son commented on his father in 1977, "I believe he was shabbily treated by all interested parties, because he refused to take sides but rather insisted that proper legal and judicial deliberations precede any decisions between the rival claims of the Communist and Nationalist Governments."[82]

Not nationalism and withdrawal from transnational connections but the desire to pursue new opportunities as a family has been cited by Sherman Cochran as the reason for prominent entrepreneurial families like Liu Hongsheng's family in Shanghai to stay and regroup in China after 1949. According to his interpretation, "they believed that their brand of capitalism was compatible with communism."[83] Hsia Pin-fang was not a capitalist but a professional with an extraordinary set of skills who opted out not only from extreme political choices but also from his banking profession. Between 1952 and 1967 he found new employment with the essential oil firm Magnus, Maybee and Renard in New York City. Lacking any documentary evidence for the years after 1951, it is difficult to speculate why Hsia left the financial sector at the peak of his career despite so much professional experience. Immigration regulations, difficulties due to his past professional involvement with "red" China,

---

81. The Editorial Committee on the History of the Bank of China, *A History of the Bank of China (1912–1949)*, 225.

82. Y. Edward Hsia, M.D., to Lawrence J. Kipp, Librarian, Baker Library, Harvard Business School, April 27, 1977, case 4, HPF Papers.

83. Sherman Cochran, "Capitalists Choosing Communist China: The Liu Family of Shanghai, 1948–56," in Brown and Pickowicz, eds., *Dilemmas of Victory*, 384.

disillusionment, ill health—all of these issues might have influenced his decision to completely sever his professional ties with the world of finance. According to his obituary in the *New York Times*, he became an American citizen only in 1969, one year before his death, indicating possible political trouble with naturalization due to his past engagement with China.[84] Hsia Pin-fang's choice of independence from Communist and Nationalist politics vindicated his professional ethics but ultimately came at the cost of his professional career and identity.

---

84. "Pinfang Hsia, 68, Bank of China Aide," *New York Times*, December 23, 1970.

GLOSSARY

Andō Rikichi	安藤利吉
Baisha	白沙
Bangzhou	邦周
baoli	暴力
Baosheng yinhang	寶生銀行
batou	把頭
Bei Zuyi	貝祖詒
Beijing (Peking)	北京
Beiping (Peiping)	北平
Bian Baimei	卞白眉
bianli qiaohui, fuwu qiaobao	便利僑匯, 服務僑胞
Bo Yibo	薄一波
Cai Guoyi	蔡國儀
Canton (Guangzhou)	廣州
Cathay Insurance Co.	國泰保險公司
Chang Fah-Kwei (Zhang Fakui)	張發奎
Changfeng	昌豐
Changjiang sanjiaozhou	長江三角洲
Changlu	長蘆
changzhang	廠長
Chen Changtong	陳長桐
Chen Cheng	陳誠
Chen Gongbo	陳公博
Chen Mu	陳穆
Chen Qicai	陳其采
Chen Rong	陳容
Chen Xin	陳炘
Chen Xiping	陳西平
Chen Yi	陳儀
Chen Yun	陳雲

299

Chen, K.P. (Chen Guangfu, Chen Kwang Pu)	陳光甫
Cheung Pui Kai (Zhang Peijie)	張沛堦
Chiang Ching-kuo (Jiang Jingguo)	蔣經國
Chiang Kai-shek (Jiang Jieshi)	蔣介石
China Industries, Inc.	中國工業投資公司
Choa Lap Chee (Cai Lizhi)	蔡立志
Choa Po Yew (Cai Baoyao)	蔡寶耀
Chongqing (Chungking)	重慶
Choy Sing Nam (Cai Shengnan)	蔡昇南
Chrysis Corporation	格蘭雪斯公司
da laohu	打老虎
Dagong bao (Ta Kung Pao)	大公報
Dahe Property	大和物產
Dai Anguo	戴安國
Dai Li	戴笠
Dai Tōa kyōeiken	大東亞共榮圈
Dalian	大連
Dalu yinhang	大陸銀行
dang zhibu	黨支部
Danyang	丹陽
Dapu	大浦
Dayu Tea Company	大裕茶行
Deng Xiaoping	鄧小平
Donghua yiyuan	東華醫院
Dongya Corporation	東亞公司 (東亞企業有限公司)
Du Yuesheng	杜月笙
Duan Qirui	段祺瑞
fabi	法幣
Fan Xudong	范旭東
Fang Yuanmou	方遠謀
Fei Yimin	費彝民
Feng Yuxiang	馮玉祥
Fu Zuoyi	傅作義

fushi	腐蝕
Fuxin	福新
Gong Yinbing	龔飲冰
Gong You Yuan	公有源
gongsi heying	公私合營
Gu Zhun	顧準
guanliao zhuyi	官僚主義
Guo Bingwen	郭秉文
Guo Dihuo	郭棣活
guofen lideshui	過份利得稅
Guofeng	國豐
Guohua shangye yinhang	國華商業銀行
guohuo	國貨
hanjian	漢奸
Hankou	漢口
He Lian	何廉
Hengfengtang	恒豐堂
Hirohito	裕仁
Ho Fuk (He Fu)	何福
Ho Hung Pong (He Hongbang)	何鴻邦
Ho Hung Sun (He Hongshen; Stanley Ho)	何鴻燊
Ho Kom Tong (He Gantang)	何甘棠
Ho Sai Iu (He Shiyao)	何世耀
Ho Sai Ki (He Shiqi)	何世奇
Ho Sai Kim (He Shi-jian Edward; He Shijian)	何世儉
Ho Sai Kit (He Shijie)	何世傑
Ho Sai Kwong (He Shiguang)	何世光
Ho Sai Lai (Ho Shai Lai; He Shili)	何世禮
Ho Sai Leung (He Shiliang)	何世亮
Ho Sai Wa (He Shihua)	何世華
Ho Sai Wing (He Shirong)	何世榮
Ho Tung, Robert (He Dong)	何東

Hong Kong	香港
Hong Lanyou	洪蘭友
Hongfeng	宏豐
Hou Debang	侯德榜
Hsi Te-mao (Xi Demao)	席德懋
Hsia Pin-fang (Xia Pingfang)	夏屏方
Hsu Cho-yun (Xu Zhuoyun)	許倬雲
Hu Sheng	胡繩
Hu Shi	胡適
Hu Zutong	胡祖同
Huaihai	淮海
Huang Fu	黃浮
Huang Huoqing	黃火青
Huang Jing	黃敬
Huang Kecheng	黃克誠
Huang Shaogu	黃少谷
Huang Xin	黃欣
Huang Yanpei	黃炎培
Huang Zhaohua	黃昭華
huidui ju	匯兌局
Hujiang	滬江
Huludao	葫蘆島
Hyōgi kai	評議會
Itō Kinjirō	伊藤金次郎
Jiang Bocheng	蔣伯成
jianmin	奸民
jianshang	奸商
Jianye yinhang	建業銀行
Jiaotong yinhang	交通銀行
Jidacheng Wood Co.	集大成材木商行
jieji shengdan	借雞生蛋
Jin Runquan	金潤泉
Jinbu ribao	進步日報
Jincheng yinhang	金城銀行

jingti tantu xiangle	警惕貪圖享樂
Jinshanzhuang	金山莊
jinyuan quan	金圓券
Jiuda	久大
jiufen dui	糾紛隊
jiuguo	救國
Kai Tak Airport (Qide jichang)	啟德機場
kanku yundong	砍矻運動
Kaohsiung (Gaoxiong)	高雄
Keeloong (Jilong)	基隆
Kodama Tomoō	兒玉友雄
Kōminhokokai	皇民奉公會
Kōminka	皇民化
Koo Bin-fu (Gu Binfu)	辜斌甫
Koo Chen-fu (Gu Zhenfu)	辜振甫
Koo Hsien-jung (Gu Xianrong)	辜顯榮
Koo Kwan-min (Gu Kuanmin)	辜寬敏
Koo Wei-fu (Gu Weifu)	辜偉甫
Koo Yen Pi-hsia (Gu Yan Bixia)	辜顏碧霞
Kowloon (Jiulong)	九龍
Ku, Vivien (Gu Huaiqun)	辜懷群
Kung, H.H. (Kong Xiangxi)	孔祥熙
Lei Zhen	雷震
Li Chenggan	李承幹
Li Guowei	李國偉
Li Hongzhang	李鴻章
Li Jishen	李濟深
Li Lisan	李立三
Li Lixia	李立俠
Li Ming	李銘
Li Sihao	李思浩
Li Weihan	李維漢
Li Wencai	李文采
Li Wenming	李文明

Li Xiaohe	利孝和
Li Zeyi	李擇一
Li Zhuchen	李燭塵
Liang Chuanwei	梁傳偉
Liang Guanghong	梁廣宏
Liang Shiyang	梁世揚
Liang Xichao	梁錫超
Liang Xicun	梁錫存
Liang Yinghong	梁英宏
Liang Zhenyou	梁珍友
liangtou she	兩頭蛇
lianhe peisong chu	聯合配送處
Lianhe yintuan	聯合銀團
lianying chu	聯營處
Lin Boqu	林伯渠
Lin Kanghou	林康候
Lin Mulan	林慕蘭
Lin Xiantang	林獻堂
Lin Xiongxiang	林熊祥
Lin Xiongzheng	林熊徵
lingdao	領導
Linqing	臨清
Liu Gongyun	劉攻芸
Liu Hongsheng	劉鴻生
Liu Shaoqi	劉少奇
Liu Shuting	劉淑婷
Liu Yousan	劉友三
Lixin Academy	立信會計事務所
Lo Cheung Shiu (Luo Changzhao)	羅長肇
Lo Cheung Yip (Luo Changye)	羅長業
Lo, M.K. (Luo Wenjin)	羅文錦
Lü Heruo	呂赫若
Lu Zuofu	盧作孚
Luo Jingyi	羅靜宜

Luo Meihuan	駱美奐
Ma Fulun	馬阜倫
Ma Guochuan	馬國傳
Ma Guocong	馬國聰
Ma Jueqing	馬絕卿
Ma Junlun	馬俊倫
Ma Licheng	馬立成
Ma Rongnian	馬榮念
Ma Shuzhen	馬淑貞
Ma Wenwei	馬文偉
Ma Xuchao (Ma Tsui Chiu)	馬敍朝
Ma Zhoucheng	馬周成
Macao	澳門
Manufacturing Enterprises of China	中國工業拓展公司
Manzhou	滿洲
Mao Qihua	毛齊華
Mao Zedong (Mao Tse-tung)	毛澤東
Maoxin	茂新
Meng Xiaodong	孟小冬
Mi Huasheng	糜華生
Nan Hanchen	南漢宸
Nanjing	南京
Ozaki Shiyushin	尾崎秀太郎
paijia	牌價
Pan Hannian	潘漢年
Pan Xulun	潘序倫
Pan Zongyao	潘宗堯
Pan-ch'iao (Banqiao)	板橋
Peng Mengji	彭孟緝
piguan	批館
Po Leung Kuk (Baoliang ju)	保良局
Qian Xinzhi	錢新之
Qian Yongming	錢永銘
qianzhuang	錢莊

Qiao Guanhua	喬冠華
qiaohui zheng	僑匯証
Qing	清
Qingdao	青島
Qingxin	慶新
Qinhuangdao (Chinwangdao)	秦皇島
quan guohuo	全國貨
Quanguo jinrong ye lianxi huiyi	全國金融業聯席會議
Richang	日昌
Rong Desheng	榮德生
Rong Zongjing	榮宗敬
ruoji ruoli	若即若離
sanfan wufan yundong	三反五反運動
sanfan yundong	三反運動
Sha Qianli	沙千里
Shanghai	上海
Shanghai shangye chuxu yinhang	上海商業儲蓄銀行
Shanghai shangye yinhang	上海商業銀行
Shanghai yinlian	上海銀聯
Shao Lizi	邵力子
shenghuo fuhua	生活腐化
Shenxin	申新
shenzai Xianggang, xinzai Shanghai	身在香港，心在上海
Shenzhen	深圳
shidai de xisheng	時代的犧牲
Shiego Suzuki	鈴木茂夫
shoufa hu	守法戶
Shōwa	昭和
shuike	水客
Shunji Shiomi	塩見俊二
Situ	司徒
Song Feiqing	宋棐卿
Song Hanzhang	宋漢章

Song Xiangyun	宋祥雲
Song Zheyuan	宋哲元
Soong May-ling (Song Meiling; Madame Chiang Kai-shek)	宋美齡
Soong, T.V. (Song Ziwen)	宋子文
Sotokufu	總督府
sufan fengchao	肅反風潮
Sun Yat-sen (Sun Zhongshan)	孫中山
Taihoku Teikoku University	台北帝國大學
Taishan	台山
Taishō	大正
Taiwan jiho	台灣時報
Taiwan xingzhengyuan	臺灣行政院
Tang Shoumin	唐壽民
tangdan	糖彈
Tangshan	唐山
tangyi paodan	糖衣炮彈
tantu anyi	貪圖安逸
tantu fubai	貪圖腐敗
Tianchu	天廚
Tianjin jianghua	天津講話
Tianran Cement	天然水泥
touji daoba	投機倒把
Tse Kar Po (Xie Jiabao)	謝家寶
Tse Yat (Xie Yi)	謝逸
Tseng Ling (Zeng Ling)	曾凌
Tsinghua (Qinghua) University	清華大學
tunji juqi	囤積居奇
waihui guigong, liyi guisi	外匯歸公, 利益歸私
Wang Daohan	汪道涵
Wang Guangmei	王光美
Wang Guangying	王光英
Wang Jingwei	汪精衛

Wang Kemin	王克敏
Wang Shaoxian	王紹賢
Wang Shijie	王世杰
Wang Shijing	汪時璟
Wang Xiaolai	王曉籟
Wang Yiling	王毅靈
Wanxian	萬縣
Wei Daoming	魏道明
weilianbi	偽聯幣
weizhisu	味之素
Weng Wenhao	翁文灝
Wong Kam Fook (Huang Jinfu)	黃金福
Wu Dingchang	吳鼎昌
Wu Kejia	伍克家
Wu Tiecheng	吳鐵城
Wu Yunchu	吳蘊初
Wu Yunzhai	吳蘊齊
wudu	五毒
wufan yundong	五反運動
Wuhan	武漢
Wuhu	蕪湖
Wuxi	無錫
Wuzhou	五洲
Xi'an	西安
Xia Yan	夏衍
Xia Zhongqian	夏仲謙
Xianggang jinrong gongzuo tuan	香港金融工作團
Xianming Co.	顯明商行
xie	挾
xinju	信局
Xu Baiyuan	徐柏園
Xu Bing	許丙
Xu Bing	徐冰
Xu Caicheng	徐采承

Xu Dixin	許滌新
Xu Guomao	徐國懋
Xu Jiqing	徐寄廎
Xu Kan	徐堪
Xu Teli	徐特立
Xu Xinliu	徐新六
Xu Zuoliang	徐左良
Xue Muqiao	薛暮橋
Xue Xianzhi	薛獻之
yahui	押匯
Yan Fu	嚴復
Yan Hu	嚴琥
Yan Zhuoyun	嚴倬雲
Yang Guozhang	楊國璋
Yang Jicheng	楊濟成
Yang Yongtai	楊永泰
Yang Zhifu	楊植夫
yanghuo	洋貨
Yanye yinhang	鹽業銀行
Yao Songling	姚崧齡
Ye Mingxun	葉明勳
Yichang	宜昌
yinhang	銀行
Yongli	永利
Yoshio Makisawa	牧澤義夫
Youbang Industrial Co.	有邦工業
Yu Guojun	余國俊
zengchan jieyue	增產節約
zengjia shengchan, fanrong jingji, gongsi jiangu, laozi liangli	增加生產, 繁榮經濟, 公私兼顧, 勞資兩利
Zhang Fengzhou	張豐冑
Zhang Hanfu	章漢夫
Zhang Huinong	張惠農
Zhang Jia'ao	張嘉璈
Zhang Jianhui (T.V. Chang)	章劍慧

Zhang Naiqi	章乃器
Zhang Qun	張羣
Zhang Xueliang	張學良
Zhang Yangfen	章央芬
Zhang Yingfen	章映芬
Zhang Zikai	張茲闓
Zhejiang diyi shangye yinhang	浙江第一商業銀行
Zhejiang shiye yinhang	浙江實業銀行
Zheng Tieru	鄭鐵如
Zhonggong zhongyang Xianggang fenju	中共中央 香港分局
Zhongguo jianshe yin gongsi	中國建設銀公司
Zhongguo jingji shiye cujinhui	中國經濟事業促進會
Zhongguo lianhe zhunbei yinhang	中國聯合準備銀行
Zhongguo mianye gongsi	中國棉業公司
Zhongguo nongmin yinhang	中國農民銀行
Zhongguo renmin yinhang	中國人民銀行
Zhongguo shiye yinhang	中國實業銀行
Zhongguo yinhang	中國銀行
Zhonghua renmin gongheguo chengzhi fangeming tiaoli	中華人民共和國 懲治反革命條例
Zhonghui yinhang	中匯銀行
Zhongnan yinhang	中南銀行
Zhongri maoyi xiehui	中日貿易協會
Zhongyang chubei yinhang	中央儲備銀行
Zhongyang xintuoju	中央信託局
Zhongyang yinhang	中央銀行
Zhou Enlai (Chou En-lai)	周恩來
Zhou Fohai	周佛海
Zhou Zuomin (Chou Tso-min)	周作民
Zhu Jiahua	朱家驊
Zhu Wenxiong	朱文熊
zong gongsi	總公司
zong zhibu	總支部
Zou Jiayou	鄒家祐

INDEX

This page is intentionally left blank.

CONTRIBUTORS

Kai Yiu Chan	Associate Professor of History, National Cheng Kung University
Parks M. Coble	James L. Sellers Professor of History, University of Nebraska
Sherman Cochran	Hu Shih Professor of Chinese History Emeritus, Cornell University
Karl Gerth	Hwei-Chi and Julia Hsiu Professor of Chinese Studies, University of California, San Diego
Tsai-man Ho	Assistant Professor, Center for General Education, Chung Yuan Christian University
Elisabeth Köll	Associate Professor, Harvard Business School, Harvard University
Man Bun Kwan	Associate Professor of History, University of Cincinnati
Pui-Tak Lee	Adjunct Associate Professor, Faculty of Economics and Business, University of Hong Kong
Christopher R. Leighton	Assistant Professor of History, Massachusetts Institute of Technology
Brett Sheehan	Associate Professor of History, University of Southern California
Tomoko Shiroyama	Professor of Economics, University of Tokyo
Siu-lun Wong	Professor of Sociology Emeritus, Hong Kong University
Victor Zheng	Co-Director, Centre for Social and Political Development Studies, Chinese University of Hong Kong

CORNELL EAST ASIA SERIES

CORNELL
East Asia Series

eap.einaudi.cornell.edu/publications